THE LETTERS OF JOHN MIDDLETON MURRY
TO KATHERINE MANSFIELD

Also by C. A. Hankin

Katherine Mansfield and Her Confessional Stories
Critical Essays on the New Zealand Novel (editor)
Life in a Young Colony: Selections from Early New Zealand Writing
(editor)
Critical Essays on the New Zealand Short Story (editor)

The letters of

JOHN MIDDLETON MURRY

to

KATHERINE MANSFIELD

selected and edited by
C. A. Hankin

Franklin Watts

New York

1983

First published in the United Kingdom in 1983 by
Constable and Company Limited

First United States publication 1983 by Franklin Watts, Inc.,
387 Park Avenue South, New York, NY 10016

Printed in Great Britain

Library of Congress Catalog Card Number: 83–61096

ISBN: 0-531-09801-X

Contents

Introduction

More than thirty years have passed since John Middleton Murry, in 1951, published the letters that Katherine Mansfield wrote to him during the course of their relationship. From the time of her death in 1923, it had been Murry's deliberate policy to make available to the public as much as possible of the writing Katherine Mansfield left behind. As well as publishing two posthumous collections of stories, he edited for publication *The Aloe* (an early version of *Prelude*), Katherine Mansfield's *Journal*, her *Letters* to a variety of people, her *Poems*, her reviews for the *Athenaeum* (as *Novels and Novelists*) and her *Scrapbook*. At a time when people felt that reticence rather than disclosure was the proper way to honour the memory of the dead, many considered Murry's publication of this material to be in bad taste. After enduring half a lifetime of criticism tinged with mockery – thanks to Aldous Huxley's facile portrait of him as Burlap in *Point Counter Point* – Murry showed considerable courage, therefore, in letting the world see the letters Katherine Mansfield had written to him.

With the publication of Katherine Mansfield's *Letters to John Middleton Murry*, the greater part of her writing had been made available to scholars. There followed, in 1954, Anthony Alpers' 'definitive' biography. The 1970s saw a new wave of interest in Mansfield. Jeffrey Meyers' biography appeared in 1978, and in 1980 Anthony Alpers' second, even more definitive, *Life*. But there remained one missing link: Murry's half of the correspondence with Katherine Mansfield. Without this, it has not been possible properly to assess and balance the information, especially the emotional information, provided by her letters. Although copies made by Ruth Mantz of some of Murry's letters are in the Humanities Research Centre at Austin, Texas, their inaccuracy makes them an unreliable scholarly resource. It was a considerable breakthrough, then, when the family and literary executors of John Middleton Murry gave permission in

1978 for the letters which had been purchased by the Alexander Turnbull Library in 1972 to be published.

Most editors of letters would prefer to present all the available material: in this case, the exigencies of publishing and a concern for readability determined that only a little over half the letters Murry wrote to Katherine Mansfield should be selected. Correspondence between the couple began in January 1912 and ended in January 1923. The bulk of the letters were written between 1918, when tuberculosis first forced Katherine to live apart from Murry in a better climate, and 1921, when he finally joined her in Switzerland. During these years, when she was struggling to come to terms with a mortal illness, Katherine depended on Murry's letters as on a lifeline. He responded to her need by finding time every day, if he could, to record for her something of his existence, no matter how ordinary or unimportant it might be. Sometimes he only described his meals, his surroundings, the activities of the two cats as he wrote, or his tiredness. Some of what he wrote just to fill up a page is repetitive and uninteresting; and it is material of this kind that has generally been omitted. Rather than irritate the reader by presenting abridged letters from which the trivial has been cut, I have decided to publish all the letters selected in their entirety. Occasionally a few sentences of significant information are contained in a published letter which is otherwise unimportant; while occasionally I have left unpublished or added only in a footnote, passing references to well-known people or events that are embedded in an otherwise long and insignificant letter. However, all the extant letters written at the beginning and at the end of the relationship between Katherine and Murry have been selected for publication. A brief chronology on p. 371 indicates the pattern of Murry's life until 1923; and a separate appendix lists all the unpublished letters and telegrams in the Alexander Turnbull Library.

Unfortunately, some obviously important letters are missing from the Turnbull collection; and all attempts to trace their whereabouts or their fate have failed. Murry published seven letters written by Katherine Mansfield to him in 1916: only one of his exists; fifteen of her letters written in 1917 are extant: none of his. Also missing are letters he wrote between March 2 and 10, 1920, and all except one written between September 1920 and January 1921. Whereas Murry published forty-six letters written by Katherine in the last year of her life, 1922, only fifteen of his remain. It may be significant that relations between the couple were more than usually strained during all the periods (except for March 1920 when the mails were erratic) from which letters are missing. Possibly it was Katherine who in her rejecting, angry moods simply didn't bother to save these letters. Anthony Alpers, for one, is of the opinion that Murry would not have destroyed them, even if they did reflect unfavourably on himself. Whether the missing material was never preserved by the recipient, whether Murry, or after his death someone else, destroyed it, will have to remain a matter for conjecture.

In the difficult task of selecting the letters for publication I have been guided by three principal considerations. First of all, I have been mindful that this is Murry's side of a correspondence that Katherine Mansfield's letters have already made famous. What Murry had to say to her casts a good deal of light on the close but troubled relationship between them. Katherine, never hesitant about expressing her feelings, at times criticised her husband fiercely for what she considered his weaknesses and his inadequacies. Letters written by Murry that, for whatever reason, evoked a strong reaction from her have been published. So have the tender, moving ones in which repeatedly he poured out his love and his physical longing, as well as his anguish and despair at the turn of events that was cutting them both down. Letters containing interesting biographical information about their financial affairs, their movements from one place or dwelling to another, and their relationship with family, friends and literary acquaintances, have been included where possible. Inevitably, Murry discussed Katherine Mansfield's writing. He was the first to read and respond critically to such major works as 'Bliss', 'Je ne parle pas français', and 'The Man Without a Temperament'. Generally lavish in his praise of her work, he was on occasion prepared to suggest subtle changes in a story. The weekly fiction reviews she wrote for the *Athenaeum* in 1919 and 1920 are a frequent subject of discussion. Passing comments about a review or Katherine Mansfield's dealings with publishers have not necessarily been reproduced; but all letters which make references of any significance to her work and its publication have been included.

Secondly, Murry's lifelong career as an editor, writer and critic makes the record of his early years in literary journalism interesting in its own right. As a man of letters, he gained a considerable following in his day, and some of his critical writing has worn well. Historically, Murry is an important figure because he was present at, indeed assisted in, the birth of English Modernism. Pound and Eliot were virtually unknown, James Joyce had published no fiction, D. H. Lawrence had not written *Sons and Lovers*, nor Virginia Woolf her first novel, when in 1911 Murry co-founded *Rhythm*, an avant-garde magazine of art and literature. Consciously Modernist, he wrote at the time to a friend about his artistic aims: "Modernism means, when I use it, Bergsonism in Philosophy. . . . Now Bergsonism stands for Post Impressionism in its essential meaning . . . for a certain symbolism in poetry . . . for Debussy and Maehler in music; for Fantaisisme in Modern French Literature, and generally if you like for 'guts and bloodiness' ". The first issue of *Rhythm* included a drawing by Picasso and an article on Fauvism; 'guts and bloodiness' Murry found in Katherine Mansfield's story, 'The Woman at the Store' which he published in the spring of 1912.

Many of the people Murry wrote about to Katherine belonged to the circle of friends, acquaintances and contributors that he gathered together in his early years as an editor. It was his success in this field which first brought him into close contact with D. H. Lawrence and his wife, Frieda; into the orbit of Lady Ottoline Morrell and those she entertained at Garsington; and which later gave him entrée to the group associated with Leonard and Virginia Woolf. In his position as editor of the brilliantly reconstituted *Athenaeum* in 1919 and 1920, Murry was an important and prominent figure in London literary circles. He published, according to Frank Swinnerton, 'a truly astonishing number of articles and reviews and letters written by men and women who have since taken leading places in the literary world.' Aldous Huxley was glad to be employed as an assistant editor of the *Athenaeum*, and writers such as T. S. Eliot, Virginia Woolf and James Strachey to be asked to contribute. Murry's private comments to Katherine about the literary people with whom he mixed are generally more charitable than, for instance, those made by Virginia Woolf about her acquaintances. But when it came to J. C. Squire of the rival *London Mercury* and his edition of Georgian poetry, Murry was less restrained. What his letters do reveal, again and again, is that he, like Katherine Mansfield, cared passionately about literature. If Mansfield and Murry were moralistic in their defence of their beliefs, it was because art was for them literally a religion. Towards the end of her life, Murry wrote to Katherine more about writing and less about external concerns. It has not been possible to publish every letter with a reference to literature or to contemporary writers; but anything which casts significant light on Murry as an editor and critic has been included.

A third aim in selecting these letters has been to represent as justly, and from as many angles as possible, the character of Murry as a young man. Murry was much criticised by his contemporaries, and even by Katherine, for appearing to bare his soul in public. Yet for all the self-revelation of his autobiographical book, *Between Two Worlds*, and for all the expression of his personal views in works like *Son of Woman*, he was there, as throughout his professional writing, presenting himself knowingly to the public. His letters to Katherine Mansfield, whom he loved and trusted, are self-revelation of a very different kind. They provide a poignant picture of the boyish, enthusiastic young man who was checked abruptly in his earnest yet somehow carefree espousal of literature, first by the War, then by Katherine's illness. Murry's letters show that in the early years of his companionship with her, he could take setbacks like the collapse of *Rhythm*, their subsequent inability to afford suitable accommodation, his bankruptcy, and even her infidelity, more or less in his stride. But before the War's end, everything had darkened. Working long hours at the War Office as a translator yet striving to retain his foothold as a writer, Murry found himself on a treadmill. Far worse than the physical and mental exhaustion he suffered, however, was the drain on his emotional resources made by Katherine's worsening health. After her terrible journey to Bandol in 1918, she became suddenly dependent on Murry. Lonely and frightened, she called on him for daily letters, for practical help, and for reassurance: reassurance of his continuing love and reassurance that she was not dying, that she *would* become well and live a normal life with him again.

Just how great the strain became for the man who, for all his love, was being asked to do the impossible, his letters reveal. A reasonably healthy man, Murry was now required to see life from the viewpoint of an invalid. This was not easy for one who, unlike Katherine Mansfield, was essentially un-imaginative. Painfully, he discovered that there was risk in writing enthusiastically about activities, especially social activi-ties, which he still enjoyed but which Katherine no longer could. And when, thinking of the life ahead of him, he cheered himself up by making purchases for the home that privately she knew could never be hers, he found that he had unwittingly inflicted hurt. There was also the problem of money. Brought up in circumstances which made him always feel insecure financially, his natural reluctance to part with his earnings, combined with an attempt to save for the house he yearned to own, evoked charges of meanness. There were times when Murry desperately felt that he could do or say nothing right.

As the situation grew more hopeless, Murry grew more defensive, more self-protective. He was not 'made of whipcord and steel', he told the sick woman; and indeed, he had not the resources, either emotional or spiritual, at once to sustain her and keep himself afloat. Murry, as an adult, was handicapped by the deprived childhood through which he had struggled his way to Oxford and to the profession of literature. Knowledge of the 'abyss' out of which he had climbed, and which still seemed perilously close, made personal survival his first instinct. But if he could not imaginatively enter into Katherine's suffering as a physical invalid, she, with her secure middle-class background, could not fully comprehend his fearful psychological disabili-ties. Nor could, or would, those like Aldous Huxley who, after Murry had outlived his usefulness as editor of the *Athenaeum* and husband of Katherine Mansfield, lost no time in making him the butt of jokes in private and of jibes in public.

It is his own words to the woman he undoubtedly loved that may help redress the imbalance in the public view of Murry. Like most of his fellows, he was a flawed human being: he was guilty, perhaps, of caring too much about his earnings, about his career, about his own feelings and his own needs. What demonstrably he cannot be charged with is feigning love for the brilliant, demanding woman who chose him for a partner. Weaker, and unconsciously if not consciously, struggling against the domination of Katherine Mansfield, he helped her within the limits imposed by his own personality. Understanding, at the end, she did not doubt his love. 'I feel no other lovers have walked the earth more joyfully – in spite of all', she wrote in farewell. In a very real sense, then, these are love-letters and will be read as such. They are also the record of an unusual yet enduring partnership between two very remarkable twentieth century writers.

These letters have been transcribed from microfilm copies of the handwritten originals. My principal concern as editor has been to reproduce, as accurately as possible and with as little editorial interference as possible, exactly what Murry wrote. Generally, he wrote in moments snatched from the more laborious composition of critical articles and reviews. Particularly in his earlier letters, the signs of Murry's haste are evident: inconsistency – indeed, mistakes – in spelling and punctuation; imperfect syntax; the omission of words and punctuation points; the use of the ampersand; and the adding of material in the margins of letters. 'Style is the man', we are told. Murry, when he wrote off-guard, so to speak, seems far more human than the professional critic whose six lectures on *The Problem of Style* have become a classic. For this reason his idiosyncracies and mistakes have been faithfully reproduced, mostly without an explanatory 'sic'. In the interests of clarity, however, quotation-marks have been standardized. Murry was also erratic in the way he wrote titles of books and stories. To avoid confusion, I have followed the current practice of italicising the titles of books, magazines, newspapers and plays (and abbreviations of these). Inverted commas have been used for the titles of individual articles and short stories. A problem arises with the two long stories by Katherine Mansfield which were first published in book form, *Prelude* and *Je ne parle pas français*. Murry refers sometimes to these works as they originally appeared, sometimes to their forthcoming publication in *Bliss and other stories*. For the sake of consistency, I have italicised these titles whenever they occur.

As far as possible, Murry's setting-out has been followed. His paragraphing was as erratic as his punctuation. Sometimes, when a sentence concluded before the end of a line, he began a new paragraph at the margin of the page instead of indenting; sometimes, when he did not complete a letter at one sitting, he left a gap to indicate the interruption. These idiosyncracies are reproduced, together with the lines he used for emphasis and his occasional drawings. Material written in the margins, however, has been placed at the end of the letter, without a 'P.S.', except where the meaning dictated that it should be placed at the top of the page.

Addresses Murry tended to abbreviate or leave out altogether. The missing information as to place of writing is given in square brackets. When he wrote from the office on business notepaper, the office address but not the full business heading is given. At the time of writing, Murry frequently did not bother to date his letters, although he nearly always gave the day of the week and often the hour. Some years after Katherine Mansfield's death, however, he went through the letters and pencilled in a date. It is this subsequent dating by Murry which is generally the source of the date given in square brackets. Where obvious inaccuracies have been detected, they have been corrected; and on the few occasions when Murry himself was unable to establish the correct date or sequence of his letters, internal evidence has been used to determine an approximate date, which is preceded by a question mark.

Assuming a fair amount of general literary knowledge in the reader, I have attempted to be scholarly but not pedantic in the footnotes. Where possible, I have identified places, the names of people, and references to the correspondents' own writing. When I have noticed that information contained in Murry's letters is at variance with facts cited by recent writers on Katherine Mansfield and Murry, I have drawn attention to the discrepancy. My other concern in the footnotes has been to offer a context that will make the letters more useful and more interesting. The principal background against which they should be read is, of course, Katherine Mansfield's letters to Murry. The edition published by Constable and Knopf in 1951 can still be found in libraries; and before too long the collected letters of Katherine Mansfield will be available. Rather than quote extensively from them, therefore, I have used the footnotes to indicate, where possible, which of Katherine Mansfield's letters Murry was replying to, and which letter of hers was written in answer to his. Since the dates of the 1951 edition are not always accurate, my cross-references cite both the date of Mansfield's letters and the opening words.

Katherine Mansfield's letters provide the personal context for Murry's. Perhaps also of interest to the general reader, if not to the scholar, is the social background of Garsington and Bloomsbury. With the Woolfs' circle Katherine had a link through her second cousin, Sydney Waterlow, who had once proposed to Virginia. After 1917, when the Hogarth Press decided to publish *Prelude*, the shared literary interests of the Murrys and the Woolfs brought them together intermittently – and ambivalently. Virginia visited Katherine, her rival, when she periodically returned to England; and in Katherine's absence abroad she entertained Murry, especially after he became editor of the *Athenaeum*, Virginia Woolf's comments in her published letters and diaries after these encounters are spicy and informative. They provide another set of eyes with which to view the turn of events as well as the people involved. The inclusion of 'gossip' such as Virginia Woolf's in the footnotes serves another purpose: that of conveying something of the social ambience that Katherine and Murry increasingly disliked and shunned. One of the strongest bonds between the two was an awareness that their different social backgrounds condemned them always to being trespassers on the grounds of Bloomsbury. If Murry occasionally expressed an animus in his letters against those who courted him as an editor but maligned him behind his back, Virginia Woolf's diaries suggest that his feelings were not altogether unjustified. From those readers who prefer shorter footnotes, however, or who are familiar with the information contained in them (as well as from those who seek more biographical details), I ask understanding and indulgence.

C. A. Hankin

Acknowledgements

I would like to thank first of all John Middleton Murry's literary executors, Mrs Mary Middleton Murry and Mr Colin Middleton Murry, for entrusting me with the editing of these letters. Acknowledgement is due to the Alexander Turnbull Library for supplying me with microfilm copies of John Middleton Murry's letters to Katherine Mansfield, and to the manuscript librarians at the Turnbull who kindly answered my questions. I am also grateful for the assistance of the following libraries: The Humanities Research Centre at Austin, Texas; the Stanford University Libraries (Special Collections); the Huntington Library; the University of Cincinnati Libraries (Special Collections); The New York Public Library (Berg Collection); the McMaster University Library; The British Library (Department of Manuscripts); and the University of Sussex Library. Especial thanks are due to the librarians of the University of Canterbury for their invariable helpfulness, and in particular to Jeffrey Kirkus-Lamont.

I am indebted to the University of Canterbury for providing research assistance. My thanks are due to all those people, including my colleagues in various departments, who helped with information and advice. I am especially grateful to Professor John Burrows, Head of the Law Faculty at the University of Canterbury, for his valued advice and encouragement. Margaret Scott and Vincent O'Sullivan kindly allowed me to see the typescript of the first two volumes of their forthcoming collected letters of Katherine Mansfield. This apprised me of their changes in some dates and helped solve a few knotty footnote problems. Of those who helped with the difficult task of transcribing the letters from microfilm, and with the typing, I would particularly like to thank Siobhan Brownlie, Claire Carter, Carole Acheson and Kathy Cordery. Finally, I am grateful to my husband, Professor John Garrett, for his continuing patience and understanding.

John Middleton Murry was born on August 6, 1889, in the London suburb of Peckham. While his self-educated father toiled as a civil service clerk by day and as a cashier by night, his mother took in lodgers to supplement their meagre income. Marking the family's slow move up in the world (and helping to unsettle Murry's childhood) were their regular changes of houses. For the civil service clerk, however, the real key to social advancement lay in education. Accordingly, he pushed his son academically from an early age. Though disliking his cold, penny-pinching father, Murry responded; he won a scholarship first to Christ's Hospital School, and later to Brasenose College, Oxford. As a Classical scholar at Oxford, Murry did well. In 1910 he won the Bridgman prize for an essay, and he was one of four Brasenose men to win a first in Honour Moderations. But his heart was not in Classical scholarship, nor in the goal set by his father of a secure civil service post. English literature was his first love; Modern French literature and art his second. Perhaps the most significant aspect of his Oxford life, then, in view of his later career, was the range of friends and acquaintances he made through such literary groups as the Pater Society and the intercollegiate Milton Society. When (urged on by Katherine Mansfield) he finally abandoned the idea of a conventional civil service career and launched into professional literary journalism, his university friendships came to serve him well.

January – March 1912

John Middleton Murry was only a twenty-two year old under-graduate when he first met Katherine Mansfield in December 1911. Impressed by her recently published collection of stories, *In a German Pension*, and by 'The Woman at the Store' which he had accepted for publication in *Rhythm*, he looked forward with some trepidation to actually meeting this 'terribly clever' young woman. Though excited, he confessed in his autobiography, he was 'nervous and unhappy when the evening of the great encounter arrived. . . . [Katherine Mansfield] was formidable, though not at all in the way I had been made to fear. She was aloof and reserved; and beside her I felt clumsy.' Katherine, born in New Zealand on October 14 1888, was ten months older than Murry and socially far more sophisticated. From the beginning she obviously had the upper hand. Nevertheless, the fact that she preserved the first letters he wrote to her in 1912, after his return to Oxford, tells its own story.

The five letters from 1912 are those of a boyishly self-conscious young man; one who, from the outset, treated Katherine Mansfield (who shared his enthusiasm for *Rhythm*) as an intellectual equal. The subject of writers and writing is prominent in these early letters, and it runs through the entire correspondence. So does that of houses. In March 1912 Katherine was dreaming aloud about a country cottage in Heron's Gate, and Murry in turn was hoping that he might be invited as a guest to sleep in the 'tramp-room' at Cherry Tree Cottage. Instead, to his surprise, he found himself invited as a lodger to share her flat at 69 Clovelly Mansions, London.

The relationship that was to last for the next eleven years was securely launched. Although he could not know it, Murry had embarked on an emotional and spiritual journey that was to leave him, after Katherine Mansfield's tragically early death in 1923 at the age of thirty-four, a greatly changed man from the one who had started out with her so hopefully in 1912.

[1]   55, Holywell,
                                                   Oxford.
                                                   January 27. 1912

Dear Miss Katharine [sic] Mansfield,

I don't know very much about the man Neuberg[1] – but what I do I'll try to tell you. He is or rather was one of Aleister Crowley's[2] push in the advanced spiritualist – obscene yet divine – stunt; and so far as I know he was Crowley's ἐραστής [lover]. Crowley's part being always pathic. He looks it. Then for some reason they quarrelled – over some money matter, and at present Neuberg is, I am told, holding over Crowley's head some books that he had privately published, and which are for England the ne plus ultra of dirt. I've never seen them; but they must be most amusing. One is called *The Daisy Chain* the other *Snowdrops from a Curate's Garden*. I believe he looks a very bedraggled weed but I never saw him, since when I knew Crowley in Paris he had some other fellow, Kennedy.[3]

I'm sorry I can't tell you more. Today is a good day in this bloodiest of bloody places – cold and fine; intellectually I feel just fit for this obvious meteorology. Next series of *Rhythm*,[4] I want a number of Criticisms, preferably appreciation with a sting in it, of a half-dozen of the 'big' moderns in England. Each will go in two monthly numbers – about 4000 words in all. Will you do one of them? The half dozen I suggest are Wells, Shaw, Bennett, Galsworthy, Masefield, Frank Harris. It's rather early on to worry; but I'm trying to get out a prospectus of the new volume beforehand – and very much want to fix this up.

Sorry to talk mere shop, but if you knew the ghastly life I lead here one half the day sweating over some cursed Aristotle, the rest dodging my creditors, and answering my letters, you would see its difficult to be other than dull. Your idea about the sailor man was good – I don't believe they taste nice though

                              Yours
                              J.M.M.

1. K.M. had requested information about the author of a book of poetry Murry had sent her to review for *Rhythm*. Victor Neuberg, a young poet, had entered into a sado-masochistic relationship with Crowley as his disciple and homosexual partner in occult erotic rites. After breaking with Crowley in 1914, he set up the small Vine Press to publish mostly his own poetry which K.M. is said to have admired.

2. Aleister Crowley (1875–1947), brought up in an extreme Exclusive Brethren sect, was attracted to occultism at Cambridge. In 1904 he wrote *The Book of the Law* which became the basis of a new 'Crowleyan' satanic cult. Among his sexual partners-cum-disciples in 1910 was Leila Waddell, a half-Maori violinist who was probably known to K.M. (K.M. attended at least one of Crowley's 'Evenings'.)

3. Leon Engers Kennedy, a painter and early participant in Crowley's rites.

4. *Rhythm*, an avant-garde journal of art, music and literature, was launched by Murry and Michael Sadleir in June 1911. Beginning with 'The Woman at the Store' in Spring 1912, K.M. contributed stories and poems. *Rhythm* was superseded by *The Blue Review* in May 1913.

---

[2]   13 Nicosia Rd
                          Wandsworth Common S.W.
                     [Before Tuesday, 26 March, 1912]

Dear K.M.

Here's fun for you. There's a batch of my verses[1] for you. No wonder I can't do any work if my mind's been like that all the month. Chaos is nothing to it.

It's the first time I've resurrected any of the stuff from my drawer. It is a mixture. Lots of it I abominate. One or two I like.

I was thinking of looking in on Tuesday with a batch of MSS submitted to *Rhythm*. If you get as bored as I do nowadays it'll do you good. I think about three p.m. If you're not there it can't be helped.

I searched for some of my short stories[2] but I must have left them all in London I mean Oxford, for I can't see anything at all in my box. If ever my few properties arrive from there you shall have them   I'm frightened about the devil's distraining on them in my absence. Also, I shall probably shift from Wandsworth[3] in April I don't know where. Je m'étouffe here. I shall come into London if I can get a job[4]

Yours
J.M.M.

It's bloody cold   I can't hold my pen.

1. Murry's 'Brasenose ale verses' appeared in *The Brazen Nose* in May 1911; 'Life' in the Winter 1911 issue of *Rhythm*.

2. Short stories by Murry which appeared in *Rhythm* were 'The Little Boy' in August 1912 and 'The Squire' in December 1912.

3. After coming down from Oxford in March 1912, Murry at first lived

with his parents at 13 Nicosia Road, Wandsworth Common. (Subsequently
he returned to take his Finals, gaining a 'tolerable' second.)

4. In April H. F. Fox, Murry's tutor at Oxford, arranged the interview
with J. A. Spender, editor of *The Westminster Gazette*, which resulted in
Murry obtaining his first job, as a reviewer for the *Westminster*.

---

[3]   13 Nicosia Road
                                   Wandsworth Common S.W.
                                           26 March. [1912]

Dear M.K.M.

Will you suggest the day for the visit to the pictures? They're all the
same to me. I'm lunching with W.L.G.[1] I believe on Thursday. I feel
very much as though I want to get drunk now. I was delighted to see
you, but you mustn't run away into the country yet.[2] I'm still
chuckling over the *Rhythm* set. I'm so awfully out of it.

Yours
J.M.M.

1. It was at the St. John's Wood home of Walter (Willy) Lionel George,
(1882–1926), a French novelist who collected bright young writers, that
K.M. and Murry first met. Some six years later Katherine repaid George by
using his house as the setting for 'Bliss' and himself as the model for the
emotionally empty Harry Young.

2. Katherine was planning to leave London for the country and to live in
'Cherry Tree Cottage', Heronsgate. Murry's feeling that she was withdrawing
from him led to his addressing her as M.K.M. and saying that he wanted to
get drunk.

---

[4]   Thirteen. Nicosia Road
                                      Wandsworth Common.
                                           [March 28, 1912]

Dear K.M.

Friday will be fine – I mean will do fine. Have you seen this *New
Age*[1] and *Present Day Criticism*?[2] They really have done it this time.
Good old Horace.[3] You mustn't go on imagining all these places. I'm
simply dying for sea washed windy hills – and it can't be done for ages.
There's something I want to talk to you about. Will you remind me, as
I'm sure to forget. I'll come in in the afternoon time.

I've been staining my floor all day – everything's in a damnable mess

J.M.M.

1. *The New Age*, a weekly review of politics, literature and art edited by A. R. Orage from 1907–1922, first launched K.M. on the London literary scene. The ten stories published by *The New Age* in 1910 and 1911 were collected with three others as *In a German Pension* (1911).

2. 'Present Day Criticism' was an occasional column in *The New Age* that reviewed anonymously other critical journals. The column of 28 March delivered a blistering attack on the latest (Spring, 1912) issue of *Rhythm*.

3. The column in question quoted with satiric effect from Horace's *Ars Poetica*.

---

[5]   13 Nicosia Road
                                                  Wandsworth Common
                                                      [March 30, 1912]

Dear K.M.,

Sorry I was so boring – can't be helped. Forgot all about what I wanted to say – which was I want you to have a look at a couple of things sent me for *Rhythm*, both under strong recommendation from people I believe in. One I think is rotten, the other quite good. Tell me what you think of them, as I imagine your judgement is nearer what mine would be, were I in a normal state. Let's fix up a day next week to lunch out tea out, dine out with Johnny F.[1] I'm going to try to touch Jackson[2] for a cheque tomorrow. Be charitable to a convalescent.

Your d-d house has got on my brain. I've just drawn a wonderful picture of it in words and told a friend of mine that I'm going to live there – you can run out naked in the long grass and roll, roll, right under the pine trees, and little winds creep about and pink your body all warm, and right over the wall on the right hand side is a deep place, all white nettle and convolvulus, and you don't dare jump down because there must be creepy things in the water, so you wriggle back under the tummocky grass right back to the Cherry Tree; and then you cry just out of pure joy just because you know the world is made for you and you can do anything with it: and day after day you do nothing because you can do everything and you lie on your back under the pine tree and look right up the long tunnels and little stars just twinkle down, twiddling round and round the long barrel till they drop in your face, and they sing and you shout – My God it's awful: and all at the cherry-tree, Heronsgate. Heron's gate – my god those herons just coming on a wisp of wind and flickering over the pine tops.

It's all because my gas lamp makes a hard steel mark on the roof below and I hate this bloody place. You'll be able to write masterpieces and won't, because the windy blood is all round your heart; and I shan't be able to, and shall write absolute muck and think for an hour that its good, and wake in the morning to know what a fool I've been. I'm simply bloody tonight. I found the daughter of the publican uncle, (It was a publican.) *waiting* to see me in my room. She talked to me about pure love as opposed to the other variety, and morals, and her 'boy' who is a stockbroker's clerk, secretary to a Y.M.C.A. 'Her dad was in low line of business – but she was going to marry a cultured man for love and not for money.' It all came out of nightmare book from 7.30 to 9 when I tucked her into a taxi and ran all round Wandsworth Common blaspheming – and forgot to borrow a quid.

But I'm going to take you seriously. When you're swinging on Heron's Gate you must ask me down to the tramp room I am a goodish tramp – and I shall forget everything for a bit. Or if you want an expert stainer, stain all day for his food call on me at once. And don't forget all about it[3]

Yours

J.M.M.

If Macqueen[4] ever does worry you for God's sake tell him Fergusson's in Thurso N.B and I'm in gaol for drunk and disorderly.

1. John Duncan Fergusson (1874–1961), a Scottish painter who became Murry's friend in Paris in 1910 and later art editor of *Rhythm*, first suggested the name *Rhythm*. In 1918 he, with Dorothy Brett, was a witness at the Murrys' registry office wedding.
2. Holbrook Jackson (1874–1948), editor and writer, co-founded *The New Age* with Orage in 1907 only to leave the magazine in 1908. He contributed to the Winter 1911 issue of *Rhythm*, and in March 1912 commissioned an article from Murry for *T.P.'s Weekly*.
3. Murry quotes part of this letter (making some minor corrections) in his autobiography *Between Two Worlds*, p. 191–192.
4. Willy Macqueen was a dilettantish member of Frank Harris's circle whom Katherine described in 1915 as an 'awful fathead'.

May – June 1913

By 1913, a pattern was establishing itself in the lives of K.M. and Murry: that of moving from one rented dwelling to another. Early in 1913, they went to live near their friend Gilbert Cannan, in Cholesbury, Bucks. But Murry, still trying to run *Rhythm* (later *The Blue Review*), was forced to commute from London at the weekends. A long series of separations, which they attempted to bridge by letters, had also begun in the lives of Katherine and Murry.

[6]
> The Blue Review,
> 57 Chancery Lane,
> London, W.C.
> [?6 May, 1913.]
> Tuesday 5 in the Afternoon

Tiger Darling,

   It's been raining all day; and I feel wet and miserable in soul, but not really downhearted. The bed felt terribly empty & big last night – we ought to have tiny little beds when we're apart don't you think so. I haven't done much work – it's all too clammy. You don't bear thinking about except that I see you in the corner of the kitchen with a big fire. You darling. I don't think I could have had a sweeter memory of you than that I carried away last week. It was fragrant and child-like enough to last me unfaded till Friday when I march up the hill again.

   I went to tea with Waterlow[1] yesterday to meet those Woolff people.[2] I don't think much of them. They belong to a perfectly impotent Cambridge set. Gordon[3] has just rung me up to say Beatrice is in London and could he meet me to-night. So I'm going to Selwood Terrace after I've been to the *Daily News*. I'm getting all untidy again now you're not here; but I've kept your room beautiful. Boulestin[4] has just been round. I like him very much, I think. He's working hard for us.

   We'll have a glorious time on Friday
                                            Jack[5]

1. Sydney Waterlow (1878–1944), writer, diplomat and former suitor of
Virginia Woolf, was a second cousin of Katherine Mansfield.
2. Leonard Woolf (1880–1969) and Virginia Woolf (1882–1941), who
married in 1912, were living at 13 Cliffords Inns, Fleet Street when Murry was
first introduced to them by Sydney Waterlow. Virginia gave her version of the
encounter with Murry to Lytton Strachey in July 1916: 'Katherine Mansfield
has dogged my steps for three years – I'm always on the point of meeting her,
or of reading her stories, and I have never managed to do either. But once
Sydney Waterlow produced Middleton Murry instead of her – a moon calf
looking youth – her husband? Do arrange a meeting . . .'.
3. Gordon Campbell (1885–1963), an Irish barrister, and his wife Beatrice
(later Lord and Lady Glenavy) lived at 9 Selwood Terrace and were generous
friends of Murry.
4. Marcel Xavier Boulestin, a writer, principally of cookery books, discussed 'Recent French Novels' in the June issue of *The Blue Review* and
contributed a satirical drawing in July.
5. K.M. replies early May: 'Yes, Friday *will* be fun'. Anthony Alpers in
The Life of Katherine Mansfield (1980), p. 158, gives the date of Murry's letter
incorrectly as 12 May. He also mistakenly describes this letter as the same one
written on 12 May in which Murry recounted the visit of Gaudier-Brzeska and
George Banks. These are definitely two separate letters.

---

[7]   57 Chancery Lane
                                            [London.]
                                     [before ?12 May, 1913.]

Dear Tig,

I'm writing this early because I want you to get it first thing in the
morning. I know I shall feel lonely in the evening and I don't want to
write to you if I'm feeling sad. I think this separation is beastly –
you're so very far away that I can't talk to you. And do you know I
thought you were more lovely and lovable than ever this last week-
end. O Tig, you were so sweet, and so like a little child that I feel like
crying when I write it. I adore you, darling.

But it's no use. I shall be alright if I set to work

I took the key away – what will you have done without it? But don't
be frightened, darling, it'll be alright. I'm sending you the only letters
that were not newspapers

                            Your darling
                            Jack.[1]

1. K.M. replies early ?12 May: 'The postman knocked into my dream with
your letter and the back door key'.

[8]

The Blue Review,
57 Chancery Lane,
London, W.C.
May 12 1913

Dear Tig,

Banks[1] & Gaudier[2] have just been. Of course I'm not worth a twopenny dam now. I've been crying out of sheer nervous reaction. The old lies shrieked at me + some Gaudier lies & venom. I can't do any work now. I'm just good for nothing. I don't know, but this Banks business simply does for me, darling. – I'm crying again now – O God. It'll be all over – all right when you get this; but somehow it's upset all my notions of what's right and just in the world. Am I a villain? why can't somebody stand up and say I'm not. I can bear anything almost. I'd be as poor as anything willingly but this kind of thing I cannot stand. God, is it all a joke. Or am I simply lying to myself when I say that we have struggled & fought for *Rhythm*?

Oh, I shall be alright. If you see Gilbert[3] tell him as he loves me and thinks me straight to crush that woman when he sees her – or I shall kill her. I'm not crying any more. Before they came, I was happy & thinking how glorious the weather is now I'm a bit skew. But it won't last much longer now I've had a good cry.

Letters.

Tig, I love you – but, suddenly this beast has fouled everything
Jack.[4]

1. George Banks, a mannish woman, was a cartoonist whom Murry had met in Paris in 1910. She contributed articles and drawings to *Rhythm* in 1911 and 1912.
2. Henri Gaudier-Brzeska (1891–1915), a gifted French artist and sculptor, had contributed to *Rhythm*. His love for Murry turned to fierce hatred when Katherine slighted his mistress, Sophie. He was killed in the war.
3. Gilbert Cannan (1884–1955), novelist, critic and friend of Murry who contributed to *Rhythm* and *The Blue Review*. Married to the divorced wife of J. M. Barrie, he and Mary Cannan lived at the Mill House, Cholesbury. In 1913, he persuaded the Murrys to rent the next-door cottage.
4. K.M. replies ? 13 May: 'Floryan is taking this for me'.

[9]   The Blue Review,
                                                57 Chancery Lane,
                                                   London, W.C.
                                                [14 May, 1913.]

Darling Tig,[1]

I've been working very hard to-day; for my week's books are very difficult. I've just come away from them to write this.

Floryan[2] turned up this morning. I hardly spoke to him; & I couldn't say what I wanted to (1) because I *can't* be stern to people (2) because my German always goes to pot, when I feel strongly about anything. He wanted your address because he said he wanted to speak to you

Floryan has just come; and Ida[3] is coming round in ¾ of an hour. Darling, I'm so glad about Gilbert & so grateful. Its been like a great weight crushing me. I'm alright in other ways darling. I'm coming at 6.15 tomorrow

                                                      Jack.

1. J.M. replies to K.M.'s letter of ? 13 May: 'Floryan is taking this for me'.
2. Floryan Sobieniowski (1881–1964), a Polish translator and critic with whom Katherine Mansfield became involved in Wörishofen in 1909. Cadging help, he reappeared in her life in 1912 and was subsequently listed as *Rhythm*'s 'Polish Correspondent'. In 1920 he blackmailed Katherine, demanding £40 for the return of her Wörishofen letters.
3. Ida Constance Baker (1888–1978), otherwise known as Lesley Moore or L.M., began her intimate relationship with Katherine at Queen's College in 1903. She remained a selflessly devoted friend for the rest of Katherine's life.

———————

[10]   57 [Chancery Lane
                                                   London.]
                                                [19 May, 1913.]

Dear Tig.

I was a beast this morning. Forgive me. You know I don't mean this things; and breakfast makes me horrible. I don't deserve to have a darling like you when I'm like that.

I send you a letter which you must keep. It only is definite proof of what a liar & Scoundrel Floryan is, and how he'll get us into trouble everywhere. Just write to the woman & tell her exactly how things really stood, will you not?

Also, a letter from Johnny [Fergusson] which shows the darling he is. I am writing to him tonight.

Abercrombie[1] was here when I arrived. He is a very attractive man, with a curious lined, spectacled, quizzical face. I think if I saw more of him I shd. get on with him famously.

Also, a letter from Albert,[2] which is a very welcome suprise.

I send you all my love darling; tho' I'm hurrying to the *Westminster*

Your loving

Jack.[3]

1. Lascelles Abercrombie (1881–1938), poet, dramatist and critic who contributed in 1913 to *Rhythm* and *The Blue Review*.
2. Albert Rothenstein (1881–1953), younger brother of William Rothenstein, later changed his name to 'Rutherston'. He was an artist and designer who contributed to *Rhythm* and *The Blue Review* in 1913.
3. K.M. replies 20 May: 'I am sorry for my anxiety of yesterday'.

---

[11]   57 Chancery Lane
                                       [London.]
                                       [?20 May, 1913.]

Tig Darling,[1]

I'm all late & lonely tonight; not so much that the loneliness worries me as that I keep on accusing myself for being a beast on Monday at breakfast. But do forgive me; I didn't mean it. I've read both your story & your chronicle again. They are both top-notch & it would be impossible to cut them, at any rate I couldn't do it, and I don't think that anyone would have the stupidity to do so They go in intact.

Ransome[2] was here yesterday & to-day trying to inveigle me into the country with him. I was adamant. Wilfrid's[3] going however next week-end, so we shall be alone – which is first rate. W. H. Davies[4] also was here.

I don't think that there'll be be any difficulty about placing stories of 1000 words if they aren't too 'shocking' in the sedate Saturday *Westminster*. The Royde-Smith,[5] quite unprovoked, was expressing a great admiration for yr. work. Wilfrid thinks your story *great*, & you know what I think. You're alright.

Books this week for the *Westminster* are particularly heavy; but I'll be down on Thursday at the old time. By God, I do wish I was there now.

Hake[6] was there yesterday. We talked from 9 to 12 at night; and I gave him supper. His mind is simply improving like anything. He's read all sorts of things that matter lately and too many that I haven't.

Darling, dont worry about me. I'm alright, except that now my stomach's empty. It's half past ten – people worry me so that I can't write before – and I haven't had supper. I'm going out to Sam Isaacs[7] if I can find the outdoor key.

My love darling
Jack.

Visitors today Curle[8] Swinnerton[9] Davies Boulestin Ransome Spring-Rice[10] all at difft. times

1. J.M. is probably replying to Katherine's letter of the previous day: 'I've nursed the *Epilogue* to no purpose'.
2. Arthur Ransome (1884–1967), journalist and prolific writer, especially of children's books.
3. Wilfrid Wilson Gibson (1878–1962), Georgian poet and regular contributor to *Rhythm*. After Eddie Marsh subsidised him as assistant-editor of *Rhythm*, he used a small 'cubby hole' in Murry's flat at 57 Chancery Lane as an office.
4. W. H. Davies (1871–1940), Georgian poet who contributed to *Rhythm* and *The Blue Review*.
5. Naomi Royde-Smith, editor of the Saturday *Westminster*, the literary supplement of the *Westminster Gazette*.
6. Thomas St. Edmund Hake (d. 1917), novelist and writer.
7. Sam Isaacs was a cheap restaurant where Murry and Katherine often dined.
8. Richard Curle (1883–1968), writer and friend of Conrad, was a contributor to *Rhythm*. With Swinnerton and others he frequented *Rhythm*'s Chancery Lane office.
9. Frank Swinnerton (1884–1982) was one of the prominent 'younger generation' writers who contributed to, and enthusiastically supported *Rhythm*.
10. Edward Dominick Spring-Rice (1829–1940), Cambridge-educated writer on banking subjects.

[12]   [57 Chancery Lane
London.]
[21 May, 1913]

Dear Tig,[1]

It's funny writing at 5 in the afternoon; but I'm determined that you shall have this letter early in the morning.

I got the review this morning. I didn't roar. Thank's very much, darling; it'll do fine.

Gordon turned up at lunch-time; & took Wilfrid & me out to lunch in Grays Inn. It was very good. He's flourishing & coming down on Friday in the afternoon.

I'm going to supper with Rupert[2] to-night because he's going off to America in the morning; it's all very silly but a free meal is fascinating. This extra day without you is rotten. London feels so very grey – and I get so forced back upon myself and the work that here I sit writing my column on Wednesday afternoon. The *B.R*[3] has gone to press to-day. I think its very good. Wilfrid saw it off at Secker's[4] – I suppose I knew he wood. I've been swanking about the great masterpieces you've been writing in the country; and I've got a howling respect for you. No I haven't. I think you're a nut – but I adore you even more than I respect you.

But, darling, what has been the matter with you? I can't quite tell from you're letter whether you're ill or not. My god, I hope not.

I'll bring your German dictionary tomorrow; and also a book about the backwoods of Australia for review (by Eleanor Mordaunt).[5] It looks to me that it might be good – and anyhow you'll do a good review of it. I'll order Colette Willy's books[6] for you and Ch. Phillippe[7] for me when I go to the bank tomorrow; because I've only got 4/1 left. I had supper at Sam Isaacs last night 1/3 because there was nothing to eat at home.

Anyhow I'm coming home tomorrow.

Jack

1. J.M. replies to K.M.'s letter of 20 May: 'I am sorry for my anxiety of yesterday'.
2. Rupert Brooke (1887–1915), poet, contributed to *Rhythm* and *The Blue Review*. He introduced Murry to Edward Marsh and later visited the Murrys at Runcton with Marsh and Frederick Goodyear. Murry attended a farewell supper for him on the eve of his visit to America. He died of blood-poisoning en route for Gallipoli.

3. *The Blue Review* succeeded *Rhythm* in May 1913 but collapsed, after three issues, in July.

4. Martin Secker, publisher, printed *The Blue Review* and later commissioned a book on Dostoevsky from Murry in repayment of the printing debt.

5. Eleanor Mordaunt published in 1911 a novel, *Ship of Solace*, and a travel book, *On the Wallaby through Victoria*.

6. Colette Willy (1873–1954) was one of K.M.'s favourite contemporary novelists.

7. Charles Louis Phillipe (1874–1909), a French writer of realistic novels, published *Charles Blanchard* in 1913.

---

[13]   [57 Chancery Lane,
                                                      London.]
                                          [May–June, 1913.]

Tiger Darling,

When I was eating my beef and pickles all alone to-night, I felt very very lonely; so I came into my room and tried to find some paragraphs – and that cured me a bit. Oh, but I shall be glad to think that Friday is nearer & nearer. I'm getting all untidier. I'm unshaved and dirty; but I shall be nice & clean when I come down on Friday. I'll tell you tomorrow night what train – early in the afternoon.

Gordon was miserable a bit last night; but I can't help envying him all the money he earns. He has two more cases; and I'm trying hard to write my column for 2 guineas. It's funny. Christian phoned me up at lunch time to-day because on Tuesday I promised that I wd. go to the Max. show[1] with him. So I went, though I didn't want to to-day. I couldn't be amused over them somehow. They didn't seem funny. Perhaps it was me though.

I'm all tired now. I don't want to begin writing a review; and I don't dare not to. I feel I should like just one big real holiday without thinking, just lying in long grass and swimming in a soft sea and pushing an old boat off.

Lunn's[2] just been in. Harris[3] is going offer & offer with him.

                          Love Tig my love
                                    Jack

Time Newspaper just came

1. An exhibition of Max Beerbohm's caricatures, which Eddie Marsh reviewed in the June issue of *The Blue Review*. Beerbohm's 'A Study in

Dubiety' (a caricature of Marsh and Churchill in Churchill's office) was the frontispiece of the first issue of *The Blue Review*.

2. Hugh Kingsmill Lunn (1889–1949), early admirer – later biographer – of Frank Harris, met Murry at Dan Rider's bookshop in 1911.

3. Frank Harris (1856–1931), writer and editor, contributed to *Rhythm* at a time when Murry hero-worshipped him. His magazine *Hearth and Home* published K.M.'s uncollected story 'The House' in 1912.

———

[14]   57 Chancery Lane
                         [London.]
                         [June, 1913]
                         2.30 pm

Dear Tig,

Unless I write at this absurdly early hour I know that I shan't catch the post. I am sending you a P.O. for 35/-. It wd have been £2; only I don't like to get more than £4 out of the bank, wh. less £1 Wilfrid & 10/- Wm. wd. only leave me 10/- for stamps & my fare down: so I've kept 15/-. I wish to heaven I didn't have to come back for anything at all.

I hate my room here so. It's almost impossible to do anything in it. There's something very unsympathetic about it after my blue room at Cholesbury, though I can't exactly say what it is. I'm pulling at my finger & I just remembered you – Tiger, ne fais pas ça, s'il vous plait – and I've left off *pro tem*. But I want to be back again at the Gables.[1]

We caught the train with a quarter of an hour to spare and ate oranges on the station. Why am I so rude to Lesley Moore? I don't know; but I can't help it. But I love you – you're me –

                         Jack.[2]

Will you send my glasses in the box so that I can take them back?

1. 'The Gables' was the cottage at Cholesbury, Bucks. (near the Cannans' windmill house) that Katherine and Murry took in March 1913.
2. Katherine replies in June: 'I sent your glasses yesterday . . .'.

February 1914

The *Blue Review* collapsed, as *Rhythm* had done. In December 1913 Murry, with Katherine, sought escape from both his creditors and what he now saw as the drudgery of journalism by moving – with all their possessions – to Paris. Although he embarked on his novel, *Still Life*, and Katherine wrote 'Something Childish but very Natural', their hopes of a new life came to nothing. Unable either to earn a living in Paris, or to keep on deferring bankruptcy proceedings, Murry was forced to visit London in February 1914. He wrote eight letters to Katherine between February 8 and 12, returning to Paris only to arrange for their permanent removal to London. By March he was again working for the *Westminster* as a full-time reviewer and art critic.

[15]   [9 Selwood Terrace,
                                            South Kensington,
                                                London.]
                                        [8 February, 1914.]
                                            Sunday

Dear Tig,
   I have been very well at Campbells   He's just the same; and they have given me such a jolly little bedroom.
   I rang up [W.L.] George to-day and went to lunch with him. He's just the same too   Everybody's just the same. Lesley who again is opposite me at Fleming's for tea is just the same too. London makes me frightfully vague though. I cant focus to anything properly. I want to be back again. All my work, everything I want is now 31 rue de Tournon.[1] But still I'm going to be awfully business like to-morrow, I hope. Please I'm going to buy pepper & salt trousers if I can find any. Are you happy? I've got my feet wet now – and my tooth hasn't quite stopped aching.
   Were you frightened after all? You mustn't be. Its alright. I am

determined to leave by the night train on Tuesday, unless unforeseen
events i.e. jobs prevent me.

All my love
Jack.[2]

1. 31 rue de Tournon was the address of the flat K.M. and J.M. took in
Paris in December 1913.
2. K.M. replies 9 February: 'I am glad that Campbell is looking after you'.

---

[16]   [9 Selwood Terrace,
                                     South Kensington,
                                     London.]
                                     Feb. 10. 1914
                                     Tuesday 1 a.m.

I saw the bankruptcy man[1] today and I am glad that I did for, as
long as you do what you are told, they seem to be very kindly disposed
at least to one in my situation. I think that this business at least will
turn out well enough.

As for the other, even now I am no wiser than before. I am not sure
whether my immediate preference for sticking to the *Westminster* is
not merely prudential. I think even that I would throw the whole
business over if we had not got that flat in Paris – but that if we are
really poor will hang about our necks and weaken us because we can't
afford it on less than £250 a year, & perhaps hardly even on that. I wish
that I could see my way clear.

All the while I feel that I shd. be better if I had Tig close by me. Its a
ghastly business not having enough money to afford even £2 10.0 for
an extra fare to Paris & back

I'll go on with this as a letter. I'm no use at keeping a diary. I feel
that its just irony. On Monday morning I was going about so cheerful,
spending 5.16.6 on my clothes, and telling the man at the shop to be
sure and send them early Tuesday morning, for I was leaving by the
night train, and then at 3 to see Spender,[2] & at 4 to see Richmond.[3] It's
taken me a long while to understand it. We can't give up Paris its a
symbol of something free for us; nor can I (and that is we) live there
yet.

Tig you are perfect. I had to tell the Campbells all the story of how
we met and how we lived together – two years ago – to keep myself
from feeling miserable. It certainly made me feel happy. I have a little

tiny camp bed, like the one we used to sleep in together when we first came to Chancery Lane, and I went to sleep and you ached and never said a word. Now, though we're wiser perhaps we're in something of the same hole again, & again a camp bed, and only me sleeping in it. But that's not symbolical: I need you more than ever: I feel I can't move without you. Dear heart I kiss you good-night, to wake to your morning letter. Good-night

Tig. Tig

1. When the publisher of *Rhythm* absconded in October 1912, Murry and Katherine shouldered a printing debt of £400. Unable to keep up the repayments, Murry was forced to declare bankruptcy in February 1914.

2. J. A. Spender (1862–1942), the humane and liberal editor of *The Westminster Gazette*, offered Murry in February 1914 the job of art editor on *The Westminster*.

3. Bruce Richmond (1871–1964), editor of *The Times Literary Supplement*. He said he would do his best to help Murry by sending him French books to review in Paris.

Alpers writes (p. 181) that by 1915 'Murry was now established as the *Times Literary Supplement* reviewer of French books'. He states that this work, together with K.M.'s increased allowance, enabled the Murrys to take a house (and servant) at St. John's Wood. In fact, G. P. Lilley's 1974 bibliography of Murry's writing shows that the *T.L.S.* published one review in 1914, none in 1915, and one in 1916. Only in 1917, when six reviews appeared, could Murry be considered an 'established' reviewer for the *T.L.S.* Murry, in *Between Two Worlds* (which appears to be Alpers' source), is himself astray in writing of the period at Mylor, in the summer of 1916: 'I was now well established as a reviewer of French books for *The Times Literary Supplement*'.

<hr>

[17]   9, Selwood Terrace,
South Kensington, S.W.
[London.]
February 10 1914

Darling,

I'm afraid you didn't understand my wire, it was so brief. On Monday Gordon inquired about my bankruptcy business from a friend of his who is Assistant Receiver; and this friend said the only thing for me to do was to go to see them immediately. If I didn't they wd. put out a warrant after me; if I did they wd be very nice as the bankruptcy wasn't my fault. Accordingly, this Tuesday morning I went. They were nice. They said they wouldn't make any attempt to touch my earnings, and that there wdn't be any difficulty, *if* I filed a statement of my affairs immediately. The man told me to write to all the people to whom I owed money and find out exactly what I owed and bring the results to him on Friday morning when they wd draw up my statement for me. After that, I shd. only have to attend my public examination in March. So today I've written to everybody. It seems that I can do no good by returning to Paris before Friday, as I only lose the fare; and we've got so very little money. That's why I wired. If I get the answers I may manage to do the business on Thursday morning and get off Thursday evening. Only I see plainly that I must get the business off my mind, or I shall get into serious trouble.

Then about the other, even more important business, I don't know whether I made it all plain, as I was so agitated when I wrote. It amounts to this. I can't expect more than £6 a month from the *Times*; and I can expect nothing from the *Westminster*, if I decide not to return. My other attempts to find work haven't turned out well – the *British Review* won't, & the *Nation* Editor is in Egypt so that I can have no reply for 2 months. It doesn't seem to be any use looking to that. The *Westminster*, if I decide for it will take me on, as art-critic & regular reviewer, and give me £5 a week, but I must decide within three weeks.

Darling, you must try to decide for me. I don't feel that I can face working in Paris, with only £6 a month to come in, and that quite uncertain. I couldn't do anything with that idea over my head. Don't you think that somehow we had better try to exchange our flat for a year with somebody and meanwhile work here somewhere till we've got some money to fall back on i.e. produce all we can, at least 1 novel each during the year, and then if we see a fair chance clear off to our flat in Paris for good? But write to me and tell me what you think. I know we have over a week to talk about it when I get back; but I want you now. Even that arrangement depends upon exchanging flats – but somehow that shouldn't be difficult; and then we shd. always have our home in Paris, & cd. look upon it as an enforced holiday. I shd. be happy anywhere with you, so long as you had a proper working-room. (Darling, just an interruption – I love you. I can just see you there, and now were straining against each other to make us both brave. Oh darling – you are me) But we mustn't decide in a hurry. One thing we can*not* do – that is *move* in the real sense of the word. Even if our pride wd. allow it our purse won't.

Darling, I've kissed you and I feel brave as anything
Jack.[1]

1. K.M. replies on 11 February: 'I expect I did not understand your wire quite fully'.

---

[18]   [9 Selwood Terrace,
                                                South Kensington,
                                                London.]
                                                [11 February, 1914.]
                                                12 a.m.

Wednesday Morning,
Darling,[1]
I got your letter this morning and I felt awfully sad. I wanted to come over to-day just to see you – but I don't think it wd. be right. We can't afford it, & I should have to come back for Friday morning. In the letter you got yesterday morning I explained all that I could.

Oh, darling don't imagine that I don't know the disappointment & didn't feel it myself. There's something I feel even more. Continually I have before my face the picture of how you would look if I were to arrive tonight, and it makes me cry. Yet I know you understand. Something seems determined to play with us again; but though the worries are not all over after Friday, the bankruptcy is practically cleared off; and then we shall be able to think clearly about the rest. Darling, if you can manage it, write me a word of advice about it, not that I'm helpless – but it wd make me feel as though you were talking to me about it.

Thursday, Friday, Saturday – oh, it seems long: but, darling, the end *must* come then. Don't think about the people who come & go. Shut the door fast and think of us both together.
                         Your darling
                              Jack[2]

1. J.M. replies to K.M.'s letter of 10 February: 'If you are staying so long, I had better send you this to answer'.
2. K.M. replies 12 February: 'You are good to me! Two letters this morning . . .'.

---

[19]   Lyons. Oxford St.
                                                [London.]
                                                [11 February, 1914.]
                                                5 o'clock

Darling,

   I'm here with Lesley. You will have a letter from me at the time you
get this if not before. I'm not any forrader yet about the whole
business. The question seems to me whether, supposing we could find
a decent place in London, you feel that you could work there. That's
all important. And I'm not quite sure whether you could. What do you
think; or do you think that what we ought to do is to risk everything
and hang on – now I've got to the old question.

   O Tig, I nearly came at mid-day to-day; but how could I with the
money we have. It wouldn't have been right. But darling, I love you
too dearly not to be missing you terribly at every minute of the day.
Try to think that just now I'm cuddled up with you in the morning &
the alarm has just stopped sounding. My head is on your breast, and
I'm very sleepy and warm. You're more awake, because you always
are; but I'm just only awake enough to be trying to kiss you lazily, and
then my head flops down to snuggle between your breasts.

   For thats where I am really, darling.

                                                Jack.[1]

   1. K.M. replies 12 February: 'You are good to me! Two letters this
morning . . .'.

---

[20]   [9 Selwood Terrace,
                                                South Kensington,
                                                London.]
Bedtime. Wednesday   [11 February, 1914.]

Darling,

   There's only one more bedtime here, and the next I shall be in the
train on my way to you. The day has been slow, slow beyond all
telling. I spend the time mostly mooning in a chair; the rest wandering
about London. I go to bed only with the expectation of a long letter
from you in the morning. This morning I was disappointed; but I see
now why it was. My telegram about the bankruptcy did not reach you

till late on Tuesday, and then you were expecting that I should be on my way back to Paris by the night train, so that you were not going to write and my telegram only left you a few minutes before the post. Oh, but I want something longer to-morrow, please. I wonder. Tig, did I tell you that on Monday morning I had bought all my fine clothes, my shoes, my black overcoat, my blue jacket and my white trousers – and in the afternoon I got my news. Wasn't it just my luck?

Tig dear, you do love me awfully don't you? and you do think that I'm trying to do everything as well as I can don't you? Because if you didn't, or if I thought that you were going to be sad with me, I should be terribly miserable. But that's silly isn't it. I know you think I'm doing things right, because I am trying to, my hardest.

There's nothing to say, darling – for nothing happens. Gordon has helped me awfully, though sometimes I feel mad hurt with him because he plays with his baby, instead of looking grave about our affairs. I am a silly chump. He has been splendid to me, more than any friend I cd. imagine. I'm just going to bed.

I have horrible thoughts of you sometimes getting frightened in the flat. But, darling, don't. Its really safe. Perhaps I should convince myself, if you didn't sometimes seem to be so tiny that no-one could take you for a grown-up woman, but only something to be taken in my arms. You are such a wonderful child. I shall never see you grown-up. That photo of you I've got in my pocket-case, is wrong, I see now, just because it hasn't got enough of the child.

Tig, I am going to bed with you, only you, in my eyes.

Jack

---

[21]   [9 Selwood Terrace,
                 South Kensington,
                   London.]
                 [12 February, 1914.]
               Thursday morning 10 a.m.

Darling,[1]

I have just had your letter. Do you think I didn't hate the postcard as much as you did. Only what was I to do? I was sealing up your letter, when Beatrice[2] gave it to me to send to you with her initials on the other side. It seemed so utterly foolish, considering what I was writing about. But I couldn't help it.

O, Tig, don't think for a moment I'm wanting to stay on here till the exchange. All I want to do is to get back. Then we have a long while to think out, and if we decide for the job. Then we can both come over and live somewhere and try afterwards to let the flat or exchange. If I'm making a little money we can afford to do that and even have the flat empty for some time. But I shouldn't think that it would be hard to let

But its only together that we can really see straight. I'm just going off to see if I can finish up the bankruptcy to-day Thursday. There's a 1000 to 1 chance.

Anyhow I'll write by early morning post which is delivered in Paris in the Friday evening.

Jack.

1. J.M. replies to K.M.'s letter of 11 February: 'I expect I did not understand your wire quite fully'.
2. Beatrice Campbell.

---

[22]
[9 Selwood Terrace,
South Kensington,
London.]
[12 February, 1914.]
7 o'clock
Thursday

Tig darling,

I have just got the bankruptcy business over, and I am coming by the 10 a.m. train tomorrow morning Friday which gets in about 8 o'clock or a little before, just after half. past seven.

Darling, I shall be happy to see you again – then we can get every thing right.

Love – to catch the post

Jack.

February 1915

1914, in the aftermath of their return to Paris, proved to be for Katherine and Murry an unsettled year. As Murry put it: 'The times were out of joint. There seemed so little to cling to'. While he became engrossed in his intellectual friendship with D. H. Lawrence and Gordon Campbell, Katherine turned emotionally to the romantic figure of Murry's Parisian friend, Francis Carco. Believing that the time had come to leave Murry, she arranged to join her new lover in France. On 15 February 1915, Murry saw her off – not jealous, but quietly confident, as his five letters show, that their relationship would endure. He was right. The affair was a fiasco and ten days later Katherine returned to him and Rose Tree Cottage.

[23]   [Rose Tree Cottage,
                                          The Lee,
                                    Great Missenden,
                                    Buckinghamshire.]
                                    [15 February, 1915.]
                                    Monday Night. In the shed.

Darling,
    Its better that I should be in my shed when I write to you, because I'm used to being alone there and I feel fairly cheerful, nothing worse than a kind of strangeness. Inside the house its quite different – very cold, in a very lonely way; but that was inevitable. The only drawback is that if I write while I'm still in my shed, it won't quite be true, because I know it will feel very different when I've gone back into the house and rattled a Primus stove about to heat the hot-water bottle without whose company I don't dare to go to bed. You must remember that when I say that all that I feel just now is a kind of strangeness, not very much unlike what I've had before, and tried to describe to you as the going-in-to-examination feeling, – a kind of apprehension, when, without being actually uneasy, my mind keeps harping on the

thought of how uneasy I shall be – *when* I shut my shed door and go in to the empty bed-room.

The more I try to describe to you how I feel the less certain am I about it. But I think that it is not unlike the physical sensation I have got as the result of 'Belguins' or whatever they are. They have dried up my cold without letting me forget that I have one.[1] Similarly, in my shed I don't feel violently that you are not here, but something keeps on reminding me that I'd better not go into the house expecting you, or shouting out 'Tig', because I shall only get an echo, a very chilly echo, in reply. But in spite of the incessant warning I can't quite believe that you aren't really there. Just to write these words is the nearest I have come to actually believing it. Besides that I instinctively try to present to myself what ten days really means – and that's the hardest thing in the world; for there are all kinds of ten days.

But I'm not sad, or miserable, darling – only just vaguely uncomfortable, anticipating uneasiness, like a cat incessantly turning round to see whether his tale [sic] is really there. How long this will take to get to you!

Jack.

just a word to say that I'm on my way to the Lawrences[2] for 3 days will write tonight.

1. Murry was going down with a violent attack of influenza, and he went to the Lawrences to be nursed. Lawrence later fictionalised his care of Murry at this time in *Aaron's Rod*.

2. D. H. Lawrence (1885–1930) and Frieda Lawrence (1879–1956) first met Katherine and Murry in 1913 at the office of *Rhythm*. A close but difficult relationship developed between these two couples – especially between Lawrence and Murry – who lived near each other for periods from 1914 –1916. Unknown to Murry, Lawrence was in 1916 writing him and Katherine into *Women in Love* as Gerald and Gudrun.

---

[24]   Greatham
                                        Pulborough
                                        Sussex.
Tuesday   16 February, 1915.

Darling,

You see that one night alone was enough. I had to run off to the Lawrences, feeling that they might be kind to me. They have been –

and I will remember it in their favour. You see its no use plunging into solitude after having been with you – but in a few days I may very possibly be quite sick with the L's (or they with me) and then to be alone in my shed will appear delightful. Anyhow I couldn't work – my cold has got quite bad again, so a change of atmosphere will do me good, I think. Of course this cottage is a palace. One enormous dining-room with great beams, the size of a good barn, three bed-rooms, a bath-room and a wonderful kitchen. For comfort it beats Mary's Mill,[1] (though it is after Mary's style) because its not over-crowded with things. I must confess I envy these people their money. Its the kind of cottage we could live in so much better than they. However, we were born to be poor. Its horrible to think that I'm already getting quite sick of our cottage at the Lee,[2] but there it is. It seems as though we shall never be satisfied without perfection, that we can never afford.

That sounds very gloomy, but I'm not – only worried a bit by the cold. Rather I'm glad that I'm not sleeping alone in that cottage tonight. I walked here 4 most confusing miles from the station, and at length in despair and in total darkness, I knocked at this door to ask the way. I was pleasantly bouleversed to find Lorenzo[3] at the door. Inside was a lady called Cynthia Asquith[4] – not born but married Asquith – who was rather nice of the clever kind; much better than the women the L's generally pick up, though there was a great deal too much 'Lady Cynthia' about it all. L. enjoys it a bit, himself – while Frieda almost wallows.

I am eagerly waiting your letter to me. L says he saw you in London last night.

To be continued tomorrow morning.

Wednesday Morning.

Darling Tig – Someone is going to London, so that I have a chance of sending this little letter off earlier. I will write again by the 7 o'clock post tonight.   Jack.

1. The mill house of Gilbert and Mary Cannan at Cholesbury.
2. In October 1914 K.M. and J.M. had moved to Rose Tree Cottage at The Lee, in Buckinghamshire. For a time the Lawrences lived only three miles away in Chesham; but in January they moved to Viola Meynell's cottage at Greatham, near Pulborough, in Sussex.
3. An affectionate name for D. H. Lawrence.
4. Lady Cynthia Asquith (1887–1959), married to the Hon. Herbert Asquith (son of the Liberal Prime Minister), was introduced to Lawrence in 1913 by Edward Marsh and became his generous friend.

[25]   Greatham
                                    nr. Pulborough
Wednesday afternoon   17 February, 1915.

Tig Darling,

I'm very glad I came here, now, for I don't think I could have stuck out existence at the Lee. My cold began to give me a thorough exhibition of its possibilities.

At present I am waiting for some news of you, – but I shall get a letter before you get this. Having a cold, naturally all my news would be concerned with that, and the one colossal fact is that I have only one clean pocket handkerchief to face the world. The lady of high degree left today and left me wondering (as I've done before) how women who have such a lot of knowledge can be so essentially stupid & useless. It was an amazing exhibition of ineffectuality. This afternoon we had to go to Monica Saleeby's[1] cottage (she lives next door) for coffee. What I cannot imagine after seeing her is how she ever managed the aesthetic-sugeric [sic] stunt with the bearded doctor. She's fat, quite amiable & kindly, and perfectly stupid, *so stupid* that Frieda L. seems a paragon of wit and ingenuity beside her. Then there is the famous Sebastian[2] – again an amiable fellow utterly dull. I am afraid his amiability mainly consists in the pleasant conceit of myself he manages to give me, by hanging onto my words in awestruck reverence. I like people to do that. I feel a great man again, when they do it while I have a cold. I imagine that I told you that this cottage was palatial – therefore annoying. But I must say the L's deserve their luck, for they are being very nice to me, me without an idea in my head, breathing grampously thro' my open mouth, and generally behaving like a fish on a fishmonger's slab.

But I shall leave the cold at Greatham so that you will have quite a nice boy when you get back.

But what's the use of all this except to say that I am waiting for your letter. I hope that the fine weather yesterday made the Channel tolerable; but you see that I don't know how you are getting on now. I'm not worried, but just now I feel at one end of a broken telephone wire.

                        Jack.

1. Monica Saleeby, daughter of Wilfrid and Alice Meynell, and wife of Dr. Caleb Saleeby, a well-known popular science writer. It was at their home that

K.M. and her first husband, George Bowden, had met in 1909. By 1915, however, the Saleebys' marriage had collapsed and Monica was suffering from a nervous breakdown.

2. Possibly W. J. H. ['Sebastian'] Sprott (1897–1971), who became known in Bloomsbury circles as a friend of Lady Ottoline Morrell, J. M. Keynes and later E. M. Forster.

---

[26]　　　　　　　　　　　　Greatham.
　　　　　　　　　　　　　　[Pulborough]
　　　　　　　　　　[Thursday,] Feb. 18. 1915

Darling Tig.

I enclose a registered letter from Carco.[1] It appears that the right address in Elgin Crescent was 95,[2] not 91, and the man was there on Monday. I have just had a card from him & have written to arrange a meeting as I pass through London home. I don't quite know when I shall go – probably as soon as my cold is quite better.

Nothing has happened since yesterday. The Lawrences continue to be very kind to me, except that Frieda has ferreted out my novel[3] which she reads in secret somewhere. That annoys me, though I don't know why it should. I feel exactly as I did once when I got ill at Oxford & Fox[4] took me away to his house to stay until I was better. The feeling is a kind of pleasant irresponsibility. The cottage is light & pleasant; & I have a convincing excuse for doing nothing. I am still waiting for a letter.

(I've just come back from a short walk since writing what goes before – and, inevitably Frieda has read what I've written before. I can't help thinking that it serves her right.) When I say that I am waiting for your letter, I don't mean that I'm worried at not getting one, for I have calculated the time and don't expect anything until tomorrow morning. Let it be a long one

　　　　　　　　　　　　　Jack.

1. Francis Carco (1886–1958), bohemian French poet, novelist and contributor to *Rhythm* whom Murry first met in 1910, and whom K.M. met in December 1913. Imagining herself in love with him after a passionate correspondence, K.M. had left Murry to join Carco in the war zone at Gray, in France. The affair was a fiasco.

2. 95 Elgin Crescent, London, where Murry was to take rooms in March, 1915.

3. *Still Life*, which was begun in Paris in December 1913 and published by Constable in 1916.

4. H. F. Fox, Murry's admired and kindly classical tutor at Oxford.

---

[27]   Greatham, Pulborough
                                        [19 February, 1915.]
Friday.

Dear Tig,

I haven't had a word yet, though I did expect something this morning. I shall begin to be worried if nothing turns up tomorrow, because after that is Sunday, and I can't get the letter, even if there is one. And that means waiting till Monday.

But you mustn't be worried, if you get this when you have already sent me letters, because it is very possible that the posts are entirely disorganised, and there may be any amount of delays.

Now there is nothing to say, because I am waiting. My cold is getting better; but I want news of you. Lawrence is plainly writing you a line just now.

                        Jack.

From March 18 to 31, Katherine made another visit to France where Carco (still at Gray) had given her the use of his Paris apartment. Now her mood was different. Once again in love with Murry, she wanted to write, and in fact began the first draft of *The Aloe*.

[28]   9, Selwood Terrace,
                                        South Kensington,
                                        [London.]
Friday   [19 March, 1915.]

Dear darling,[1]
    I don't think there is very much fun to be had out of furnishing rooms alone.[2] It just seems like a great waste, of energy & money & time. There's no-one to enjoy it.
    I'm dog-tired. In the middle of the day I sent you a cross p.c. about the man who was to have upholstered the sofa. In case the p.c. does not reach you, I asked where he was to be found. I hunted all over Baker St. for a couple of hours in vain. Please give me some directions that will do.
    I was at the job of finding cheap furniture all day to-day. Its cheap & nasty; but it can't be helped. We couldn't afford better. Then I've been putting up shelves in the kitchen. I bought a chest of drawers for 16/- (wh: I shall have to paint to-morrow) but I can't find a cupboard anywhere.
    No, I'm not going on with this now. I'm too tired

1. K.M. replies on 25 March: 'Yesterday I had your letters at last'.
2. At 95 Elgin Crescent.

---

[29]
9 Selwood Terrace,
South Kensington,
[London.]
[20 March, 1915.]
Saturday Night.

Tig Darling,[1]

I was so tired last night that I could not get on with the letter I began. I'm pretty tired again tonight, but not so much in the head. I'll tell you all I did to-day, & yesterday.

Yesterday I started out to find a chest of drawers cheap. The Harrow Road was useless, Fulham Rd no better, and I woke up, and went in a kind of desperation to that shop that is at the corner of Edith Grove, where I found a plain servant's chest, big, for 16/-. Then I had to hurry off to the *W.G.*[2] My hat blew off in the road, and skiddled into a pool of black mud as soon as I got outside the shop. So I had to carry it in my hand all the morning. When the *W.G.* was done, (Naomi[3] very off me. Spender very well inclined) I went off to the imaginary King,[4] South St., Baker St., and after wearing my legs out and getting very cross, went to sale, (the big lamp people in Oxford St) & bt. 3 incandescent burners. Then off to Holland Park, where I got 2 wooden mantelpieces out of an oil shop for shelves. Then in a cheap furniture shop I found a new kitchen table (ugly as sin) & 2 kitchen chairs (uglier, but paint will do wonders) 10/- the lot. Then I started in on the carpentry. But I only got one shelf up when I had to go. But I went back to Gordon's happy for the furniture from the country had arrived. It looked nothing in the rooms; but still there it is. Somewhere in that day you have to sandwich curtain rods and carpentering tools (3 visits to the ironmonger) – quite enough. The ironmonger did not stock the decent shades of Ripolin[5] so

This morning I began with a search for the head Ripolin office. I got what I wanted – a good yellow, & good blue & white (4/-). Then off to Norman Franks, where I stocked myself with fairly decent things (not very original for 10/-. Then to Whiteleys for a kitchen cupboard. Terribly expensive. The only good sized one 18/-. I bought a tiny one for 7/6. At the back of Whiteleys in a disgustingly dirty shop I caught sight of a sort of corner cupboard without a door, but the shelves were all like Arthur's[6] letter rack, slanting downwards, so I went away. After a while I thought that by a bit of carpentry I could change it. So I went back: the man was out. I spoke to three small boys who seemed to be in charge, and eventually left a note to say that if the aforesaid (filthy) cupboard was brought round to 95 Elgin before 6 oclock, I would give 3/- for it. Then off to the oilshop to buy brooms & pails & bowls 10/-, white paint & brushes from the ironmonger. When I got back the cupboard had arrived. The bosom[7] – name Mrs. *Sprinks* – had paid for it. No doubt she's made up her mind that I'm a hopeless fool to pay for that. Then 3 solid hours carpentry – after getting your letter from Victoria – I bashed the thing in to shape – took it all to pieces & put it together again, put up the second shelf, and made the floor unimaginable. The filth out of that old cupboard got into my eyes, my lungs & my nails while I sandpapered it more or less clean. But I was very pleased with the job at the end. It was worth 13/- now I thought. Then I began to paint, gave the shelves their first coat, when in came Lawrence, Frieda, Horne[8] & Kottilianski.[9] That took ½ an hour. They didn't go till 5 past 7, and I still had to give the first coat to my cupboard Then I was unspeakably filthy. I used my new towel & hanselled the bath. You get oceans of really hot water for a penny I got out of the bath at ten to 8 and sprinted for my life home. Did the whole journey in 19 minutes.

Aren't I a good Jag? Two days and I haven't been woolly a bit, but working very hard. Tomorrow morning Sunday I'm promised to search out the L's at Temple Fortune Hill chez Barbara Low.[10] It is a nuisance seeing what I might do at the rooms – but anyhow I'm going back to give my things another coat of paint first.

Please think I'm good, my darling.

Tag – Boy.

1. K.M. replies on 25 March: 'Yesterday I had your letters at last'.
2. *The Westminster Gazette.*
3. Naomi Royde-Smith.
4. An upholsterer named King whose shop was in South Street, off Baker Street.
5. Ripolin was the proprietary name for a brand of enamel paint.
6. Arthur, Murry's younger brother, who at K.M.'s instigation later changed his name to Richard.
7. The 'bosom' was either the landlady or the household help at 95 Elgin Crescent.
8. Horn, who worked with Koteliansky at the Russian Law Office, had gone on a walking tour with Lawrence in 1914.
9. Samuel Solomonovich Koteliansky (1882–1955), affectionately called 'Kot', was a White Russian Jew who came to England in 1911. After meeting

K.M. at the Lawrences' in 1914, he remained her devoted friend. A translator of Russian literature into English, he later collaborated with K.M., D. H. Lawrence and Leonard and Virginia Woolf.

   10. A Freudian psychoanalyst whom Lawrence met in 1914.

---

[30]   95 Elgin Crescent
                                                              [London.]
                                                      [22 March, 1915.]
Monday Night. Half past ten.

Tiggle Darling,[1]

How wonderful were your letters this morning – they are so wonderful that they are almost you. And I haven't written half so many or half so long. But I wrote immediately, the same night that you went, so that I can't understand why you haven't got one.

But, darling, if my letters are funny or cross or dull, like this one, remember (I'm not asking for pity) that they were written while I was dropping with fatigue. I've never felt so tired as I have doing these rooms – it was because I couldn't get decent rest on C's couch.[2] I had four nights of that. This is my first night In the rooms. I've just stopped work on them. Oh dear, how bare they look. Bare, but good. They swallowed up our sticks, and the one or two bits I could buy. Now there remain 8/- and the rent to pay, I suppose, to-morrow. So I shall have to review four novels tomorrow morning early. Honestly I rather enjoy being so hard up. It made the penny bazaar I went to to-day terribly important. But what's the good of a palace without my princess, my wonderful. Oh, Tiggle, we are the lovers of the world.

> We are the lovers that were dreamed by God
> When first he set his image on the clay
> And made it man & woman: on that day
> He dreamed a spirit should inspire the clod
> He fashioned human

No I'm no poet tonight, I'm a painter and polished by profession and mind. But the poem shall be made to you – my queen. Oh! What shall I call you – are there no new words for that wonderful firm breasted child woman that has lain in my arms, that darling queen who is all things in her one perfect self.

I would not have thee nearer than thou art
E'n thus do all perfections shine in thee
Like to a gem to whose translucent heart
The myriad rays return and severally
Unite in one remote and flawless flame

Another beginning . . .

Darling, I haven't anything to say but that I love you. But I think I shall say it properly soon. Its no use to tell you how I have been running all over London, to tell you again how the curtains don't fit, and how I have to use the blinds that were (providentially in the rooms) – it's no use because there's nothing true in it. Its not me at all; I have spent 4 days in a dream. Tomorrow I begin to live again, discreetly, and not tempting providence by a premature turn on the roundabout. But there it is, what was to be done has been done – all save the sofa, you black angel.

More to the point, tomorrow I will begin to write real letters, I hope – not hallucinated effusions like this.

I wrote to Orage[3] a really very nice letter – I got a reply 'No thanks'. I won't pretend I'm not hurt about it. I am very deeply hurt. And it rankles nastily in my brain. I had never dreamt that it was possible that he should give me a slap in the eye like that. It was not right, anyhow. No, Orage may be a brainy fellow, as he is, but he's not one of my kind. My kind don't, can't do things like that. I'm very sorry about it and sore. Just at the moment when I'd really hardened myself against people, I was foolish enough to let myself go because you believe in him.

For God's sake don't think these last words are against you. Only now I feel sure that what you admire in Orage – or rather your admiration – belongs to you of three years ago.

Perhaps I'm all wrong; but I could never bring it off with him now – never never.

Yes, you can see I'm hurt – I can't let the thing alone. It tapped in my brain all day 'Fool, fool'. I'm made to be a lonely one, now – lonelier, I believe, than you even.

Self-pity damnit, you mean little swine of a J.M.

Tig darling, its all because I'm tired out – but why should it make lumps in my throat because a man won't see me? *Please* never breathe a word of what I've written, or ever suggest in any way to him to make advances. Kaput!

Bogey.[4]

No curtains yet.

1. Murry replies to K.M.'s two letters of 19 March: 'I have just had déjeuner', and 'I went to Chartier to lunch'; 20 March: 'I don't know what you think of yourself'; and 21 March: 'Still no letter'.

2. Murry had been staying with the Campbells at 9 Selwood Terrace while he was furnishing the rooms.

3. A. R. Orage (1873–1934), editor of *The New Age* from 1907–1922, first accorded Katherine Mansfield recognition in England when he began publishing her stories in 1910. In spite of a falling-out when K.M. moved to *Rhythm*, it was he who in 1922 introduced her to the teachings of Gurdjieff and encouraged her to join the Gurdjieff Institute at Fontainebleau.

4. K.M.'s reply on 27 March begins: 'I'm doing the unpardonable thing – writing in pencil . . .'.

---

[31]   95 [Elgin Crescent,
                                                  Notting Hill Gate,
                                                  London.]
Wednesday Night 11.45.   [24 March, 1915]

Tiggle Darling,[1]

Kottilianski has been here. He has just gone; but I was glad of him.

Darling – a letter came from you this morning. You had just got the first of mine. I feel that it must have been a bad one. Forgive me. I don't remember what it was about; but I know that I was tired with much work on the rooms, and what I wrote then wasn't really me. It was true, of course, but it was true of a weary Jack navvy. But was it really so bad that it made you think that I wouldn't want you to say that you loved me? It must have been. Tear it up and forget it.

This morning, too, came your letter about the Zeppelins. That was wonderful. I felt them all – and again through you I got something out of the war. Please write me letters like these, letters that you write when you just think I am Bogey.

Now I will tell you what I did today. I got up and had my bath at nine. (You can get a terrific hot bath here for a penny, only so hot that it makes you sleepy). Then I made my breakfast – two eggs. When I sit alone in the little kitchen it makes me think always of Clovelly,[2] when you left the little blue note 'This is for you' with my boiled egg. Then I began to sweep & polish the floors, to tidy, to wash up – and by the time I had washed again it was eleven o'clock. I began to write a notice of the National Portrait Society. It came slowly with many cigarettes, but there it was done (quite well) and at 1.30 I had my lunch (sardines & some fine coffee, out of the little tin you sent with me). I meant to work at the novel; but then I hadn't settled the curtain problem. I had only the dirty old blinds up. Suddenly I thought – they may not be big enough as they are, but what if I cut them off and made 4 ½-curtains. I measured them – they were just right. Then I began to feel happy. I didn't know why, and wondered about it even while I was feeling happy. At the same moment I wanted a lamp to work with – and I began to feel that I could work. I counted my money – 13/6, and the landlord was coming that afternoon for the rent. I found a great book that I didn't want to review, and another that I did, snatched up the curtains, ran along to the coal shop and ordered a half-hundred to be sent at six, jumped on a bus to Oxford Circus, and began to read the book I did want to review hard. I had three quarters finished the story when I got to the circus. I must finish it before I sold it. I went into Lyons and had a tuppenny cup of tea. I felt really poor, and happy. The lamp people hadn't got what I wanted ready. I was disappointed, but hurried along to Thorpe.[3] At the corner before I got there a band began to play. I had to stop and watch with my curtains over my arm. It was soldiers, and I began to walk beside them like a little street boy. I felt I was like a little street boy; but I had to hurry on to Thorpe's and after all, I said to myself, I'm not looking so wonderfully reputable that it matters. (I hated myself for thinking that). Just as I was hating myself particularly, I found myself looking into Floryan's eyes. There was no help for it. And besides I felt that it was no use having a grudge against him. Floryan was Floryan, after all. He asked how you were; told he was very *bussy* – he don't talk a bit better English, now – as secretary to the Polish Committee, that he was publishing a pamphlet on Poland next month, that he had translated all Synge's plays into Polish and they had appeared at Warsaw, that next month his translation of one of the Wyspianski[4] plays was to be produced at the Little Theatre – and so on. Altogether I was made to feel that he was very important. I gave him my address – why not, I said to myself – and dashed into the tube for Campbell's. There I told Beatrice what I wanted done to the curtains, and she and the nurse tackled them while I waited, having first run out for green cotton. I got back in time to catch the coal man. From Beatrice I learned that Kot. had been trying to phone me yesterday; so I phoned him and told him to come round tonight. (Also I picked up the *New Age*. Why is there nothing of yours in it? Without your stuff it is only an offence to me now).

I sewed up the ends of my curtains tight and then went out to buy little rings. I bought a duster, a packet of screws, two candle shade holders and two candle shades at the penny bazaar (It fills me with a deep satisfaction to buy things at the penny bazaar) – 7 candles 2d – 3 doz curtain rings 3d – and a packet of needles 1. When I came back inside Mr. Jarvis was there. I talked to him about his garden, and then I found that he didn't want any rent till next week – 10/6 made in a moment. Then I found that the hems of the curtains were enough to put them up, without sewing on rings. I got them up, washed up, laid my first fire, and had nearly finished my supper when Kot. came.

Isn't this all silly? But I thought you would like it. I forgot about the old man above. He's a fraud & a nuisance. The moment he heard me come in he crawled down with the same tale about being lonely – his niece had gone out – left him no food. I felt it was critical when he asked me point-blank was I going to have a cup of tea.

I've had it already, said I

He stood in the kitchen, muttering. I pretended to busy tidying. I don't want to intrude, he said. I said very quickly & nervously that I was always busy in the evening: 'I have to write in time for next morning's papers.'

I don't want to intrude.

More tidying – plainly unnecessary. I could not look at him.

Would you mind making me a cup of tea?

'No . . . I don't mind.' Pouring spirit into the primus. 'But I'm very busy. I've got friends coming – and I'm just now going out. Can you not make it yourself. I'll leave the kettle on'.

No, that wouldn't do for him. I'm much obliged, he muttered and crawled out of the room. In relief I sweated. Then I heard his step shuffle softly back – he wears list slippers – My God.

I shall have to wait till my niece comes back, then. She went out without my knowing.

Can't you get your niece to leave you some food?

Yes, I will another time . . . Would you mind giving me a bit of something to go on with?

I was really angry, nervously angry. I cut off two slices from the loaf and spread them viciously. I could not look at him. I took up a paper bag that was on the table and put them in, twiddled the corners, and gave them to him just like a man serving in a shop.

I'm much obliged, he said and shuffled away. I heard him talking to himself as he went away, I was furious, above all with myself. But how was I to know he was such a deadly fraud. I believe he's a liar as well. I made up my mind to buttonhole the niece on the stairs, and tell her that it must not happen again. But she came in while I was at the Penny Bazaar, and I couldn't go up & tackle them both. But my mind is fixed. If it happens again I shall tell him point-blank. I can't have my life ruined by an old dotty – if he's not worse. Its no use to be friendly with that kind of man. But you'll know Tiggle what it cost me, even to do what I did this afternoon. I'll settle his hash, very soon; & they can be my deadly enemies for all I care. If they – he – makes me really uncomfortable again I'll tell Jarvis that they must go or I shall. I really feel competent to do that now.

Tig, I think you would like the one room with the half curtains – and all the furniture except the bed. I felt you while I was doing it in everything. You would like the kitchen too. I've put you into that – but the bedroom which should be the best room of all, is empty. There's a wonderful bird who sings me awake in the morning. Just when I'm in bed at night I feel lumpy in the throat – I can't help it. Then I go to sleep and wake up to the household jobs.

To-night I had a cheque for £4.9.0. I've more than £5 now. I shall be able to pay the rent of the cottage on the day next week. It worried me a bit – and I'm living on very little If you want any more before the 1st – shall I send it? or can you borrow from Beatrice Hastings?[5] Don't be afraid of doing that, because I shall have saved something decent in a few weeks – what a terrible long time that sounds. I can't write about you – you're perfect – and if I really try to, I begin to see you and then its all up, with me. And now I don't know whether I ought even to have told you that. But if I didn't, you wouldn't know – you wd. know, but you wouldn't believe it, and that wd. make you sad, sadder than you are when I do write those things.

Bogey.[6]

I send you all about a murder case. Its amazing.

1. J.M. replies to K.M.'s two letters of 22 March: 'I have just had your first letter . . .'; and 'When I wrote to you this afternoon, I was not a nice girl . . .'.

2. 69 Clovelly Mansions, where Katherine first took Murry as her lodger.

3. A book dealer at 93 St. Martin's Lane.

4. Stanislaw Wypianski (1869–1907), a Polish dramatist to whom – influenced by Floryan – Katherine addressed her poem, 'To Stanislaw Wypianski'.

5. Beatrice Hastings (1879–1943), a South African-born journalist, (separated from her husband) lived for a time with Orage and contributed maliciously clever articles to the *New Age*. After leaving Orage in 1914, she moved to Paris, taking up with Modigliani, among others. At first friendly with Katherine, (who privately called her 'Biggy B') she later turned jealously against her.

6. K.M. replies 27 March: 'I am really worried about money for you'.

---

[32]   95 Elgin Crescent
                                        [London.]
                                    [25 March, 1915.]
Thursday: 11.45.

Tiggle,[1]

This morning I got the letter you wrote on Monday. I think those Zeppelins must be terrifying, really – and just before your letter came I read in the stop-press of my morning paper that another one had been signalled coming towards Paris at 10.30 last night. But there was nothing in the evening paper about it. So perhaps it didn't come. I hope not; for though its silly, I'm always thinking that if they do kill anybody it must be you. I had a terrible turn when I saw the placard on Monday (it may have been Tuesday)

ZEPPELINS OVER PARIS
ONE WOMAN KILLED.

If they had only put THE in front of the second line, I shd. have been done for, for a dead snip. It made me very sad to hear that about Beatrice Hastings, because I know she must have come near being a fine woman; and I know too that what really upsets you in her now, is the completeness of something which was – perhaps only a little bit – in you, that used to terrify me and almost killed me dead – I mean the Cabaret bit. You see Beatrice (tho' I never have seen her) seems to be a smaller specimen of your kind. Well, they don't turn up very often. They're absolutely different from women in general; and all women in general are against them. Its easy to see why. It's not because you criticise them or are clever; but because they see in you the ideal they never can attain. You are as I said six weeks ago – the eternal woman. The others are wives or mothers or Rebecca Wests[2] – all of them are females. All their activity consists in feverish reactions because they

haven't a man or a baby in bed with them at night. When they have –
well they don't have any activity at all. They're negatives – in you they
come up against a positive and they hate it. They put up right & wrong
against you, whose greatness is that there is no right and wrong save
what you feel to be you or not-you. Well with so much against you, it's
a hard row to hoe, to be really *you*. (You is a type – the wonderful type
from Aspasia[3] to B.B.[4] Colette Vagabonde,[5] and you above all
moderns) Naturally the tendency is to be extravagant and outrageous,
retaliating against the hostility that puts up right & wrong against you.
You by the sheer fact of your genius – genius is with you only being
wonderfully what you are – have got through that without hurting
yourself, and are very near to getting absolutely rid of your wickedness (that's only a figure of speech). Because of that, you'll stick to me:
not so much because you love me, which you do, but because you
know that you are more the real you, the good you, with me. I stick to
you because I adore you, and you are the only woman I have ever seen
and the only one I ever shall see. No woman could take me away from
you. I could prove it logically almost, but that's off the point.

Well B.B. just hadn't enough to pull her through. When she said
she left O.[rage] because he wasn't passionate enough – that was a lie, I
know. She was only excusing herself. It wasn't a failure in O. but in
her – and I think I could tell you the reason why she failed, but again
that don't matter.

The point is that I'm always thinking about you and I feel that I
know more about you than you do yourself. (You think that is swank).
I will put it more acceptably when I say that I know how big you are
better than you do now. I used to know much less of course.

I mustn't go on gassing like this. To-day I've been trying to take up
my novel again. It was awfully hard work, and then I couldn't get
going – and that is more tiring than anything I know. And so I am tired
now. I am missing you badly – but I couldn't help doing that, could I?
Life gets frightfully empty when you aren't here. It might be alright if
I could then make up on the roundabout what I lose on the swings.
Most likely I will tomorrow. I'll tell you. I wish we had hundreds and
hundreds of pounds and that I was there with you. I hope my good
letters have begun to arrive.

Tiggle – why aren't you in my arms in my big bed tonight?

Boge.

1. J.M. replies to K.M.'s letter of 22 March: 'When I wrote to you this afternoon, I was not a nice girl . . .'.

2. Probably a reference to the liberated, amoral female protagonist of Ibsen's *Rosmersholm*; but possibly also a reference to the novelist Rebecca West (b. 1892) who deliberately took her pen-name from Ibsen's play.

3. Probably a reference to the famous courtesan of Ancient Greece whose beauty, culture and wit so captivated Pericles that he made her his life-long companion.

4. Beatrice Hastings.

5. Colette's novel about her music-hall life, *La Vagabonde*, was published in 1910.

---

[33]   95 Elgin Crescent
                                                    [London]
Monday,   [29 March, 1915.]

Tiggle darling,[1]

The letter you got just before this was written on Friday and not posted until Monday. In my terrible hurry, going to the Lawrences I forgot it.

I came back this morning and found two of your letters – one when an Alsatian woman had managed to defraud you of one of mine, and the other when you had got it. I'm terribly glad it did come.

I don't know what to write at this moment (1.30). There's nothing to say about the L.'s. L. talks an awful lot about you and me, and I'm sure I don't understand one-tenth of it all. The other nine-tenths are wrong; but I don't trouble to correct it. You see there is good feeling (as Kot wd. say) between me & L. & nothing else really matters. I wouldn't gain anything by trying to put him right. For instance, he says that it gave him quite a shock to discover how crude I was physically, apparently as between you and me. I listened; but it didn't give me a shock at all, for I haven't the least idea of what he was driving at. I suppose he meant something; but I'm not quite sure.

So there's really nothing to say about my week-end. And about my return, nothing. One thing is over everything – the ghastly cold weather. It's always just beginning to snow; and if it doesn't bring it off it's because it's too cold. The stuff just gets frozen into ice before it gets going at all.

I don't understand Orage a bit – and there's the end of him. Perhaps he is too old and in life has gone a bit bad. I don't know. Now I laugh at myself for being hurt. What does it matter? Only its funny the way I go about saying to myself I won't be hurt any more (just as I said in that auctioneer's shop I won't be swindled) and I always let myself in. Its nothing to be proud of; I suppose. But I don't get angry with myself. I only laugh. Perhaps I am simpler than they are. And to be simple is a good thing, Tiggle, I know. I am so much better than I was – not good yet, of course, but really better than I was. Now there's a bad pride still in me, but perhaps that will go soon – and then I shall begin to be something. It sounds like Snodgrass in *Pickwick*, who 'took his coat off and loudly announced to the bystanders several times that he was going to begin.' Then, sometimes, I think I'm a funny little chap – just like that – and give myself a small pat on the head or a pinch of the ear and say 'You'll grow up one of these days' – but I never shall, never. I shall only become a funnier little chap. But you'll stick to me. I know that somehow, and don't think about it very much. I stand for the good in you & you for the good in me. We can't leave off now, nor ever, so long as it is good: and I can't imagine that it can ever be otherwise

How little I do think about now, to be sure. I don't think you would find me talking very much, nowadays. I feel quite extraordinarily calm and peaceful. But I do want you. Its wonderful to think about that – to have somebody near me who understands me as you do, and will tell me the truth, and do true things to me. Even now that I begin to imagine our caresses, my head snuggling against your wonderful breasts, my lips feeling slowly over them till I kiss – it is all so true. Do you understand what I mean. The word is funny. But I mean its not just desire, or wickedness, or excitement, but the being of two good souls and bodies together & making suddenly a better thing. Now I would have you back. Something in me says why is Tig not here now? and another thing says why should she be – she is there and Tiggle – more truly Tiggle for being there. But those two things do not really drag me different ways. I can wait, quite content and happy, till you come: simply, I suppose, because I have no shadow of a doubt any more either of you or me.

Good-night, darling

Boge.

1. J.M. replies to K.M.'s letters of 26 March: 'I am in such a state of worry and suspense . . .'; and 27 March: 'I'm doing the unpardonable thing . . .'.

May 1915

After her return to England Katherine was unable to write in the rooms Murry had taken at 95 Elgin Crescent. So she went once more, on 5 May, to Carco's vacant Paris apartment. She came back to London on 19 May. Shortly afterwards the Murrys took a house Katherine did like at No. 5 Acacia Road, St. John's Wood.

[34]   95 Elgin Crescent,
                                                    London
                                               [5 May, 1915.]
                                          Wednesday Morning

Wig darling.

There you are and here I am. It seems rather strange. But this time I don't really feel that you are very far away. We parted, as Kot wd. say, in such a good mood. And I can't find anything to be miserable about, because I'm so convinced we did the right thing: I can't even make any heroics about it; its as though you had gone down to Brighton for the day. Only whenever I think of you, I smile – I don't feel sad at all – smile because all my memories are of the wonderful Wig and not a bit of the Wigged one. The other times you went away I was always sad when I thought about you. It shows the difference.

After I got back yesterday, I stayed in all day. I worked at my novel in the morning & wrote an article for the *Times*[1] afterwards. I was so tired and lazy in the afternoon that I went to sleep. Yesterday was very warm, but it never got any clearer than it was in the morning – and I had to light my fire. Today its bright & warm, a most wonderful day, the image of that day when you and I went to Paris together, *3* years ago to the very week. And really in myself I feel young as I was then. I want to take life into my arms – to walk, run, scamper hand in hand with you. No-one will ever be able to touch *us* when you come back. Yes, I'm really happy.

Even I almost envy you Paris – and nowadays I have to be very insouciant to do that. I could loll about under yellow green trees and drink the stickiest sirops today. In fact I could do almost anything instead of reviewing the 5[?]brevier novels I got last week. Il faut travailler, quand même. And then I must tell you I work at my novel with ten times the absorption & conviction now that I know you are working at yours. I'm getting towards the end of the first part.

Last night I got my W. cheque. It was what I expected £5.1.4, so that I can stick £2.10 in the bank almost immediately. That makes me cheerful a bit, too. There's one fly in the ointment. I see from a *Times* leader to-day that there's a good chance of conscription[2] after all. I don't want to go very much; but if we all go – well, I won't grumble so much. But its probably a false alarm. I do feel inclined to damn the silly old war.

Good bye Wig darling

Boge.[3]

1. George P. Lilley's *Bibliography of John Middleton Murry* records no contributions to the *Times* newspaper before 1918; nor is any review for the *Times Literary Supplement* listed in 1915. Some of the articles Murry mentions writing, therefore, were either not published or have not been traced.

2. Conscription was not introduced in England until 1916. Murry counted himself lucky to be declared physically unfit for active service in 1916, taking instead a job at the War Office.

3. K.M. replies on 8 May: 'I shall write you my letter today in this café Biard . . .'.

---

[35]   95 [Elgin Crescent,
                                                         London.]
                                                   [7 May, 1915.]

Friday.

Wig darling,

Wonderful weather – you just managed to get off in time to be able to say there never is any summer in London – and a busy day. Its now ten o'clock and I have not been home since I went out to the office this morning.

First when I got to the office, *another* letter from the President of the Royal Institute protesting against my criticism (I said 'The only thing to be said about the R.I is R.I.P.') and threatening a libelaction. Still Spender was as nice as could be expected under the circs. Nothing in the Saturday *Westminster*, alas! Then I went to see Kot. to find out when the L's were coming, and he said 6. So I went off and did the International Society.[1] Came back to Kot, and we went together to a man called Basil Procter (– I think one of the Meynell[2] young men –) with whom the L's are staying. The L's weren't there so K & I went and had cider in a pub. and sat in the gardens in Leicester Square – I've never known anything more like Paris than it was this afternoon. We came back & found them. They were very surprised that you had gone – and, I'm sure, privately convinced that you had gone off to F.C.[3] Frieda I wouldn't mind betting thinks you're playing the devil with loyal and unsuspecting me. But, poor dears, they can't help it. They can't quite understand us yet. But L. is a really good soul. K. said he'd heard of a new place for dinner called 'Isola Bella' – lo and behold it was the old Savoyard – not very much metagrobolised, only they've put a picture of Lake Maggiore where the woman with the baby used to be. So I told them all about that wonderful time when we had tea together. After dinner I bolted off to write this letter. On the way the papers came out crying that the Lusitania had been torpedoed with 1900 people on board. Then I remembered it was Arthur's birthday tomorrow, and that I must take him out for a special treat. I suppose there wasn't very much really; but it seems to have been a dayful. But all day I've been very chirpy (in spite of the libel action) very confident about us and a glamorous future.

At the present moment just because I've been thinking about you I want you physically. Are you like that – or is it wicked & sordid to confess? I can't help it. I want to be your lover. Its wonderful summer and its got into my blood. But I can't feel sad, my wig.

Are you working hard?

Boge[4]

(Did you get the *D.N.* [*Daily News*] I sent you this morning?)

1. Murry's review of the Spring exhibition of The International Society [of sculptors, painters and engravers] appeared in the *Westminster* 19 May.
2. Viola Meynell lent her Greatham cottage to the Lawrences for six months in 1915. Living next door in her parents' house, Viola 'overlooked and underheard' the battles between them. Lawrence's response to the Meynells' generosity was to misrepresent their family and environment in his story '*England, My England*'.
3. Katherine responded: 'F.[rancis] C.[arco] as you know simply doesn't exist for me'.
4. K.M. replies 8 May: 'The lamplighter is just going his rounds . . .'.

[36]   95 Elgin Crescent
                                                         [London]
Saturday Evening   [8 May, 1915.]
Wig Darling,[1]

I got your letter this morning. I wish you were here now.

The Lawrences have just been. Yesterday, thinking that I ought to be nice to them, I invited them here to supper tonight at 7 o'clock. All day I've been with my brother because it was his birthday, and did not get back till 5.30. Then for an hour and a half I slaved to get supper ready. They turned up with an extra man at 8.30. Isn't it silly that that should upset me? I should have been alright if Frieda hadn't been there. I was hurt that they were late, seeing that they knew I had to get it all myself, but to find Frieda fatuously laughing on the doorstep, as though it were so very Bohemian to be an hour and a half late – no, that was a little too much. After an hour of it, she decided that I was dull, and to prove to me what a party should be began to sing German sentimental songs in that idiotic voice of hers. Lawrence kept on saying à propos of the cottage in Bucks, you & I and Katherine & Frieda will never have so good a time as we did some of those evenings at your cottage. It makes me think furiously. He must be blind to certain things. I do look back on some moments with a kind of feeling that it won't happen again – but on the evenings in Rose Tree Cottage, never. I think I have fifty times the capacity for delight now that I had then. But I do like Lawrence; though I *feel* that he is deteriorating – really getting feeble. Frieda is the Red Woman, the Whore of Babylon, the Abomination of Desolations that was to Fornicate in the High Places, and the Holy of Holies. I've just remembered that bit of Revelations – isn't it really Frieda, spiritually speaking?

I feel inclined to write a play about the evening – called 'Un Peu de Charcuterie' – I got some from Appenrodt;[2] of which the aforesaid F. wolved over one half before anybody else had even begun to eat – and then she said that spring-onions (also provided) she could not eat because they were vulgar. Then the strange man they brought was continually saying quite unintelligible misfires in French & German and asking Frieda if it was right. You've no idea of the bestial cumulative effect.

I met my brother at S. Ken. I was surprised he was late. He didn't turn up till 12.10. Then, the moment he saw me he began to cry. So I had to walk him down to Thurloe Square to find out what was the matter. He'd got on to a 19 bus – and it had taken him to Sloane

Square. He hadn't any money & he made sure I would be gone. So he had run all the way from Sloane Square to S. Kensington (– and he didn't know the road at all –) as fast as he could. It was a melancholy & typical beginning. I used to be just like that. But he had a lemon squash which seemed to revive him, and then we rowed for 2 hours round the Serpentine. It was wonderfully beautiful in Kensington Gardens to-day. Then a good Dairy Express Lunch; then he came home with me to tea and then had to rush home. But as he said while he was having tea in our kitchen. 'I *think* I've enjoyed myself to-day'; which seems to me a masterpiece.

My mother sent me a note asking if you would go to tea with her on Wednesday – 'She hasn't seen you for so long' – but I'll say – unless forbidden – something nice from you when I go.

Goodbye, Wig darling, – I'm quite alright now I've talked to you
Boge,[3]

1. J.M. replies to K.M.'s letter of 6 May: 'I cannot tell you how beautiful this place is by daylight'.
2. A delicatessen.
3. K.M. replies on 11 May: 'I have just got your Saturday letter . . .'.

[37]   95. [Elgin Crescent,
London]
9 May, 1915.
Sunday

Dear Wig.

I just had a funny thought. I was cooking a bloater for supper, just now, and I wondered how you did without a gas-stove. I felt sorry for you because you hadn't got a gas-stove. Oh – I'm too silly. Fancy putting that down.

I've been in all day – Sunday – working for the *Daily News*. In twenty minutes I am going out to see the Lawrences; but I know I am going to be offensive to Frieda, for plainly I hate her. I shall have to be very careful. Part of the afternoon I spent sewing a button on my trousers, a tape on my pants, & sewing up the waistcoat pocket of my old flannel suit. I did it all beautifully, especially the white-cotton hemstitch that shows on my flannel waistcoat pocket.

To-day's been windy, sunny, & cold. At least I think it has been cold, because I left off my pants first thing in the morning and had to put them on again in the evening. (What an awful lot there is about pants in this letter). Early in the morning I went out to buy some tobacco from the sylph I told you about. She's very cold to me, not cold – I don't mind that – but she despises me profoundly. I wouldn't go there at all, only it's the only shop open on Sunday. I always drop my change; she makes me so nervous.

What else have I done to-day? I can't think of anything. I thought about you several times. First, as I do every morning, that you were very wigged to take away the sponge – but I am getting quite expert in bathing myself with my hands. Then when I did my sewing I thought it was sad that you weren't there to show it to, because I'd done it better than you could, at any rate as well. I'm always thinking about you when I think of anything at all; but except when my thoughts are passionate, its wonderfully calm and happy to think about you. I just smile a little, and feel that I were talking to someone quietly in a boat (I think in Venice) on a midsummer night. It is wonderful to be so secure and beautifully – tender or sensitive, I don't know the word.

But this has been a quiet day. I've got nothing to tell you except what I know you can read in every word I've written.

Boge.[1]

1. K.M. replies 11 May: 'I have just got your Saturday letter . . .'.

---

[38]

[95 Elgin Crescent,
London.]
[11 May, 1915.]

Tuesday.
Wig darling,[1]

I've just got your letter of Sunday evening, saying that you haven't had a letter from me. Darling, I write to you every night by the 12 o'clock post. Perhaps they would get to you quicker if I put the arrondissement on the envelope. I have quite forgotten which it is, so please tell me in your next letter.

I went to see Lawrence last night as I said. He was very sad. Poor devil he is so lonely, with that bitch of a Frieda, always playing traitor, and hurting him in every secret and intimate part of his soul. It's no good until he can get away from her – she's really wearing him out. No, it depressed me terribly to be with him last night. It was all so unreasonable & cruel, – but it's no use to go on with that. But I think I shall ask him to come away with me for a fortnight's holiday during this summer to see if I can urge him to the point of leaving her. Not that I think I can do very much directly; but I have an idea that he might be happy were he away with me for a bit, because he would know that I was loving him. It does make a difference. – Wig, how wonderful *we* are!

Well, I'd been talking to him for about an hour, Kot being the silent corner-man, Frieda happily away at a concert, when who should turn up but Gilbert & Miss Muir[2] – you remember Miss Muir, who walked over with me & Gilbert [Cannan] one day when I was staying with G [Gilbert] & M [Mary] & you with the L's. Gilbert was in a very good mood. I liked him more than I have at any time during the last 2 years. Yes he was very good and I was happy that he was still our friend. I lunched with him to-day, and amiably gave him a piece of my mind about himself & his writing. He took it awfully well. He seems to have a respect for what I say – perhaps that's why I'm liking him now. Tomorrow I'm going to tea with Miss Muir & him. She's nice, I think, – at any rate she got me by admiring you – not in the silly envious coarse way of Frieda, but sincerely. She thinks you're very beautiful and that we're an awfully fine pair. Perhaps I tumble into that kind of trap too easily. – I don't know, but I like tumbling.

Gilbert's going to see Pinker[3] about my book so with D.H.L. too, something ought to happen. Won't it be fine if we both appear together. Tig and Wig

I didn't make the books big enough to write titles on.

Oh, about that supper. It was D. S. MacColl,[4] Aitken,[5] Muirhead Bone[6] & me. They were very nice, particularly nice to me. But I thought them all a bit stupid. I couldn't talk to them at all. I wasn't nervous or bored, but I just couldn't. They're alright, but they aren't my tribes. And, I can't believe Muirhead Bone is as big an artist as I thought he was. He must be a second-rater with a great technical skill.

Jarvis has just been for his 10/6, chatting away – saying the same thing a half-dozen times: but I can't help liking him.

Wig, Wig, Wig

You are a darling

I love you

Boge.[7]

1. J.M. replies to K.M.'s letters of 9 and 10 May: 'Instead of having dinner today I ate some bread . . .'.

2. Molly Muir, an attractive friend of Gilbert Cannan's.

3. J. B. Pinker (1863–c 1940), a leading London literary agent who became D. H. Lawrence's agent in 1914, and later Katherine Mansfield's.

4. Dugald Sutherland MacColl (1859–1948), painter, art critic and supporter of the New English Art Club.

5. Probably Conrad Aiken (1889–1973), poet, novelist and critic.

6. Muirhead Bone (1876–1953), a Scottish painter whose work Murry had reviewed for the *Westminster* twice in 1914 and again in March 1915.

7. K.M. replies 13 May: 'This is about the 4th letter I have written and torn up'.

---

[39]   [95 Elgin Crescent,
                                                                 London]
                                                          [13 May, 1915.]

Thursday,

Wig darling,[1]

Yesterday I was in a bad mood and did nothing. To-day I wasn't in a bad mood & did nothing . . . I don't know why but I can't do any reviews just now. Just after I wrote to you yesterday – that is at 10 o'clock, I went to bed. It seemed the only tolerable place. I didn't wake up until half past eight, and then I found to my joy that my vulgar swelling had begun to disappear.

It began to rain last night; it was raining just as hard this morning, and it has rained all day. I worked at the novel in the morning, and in the afternoon I braved all the rain and went to see my mother, who talked to me about the theatres she used to see when she was a girl, and, most strangely, of the 'Walk of London', [i.e. *Walker London*] and how beautiful was a young actress in it called Mary Ansell.[2] She wore a sailor suit and a white yachting cap with a bunch of coloured ribbons over her ear, and she looked so charming that my mother has never been able to forget her. I must tell Mary that when I see her again: I like the idea of the yachting cap immensely.

I suppose the rain will stop the anti-German riots which, to me, seem perfectly disgraceful. It's enough to make anyone believe that we deserve all we get – Lusitanias and everything. There's a photo at the back of the *D.N.* I send you – showing four policemen *just looking on* while some poor unfortunate German's whole house is plundered. It's pretty damning evidence against England, I think.

You are a poor Wig with those Apaches & Fantômes worrying you at night.[3] When you tell about those things I want to dash along and cuddle you – you seem so small . . . But don't go overdoing it about the money. There's no need. If a pound will be any use, I'll send it immediately, for I shall surely be getting some money next week . . . If you do have the chance, you might send me a word about any book – or subject – which might make a good *Times* article. Its all in the good cause.

Kot's sitting in my chair with its new blue cover. It looks very nice. He's reading Samuel Butler. He wears eyeglasses now. If you want anything to read tell me. I wonder if you'll be able to get those Henry James' books in Tauchnitz. It would be a good idea if you could. I'd love to read the *Golden Bowl – The Spoils of Poynton* and all those. So you'd better have that pound.

What a silly stupid letter – but there's been a sheet of rain between me & the world all day, besides that my brain won't work at all at any thing. If I read any thing its just a lot of printed signs – very bad case. I'm cheerful but deeply disgruntled – I don't know why. Good-bye my darling – but when are you going to send me a bit of your book? Oh, I kiss you, Wig, Wig I want to be your lover, Boge.[4]

1. J.M. replies to K.M.'s letter of 11 May: 'I have just got your Saturday letter, and you can imagine what I feel about the supper party and about Frieda'.

2. Mary Ansell was the maiden name of Mary Cannan. An actress when she married her first husband, J. M. Barrie, her first big part had been in Barrie's play, *Walker London*.

3. Since childhood K.M. had suffered 'nightfears'. In her letter of May 9 she tells of seeing a detective movie whose hero was 'an apache called "L'Fantôme" '. On May 11 she wrote to Murry: 'At half past ten I shut up shop and went to bed, but not to sleep. The three apaches of the cinema, L'Fantôme, Bébé and le faux Curé, tried the key of the door all night'.

4. K.M. replies 15 May: 'I got very sane after I had written to you yesterday'.

[40]   [95 Elgin Crescent,
                                              London.]
Saturday Morning,   [15 May, 1915.]

Wig darling,[1]

I'm hoping while I write this that it will never get to you, because you'll have had my wire and been able to come back.

Your letter this morning was terrible. I don't know *when* you wrote it, but you had torn up 3 already. Oh, darling it was awful to read. I don't know what to say except that we mustn't be apart while you're like this. It isn't right. Come to London again and we'll find a room somewhere, where you can work all day – or I'll go back to the country so that you can have these rooms until your book is finished. But I can't bear the thought of you ill over there – so far away.

And now I wonder whether the wire has got to you, and whether you will come back if it does. You see I've only got that awful note – and I know I shan't hear from you again – I can't hear from you again – till Monday. Oh Tig – I wonder whether you will wire in answer so that I get it to-night.

Oh my precious – life seems so cruelly hard to you that you can't bear it alone. The last words of your letter were 'I am ill & alone – voilà tout'. Tig, you must know what that means to me. You must be coming home. You wouldnt just write that and stay. Oh darling I can hear your tears in every word of the letter – and I can't do anything.

No, I've got nothing even to say. I just wonder whether you are coming, and how I shall wait until Monday.

                              Boge.

1. J.M. replies to K.M.'s letter of 14 May: 'This is about the 4th letter I have written and torn up'.

December 1915

Katherine and Murry spent a happy summer at the St. John's Wood house. The Lawrences, living nearby, launched, with Murry, the short-lived magazine, *Signature*. And visiting on leave from his British regiment was Katherine's brother, Leslie. The New Zealand of her childhood was brought back to life for Katherine as brother and sister talked endlessly about places and people they had shared.

Leslie's accidental death in October 1915 came as an overwhelming shock. Unable to remain in the house with its recent memories of her brother, Katherine, escorted by Murry, set out for Bandol in the South of France. She was alone there from December 7, when Murry returned to England, until January 1 when he rejoined her at the Villa Pauline.

[41]   Marseilles
                                [7 December, 1915.]
                                Six o'clock.

Dear Tig.

Just one line with your letter – and something I shan't need for confitures. Darling – I love & love & love you.

My train goes in a hour. I'm at the Café Noailles – you remember. I have got myself a corner seat in the train – and I am going by Havre & Southampton, because its quicker & cheaper.

Don't forget your agreement my darling – not to hesitate a moment before writing to me for anything whatever. And don't stay a moment longer than you want to. Good-bye darling
I will write from Paris   Jack.[1]

1. K.M. replies on 8 December: 'The "comfortable party" brought me your letter this morning . . .'.

[42]   *But don't*   c/o Kot.
                       write there.   [London]
Sunday   [12 December, 1915.]
Wig darling,

I have been waiting for a letter from you – but nothing has come yet. Probably the posts take longer than we imagined – but I shall get anxious soon.

I am now in that room of which I spoke (41 Devonshire St.);[1] but I don't like it very much. However, before taking it I told them plainly that I would only stay until I had found a studio. The room is a rather pretty little attic right at the top of the house – but it isn't very clean, and it's a terrible trouble doing for one's self. Kot, as I told you is very angry with me for being here at all; and I am sure he will compel me to find a studio within a week. The chief trouble with this room is that, in addition to its not being quite clean anywhere, the bed is only an apology, lumpy and hard – in fact a disreputable example of the old familiar kind of chair bedstead. There are a few draughts as well. However, I'm not at all sad, except at having received no letter from you.

Goodyear[2] has been here on 5 days leave. His boat left Le Havre at the same time as my own; but we didn't see each other until we met at Campbell's on Friday night. On Saturday G. stood me a dinner at Treviglio's, after I had taken him to see Lawrence, and then he came back with me here and stayed the night. Now, as an old campaign.

He can sleep, even on a dirty floor, with the greatest satisfaction. He is now sick of the war and desperately anxious to be a free man again. But he has become awfully nice – really one of us; and he tells some very funny stories of his experiences. He lives with a Welsh brewer in a lovely cottage, belonging to a French peasant on whom he is billeted, and they spend all the time devising how to steal the necessary stores from the quarter-master sergeant. I have given him your address and told him to write you immediately.

I think that Lawrence was really & truly pleased to see me back again. I feel that he is very fond indeed of you and me – and that he feels that we are the only people who really care for him in the way he wants to be cared for. Our going away had depressed him very much: already – I have been to see him twice – I notice that he is much more cheerful. Kot is also happier, I think. Lawrence is writing to you to-day.

There is a mangy old cat on these stairs – very frightening at

night-time. But he has chummed up with me, drunk my milk and
eaten my sausage (he was so starved that in his ravenous appetite he
made a beastly mess on the floor) and now he sits in front of my fire
wagging his tail for the first time, I should think, since the war began.
I am glad to have him for all his manginess – only I dare not touch him
yet.

My first two nights – I was ashamed to say so – I stayed at the
Campbells. Gordon is now completely done for, and terribly depressing. I think he is really a lost soul. Biddy[3] is lovely as ever – she has had
her photograph taken with yr. locket round her neck. Shall I get you
one of the photographs? They aren't very good because she was
frightened – and Paddy[4] who is in the photograph too was more
terrified still. O Tig, why haven't I got a photograph of you as a baby?
All my mind will insist on picturing you as one. You are always rising
up before my eyes as you must have been when you were three years
old, with those wonderful darling fingers, that bend as no woman's
ever could. That little tiny crook in them is almost making me cry now
– with love and pride and delight. When you get to these words, just
hold up your finger and bend it as you do for me – and think that there
is only one who carries that beauty locked in his heart for ever – that he
is wicked at times and cowardly and cruel through cowardice, and yet
loves you with some power that you have given him, so much is it
beyond his own compass. Darling.

I am very anxious about your money. Please when you write explain
to me exactly how it is going and how much you would like. I'm sure I
can get it from anybody – *Times*, *Westminster* etc.

Kot has just been in to see me for a minute or two; and in the
interval I have been looking up the Jiggisons in the little red-book. I
haven't been able to get the Weekly *Times* – but the *Literary Supplement* was sent on Friday. The *Times* will follow tomorrow, Monday.

To-night, I am going to the Dreys[5] for dinner. I don't want to at all;
but I have to keep my promise. Besides I have to soften the resump-
tion of my job I will tell you in my tomorrow letter of what happens.

To-day it is very cold here in London. Before midday it even
snowed a little.

My darling – for my sake, next time you go out wear your goblin
hat. I want to think of you in it, then you are most mine.

Jag.[6]

1. The house at 5 Acacia Road had been given up (although Koteliansky rented rooms there until his death). So Murry once again had to look for accommodation.

2. Frederick Goodyear (1887–1917), Murry's friend from Oxford, wrote the manifesto to the first number of *Rhythm*. He and K.M. had liked each other since their first meeting in 1912. His letters to her indicate a continuing mutual attachment: 'You're a genuine old Darling, for all your mendacity, and by not writing to me you cheat yourself of a certain amount of love. Always collect love like postage stamps. Lots of kisses, he wrote in 1916. In his next letter he said: 'All the time I have known you you have been fixt up with Murry, & that's been final so far as I was concerned, though it has made things very awkward between us'. Goodyear's death on active service was a great blow to Katherine.

3. Brigid Campbell (1914–1944), the daughter of Gordon and Beatrice.

4. Patrick Campbell (1913–1980), son of Gordon and Beatrice, who later became a well-known journalist and television personality.

5. O. Raymond Drey (1885–1976), a friend who as an art and theatre critic had contributed to *Rhythm* and *The Blue Review*. In 1913 he married Anne Estelle Rice (1879–1959), a magazine illustrator who contributed to *Rhythm*. She became a close friend of Katherine's, painting her portrait while they were both at Looe, Cornwall, in 1918.

6. K.M. replies 15 December: 'The maid came back with the wire'.

---

[43]   23 Worsley Road
                                                 Hampstead. N.W.
                                                 [London.]
Thursday – late afternoon.   [16 December, 1915.]

Wig darling,[1]

This morning I had two letters. When you wrote them, you had not yet got one of mine – the other arrived as you were writing. Both your letters made me sad; for in both you were ill. Oh, my dear darling, can you understand – of course you can, better than I – how small and infinitely precious, infinitely fragile you appear to me? I am afraid for you, and our letters take so long. You say that perhaps when I get your letters, you are no longer ill. I feel that you may be worse. I feel, too, all the love that your letters bring, and I wonder are mine strong enough to carry something back to you. Because of my love for you & yours for me – Tig, precious, it is for *Toujours* – it has *Toujours* written upon it – because of our love, I feel a stranger in my own land. This England is my own land, I know, but yet the persons in it, even those who are in some way dear to me, seem to be blunt of understanding. They seem to laugh when they should not, and to talk when they should be silent, and not to know how precious is the thing of ours I carry in my heart. To me it is something that I must bear in my cupped hands ever so lightly, like a flame – (not that it may be blown out, but that it burns so brightly that they could not see it at all,) or rather like that little bird you carried in the room at Cholesbury, or even like O'Hara San[2] herself who is to me so delicate that I dare hardly breathe when I smoothe her hair. I wonder now, sitting here, whether you and I in our common love are not too fine for those, even those, whom we call our friends. Wouldn't they be somehow different, Wig, somehow more sensitive if they really knew. Or do we suffer just because we have been chosen out of all others to keep the one flame alive until we too have given it over to others? I feel myself somehow aloof, terribly apart, though I would be of them. I try to conquer myself to work with them. But I am not I any more, I am you, and our common spirit will not submit. All our friends hurt me; Kot very deeply – Campbell insufferably; Lawrence least of all – but all of them hurt. I wonder are we, am I, as selfish and hard as they are? Perhaps, but I do not believe it; and now I seem to discover that even those silences & gruffnesses wh: you do not like in me – they are going away, dearest, I am sure, so that I may be a new Jag to take you into my arms at meeting – were a God-given protection against the unmeant brutalities of people.

And now I am afraid you will think I am sad on my own account as well as on yours. It is not true, at all. I am sad for your illness, my nut brown goblin (and this morning I called to you in the dark, whistled my empty windy whistle to you, as you swung so sadly on that gate, and I think you must have heard) but in what I have told you before I am not sad. I am just laying my head upon your cool and wonderful breast, and telling you what I have found in the world to which I was sent. For you and I are not of the world, darling; we belong to our own kingdom, which truly is when we stand hand in hand, even when we are cross together like two little boys. Somehow we were born again in each other, tiny children, pure and shining, with large sad eyes and shocked hair, each to be the other's doll. I cannot speak save to you – and to you I have no need of words.

Oh, my dearest – I must not write any more like this; I do not believe it will make you happier, but rather sadder, for something in real love is sad – that knowledge of apartness, of an enemy world in which we dare not stay too long for the peril of our souls. And that is the sadness that has hold of me tonight. It is not sadness at all, but the final triumph of our love. Darling it is *toujours*. If you would not say the word now that I have opened all my heart, I feel that I should die. But I hear you saying it: I even see your lips shaped to the word.

There I go again. I will not. Dearest, I am sending you the money I spoke of, in this letter. Tomorrow I will send you a couple of Colettes rescued from the ruins of 5 Acacia Road. To-day I sent you another *Literary Supplement* & the *Daily News*. How long will you stay?

Jag.[3]

1. J.M. replies to K.M.'s letters of 12 December: 'I really do think I may expect your first London letter tomorrow . . .'; and 12–13 December: 'I have just put on my spencer . . .'.
2. Katherine's Japanese doll.
3. K.M. replies on 19 December: 'I have just got the letter that you wrote me on Thursday night . . .'.

----

[44]   23 Worsley Road
                                             Hampstead N.W.
Saturday.   [London.]
                                          [18 December, 1915.]

Wig darling,

I am worried because I received no letter from you today. In the last two you were ill, and now I am afraid. Perhaps I shall get something even yet; but tomorrow is Sunday, and then I can hope for nothing till Monday. Because of this, I feel I can write nothing that is not melancholy. Therefore I had best tell you all that I have done to-day.

Last night I received a letter from Lady Ottoline,[1] whom Lawrence must have told of my return, asking me to go there for Christmas. The only thing that prevented me from saying 'Yes' immediately is a queer little idea at the back of my mind that you will be with me at Christmas. But, of course, that is preposterous – and tonight, I shall write to her and say yes, thank you very much.

This morning I was waked, as always now, by the woman coming to light my fire. Then my hot water is put on the fire in a little black kettle; and by the time it boils I get up, wash gingerly and dress. Then in comes my breakfast (7d. a whack) – pot of tea, bread & butter, bacon, fresh egg (supplied by myself) and Cooper's marmalade *ditto*. Then out. This time I walked down to Belsize Park Tube Station to see about that studio. I'm afraid there's no chance and that the Belgian Bastards[2] have it. However the agreement is not yet signed, and as the wall-eyed agent (you remember the man who sent us to that funny little derelict house in Pond St. wh. frightened us) wisely said: 'You never know'. However he has promised to let me know definitely on Tuesday next.

Thence on to Kot's in the hope of a letter – none. Then out to the cleaner's for my grey hat. They didn't make much of a job of it, though they charged me 1/9. Back to Kots who is very angry because it is proposed to amalgamate the relics of the *Signature*[3] with some kind of subscription magazine which Clive Bell[4] is bringing out. After a futile argument, in which Kot talks easily of a lot of money when we haven't got any between us – I left to stand at the corner of Tottenham Court Road and wait for Frieda to ask me to take Lawrence's place at a lunch with Monica Saleeby at Chantecle (L. is in bed with a bad cold). Waited twenty minutes in the cold before she deigned to appear. Then had to face not only Monica & Frieda but Anna Hepburn[5] and an Armenian called Kewyewmjun[6] (that's how it was pronounced) – a vile experience. The Armenian was another Willie Macqueen – at present he is the L's darling – but that will only last a day or two – he is just a low swindler of a peculiarly hateful kind. Hair brushed back, semi-Oxford manner, probably makes his living in Leicester Square.

Thence, fed up with the world, to a picture exhibition not wholly bad in Fitzroy Street, and in the Tube at Warren St home. Bought an Ingersoll watch for 5/-. Could not find Weekly *Times* anywhere – so bought the Weekly *Daily Sketch* which I am sending you now. In fact I'm just going out to post it. But I can't write without a letter from you. I'm too much afraid. I love you

Jag.[7]

1. Lady Ottoline Morrell (1873–1938), half-sister of the Duke of Portland and married to the Liberal M.P. Phillip Morrell, met Murry – through the Lawrences – about December 1915. The enthusiastic hostess and patron of numerous writers and artists, she entertained generously at Garsington Manor, Oxford. Among the many guests at her Christmas house-party in 1915 were Clive and Vanessa Bell, Lytton Strachey, Maynard Keynes, George Santayana, Lord Henry Bentinck and Murry. Katherine Mansfield became friendly with Ottoline after returning from Bandol in 1916.

2. Belgian refugees who were seeking accommodation.

3. *Signature*, a fortnightly periodical launched by Lawrence with the help of Murry in October 1915, survived only three issues.

4. Clive Bell (1881–1964), one of the 'Bloomsbury' group, and a writer on art and literature. He had married Virginia Woolf's sister, Vanessa, in 1907.

5. Mrs Patrick Hepburn, who wrote poetry under the pseudonym 'Anna Wickham'.

6. Dikran Kouyoumdjian (1895–1956), an Armenian who as 'Michael Arlen' wrote the facile, best-selling novel of 1924, *The Green Hat*. He was a potential member of Lawrence's utopian colony, Rananim.

7. K.M. replies on 23 December: 'I had 2 short notes from you this morning . . .'.

---

[45]

23 Worsley Road
Hampstead
N.W.

December. Sunday.

[London.]

[19 December, 1915.]

Wig darling,

Of course I couldn't hope for a letter to-day; but somehow the gap seems terribly long. This is the third I have written without one from you. I try to convince myself that [it] is all a matter of the Christmas & Sunday posts. Tomorrow will tell me. Still, to write at all, I have just to tell you what I have done since yesterday evening.

After I wrote to you, I went round for an hour to the Lawrences, more with the idea of getting a free cup of tea than anything else – (I am becoming an expert in the matter of free meals, nowadays). Lawrence has been in bed, on & off, with a cold during the last week and he was in bed again when I arrived. He has given up his flat and sold the furniture, as from Wednesday next; then he is going to his home for Christmas, and then – well, I have to go to J. D. Beresford[1] this afternoon and see if there is a cottage for him in Cornwall. At all events he is going somewhere into the country. But he still talks ardently of Florida, having somehow gathered together one hundred pounds: and he expects that I should find as much again. But I have learnt, I think, that Florida is a state of mind, not a place – so I don't commit myself & just wait until the crisis has passed. However, they are both extremely nice to me, L. of course in particular. I got my tea, which was lucky as I didn't arrive until a quarter past six, and made myself some toast. At 7.30 I started away to go first to the post office to post that Weekly *D. Sketch* I sent you yesterday, which I couldn't get into the ordinary red pillar-box (I stuck it in one at the end of this road and couldn't get it out again for a long while) and to take my nightly sausages and mashed at a café opposite the Tube Station (S & M. 7d Coffee 2½ roll 1d. = 11½ for dinner). That just reminds me that they don't open on Sunday – so that I shall have a pretty problem in feeding myself to-night. Then I came back to my rooms, where there is always a good fire (7d. a scuttle) and read *the Possessed* until bed-time. This morning I got up at my usual time 9.15, and read another Dostoievsky, *L'Adolescent*, until 1 o'clock, when I thought hurriedly how I was going to get lunch, and decided to walk to Campbell's. I arrived in time for an enormous whack of cold beef & potatoes and bread & butter pudding (a thing I could never eat before – I must be getting an appetite). Biddy was crying all the while. She got your post-card, but nevertheless she is very melancholy about her teeth, which insist upon coming.

Then I marched all the way back and here I am at 4.30. I'm not thinking about anything. Somehow not getting a letter from you makes me feel numbed. I haven't the inspiration to write. And this like yesterday's letter is only something for you to read in the morning, and think what a half-life it is for me without you.

Oh, my darling – you know how awful it is waiting for a letter – and your two last said you were ill!

Jag.[2]

1. J. D. Beresford (1873–1947), novelist and senior reviewer for *The Westminster*, had contributed to *Rhythm*. Murry arranged in December 1915 that he lend the Lawrences his house in Cornwall for a few months. In 1922 Beresford was one of the Ouspensky – Gurdjieff circle that K.M. joined.
2. K.M. replies on 23 December: 'I had 2 short notes from you this morning'.

---

[46]   23 Worsley Road
                                            Hampstead
                                            N.W.
Monday Morning. 11 o'clock.   [London.]
                                            [20 December, 1915.]

Dear darling,[1]

I waited three days for a letter from you and then on Sunday Evening, Kot brought me the letter you wrote on Tuesday last, saying you had never heard from me, and that you were going to wire.

Oh, Wig, it isn't true that I'm cruel. I have written to you everyday – one day I couldn't – and to make up I wrote two the next. Oh, darling, if I'm guilty I don't want to be spared, but it *isn't true*. Now, I feel quite crumpled up. Last night your letter nearly drove me out of my mind. I rushed off to Charing Cross to send you a wire, but it didn't do me any good: terrors were chasing through my mind – and they are there still. To-day's letter – it was one written on Wednesday, saying you had received my letter of Monday – was so short. I try to tell myself why – and no matter what answer I give it tortures me. Either you are too ill to write, or you have been so terribly hurt that you don't want to write to me any more. Oh, Wig – I don't know what to do. It is like some cruel fate – I know I have never loved you so utterly, so wholly, so unforgettingly, as in the past week. And I was so happy in the thought that some of my love had flowed over into my letter. Towards the end of last week I kept saying to myself, 'now she will have my Wednesday letter' – and I cried because I could see it making you happy – and now its all dreams.

Wig, I don't know what to say. You have been hurt and I can never take the smart away. If I felt that I had failed it would be less. But something has conspired against us.

I feel I have nothing to hold on to now. I am quite alone, even here – before I thought that I had your hand in mine – but now its all a dream. I don't know.

Then I say to myself – perhaps to-day She is happy. Perhaps some of my letters, my real ones, have reached her – and she is laughing & crying with me again. Oh, if I could only believe it, I would leap & laugh – but I can't believe it.

And all your letters came from so long ago. Wednesday letter on Monday – what may have happened since! I still dream that some of my love may have made you happy – but the dream does not last a second of time. No I am losing faith in love – the only thing in which I did believe – it did not come across to you. Still I think, she will answer my wire and I shall know now. And then I read in your letter that you cannot send a wire.

Oh, Wig, I shall have no answer to *this* letter for a week – what shall I do till then?

My darling – oh if I only knew some one word that would be so living & sweet & dear that it would smoothe your hurt away! But what is hardest of all to bear is that the happiness & the confidence that we were together secretly, apart from the hateful world, which was with me all the week, should suddenly have been taken from me. Without your love I am nothing – and I am nothing now.

And then you are ill, terribly ill – what can I do – why in God's name are we apart? Why, why why – I would have guarded you so. In my wire I asked you should I come? Perhaps you will answer. I could come. Darling, Darling, oh can't you feel even these kisses and these tears?

Jag.[2]

1. J.M. replies to K.M.'s letters of 14 December: 'Don't you worry about me . . .'; and two of 15 December: 'I have opened my letter to say that now another day has come and again I have no news'; and: 'The maid came back with the wire'.
2. K.M. replies on 24 December: 'Yesterday I had *four* letters from you . . .'.

----

[47]   23 Worsley Road
                                           Hampstead
                                           N.W.
Monday. 6 p.m.   [London.]
                                         [20 December, 1915.]

Wig darling,

I wrote to you early this morning. To-day to fill up the interval of waiting for answer to my telegram, I have been everywhere in Hampstead & Highgate, looking for a studio, even for rooms. I haven't found anything yet; but of course I shall soon. And the suspense of waiting must be filled up somehow.

Oh, my darling, since your letter of last night, I have had no heart at all. Everything round me has been like a grey mist and no place for me to hold fast. Every moment that I am not doing something active and definite, I just see nothing but your face, when you found no letter and turned over to the wall and cried. I ask myself how can I comfort you? and something echoes and echoes that I can't, that it all has happened irreparably, that you trusted in me and I failed when I was all you had to lean on. And yet I can't believe it, for I know how I am utterly swallowed up in my love of you. I have carried your presence everywhere with me during the last days. I have talked and whispered, danced and whistled to you, all in secret so that only you and I could understand. I have found my goblin swinging on a lonely gate, and taken her hand and run away away from the world. I have pressed your darling head to my breast and laid mine in yours. I have kissed your lips & your eyelids, and held your face between my two hands. And now, I feel that it was all some sick imagination. You were not there, you did not feel, and I gave my inmost heart away to the cold winds & the grey air.

And I ask myself – what could I have done, that she should never have been hurt? No, it is something beyond me that fails. My heart has been full to bursting, and every time that I have written to you, my throat has been full of tears, warm tears that were sad & happy at once. This morning, when I wrote, I could not see my words, for the tears in my eyes. But they didn't make rainbows as they used to only a few days ago, when all my sadness was only an extreme happiness, and I was so foolishly sure that every warm thought of mine came all the way to you as warm. That is all gone away from me now, and I feel as helpless, as remote, and as hungry for you as I did that day in Runcton, when I went away and you cooeed and I did not answer.

There's a devil at the back of my brain, who keeps on saying: 'You have lost her – it will never be again.' Oh, Wig, my darling, my precious, my goblin – that can't be true, can it? All of me is yours, is you: I do not live save in the full knowledge of our wonderful love. What will there be left for me? Oh, my darling – perhaps my hurt is less than yours; perhaps I do not know how you have suffered – but I have suffered, and I am suffering now, just as much as I can bear. I know I am not worthy of you & that I am only a *little* man – but yet darling, I have given you all my love. If I had held any back, if for one second since we parted, I had not been hungry for your presence again, then I would not complain, or write this pitiful letter to you. You have taught me so much, Wig, will you still be hurt just because there is something left to learn?

Perhaps the wound will be so old and deep and ineradicable when this reaches you, that you will just smile at my words – that bitter smile of which I am in terror, as you have learnt to smile by disillusionment. Oh, Wig, if I could only make them alive; but they faint & die on the way, and I feel that it is useless. I would make you a drawing; but I haven't the heart. And I feel you would just turn away. Oh, my baby – I am yours. I will guard you and cherish you & give up my life to you, if only you will say something to let me know that our love is joined again. And even if you do not, I cannot change: I am still yours for ever – *TOUJOURS*.

Jag.[1]

My darling – all I know is that you are *very* ill. If your wire, says *come* I will somehow come and fetch you back again. This awful horror can't

go on. But tell me *the Truth* about your illness. I am in the dark &
afraid.

Jag

1. K.M. replies on 24 December: 'Yesterday I had *four* letters from
you . . .'.

---

[48]   23 Worsley Road
                                               Hampstead. N.W.
                                               [London.]
                                               [20 December, 1915.]

Monday evening 10 p.m.

Wig – I know its silly to sit down and write again to-day but what am
I to do? I have had no answer to my wire. Perhaps you couldn't send
one, as you wrote that you could not on Wednesday. But that is worst
of all – that you should be so terribly ill. Oh, Wig, I pray that there will
be some answer tomorrow morning. Perhaps this address had not
reached you yet and you telegraphed to Kottilianski.

I could not just go out and eat and come straight back here. Je
m'énerve, to-day when I am alone. I went to the Lawrences for an
hour. They had got your letter to-day. They did not show it me. I
didn't ask to see it; I couldn't look at what you wrote to anybody else –
and perhaps you told them not to show it. But Lawrence went for me,
about you, terribly. Had I been alive I should have been hurt; but I'm
not alive to-day. I'm just numbed. He said that it was all my fault, that
I was a coward, that I never offered you a new life, that I would not
break with my past, that your illness was all due to your misery and
that I had made you miserable, by always whining & never making a
decision; that I should never have left you there. I do not know how
much of it is true – perhaps all, perhaps nothing. I can't really think
about it, tho' I try. To me we seemed to be so happy together, and that
happiness made me feel happy even when we parted. It breathed out
of your first letters.

Wig, do you just treat me as a child? Do you make your letters seem
happy to deceive me? Do you just pretend to be happy in order to
make me happy? And what has happened – is it that you were
unhappy all the while & now do not care to conceal it any more?

Perhaps I am just blind. Lawrence says to me that your superficial happiness never deceived him. I don't know what to answer, except that he never knew you. Was all our secret life together just a game you played to amuse me as a child, so that I should not know how sad at heart you were?

Lawrence confuses me utterly now. Another day, I should not have cared, for I should have felt in my heart that you and I understood each other, and that we couldn't tell our secret to anybody. I should just have listened with a smile, with my love curled up warm in my heart so that I could touch it and feel safe, while he said monstrous things. But to-night I have lost my treasure. He says these things and I feel that perhaps some of them may be true. There is nothing curled round my heart to make me feel miles away from the world he talks about. He let drop by accident that you had written that 'there was nothing for you in life'. And now instead of my warm love, that creeps about me like a poison, and I feel that so soon as you have said that there is nothing for me. He says to me 'that unless I promise you happiness, I will lose you', and even though happiness for him means Florida, I feel that there was something in your letter made him say that.

Oh, darling, is there nothing left of that which was *ours*. I know that Chummie's[1] death was terrible, and that the pain tugs at your heart for ever; but I trusted that even then we should be yet greater lovers than we were. And now I think that all that was just my own brutality – my insensibility.[2]

1. Leslie Heron Beauchamp (1894–1915), only brother of K.M., whom she affectionately called 'Chummie'. Arriving in England from New Zealand in February 1915 to train as an officer in a British regiment, he spent some happy periods of leave with Katherine. She mourned his accidental death in France inordinately.
2. K.M. replies on 25 December: 'The rain is pouring down . . .'.

---

[49]
　　　　　　　　　　　　[23 Worsley Road,
　　　　　　　　　　　　　Hampstead, N.W.,]
　　　　　　　　　　　　　London.
　　　　　　　　　　　　[21 December, 1915.]

Tuesday evening. 5.45.

Wig darling,[1]
　I have just had your wire. Oh, do you know how I feel. You were

wonderful to put 'always' – that is the same as toujours. You can never take it back now.

I had a ghastly time in the evening after I had written the letter which is on the other sheet. This morning I rose early and rushed down to Kot's to see if there was anything for me. Perhaps a letter, and I thought too that you would not have my address in time to send straight to Hampstead. There was nothing. Oh, Wig – it was awful. I went straight off to the Consulate to have my passport visaed for my one idea was that if I had no reply by to-night I would set off in the morning. They were kind to me at the Consulate – but now it is stricter than ever, and though they said they would give me a visa at once, I had to go to the Foreign Office and get my passport endorsed. I can't really remember what happened then. I was a kind of nervous maniac – and I told them all my secrets. At half-past three they endorsed my passport. They must have been convinced.

I could not wait. I was too dotty. So at midday I went back to Kot's to see if anything had come at all. I did not expect anything; but I could not stay away. And wonder of wonders, there was a letter. You were not happy – but at least you were happier – and you were not so terribly ill. And it began *Dearest Boge* – you know what that meant to me. My heart seemed to work free again; it has been under a huge weight since Sunday. And now when I have come home again, I find your Telegram. Those words of yours are curled up in my heart again and I feel that my head is laid between your breasts. Besides I know that you have got some at least of my Worsley Rd. letters – and I know the kind of letters I have written every day – then the good ones, those in which I got free of the world and bathed myself completely in our love, began. I even feel that I am somehow forgiven.

In your letter today you speak of having got my pencil letter. It was the last of my bad ones. They were those in which I seemed not to be able to touch your hand. Then I was lost, and I could not hear your voice. That very day I began to live wholly in your presence again – and you were with me all the week until that awful Sunday night. Now your letter tells me that you are returning to me again, and the wire sings that we are 'us', once more.

You wrote: 'I feel very sober today. I'm afraid you will think my last letters very silly. They won't happen again. I understand you far better now and I'll not ask for the moon either.'

Tig, my precious, you must ask for the moon. Even if I can't give it, yet to feel that you will not ask it of me is terrible, for, darling, I am learning. I do not want for a second to excuse myself. But a little man like me does not learn to love you in a day – not even in three years. You were set so high above me that I only dared to see in you the things I would understand. But I am learning. I have learnt much in three days: you will not find me the same Jag – but something truer, more grown and more worthy.

Oh, my darling, I pray you not to give up expecting everything of me. I will give. I can, if only you will believe that I can. Oh we will walk & talk – my darling: come back and let me love you.

I have just put a line under those words. Now, the one terrible thing that divides me from utter surrender to the happiness of loving you, is that thought that you will give up asking all. Oh, Wig – just think of me – hold me before you – and say you will ask everything – and that you will come soon for me to give.

Jag.

1. J.M. replies to K.M.'s letter of 16 December: 'I am better but still in bed . . .'.
2. K.M. replies on 25 December: 'The rain is pouring down . . .'.

---

[50]   23 Worsley Road
                                  Hampstead. N.W.
                                  London.
                                  22 December, 1915.
Wednesday. 7.30.

Dear darling,[1]

I feel so miserable without you to-night. It has been round about me all day. Yet I was happy enough with your telegrams last night – a second one, all in French, came very late at night, quite unexpected – but it didn't last with me, somehow. I think that your illness and your awful loneliness has shaken me. I have lost the old confidence. I want terribly to be near you, to have the warm comfort of your actual presence. Without you, I am lost.

And your letters – just one word or one sentence of them – stab me. When you wrote in your Friday–Saturday letter about the villa at 88 francs, when I read 'But no, I won't speak of these things – for its useless and foolish – I'll remember that England and the Printing Press won the day and left me on the field' – oh, Wig, that has haunted me all day long. Why did I leave you? I keep on asking myself the question, and I find no answer. I can remember nothing of what urged me back. It must have been strong and overwhelming – but it is all gone. There is no printing press – that vanished like smoke. There is no England. There is only you, whom I left. Why, how, did it seem all so simple & natural then, and now it's like a nightmare that never ends?

Wig, is it all too late. Could you not even now get a villa? and I could come. I should not go away again. England is simply a foolish word without you. You are everything – everything. Will you not get a villa – surely you could find one; I could find the money to come, and even if I could earn nothing, I might live on only a tiny bit of your money. Surely it isn't too late. Or [do] you mistrust me now, for a coward

Darling, for an hour I've stopped, just thinking – shall I borrow the money and come to you now? Shall I wait in the hope that you will come back? Shall I wait a little while until you have found a villa and then come? – for I should have nothing at all & could not afford to stop in the hôtel.

These three chase one another through my brain incessantly till I am dizzy with them. I don't exist any longer – but I am only a torment of longing to be with you. And then, if I come – I am terrified that I should be a burden.

Your Sunday letter has just come, while I was writing. Another stab. 'I have a présentiment that I shall never see Albion's shores again' Oh, Tig, if its only a jest, it nearly tears my heart out.

Darling, will you promise me this – that you will try to get a tiny villa for us both immediately – that if you can you will telegraph to me 'Come immediately. Ill.' (Then they will visa my passport immediately. I have arranged with the nice man who took me last time) I will borrow £10 – Lorenzo has £100 – and come, just as I am. I will be there within 3 days of when you wire. I can't live away from you. I don't desire even to be alive. It is one incessant hunger. Oh, my Tig, *I implore you to do this* if you can. We could live in a villa for £3 a week, easy, couldn't we darling?

Wig, I want to sit by you, to hold your hand, to talk all my heart to you. I have only just learnt – oh Tig, the things I have to tell you or my heart will burst. And don't think I will fail again – never, never. We will live like little goblins in our nest and go hand in hand for ever. I have lost the world in finding you. I have not cared to do anything since I left you. Journalism is past. I am only a lover after all. Tig, Tig, do this for me. Even though you have found me wanting, give me this one chance more. We will go from sunshine to sunshine.

If you cannot do this, then come back to me. I will make a nest – where we can talk. Its to talk to you, to hear your voice, to pour out all the things that have been crushed to death in my heart – all the things that I was too hard to give.

I must, must be with you   Jag.[2]

1. J.M. replies to K.M.'s letters of 17 December: 'I am afraid the courier is past . . .'; 18 December: 'I must write a little more for "le temps" is so exciting'; and 19 December: 'From sheer laziness I am sitting up in bed'.

2. K.M. replies on 27 December: 'Even if you never came I cannot but love you more . . .'.

———————

[51]

23 Worsley Road
Hampstead
N.W.
[London.]
[23 December, 1915.]

Read the other letter first. –
this is all wrong.

Thursday Afternoon 5.30.

Dear Love,

I have sent you to-day, *Oliver Twist*, *Sketches by Boz*, and *The Essays of Elia* – also the *Times Literary Supplement* and a letter from Lesley Moore which was sent registered to Kot.

Wig – if there isn't a villa, what will you do? Are you going to stay out there a long while? Or will you come back soon? I don't know why it is; but now I can't do anything without you. I've become all nervous. You see, dear heart, you don't tell me what it is in your mind to do, whether to stay or to come back – and I can't bear the thought of being apart from you much longer. If you decide to stay, then I must come out to you. If you will come back – then I will find some lovely rooms. But now I don't know which it will be. When you write you speak of *my* studio. So I've given up looking for it. I thought that it was our studio. What's the good of a studio *for me*?

No, I am very miserable with the suspense. I can't do anything definite; and so I just sit in my furnished room and wonder, wonder . . . You see, even if you said you would come back when you could; or if you said that you would find a villa – then the vagueness would go and I should be able to act. As it is, I just spend all my days as though I were on the platform, waiting for a train, that will take me I don't know where. If you were coming back I would go ahead and find a place – if you were staying I would borrow the money somewhere. Wiggy – you are warm to me, darling heart? You do want me still, don't you?

Lawrence goes away to-morrow morning to live at the Beresford's house in Cornwall. He has left his Endymion rug, his clock, his fender, his kitchen table & chairs, and a camp bed, for us. I have stored them in Gertler's[1] studio – until I know what is going to happen. It would not take much more to set us up, if you were coming back, in two of those rooms above the shops in High St., St. John's Wood 12/6 a week. But that was some days ago and I haven't gone any farther with it.

I haven't done a single stroke of work of any kind since I came back. Perhaps I never shall any more.

Darling, I was just staring absently at the blotting paper of my pad in front of me, listening to the ticking of L's clock, which I have hung up on my wall, when I saw something familiar in some writing at the bottom, here it is (something like)

It slowly dawned on me that it was your own dear name.

I don't know what to write anymore. You see its no good writing over and over again that I can't live without you – and that's all I have to say. The day goes by somehow – nothing happens

The thing that bewilders me most, I suppose, is that I really thought that you hated the South of France now as much as I did; and that I was just a little courier of my queen to prepare a place for her, and strew the road with palms. And now, I suppose, I am dazed by the sudden knowledge that you think I am doing it for myself alone. At any rate, I shan't do anything more. Perhaps the reason is that I am so selfish that I saw only my own desires. I don't know. I am just bewildered. I feel rather like an old clock that is running down.

I suppose I am only going through one hundredth part of what I made you suffer – but I feel mine is about as much as I can bear. I sit for hours giddy just with the longing to see you once more – and I suppose that makes me tired. Then I am tired with my own ind e c i s i on. I want either to go right away – perhaps to some up-country station in your back-blocks – or I want to stay in England. Only before either of those things, I want to be with you. Therefore, if you decide to stay, I must come, even if I starve for it. Tig, my precious, my darling, do you know what it is to die of love. I'm beginning to understand it.

Jag.

1. Mark Gertler (1892–1939), a talented Jewish painter, had met the Murrys in 1913. At the Cannans' 1914 Christmas party, he acted the role of Katherine's lover (too realistically for the comfort of some guests) in an improvised play dramatising the strained relationship between the Murrys.

---

[52]   [23 Worsley Road,
                                  Hampstead, N.W.,
                                       London.]
                                  [Thursday, 23 December, 1915]
A quarter of an hour later.

Oh, Wig, what a heavenly letter you sent me[1] – it was written 'Sunday before Xmas' – that very day when I telegraphed to you. Darling do you think I'm mad? In 2 minutes – all that load that has [been] pressing on me for days and days – is utterly lifted. I am back again in the old confidence. I wrote you all my secret heart and you *knew*.

Darling – now I feel I can work, do anything, wait till you return, be good, brave, everything that you would have me. I want you back, terribly of course; but even if you stay, I know you are mine, and I am yours. I should be always preparing my heart for you. For I have many things to learn. You see, Goblin, I never knew how much I loved you before – I never realised all the things that stood between us, all of my own making. I never knew that my very life from minute to minute utterly depends on you.

You may not think this will change me but it will. Oh, [I] am a different Jag, altogether, even now. I have found our truth – I have learnt that there is nothing in [the] whole world can weigh for a second against it.

Wig, forget all my latest letters – even that of yesterday in which I said – 'Find a villa'. It was mainly cowardice. I was frightened that you were loving me less while I was not with you. I could not bear it. Now I have your arm round my neck – and I am so happy – oh, my darling if I could only tell you how wonderful it is, like a golden sunshine flooding right into my heart. If you want me, I will come *immediately*. If you do not, I will find a lovely little cave for us in London – so that when you are tired of the South, you may come back to me.

But I know that our love is enduring now. It will last longer even than we ourselves.

My darling, forgive me my letters of the last few days. I was so miserable that I could not even speak out the troubles of my heart. Now they are gone for ever.

Jag.[2]

1. J.M. replies to K.M.'s letter of 19 December: 'I have just got the letter that you wrote me on Thursday night . . .'.
2. K.M. replies on 28 December: 'I ran about yesterday and surveyed the land . . .'.

---

[53]

23 Worsley Road
Hampstead.
[London.]
[23 December, 1915.]

A little later
Thursday

Dear darling,

Do you want any more books. I will send immediately – or anything at all. You have only to ask. How I love you and how happy I am.

I suppose that I am going to Lady Ottoline's for Xmas – a very sober affair – Bertie Russell,[1] me & Clive Bell. Feasts of intellect, I don't think

Jag – Boge.

1. Bertrand Arthur Russell (1872–1970), the Cambridge philosopher and writer, had become an intimate friend of Ottoline Morrell in 1911, and was a regular visitor at Garsington. Towards the end of 1916 Russell began meeting Katherine in private. A brief correspondence ensued.

---

[54]

(Address as usual, 23 Worsley Road)
Garsington Manor
near Oxford
Sunday after Christmas.
[26 December, 1915.]

Wig darling,

I hope that my last two letters have reached you – but I am afraid that they may all arrive at once, and leave a day blank – for the posts are awful. Saturday was Christmas day; to-day is Sunday; to-morrow, Boxing Day – a bank-holiday. Its too awful. But perhaps they're not as bad as I fear. And I think you will know, darling, that I have done mon possible to ensure that one should arrive every day.

I shall leave this place on Tuesday morning. I am not having a bad time – but I do wish you were with me. Its so strange to go for long walks with people like Lytton Strachey[1] & Clive Bell, and spend the whole time talking about everything under the sun, just for the sake of talking. It is so strange that at moments while its going on I become quite bewildered, wondering whether I've suddenly grown years younger, or have been knocked suddenly tumbling into a different world. I think that the people like me rather – they seem to be rather deferential to what I say – and that's such a queer, utterly un-Jag-like feeling. But at any rate its better than being completely out of it.

I've come to the conclusion that the reason for it all is that they have a suspicion that between me and you there is actually happening that incredible thing called a *grande passion* – I suppose that is what they call it. And I imagine that something of the glamour of it hangs about me nowadays. I mean that I carry you about with me, and they cannot fail to notice it, and to respect and admire it.

But perhaps it's because I'm so conscious of you that I don't care a rap whether they like me or not, and my indifference is enough to make them more eager to get hold of me. In any case, though they are rather a close corporation – most of them have known each other for ten years or more, they are a fairly decent lot, fantastic and fin de siècle, perhaps, but pretty good underneath.

But for all that I am very much like a babe in the wood. I live in a little top room in a cottage (where I am writing now) and when I come back to it, I feel that you and I are snuggled up together – and the birds cover us with leaves – fat and friendly robin red-breasts who have been told by our fairy mother to look after us well. And I can whisper to you all night long. Oh my precious how wonderfully we will curl up each against the others body when you return. You will lie in my arms and my hand will so gently cover your breast, and your little Tig-feet will be all mixed up with mine. You will be cold, for a moment, as you always are and then you will grow warm and pink like a baby. I know how your eyes open wide, and there is a pink, bright mark across your cheek, when you are suddenly waked from sleep. You are dreamy and soft and sweet like a tiny child, and your fragrance – Wig, your sweet smell, fresh and heavy, that makes me drunken with you – it comes all about me so soon as I begin to write about it. And I shall take your darling hands in mine, those tiny, absurd, beautiful hands, that seem to me to have your very soul in them. You *are* in your hands as you are in your eyes, and in your mouth, and your ears and the wonderful back of your neck, in your breasts. Perhaps that is the secret of your body, my darling, that each part is not only perfect – perhaps there may be other women's bodies that are perfect but they are cold and uninspired – but in each is to ken the whole of you – the spirit in you that I call 'goblin' because I have no other word to show that it was not born of the world, that it belongs to other kingdoms that only you knew once upon a time, but now you have taken me and made me free of it.

Oh, my darling, how you are with me tonight.

Jag.

1. Lytton Strachey (1880–1932), eminent biographer and critic who was a central figure in the Bloomsbury group, and a frequent visitor at Garsington. He first met K.M. in November 1915 at a party given by Dorothy Brett and wrote afterwards that she 'took [his] fancy a good deal'.

---

[55]
                                    23 Worsley Road
                                    Hampstead, N.W.,
                                    London.
                                    28 December, 1915.

Tuesday night 10.45

Wig, my darling love.

I am full of hope that I shall be with you before this letter and that we shall read it together and laugh tears. Therefore it must be short. A long letter would make me feel that we should be kept from each other.

I came back from Garsington to-day. There this morning I had both your telegrams saying that I should come. When I arrived here another came – imploring me not to. That one finished me. It seemed suddenly so childish – not childish, but criminal – to stay away from you a day longer. Whatever happens I must be with you: we will live together in our villa, until the summer comes. Oh, how we'll be happy & careless.

I have to go to the Consulate tomorrow morning (Wednesday) – I shall start on Thursday. I have just a tremor of terror that they may make difficulties – they have passed so many new laws in the last few days. I hope & pray they won't & with your telegram I think I can persuade them. Oh my darling – may it all come true & on Saturday – I shall be holding your darling face in my hands   Jag.

July 1916

Murry joined Katherine at Bandol on 3 December. They spent three happy and productive months, she writing *The Aloe* and he *Fyodor Dostoevsky: A Critical Study*. It was at the urging of the Lawrences that they returned to England in April 1916, taking a cottage near them at Zennor in Cornwall. But the relationship between the two couples did not work out: in June the Murrys moved further away to Sunnyside Cottage in Mylor. Dissatisfied now with her life, and with Murry, Katherine paid several visits that summer to London and to the home of Lady Ottoline Morrell at Garsington. She arrived for her first long weekend at Garsington on 13 July – dependent, as always, on letters from Murry.

[56]

[Sunnyside Cottage,
Mylor,
Cornwall.]

Thursday Morning   [13 July, 1916.]

Wig darling,[1]
    I've just got the note you wrote on Wednesday. It is too awful. I posted the book on Tuesday, *after* I posted you a long letter explaining everything about the boat. I cannot understand why you didn't have it on Wednesday morning.
    We seem to be fated to suffer because of letters when we are away from each other.[2] Now I don't even know whether the letter I sent on Wednesday has reached you. If the other one didn't why should this. Anyhow I'm going out to send you a telegram.
    It is too awful. Only last night when I was sitting in your room, I was so happy about us. It suddenly came over me that the war must end, and that we were really free. We could always spend half the year in France, in every kind of out of the way place. We have really achieved what we used to dream of as an ideal. But now the fact of my letter having gone astray seems to have upset it all.

It hasn't really, I suppose, but I feel so miserable & depressed – particularly because you wouldn't send me a word about yourself, on purpose. I know it must have hurt you not to get a letter. 'Really you *do* rather offend me'.[3] But why wouldn't you give me credit for having written & posted it? Did you really think I would *pretend* to have done so? That worries me.

However, in spite of myself, I'm hoping that everything is alright and that the letter really did arrive at last. I can't believe it was lost. These things don't happen. I shall simply go on as though it had turned up.

I did my *Times* article yesterday. In the afternoon I went out in the boat. I'm rather chary of venturing too far into the open, knowing what it costs to get back. It was just as well, for yesterday when I had sailed as far as Restronguet creek, that is the next one to ours going towards Truro, I suddenly discovered that I had left the rowlocks behind. Luckily I wasn't more than a half mile from the shore. So I stood up in the boat, just like a shipwrecked mariner and paddled with an oar first one side & then the other until I got to land, then, feeling very much like Robinson Crusoe, I hunted about for some pieces of stick & made myself rowlocks – and so home. At all events I learn. I shall never forget rowlocks again.

The syringa is wonderfully out. I smell it religiously every evening – yesterday it was faint & lemony; faint I think because we have had too much rain. But it reminds me of our magnolia at Runcton, and for some reason I always feel sad when I think of Runcton. To get over that I went to the back, to the bed that I was digging before you went away, and began to plant late cabbages. I don't believe that any self-respecting late cabbage ever comes up if planted in July, but I had to plant something. I feel miserable, besides, if I have a bed with nothing in it. Then I tied up all the beans to their sticks: some of them are terribly lazy at climbing. I look hard at them every morning & sometimes they don't seem to move at all: perhaps they were longing to be tied up.

I bought 3 flower pots yesterday to put my dahlia seedlings in – and I think I shall get some more & put the stocks in. Then they'll grow quickly and we shall be able to plant them out in the garden.

I come down from your room into the kitchen every night at about half past ten. Last night my milk boiled over while I was reading and of course the primus flared up & smoked. To clear out the room I opened the door. In about ten minutes in came a big thing between a great moth & a dragon fly, and began to buzzzz about the room. I didn't like it at all & tried to kill it, with your felt hat. The more I swiped at it the more it buzzed at me, until suddenly I made a great hit at it and the wind I made put the lamp out. I was frightened – it was pitch dark & buzzzz – all the while. I knew if I lit a match the thing would come straight for the light, and I nearly dropped the lampglass. However I got it alight, and made another great swipe at the thing. I don't think I killed it, but it didn't buzz any more – so I didn't mind. But I felt rather like Pyotr Stepanovich & Kirillov.[4]

I am working as hard as I can at these translations,[5] so that we can have a really free time when you come back. You say I didn't write a personal word. What can I write? That I love and adore you – but darling, you know it. You are the only soul in the world: without you I am quite alone. That I miss you terribly. I don't want to say that. For though I do miss you awfully, I should be quite happy, really quite happy, if I knew that the change was doing you good. But I don't see how it will, if you have to worry so much. Oh, curse the post. When I think of that letter I am mad with rage & despair.

Good-bye, my darling – but please believe that though I may be a funny boy, every morning I write you a long letter: and do you write me one in return.

Jag.

1. J.M. replies to K.M.'s letter of 12 July 1916: 'This morning I received a book . . .'.
2. K.M. was visiting Ottoline Morrell at Garsington.
3. K.M.'s letter concluded: 'You are a funny boy, and you *do* rather offend me'.
4. Characters in Dostoevsky's novel *The Possessed*.
5. Murry was later taken on as a translator at the War Office.

January – April 1918

In September 1916, after Murry had obtained a full-time job at the War Office, he and Katherine took rooms at J. M. Keynes' house in Gower Street, Bloomsbury. But Katherine felt spied upon by Dorothy Brett and Dora Carrington who also lived there. In February 1917, therefore, she rented herself a studio in Church Street, Chelsea, while Murry moved to 47 Redcliffe Road, Fulham. An unsettled year ended with a spot on Katherine's lung being diagnosed. Happily, she acquiesced with medical advice to escape from the English winter to the kinder climate of the South of France.

Her departure alone for Bandol on 7 January 1918 was actually the beginning of a protracted nightmare. After a wretchedly cold three-day train journey, she arrived to find that wartime conditions had utterly changed the place. Hating the French now, and desperately unhappy, she became dependent on Murry's letters as her illness grew worse.

He, immersed in his work at the War Office as well as reviewing for the *T.L.S.*, could do little more than react helplessly to Katherine's bad news. He lived in her alone, he said; it was she who was 'keeping his flame alive'. Murry's letters tend to echo Katherine's: bewailing her physical sufferings, praising her writing, sharing with her the solace of reading, and hoping desperately for her safe return to England.

It was late March before she obtained permission to travel to Paris on the first stage of her journey home. In Paris, she was trapped for three weeks with L.M. (who had joined her in February) by the great German bombardment. Finally, on April 11, she returned thankfully to London.

[57]   47 Redcliffe Road
                                   Fulham,
                                   London.
                                   [9 January, 1918]
                                   Wednesday night. 9 p.m.

My precious darling,

I had your wire last night saying you were safely at Havre; so I imagine that while I am writing now you are safely lodged in the Marseilles train, with a white pillow as per instructions under your head. But I am rather frightened lest the cold should have caught you in Paris. It has been terrible. The Lord knows how many degrees of frost, and a wind that was simply unspeakable. Last night as I rode from the office to the Good Intent[1] on Number 11 bus, I firmly decided that this was the most awful wind I had ever known; and as we swept round the dark purlieus of Pimlico, I kept fancying in spite of myself that round the corner I should find a waste of ice, absolutely illimitable, stretching far beyond the Poles, and that London & the houses was really only an illusion: we really lived in some kind of place like Seraphita,[2] only worse. However, it is said to have thawed to-day: certainly the wind has dropped. And so grateful am I, I don't feel inclined to ask for more.

You know its very funny; but this life at the office is such a half-life, that I hardly realise that you have gone – much less than I did while I waited on the platform. After my dinner, I come back here and begin to read the thousand and one books I have to read for review – and then its bed-time – and then I'm hardly awake before I find myself in the train at S. Kensington once more. Just before I go to bed I feel a tinge – a vague tinge (rather like the feeling I so often get of not having had any sugar) of loneliness, but I don't have time to feel anything really. At least the moments are so rare. Just before I went to bed last night I had a tremendous feeling for Rib.[3] I had already been rather pitying him in the cold, saying nothing: and I had put him in a little place between the coal-box & the fender, where he could be warm without melting. But I couldn't leave him there. I had to take him to bed. He was suffocated. but warm. And when I woke up in the morning, his hair was standing right up on end – *just as though he were* [a] *real one.* I thought he was going to rub his eyes and say something – something terribly like us; but he didn't. But still, he enjoyed himself . . . Now I come to think of it, I forgot to remove him to his proper place. Mrs. Hardwick[4] must have said some queer things when she found him.

I said I was going to give you something like a diary. A quoi bon? It would sound so stupidly monotonous. I wrote an article for the *Nation* on Monday night; and read a book for the *Times* to-night. The book is rather good, very good in fact, within its limits. *Gens*, by Pierre Hamp.[5] The man evidently has a social conscience; but he also has a literary one; and though most of his tales are about girls who are forced on to the streets, he tells them well, in a curiously concentrated way with a just ear for the significant words. I shall send it to you when I have finished doing it for the *Times* because I would very much like to hear your considered opinion on it. Beyond this, I have done nothing. I haven't got my rooms any more tidy, for the reason that Lesley and I decided that Sunday was the best day for her to come, as it gave her an extra day in the country. So till then I put up without shelves & without order.

To-night I received a letter from Marjorie Waterlow asking where you were, and saying that she had heard you were very ill, and had gone to your studio & found it deserted, and at the same time asking us to dinner on Saturday with Lowes Dickinson,[6] who desires very much to meet us. I don't know whether I shall go. I rather incline to the plan of sitting tight and doing as much in the way of articles as I can, until I have a supply in hand. When the extra money begins to flow in automatically again – then I may go out once or twice a week. However, *we'll see.*

I feel about ten thousand miles away from my land of poetry: but I've been there – authentically – & survived, and so I look on life very differently. Besides there is no doubt that peace is in the air and that it will come this year. Meanwhile I fancy I'm storing up the material for a real poem on Ribnikov: though it hasn't shown the faintest sign of materialising yet. Perhaps one of these days – in fact certainly – I'll have a Sunday free & then *we'll see* what happens. Follow the line I have just made and you'll see how very nearly I approximate to Mr. Asquith[7] under the influence of the office.

No, I can't and don't believe you are really away: and when I do, I'm really glad that you are. The real Boge is in cold storage at Watergate House,[8] there's no doubt of that: but the thought that you are in the sun, thaws him a little. However what there is of him is wholly yours, my precious darling.

You must write me much longer letters than I write you: because you can, and now you have everything to give. My letters will only be little flag wavings: yours must be music, and bugles, & songs. It's only fair after all. Make allowance for me. Think always that behind all my rather hasty scrawls is a burning & devouring love of you. Only, like the tortoise in his winter quarters, I can't speak.

Your Boge.[9]

Strange that I have had no reply from the hotel yet. I hope to goodness everything is alright: and that you will send me a wire from Bandol. Oh, my precious love!

1. An inexpensive Chelsea eating place.
2. A character in *Seraphita*, Balzac's novel set in Norway.
3. Rib, Ribni or Ribnikov was one of K.M.'s Japanese dolls, named after Colonel Ribnikov, the Japanese hero of one of Aleksander Kuprin's short stories.
4. Murry's 'daily' help.
5. Pierre Hamp (1876–1962), a minor French novelist whose book, *Gens*, appeared in 1917. Murry's review is not listed in Lilley's *Bibliography*.
6. Goldsworthy ('Goldie') Lowes Dickinson (1862–1932), Cambridge historian and friend of the Woolfs. Leonard Woolf would probably have agreed with Murry's subsequent assessment of him (13 January); for he commented in *Beginning Again*: 'There was a weakness, a looseness of fibre, in Goldie and in his thought and writing . . .'.
7. Henry Herbert Asquith (1852–1928), Liberal Prime Minster of England from 1908–1916.
8. Murry worked at Watergate House in Military Intelligence from September 1916 to February 1919, rising to the position of Chief Censor.
9. K.M. replies 14 January: 'The Lord took Pity on me today and sent me a letter from you'.

---

[58]

47 Redcliffe Road
S.W. 10.
[13 January, 1918]

Sunday Morning:
My precious darling,[1]

I am anxiously waiting for some sign or token that you have arrived at Bandol. I got your wire and your letter from Paris both together on Thursday. On the same day I got a letter from the Hôtel which I enclose. It didn't seem very encouraging: but long before this will have got to you, you will have found out whether they really charge 12 francs a day by the month. When one thinks about it and compares it with English prices, it doesn't really seem so bad. But it is rather stiff. However, there's no need to worry about money. If yours leaves you tight, I can perfectly easily send you the necessary. I was thinking that if Marie was still there she might consent to live with you as a bonne in a villa after a time. However, you will decide all these things. Your Paris letter sounded splendidly happy: so of course I immediately got cheerful also. But now I really want to know whether you have arrived quite safely.

As I feared, the Ma Parker[2] arrangement ended in disaster. The next night Mrs. Hardwick gave me notice. It was all I could do to persuade her I hadn't meant to insult her: and that took about a quarter of an hour. Of course, there was no choice for me. I had to write, as nicely as I could, and tell Ma not to come again. Mrs. H. really is rather trying with her execrable temper; but she is honest; and I can't risk being left without anyone at all. I should never find a substitute. The final arrangement is that she should spend one day a week really cleaning all my things while I pay her 10/- a week. But I'm sorry to lose Ma.

Lesley has been here this morning, having returned from the country yesterday. The day of helping me get straight hasn't come off yet, because her woodman hasn't provided the shelves: so it has to be postponed until next Sunday. It's rather a nuisance; but it can't be helped. By the way, she left our copper kettle behind in the studio: but, luckily, I got wind of it before the next tenants had stolen it; and now it is in Walter's[3] keeping against the time when I go to retrieve it.

Last night I went to Sidney Waterlow's to dinner. Lowes Dickinson was there. He's rather a nice, certainly a very kind, sort of man. Kind to the point of gentleness. But feeble also. However, on the whole, a very good specimen of the Cambridge don. We had a good evening together: which chiefly consisted in guessing quotations. Which is a really interesting passe-temps. Either L.D. or Sidney would read a short passage (if possible not *very* characteristic). And the other two first had to date it and then give the author. On the whole I was rather good at it. But we (Sydney & I) were completely knocked out by a couple of sentences from the beginning of the *Winter's Tale*. I can't find my (your) Shakespeare now, or I would copy them – it was just a couple of sentences ending 'we shook hands as over a vast'. We both insisted they were 19th. century. Camillo . . and embraced as it were from the ends of opposed winds. The heavens continue their loves.[4]

Sydney was very anxious about you; but he is very glad you are in the South. And when Marjorie (poor 'Marge') suggested you would be lonely, he said it was a very good thing, because you would be able to do a great deal of work. In Sydney, we have someone who believes in us both. He thinks, I am sure, that we are going to do tremendous things. Which is comforting.

Sullivan[5] came round on Friday night. He was very nice, as usual. But we didn't get going at all; because he would talk of Rémy de Gourmont,[6] of whom I don't know very much, and whom I don't in any case, think very important. Still, it was very pleasant. That same day, when I was going out of the office for my lunch I found a small boy, I suppose about 7 years old, with his bare legs and bare breech showing through the most awful rags of trousers I have ever seen. I gave him sixpence and was going on my way: when I suddenly had a terrible pricking of conscience. So I pelted after him and took him into a restaurant in Villiers street. There I gave him a good feed; and then I took him off to the Stores and bought him a pair of breeches. The strange thing was that there wasn't a single pair his size that would go round his belly. Eventually, I and the man in the shop, who is very nice, managed to find something. I don't know what the boy's name was. He lived in the Caledonian Road – 'down Cally' as he said. He had 2 brothers & two sisters. His father was a soldier in Egypt: his mother worked on the railway. So she must have been pretty well off, only she had to get up at 5 in the morning. I asked him whether she was kind to him: he replied 'She don' it me'. Which, for its implications, was pretty awful. Yet, even now, I don't know whether he was pulling my leg. I have a faint suspicion that he knew a thing or two about begging. He would not throw his filthy rags of trousers away. However, it doesn't matter. But I can't get over his enormous belly. I seem to remember that you once had a little town boy called Walter,[7] and that he had an enormous belly. There's something horrible about it, as though these children weren't real children, but fat, puffy, things like mushrooms grown in the dark. Terrifying.

I had a letter from H.L.[8] asking me to dine with her & Brett[9] on Wednesday. I suppose I shall have to; it will absolve me from a week-end at G. for a long while to come. I enclose her letter. It looks as though she were now beginning to attack me for eating so much. But why does she imagine that I'm taken in by such guff about Keats. '*So human & wonderful*' – she couldn't possibly reveal the emptiness of her mind more thoroughly. And does she expect me to cure her depression! No, I'm rather – in fact, very – hostile to H.L. nowadays.

I'd sooner cut my hand off than introduce her either to Johnny [Fergusson] or Sullivan.

I'm a very dull dog. Sheppard[10] has gone away on leave. And my time is so taken up with articles that I don't have time to be anything else but dull. I've promised Sullivan that I'll go round to his rooms one evening soon. Massingham[11] has accepted (at least I think so) 'O unreturning travellers'.[12]

I'm rather on edge about peace. One morning I believe it's coming; the next that it is being thrown away. And that's unnerving. The food problem is getting acute here. Luckily the other morning I was successful in the bacon-fight at the Stores and got a chunk 6/- (2/6 a lb) which I have boiled and which may last me a long while for breakfast. To-morrow, I shall try the butter-fight, for I'm coming to the end of the superb supply you gave me.

My precious darling – I'm beginning to miss you. It's as though something used to sparkle on the dullest day – and now it doesn't. But perhaps my consciousness of that is due to my not knowing whether you arrived safely. But to think that you were here, and we were lovers, only last Sunday!

O Wig I adore you. You are absolutely unique – the light of my life. What a life we shall have together when the sky lifts off my head

Good-bye, darling.[13]

1. J.M. replies to K.M.'s letter of 9 January: 'I shall not be able to write you a "proper" letter until I arrive in Bandol'.

2. Ma Parker had been K.M.'s 'daily' at the end of 1917. She was the model for the grieving charwoman in 'The Life of Ma Parker', published in January 1921.

3. Murry probably refers to Walter de la Mare (1873–1956), poet, contributor to *Rhythm*, and friend whom Katherine remembered in her will.

4. See *The Winter's Tale*, Act I, scene i, line 20.

5. J. W. N. Sullivan (1886–1937), an Irish scientist who became Murry's friend and confidant in 1917 when they both worked at the War Office. Later Murry's assistant editor (with Aldous Huxley) on the *Athenaeum*, he married Katherine's schoolfriend, Evelyn Bartrick Baker.

6. Rémy de Gourmont (1858–1915), French essayist, critic and novelist associated with the Symbolist movement. Murry reviewed his *Lettres à L'Amazone*, and *Pendant la guerre* for the *T.L.S.* on February 28, 1918.

7. In 1909, after K.M. had suffered a miscarriage in Bavaria, L.M. sent her a sickly slum child named Walter to care for.

8. H.L. (Her Ladyship) was a term for Lady Ottoline Morrell that Katherine and Murry frequently used in their letters.

9. The Hon. Dorothy Brett (1883–1977), daughter of Lord Esher, was a

'liberated' Slade painter called 'Brett' by her friends. These included Lady Ottoline Morrell, D. H. Lawrence (whom she eventually followed to New Mexico), Katherine, and Murry. Murry's serious flirtation with her in 1920 deeply upset Katherine.

10. J. T. Sheppard (1881–1968), a classical scholar who, after meeting Murry at Garsington in 1917, helped him to obtain a post as a translator at the War Office where he himself worked. Later employed by Murry as a regular reviewer for the *Athenaeum*, he became Provost of King's College, Cambridge in 1933.

11. H. W. Massingham (1860–1924), political journalist and editor of *The Nation* to which Murry contributed after 1918.

12. Murry's poem 'To My Dead Friends', which begins: 'O never-returning travellers, O friends', appeared in *The Nation* on 19 January 1918.

13. K.M. replies 18 January: 'I jumped out of bed this morning as though a bull had brought me your telegram on his horn . . .'.

---

[59]

[47 Redcliffe Road,
Fulham,
London.
14 January, 1918.]
Monday night. 11.45.

Wig my precious,[1]

I got your Bandol letter this evening. I won't talk about it now because this is only a fragment written, while the kettle boils, to go with a letter to-morrow. I have just been writing a political article for the *Nation*. As I got up from my chair, I saw your letter lying on the little round table in front of me. I had to kiss it: then I stood by the fire and looked at the clock, and loved you so much that I thought my heart would burst. I wondered whether something would tell you that I was full of love of you, wanting you to know I loved you so deeply, at a quarter to twelve on Monday night. Then I got down your photograph. It's stuck in a corner of the looking glass. And I was knocked all of a heap by your beauty again. It's the photo where you have the black jacket on, and the marguerite in your button hole. And there is all that wonderful, secret child-ness, trembling about that impossibly delicate mouth. You darling, darling, darling. That's only the first words of what I said to you. You exquisite, incredible woman.

At that point his kettle boiled and he, being tired, had to go to bed. One thing before he goes, however. *Don't worry about money*: just ask for as much as you want.

To-morrow I shall let myself go on the matter of that journey. Tuesday morning on way to office.

I have decided to post this now – all alone. I shall send my long letter on Wednesday, darling.

Boge.[2]

1. J.M. replies to K.M.'s letter of 11 January: 'My enthusiastic letter from Paris has been on my mind ever since'.
2. K.M. replies on 18 January: 'I jumped out of bed this morning . . .'.

[60]   [47 Redcliffe Road,
                                         Fulham,
                                         London.]
                                         [15 January, 1918]
                                         Tuesday evening. 8 o'clock.

My Wig, my precious Wig[1]

I have just had your second letter, written on Saturday. How I curse myself that I haven't written every day since you went. But I will: I made up my mind to it this morning. Even if its only a tiny word – something will come every day. Thank God, your letters seem to come quickly. Let me hope it is the same with mine

Darling, I won't say I'm terrified by your journey, because you'll do something desperate to reassure me. But I am – I can't help being – worried about you. Oh, you are so tiny, such a fairy child, and so far away! My heart aches. If only there were some means of whispering all my love to you now so that you could hear just as I write . . . If only I knew that you were well; instead I know you are ill . . . If only I could send Ribni even to you just to make your heart warm . . . If only I could come myself to you. All these thoughts buzz in my brain.

That journey! My precious, it is a nightmare to me. It seems to me now that it must have killed you. Oh, I wish that you had never, never gone. Everything seems so terribly to have changed; and what we thought would be a triumph ride into the sun, has been something utterly different.

I am frightened for you. But because I say this, I beseech you, Wig, don't tell me anything but the truth about yourself. I know you are telling me the truth now, and though it frightens me, it makes me warm, because I think that love can go no farther.

Write to Madame Geoffroi[2] 1 Avenue Victor Hugo, Carpentras,

(Vaucluse). I shall feel better if I know that she would look after you. But how shall I feel really better until I hold you tight in my arms again? And yet I daren't say I want you back, because you will come back. I want you back terribly: not because I miss you terribly, not because days without the sound of your voice are lonely days – all these things would fade away, if I knew you were well and happy, if I knew there was sunshine and that you were breathing it in. I want you back because you are small, and ill & so far away; because you are the only thing in the world, because you are the whole world to me; because you are so fragile, and the thought that I cannot look after you at all, even in my clumsy way, torments me.

Perhaps the weather will change. It must. It's not so cold in London now; though there is a deluge of half-melted snow pouring from the sky. What's the good of the South if the sea is grey?

Darling, look here. I don't want you back, so long as you are really well. If you are strong and can work and are happy, I would not say a word to bring you back even in April. I love you too much. But if you would say you were coming back then, such a thrill would go through my heart that it might burst.

Wig, don't worry about me. I swear to you, straight dinkum, that I am absolutely comfortable. I never see anyone in the evening: and I like that. I am full of your presence; and if the office weighs me down all day, I bound up again in the evening. I can talk to you then. And what is the use of anybody if it's not you?

I'm very comfortable, and just now, ever since you've gone, I've been working hard at articles for the *Times* & the *Nation* so that we shall soon be swimming in funds again. Take it for granted that I could not be more comfortable. You saw the rooms. I could not ask for more. My one, my only anxiety is for you.

Oh, if you could only feel how warm my heart is for you, warmer than any nest!

Boge.[3]

1. J.M. replies to K.M.'s letter of 12 January: 'You are to write as often as you can – see?'.

2. Madame Regine Geoffroi, married to a doctor who was mayor of Carpentras, had met the Murrys during their 1916 sojourn in Bandol.

3. K.M. replies 20 January: 'I LOVE YOU. I AM EVER SO MUCH BETTER . . .'.

[61]   [47 Redcliffe Road,
                                   Fulham,
                                   London.]
                                   [16 January, 1918]
                                   Wednesday Night. 10.30.

Wig my precious, my darling[1]

I am frightened to death about you. I am angry & bitter with myself
for ever having let you go, or let you go alone: and I am frightened,
frightened. Above all, because I can do nothing. It's no use heaping
reproaches upon myself I know; but I ought to have risked everything, even your disappointment which I can't bear, to keep you from
going alone. Instead, I did what I always do, trusted you would be well
simply because you were where you longed to be.

To-day I have telegraphed Madame Geoffroy,[2] begging her in the
name of our friendship to visit you immediately. I have also sent her a
registered letter. If the wire gets to her I feel sure she will go: but I am
so frightened that in spite of myself I fear that she may be gone. In
your Saturday letter you said you were writing to her: and I have a
faint spark of hope that you may already have asked her, and that she
may even be on the way.

Lesley can come if you can get a medical certificate signed by a
British Consul. But that seems to me like a grim joke: however, I
wired that to you to-day hoping perhaps that it might be possible.

Oh, my darling: I can't write what I feel, because I am afraid, and it
would only terrify me more if I were to write. I feel so bitter that life
should torture us in this way; so bitter that I have not written every
day, that I have to work on and on, that I can't move hand or foot.
Perhaps if I didn't have to work, I should go stark, staring mad. And
there Ribni sits in the shell-back opposite me while I write, looking as
though you had never gone, as though you were in the next room just
waiting to burst in upon us.

Perhaps, I say to myself at some moments, she is not badly ill. But I
don't believe it. When you say the word *malade*, the sky falls on my
head. Parceque je suis tellement malade: it has gone echoing through
my brain all day long. That and the eternal click of my typewriter. My
God, talk about irony. Was ever an irony ever conceived like this
which sends my fingers racing over the typewriter, my brain careering
through the German papers, and parceque je suis tellement malade
thrusting up every now and then and tearing at my soul? Probably it

was the best account of German politics I ever wrote: the perfect irony demands it.

I don't know what to do or say: I have suddenly been cut into two halves. But for God's sake get a doctor, even the Bandol doctor, now: don't worry about money. I can send you as much as you want in a week.

O my darling, you know my love for you. I can't speak it, because I am turned to stone with fear. The only thing about me is my love for you. I don't know who to pray to; but I want to bash my head against his altar for you. If only I could believe that Madame Geoffroy was with you: if only I could believe there was sunshine: if only – my letters are all if only now. If only you had never gone. My heart trembles when I think how long we waved to each other while the cursed train rolled away.

O Wig –

Boge[3]

Will there be a letter to-morrow. I wonder.

1. J.M. replies (again) to K.M.'s letter of 12 January: 'You are to write as often as you can – see?'.
2. Murry sometimes misspelt the name as 'Geoffroy'. K.M.'s letter of 18 and 19 January tells how Madame Geoffroi's visit, in response to his wire, exhausted them both: 'It was a *bit awful* . . . What a pilgrimage of love on her side! And how *I* bore the conversations I have no idea. I simply died with them and rose again – died and rose again . . .'.
3. K.M. replies 20 January: 'I LOVE YOU. I AM EVER SO MUCH BETTER . . .'.

---

[62]   [47 Redcliffe Road,
                                       Fulham,
                                     London.]
                                 [19 January, 1918.]
                                Saturday. 10.45 p.m.

Wig, my precious.[1]

When I came in to-night, I had both your Wednesday letter and your wire: Much better, seen Madame Geoffroi. The letter made me very, very anxious: the wire calmed me down. But hadn't you really better have Lesley Moore [L.M.]. I know it's difficult; but I don't think there's any doubt that she'll be able to come to you if you can get a medical certificate signed by a British Consul. I know that sounds frightfully hard; but couldn't Madame Geoffroy help you? But then I don't know whether you really want L.M. She has been here to-night. She is urgent to go, but seeing your wire, has decided that there's nothing to do till Monday at any rate. She has an idea that she might be able to persuade the French Military Permit Office to let her go without the certificate, even though she failed before. I am divided in mind. On the one hand, it would lift an enormous, incessant load from my mind if I knew she was with you; on the other hand, I don't know whether, if she came now, you wouldn't be angry.

Oh, my darling, for one thing in your letter I am angry with you. You say: 'Oh dear! a panier of wood only lasts two days, *try as I may to economise*'. Really it's cruel of you – it's just the kind of thing I would say. For God's sake burn all the wood in Bandol if only you can get your room warm. On Monday morning next, without fail, I shall send you £5. What does economising matter! And then you tell me you're much worse than when we went to Harvey Nichols![2] Oh, Wig, after this month there will be plenty of money, plenty. And I have still got, besides the £5, enough to send L.M. off to you. Make it a rule to burn a panier of wood everyday.

I am just going to get up to read that Wordsworth sonnet.[3] It'll bring me near to you. I found it after a long search. Yes, it is true. They are corrupt, mean, less than human. They do not know what fineness of soul is. But, darling, that's not, after all, a change of front for you, is it? You loved the French country, the French air, the French sun; but you were only a little less frightened, less horrified of the people than I. And I believe too that you stood up to them only to save me. They are cruel, & hard, & mercenary. You and I belong to a nation which, with all its great faults, is not any of these things. The only thing that can save a people, just as it is the only thing which can save a human being, is love. It sounds sentimental but we know it's true. And there's devilishly little love in F. How strange it strikes one, when one finds even a faint trace of it in their books! Can you imagine a Frenchwoman writing the *Aloe*?[4] Of course, there are exceptions. Péguy[5] was an exception (and he paid for it, by God). Madame Geoffroy is, I think, in her heart an exception. But darling, when you and I are together, we'll take their sun & their flowers and live to ourselves. They can't hurt us then.

But how sad it all is. Are they going to let the whole world come to this? I don't know. I don't know whether there is the will to peace here even. So much depends on Labour; and I *can't* believe in Labour. And then I can't make up my mind whether Germany wants peace or not – I mean the German Government. I grope in the dark after signs.

I'll send you a Dickens and something else on Monday & I'll also send you the *Daily News* every day from Monday onwards.

Your studio – I was going to tell you yesterday – has been let. The agent sent in a bill for £3 commission. That was why I broke off. But to-day he has sent a letter saying Miss Wright is going to pay that so that I have only to pay the £4 rent from Dec. 25 to Jan. 18. So we're well out of that. I'm looking after myself really well – cross my heart Straight Dinkum, I am. If you don't believe me I'll make Sullivan tell you.

Darling, I am worried about you still, really worried. I want you in my arms. I shall never feel you safe till I hold you again; and then I shall never let you go. Has the weather changed to warm as it has here?

Wig, you know I love you, love you, love you

Boge.[6]

1. J.M. replies to K.M.'s letter of 16 January: 'I had a very gay letter from Marie today . . .'.

2. A London department store where they had shopped on 28 December 1917.

3. Sonnet XV in Wordsworth's *Poems Dedicated to National Independence and Liberty* reads:

> Great men have been among us; hands that penned
> And tongues that uttered wisdom – better none:
> The later Sidney, Marvel, Harrington,
> Young Vane, and others who called Milton friend.
> These moralists could act and comprehend:
> They knew how genuine glory was put on;
> Taught us how rightfully a nation shone
> In splendour: what strength was, that would not bend
> But in magnanimous meekness. France, 'tis strange,
> Hath brought forth no such souls as we had then.
> Perpetual emptiness! unceasing change!
> No single volume paramount, no code,
> No master spirit, no determined road;
> But equally a want of books and men!

4. *The Aloe*, which K.M. commenced in 1915, was revised as *Prelude*. A limited edition of *The Aloe*, edited by Murry, was published by Constable in 1930.

5. Charles Péguy (1873–1914), French essayist and poet who died in action

leading his company at the battle of the Marne. Murry published an article on Péguy in the *Quarterly Review* of January 1918.

6. K.M. replies 24 and 25 January: 'I *must* add this to today's letter'.

[63]   [47 Redcliffe Road,
                                   Fulham,
                                   London.]
                                   [20 January, 1918.]
                                   Sunday Night. 9.40.

My precious darling,

Will you tell me if this letter gets to you at the same time as the one I wrote last night, which I posted early this afternoon, because, if it does, I might as well write a long one on Sunday instead of two short ones. What I want to arrange is that you should get a letter (if I'm terribly hard worked it may be only a postcard) every day. So if you'd just tell me whenever two come at once, I may be able to get it right by rearranging the times when I post them. The P.O. here can't tell me anything. They just say that no-one knows when the mails go to France, and that you have to take your chance. It may be true; but I suspect it isn't.

Arthur has been here to-day. He wanted your address so that he might write to you; but I turned the subject of conversation, because I didn't want him, or my mother, to see that you were still Madame B.[1] So that you must take the will for the deed on his part. He told me a story about Wordsworth – where he can have got it from, I don't know. It's stupid, but characteristic, and it makes me love the old fellow rather. One day Wordsworth was dining with a friend. Some rather aged, yellowish peas were served. The friend in order to turn it off said to W. 'Forgive me, but I forgot to send these peas to Kensington'. 'To Kensington', says W. 'Why pray?' 'Because that is the way to Turnham Green'. W. thought this an extremely good joke, resolved to remember it, and to let it fly on the first opportunity. It came very soon. He was dining with a friend whose peas were also rather passé. He turned to the lady of the house. 'Madame, I'm afraid you forgot to send these peas to Kensington'. 'To Kensington, Mr. W., why pray?' 'Because that is the way to make them green'. And he roared with laughter.

Lesley also has been here. She is evidently very upset with anxiety about you; but for some odd reason (not so very odd) I am impelled with her to take up a very impassive attitude about you. I dislike the kind of her anxiety so much that there are moments when I assume almost a callous air about you, my darling. I say: 'I'm sure she's better'. Then she says: 'Do you believe what she says' (i.e. in your wire of yesterday) I reply, very short: 'Absolutely'. If I'm not careful I shall fall into my old habit and regard her as a kind of ghoul, fattening on your illness, although I know it's wrong & that she's really a brick. But something makes it quite impossible to unburden my heart and my anxieties to her. I am all but silent when she is here. And when she asks: 'But don't you think it's likely Madame Geoffroy has been a disappointment?', I say 'I know she's devoted to Tig & Tig's devoted to her', although I'm asking myself exactly the same question. I can't make up my mind whether I am unfair to her, whether it is in fact that I resent anyone else than myself being so concerned about you. There's something of that, I'm sure, because when I said 'Don't you think, instead of hesitating, the best thing to do would be to send her a straightforward wire: "Would you like Lesley to come?"' and she replied: 'Whatever she said, I know she wants me' – I had a kind of jealous resentment.

Oh, that old marché of which you sent me the picture and the neat little station with the stupid train! To think that the place where we were so happy, where we entered on the phase of our perfect love, should have become morne and desolate. Those wounded mangy sheep!

My precious, I hope & pray that your weather has changed. It is really almost warm here in London now, warmer, at any rate, than it has been for two months. Oh child, you small and tiny jewel, why can't we speak to each other? Why do we have to wait so long for the answers. Darling, je t'adore

Boge.[2]

1. K.M.'s divorce from George Bowden, whom she had married in 1909, and left after one night, did not become absolute until April 1918.
2. K.M. replies 26 January: 'I seem to positively *eat* writing paper . . . .'.

[64]   [47 Redcliffe Road,
Fulham,
London.]
[5 February, 1918.]
Tuesday 8.30

My precious,[1]

This evening I got the letter that was missed out yesterday (Tuesday night – Wednesday Jan 30) and one written on Friday, Feb. 1. I shall always put down on the top of my letters the exact ones which I receive, just so that you can see that everything does come along, tho' in a very queer fashion.

My darling, don't worry about me. I only told you I had a cold in the head, because I had got one. A cold in the head is nothing at all – at most a nuisance for a night or two. And now it's almost gone – quite gone I think really. But when you say (Friday) that your wing hurts you horribly that is frightening. O Wig, do be careful of your infinitely precious body. Though I'm a turnip, living a turnip life, I live in you alone. Think always – what is the exact & sober truth – that in looking after yourself, you are keeping my flame alive. Every time you think and save yourself some exertion, you are saving me. How I realise that I should never have come through this night-mare without you. To-night, yesterday's depression has quite gone. It disappeared just before I went to bed. I had been working late on an article for the *Nation*; and I was just tidying up when I saw Rib. And a wonderful true vision of you came before me. I just had to catch him up, rather roughly, & kiss him hard. Everything was changed. I was the rich man again.

How it thrills me when you say you have been working for two days & it seems the real thing. That is very meat and drink for my soul. How we have changed – how *I* have changed, rather. There was a time when I used to feel a tinge of jealousy when you were working; now I only begin to breathe freely when you are at work. When I think how our love has made me a pure, clean artist; burnt out nearly all the rottenness in me, I feel I could lift up my voice in a song that would shake the earth. One day it will. Do you know I never think of writing but one thing – and that is love poetry. I feel I have it in me to write such love poetry as has never yet been written. Great big triumph songs that sink & swell, tremble & are still, plunging down to the depths & soaring years beyond the stars. Love poetry in which love is only the truer name for life, or rather love is the only light in which life can be *seen*. I feel that in you & me our love & our work are become the same thing, inextricably knit together. We work and that is a paean to our love, we love and that is our finest work of art. That I am held back from doing these things, that my soul strains at the leash (as it does sometimes & it hurts) seems to me now a mere nothing, or at most one extra trial to prove me, before we enter on that wonderful, unbelievable life that will be ours. I laugh inside me at the thought that a miracle is happening in the world, and the world doesn't know it. But in the time to come people will turn to what we have written and wonder, until perhaps two other people, like you & me, the dead spit of us, will recognise that once upon time you and I lived, & loved & wrote together, and the world paid no more attention to us than it will to them.

You must think, when you see those hateful French bourgeois – and its they more than anyone who are keeping the war going – that they aren't real. And its true that they are in fact only a dream. You have something inside you that not only will, but actually has, blown them sky-high.

Oh, but I want you back. This being apart is so precarious. I feel that nothing's *safe*. If I've got you in my arms, then that's all right. We *are*, like a rock; but the world, just as a great mechanical thing, is dead set on doing us down, and if we separate, it has a chance of tackling us separately. I know all that is, soberly speaking, nonsense; but then it is only the bourgeois who speak soberly. I never cease to be afraid. But I stamp my fears down and think of the future, in which I live.

Boge[2]

I will get *Nicholas Nickleby* tomorrow. What about *Edwin Drood*, too? I'll send off something else besides anyhow. Don't worry – look after yourself – we shall be together in April.

1. J.M. replies to K.M.'s letters of 29 and 30 January: 'I sent you a changeling today and scarcely a letter'; and 1 February: 'This morning I got your Sunday night, Sunday morning p.c. and Monday night letter all together . . .'.

2. K.M. replies on 10 and 11 February: 'I am just going to ignore this wire from L.M. until I hear further'.

[65]   [47 Redcliffe Road,
                                              Fulham,
                                              London.]
                                        [7 February, 1918.]
                                        Thursday 8 o'clock

My precious,[1]

Your Sunday (Feb 3) letter came this morning. Somehow it told me more nearly what you felt, and how you were, than any letter you have written me. Perhaps that was because I feel exactly the things you feel. I too have two motives for writing – happiness (Villa Pauline):[2] and a despairing 'cry against corruption'. The absolute exactness of identity between this last and my own motives struck me profoundly, rather as though I had been on the point of crying out, and you had cried instead – the miraculous, unearthly feeling of complete communion.

And – I don't need to tell you – that I fear the war: it is like a plague, or some great monster waiting. Alone, I feel helpless, (at best) fatalistic; when we are together I feel that we have such virtue in us that we shall, somehow, be able to withstand it. But being apart – it's no good, no good at all.

I wish I knew something definite, whether you will be able to manage to persuade the Consulate. I feel that you will; but until I really know, I shall be anxious still.

I don't know what to say, my Wig: I'm not depressed, I'm not happy. I seem to be in a sort of limbo where everything is half-and-half; quite obviously, there is only half of me here. I was quite calm & deliberate & sober when I said, the other day, that my soul had left me to nestle with you. It seems to be such a simple matter of fact.

I think it is a very good thing that I am working hard. I mistrust myself when I am left alone and writing articles eases the strain. Without it I should be rushing from deep depression to a sort of hysterical nonchalance, and that would perhaps break something.

But how glad, unutterably glad, I am that you are coming back. The sweetest part of my life now is when I think of us sitting together in the kitchen eating: of us lying together in each others arms, with your head on my shoulder. I dare not think.

                                        Boge.

12.15

Lesley Moore has since been here. She has sprung a complete surprise on me, & now that an hour has gone since she left I am beginning to be very doubtful.

She said she had determined to go to France. She has managed, by getting a certificate from Ainger,[3] to get a passport visa'd, and she was leaving on Saturday. It was no use; she said, my saying anything about it because she had determined to go.

I was completely bowled out. I told her that you had decided to come back at the beginning of March. That made no difference, she said, she would help you come back. I didn't, however, insist, while she was here on dissuading her.

But now I feel that she has absolutely no right to go without asking you first. I feel also that it may make it more difficult for you to return; you may well manage the officials alone on our plan, but she would complicate it. That may be foolish – I don't know. But I now feel overwhelmingly that she mustn't go without asking you. Am I right? Oh, I wish I knew. I could kill any person out of hand who made it impossible for you to return, or delayed your return by a day. I'll do all I can to prevent her.

O my precious love, I want you back. My mind is all dithering, just now. It's so hard for me to decide this thing.

Boge.

Friday Morning.

I got your M.S.S.[4] this morning. I am going to wire you. I'll write to-night

I've changed my mind about Lesley Moore. It would take the worst of the strain off if I knew she was with you.

Do all that you humanly can to come back. I know you will.

Oh, Lord I wish I could make up my mind about this. I was certain it was wrong last night; certain it was right this morning & now again I don't know

If by any devilish chance you can't get back, then I would have her with you, but if you can, I feel that she may make it more difficult.

Wig, Wig – I'm a poor rabbit of a thing – frightened of my love for you.

Later.

Lesley has just telephoned me to say that there is a chance that she may be able to get some official document from the Air Board, saying that she must get back as soon as possible. If she can do this it completely alters the situation; for that may help you to get back. If she gets it – she is going to the Air Board tomorrow morning – I am all for her going

Good-bye, my precious love.[5]

1. J.M. replies to K.M.'s letter of 3 February: 'It is early for me to be up . . .'. In this often-quoted letter, K.M. described her 'two "kick-offs" in the writing game' – one 'joy', the other 'a cry against corruption'.

2. In 1916 at the Villa Pauline in Bandol, Murry and Katherine enjoyed three blissfully happy months. The constrast between Katherine's present visit to Bandol and the earlier one was overwhelming.

3. Dr. Ainger, having diagnosed a spot on K.M.'s right lung in December 1917, advised her to escape from the English winter to the South of France. On her return from that disastrous trip in April 1918, it was he who confirmed that she definitely had tuberculosis – but agreed that she should try a 'cure at home' rather than enter a sanatorium.

4. The first part of 'Je ne parle pas français'. The wire Katherine received from Murry read: 'Story received magnificent Murly'.

5. K.M. replies 11 and 12 February: 'Your Thursday letter and the page explaining L.M. has come . . .'.

---

[66]
[47 Redcliffe Road,
Fullham,
London.]
[8 February, 1918.]
Friday 10 o'clock

My precious,

Your MS. (1st part of Je ne parle pas) came this morning. It's not only first rate; it's overwhelming. The description, no, not description, creation, of that café is extraordinary. (I've just read it again, since I began). The whole thing is extraordinary. I don't know what you're going to do at all. But I'm absolutely fascinated.

I'll try to tell you what I feel. In the first place my sensation is like that which I had when I read Dostoevsky's *Letters from the Underworld*. That is, it's utterly unlike any sensation I have ever yet had from any writing of yours, or any writing at all except D's.

Secondly, although it's unlike D. in that unearthly way he has of putting you in a place & stopping the world – everything stands still, becomes timeless, – and though you have – the Lord knows how – kept this up all through, so that the first page & the last seem to be simultaneous, happening in the same icy moment – and this is the final, large impression the whole chapter leaves, ——————

Yet, it's different. Like this. Raoul Duquette[1] isn't what he would be if it were either Dostoevsky (or me) writing, for then he would be Dostoevsky thinking aloud. But instead of this, you have got this strange person, who's strange, not, as D's man would be, because he has thought everything to a standstill, but because he is conscious of a piece out of him. I don't quite know what words to put it in. Yes, he's conscious of having no roots. He sees a person like Dick[2] who has roots and he realises the difference. But what it is he hasn't got, he doesn't know. Nor do I.

What you are going to do with them I haven't the faintest idea. But I am ravenous to know. It's all of such a different kind to any of your other work. Different, I mean, in scope & skeleton & structure, the exquisite exactness – the this & nothing else – of your vision in the detail is there just as before. How can I put it? This is the only writing of yours I know that seems to be *dangerous*. Do you understand what I mean – by the adjective? Its *dangerous* to stop the world for a timeless moment.

To put it another way. Here you seem to have begun to drag the depths of your *consciousness*. Before you did something quite different, and I am certain that you will again. But somehow it has happened that on this one occasion you were driven to make an utterly new approach, to express something different. I mean it like this. Ordinarily what you express & satisfy is your desire to write, because you are a born writer, and a writer born with a true vision of the world. Now you express & satisfy some other desire, perhaps because for a moment you doubt or have not got the other vision. The world is shut out. You are looking into yourself.

Does all that seem nonsense? I feel certain that it is true, and also I see how apposite it was I that began by likening this story of yours, though you are essentially a Tolstoy writer, to Dostoevsky.

The thing is tremendous – but my impatience to have more of it is awful.

I'm rather worn out just for the moment by the continual underneath anxiety about your return. The L.M. affair hasn't moved since I wrote this morning. If she gets that letter from the Air Board, I am all for her going. She could bring you back safely. But I shan't be any good at anything till you are back here.

Wig – if we could only hold each other tight in our arms now

When I say I'm rather worn out, of course I don't mean anything serious. What I mean is that the anxiety & the hope always moving inside me are like a little chain tethering me. Whatever I do, or write, or think there comes the jerk.

I love you.

Boge.[3]

1. The central, narrating character in 'Je ne parle pas français'.
2. Dick Harmon, an important character in the story.
3. K.M. replies 12 February: 'Your Thursday letter and the page explaining L.M. has come, and your Friday letter about my story'. About Murry's appreciation of 'Je ne parle pas français' she wrote: 'Now about your letter about the first chapter. I read it and I wept for joy. How can you so marvellously understand and so receive my love offering. Ah, it will take all the longest life I can live to repay you. . . . Yes, I did feel that. But, Christ! a devil about the size of a flea nips in my ear "Suppose he's disappointed with the second half?"'

[67]   [47 Redcliffe Road,
                                                      Fulham,
                                                      London.]
                                              February 9 [1918.]
                                              Saturday 11.30 p.m.

My precious,

I saw L.M off by the 4. o'clock train to-day: by the time this gets to you she will be with you. What decided me that it was right that she should go – though of course I had absolutely nothing at all to do with it, because she had firmly decided – was reading your story on Friday morning. You'll understand. I wobbled again towards noon – the record of what I went through is in the letter sent on Friday. The reason why I wobbled was the same original one: I felt that somehow her being there might make it more difficult for you to come back. When she told me that she would be able to get back through the Air Board, my fear disappeared.

My darling one. I want to make my mind, now that the thing has been done and I am, tant soit peu, calm again, quite clear to you, to be absolutely candid.

First, I want you back. I can't bear this separation.

Second, my fear about you is much lessened by my knowledge that L.M. is with you. But it is still there.

Third. In spite of (1) & (2) you must not think that you must come because of me. If you are not fit, if it would make you stronger to stay there longer now that L.M. is there to look after you, if in any way you hesitate to face the journey, if you think you would be able to work by taking a villa, then I *want* you to stay. For us to be parted is not a good thing; but if I know you are being cared for and getting stronger, then I can put up with it, (I won't say indefinitely because it's not true) for some months. I shall be perfectly *all right*, if you now decide to stay on. I shan't even be disappointed. I know that you love me & I know that I love you; and, though there are moments when I could cry because I haven't got you to clasp in my arms, I have to remember that I am after all almost a complete machine until the war is over, and lately, because the money has been going rather fast, I have become worse than ever.

Fourth, you *simply must not worry* about me. Everything goes well. I feed myself, I look after myself, I can truly say (to *you*) I am absolutely fit.[1] I keep very much to myself. I have to in order to do the extra work, & I have no inclination to do otherwise – quite the other way. The moment anything upsetting occurs, I will let you know. I have been nervous, very nervous, about you; but – I don't know why – it hasn't pulled me down in the least. There is not the faintest reason why I should not go on.

I think that's all. I wanted to make it perfectly plain so that you should have something to go on when you make a decision. It comes to this – that I, your faithful, passionate lover, declare that you must not come back for my sake. It's only the selfish part of my love that says: I want you back. I say that it is your duty, as my lover – my darling lover, *to think only of what will be best for you*. In that way, you will love me best of all.

What a little solemn Boge I have been to be sure! But you will read my heart in between the lines, if it's not in them. Good-night, my love.

B.[2]

1. Murry had earlier been declared unfit for military service because of suspected tuberculosis. After a medical examination in 1916, however, he was threatened with conscription. To avoid this he took a job of 'national importance' at the War Office.

2. K.M. replies 14 February: 'I had 2 letters from you today – your last Saturday and your Monday letter'.

[68]
[47 Redcliffe Road,
Fulham,
London.]
[11 February, 1918.]
Monday. 8 p.m.

My precious,[1]
I found your letter of the 7th. (the one written when you had received my 'Absolutely agree' wire) and the handkerchief for my mother & the brown bread receipt, when I got in.

It's rather ironical the way things move so much faster than letters. L.M. is, I suppose, something like half way across France by now. You have my letter telling you as clearly as I could what I thought of your story. And I am like a little man with a bag from the suburbs running up an endless moving stair. I am feeling the strain a bit this evening; and am inclined to wonder whether, if I do come through, I shan't be somehow used up. But, of course, I won't be.

Still, I must confess this to you. Don't tell L.M. I think she was very much upset with me because I didn't agree immediately with her plan of going to France. The chief reason for my attitude – this is my confession – was that I thought she wanted me to find the money. I have got as a matter of fact about £15 in hand. But I couldn't have let her have it unless I knew from you that you wanted her. Now that I work every night – I do feel that the money is too hardly earned to be spent except for what it is made for, to give you and me the chance of our own life after the war. It may sound mean – I hope it doesn't, but I feel it may – but I felt as though she were tearing away our future for some caprice of her own. Of course, she wasn't. She found the money herself – and I had nothing to say in the matter. But she may tell you that I was very queer about her going and I want to unburden myself.

And I love to unburden myself to you: you understand me. I know that even if I was mean you wouldn't mind. But I feel as though I had been working on my last reserve: that I'm perfectly willing, no, even happy to do this, if it is going to help us to be independent after the war; but if it isn't and if there's to be the same old *corvée*, then I can't face it. I don't mind where we live so long as it's somewhere deep in the country, hidden right away in a sunny place. I want to be able to live only for you and for poetry. And, though the printing press may seem a fad of mine it isn't at all. I've thought everything out. I can see no other way, no other possible way, of making even the scantiest living except by a printing press and a garden. You see I have to face the fact that my novel[2] made £8-10-0; and the typewriting cost me £9-0-0. Net loss 10/-. I can't be popular – it's no use my thinking for one moment I can make even £1 a week if I publish in the ordinary way. And, though I think you're not in quite such an awful case as me, I think its really the same. But you and I may very well find between us 250 people willing to pay £2 a year each for 4 privately printed books of ours every year, and out of that we could make £300 a year profit. It's the soberest sense I'm talking. I haven't got a bee in my bonnet or a maggot in my brain. It's a chance of real salvation. Think of that *tripe* of the Woolves![3] And so it is, my darling heart, that each £10 I make now is to me the possibility of freedom in the future. If I haven't enough money to buy a press, then I feel that the big stone will have been put on my head again. And I can't ask people any more. I hate them. Really, the blackness of my hatred of people like O.M. [Ottoline Morrell] staggers even myself. O what a silly Boge I am my darling heart. Off to a *Nation* article.

Boge[4]

Keats had £1000 to start with

1. J.M. replies to K.M.'s letter of 7 February: 'The Aged brought me your wire last night'.
2. *Still Life* (Constable, 1916).
3. Leonard and Virginia Woolf were often called 'The Woolves'. They had bought their own (Hogarth) printing press in 1917 to publish small books on a subscription basis. K.M.'s *Prelude* had been accepted in 1917 as 'Publication No. 2'. Murry wrote more charitably to K.M. about their printing on 18 March:
   'They have done 44 pages of "Prelude" & I must say they have done it *very well* indeed. There's no comparison between this piece of printing and their last. And when it's finished – which, they say will take a good time yet – I am sure you'll be very pleased. They have used a Caslon fount with the result that there's nothing shoddy or amateurish about it. One mistake (a stupid one) has been made. Instead of calling it "Prelude" simply on the half title and on the top of the first dozen pages, they have put "The Prelude". Unfortunately it can't be altered, now. But they must put a note at the end to set it right'.
4. K.M. replies 16 Feb: 'The Lord saw fit to remove the shadow . . .'.

[69]
47 Redcliffe [Road,
Fulham,
London.]
[14 February, 1918.]
Thursday 11.30

My precious,[1]

This morning I got your letter written on Sunday the 10th when you had just got L.M.'s wire. O damn! damn! I knew at the bottom of my soul that this would happen. I was against her going: above all, against her going without asking you first. But it was taken out of my hands. And when I read: 'If I had not had this telegram I should have been feeling almost happier than ever before in my writing life', I feel furious against her. You might have been writing another master-piece, – and instead you are tortured with the thought that something may have happened to me. The only comfort I can give is that this at least is not true. I am perfectly sound.

It's like, just like, that atrocious little devil of a fate who goes about upsetting our apple-cart. I don't know what to say: I can't forgive my own carelessness – I was bewildered & flustered & upset by the sudden turn – in not seeing what telegram she actually sent. Somehow, she gave me to understand that in the letters you had written her, you had asked her to come if she possibly could; and I thought you would understand when she said she was coming why she was coming. Also, I fancy she felt that by going she was – somehow – outdoing me in love. I am cruel to her; but to-day I feel, I can't help feeling, violently anti-L.M.

But perhaps the sun will put things right. Perhaps you will still be able to work. Perhaps – I don't know. I long to hear from you after she arrives. At present, I am too resentful against her for 'butting in'. She may be some use to you mayn't she? My great fear, as it was before, is that, if you decide to come back, she will merely make it difficult. And I shan't easily forgive her for misrepresenting to me what you wrote to her. If it had been what she gave me to understand it was, you couldn't not have known why she was coming.

However, I *mustn't* be cruel. There is something jolly fine about her, and I must fasten upon that. Or otherwise I shall be getting the crooked vision about her that I used to have. But it is hard to forgive, isn't it? Seeing that she gave me three days agony of distraction trying to decide, and now she has done worse to you. However, I am *allright*

& You will have someone to take care of you – there's that way of
looking at it. But I must hear from you

Boge.[2]

1. J.M. replies to K.M.'s letter of 10 February: 'I am out of breath . . .'.
2. K.M. replies 19 February: 'I want to tell you some things which are a bit
awful . . .'.

---

[70]   47 Redcliffe Road,
                                      Fulham,
                                      London.
                              [15 February, 1918.]
                                  Friday 8.30

My precious darling,

Your stories[1] came safely this morning. I hadn't time to read them
before I went to the office; so I took them with me and read them at
lunch. After which I sent you the shilling wire.

They are quite first-chop. I wasn't prepared for the tragic turn of *Je
ne parle pas*, and it upset me – I'm an awful child. But it's lovely,
lovely. I must read it right through again to taste fully the growth of
the quality of that ending out of that beginning. The lift is amazing.
And how the devil you got that sharp outline for Mouse I don't know.
And then there's 'Sun & Moon' – with the little grey whiskered man.
It's quite perfect, and the symbolical value it has stretches out
illimitably. It's so damned true of us now, isn't it? These people think
we can be fed on broken meats, and that we can feel delight in
ice-houses when the roof has been pushed in by their hateful spoons.
Save that we walk away hand in hand to our secret darksome cave – it's
all true. Go on, my darling, stick to it if you can with L.M. there: what
a writer you are!

Well, well, it's no use talking of L.M. She played me in or up
completely. When you tell me that you asked her *not* to come on yr.
account, well then I feel vicious against her. But this will be all in the
past when you get this.

After three weeks warm weather it has begun to get cold again here;
but, of course, nothing like so cold as it was the day you went away. I
haven't been such a good little machine this week as last. I've really
done nothing except a *Nation* article on Monday. On Wednesday I
really was done up, dead to the world, codfish eyes, and a face like an

artichoke. Purely mental, understand, physical turn out spanking. On Thursday I was inclined to be feeble and laugh helplessly (of course, I didn't) and I felt on the whole happy & careless, rather as though my mind had gone off on a spree and How the deuce do I know when it's coming back, & why should I care, anyway? To-day, returning sanity, but still rather weak in the head. Before I go to bed to-night I shall have pulled myself together. It's an odd experience, and though it's not really fair I put it down to the tax on my nervous energies that the L.M. affair put on me, so that when it came to Wednesday, I just flopped like a cuttlefish on to the typewriter. But this work of yours is a tonic. I've told you the exact truth of the last 3 days, because its our bargain. But you must understand that physically I'm in perfect health, and I stood it like Sun^2 himself would stand that disaster.

And I want you to promise me that if you think you will be able to work better by staying down there & turning L.M. into an abject slave – It's the very best you can do with her and better than she deserves – you will do so. Don't come and be caught by an ugly March wind, my darling, unless you really must. If you can't work down there, then you're better here. And you know how I should hug you. But if you can, and if you are looking after yourself and getting strong, then it's your duty to me as your Boge to stay

Goodnight
Boge[3]

Rib says: 'That was a good story she gave me, especially the bit about the nut-door-handle.'[4]

1. The second part of 'Je ne parle pas français' and 'Sun and Moon'.
2. The protagonist of 'Sun and Moon', a sensitive small boy.
3. K.M. replies 19 February: 'I want to tell you some things which are a bit awful . . .'. Turning away from the news that she has begun spitting 'bright arterial blood', Katherine says of Murry's reaction to her writing: 'I had your letter about the 2nd part of *Je ne parle pas*, and I feel you are disappointed . . . Is that true, and if it is, please tell me why'.
4. Central to 'Sun and Moon' is an ice-cream pudding, shaped like a house, with a door-handle made from a nut.

[71]   [47 Redcliffe Road,
You told me   Fulham,
to put two lines   London.]
Remember?   Monday Feb. 18. [1918.]
                             11.30

My precious darling,[1]

I got your Thursday letter to-night. I'm overjoyed, absolutely triumphant, that you have decided to come back. When I wrote to you and put everything as calmly as I could, in the letter you had before you wrote, I had a sinking feeling because I was making out such a good case for your staying at Bandol. Oh, Wig – when you are back, when you are back. You wonderful, beautiful Wig.

I've done with L.M. absolutely. She is a ghoul: spiritually a real ghoul. I knew all the while that she really wanted to batten on your illness; but she played me up completely by telling me that you had written to her begging her to come. However, don't let's think about that.

I want you back as soon as you can come, of course – but please don't put it off too long. However, I'll wait quite patiently for the wire. But if she comes back without bringing you safe & sound I'll shoot her.

Don't think I'm too busy to hear about your work and your ideas of work. I won't tell you again, because I've told you enough already, (and I don't want to give you a too swelled head, like Rib has got through being alone with me,) but to hear about your work, & to read your stories has done more than anything else to keep me going. Apart from the direct delight I have in the wonderful things you have done, I am flooded with a belief in *us* & *our star* when I read your work. I perfectly understand your point of view about the new approach being necessary for everything. It is. But don't be afraid of letting byegones be byegones. Your byegones would [be] enough equipment for four writers of genius. Don't start taking *The Aloe* and rewriting it all from the beginning. Corriger une oeuvre dans une autre. *Everything* you have done since we were in Bandol together has been first chop of its kind. You have no right to demand that everything should be first chop of the latest kind.

They're just sounding the All Clear. There's been another old raid. Three running that makes. But they aren't very bad ones now. I should imagine our defences must be good. But why they should always choose the nights when I'm writing an article to bang away I don't know. I suppose it's because they realize the effect my profound utterances in the *Nation* have upon English opinion.

Forgive me Wig I forgot to send off the *T. Lit. Sup* & the *Nation* to-day. I was so busy registering myself for food & butter that it quite slipped my mind. They will go off to-morrow. Thumbs down for Mac[2] & your Pa – hooray!

You see from the cheerful flippant tone of this letter that your decision has made a new man of me. I couldn't tell you how full of secret smiles I am. It's the india-rubber ball in the Tchehov story. My lovely, precious darling, good-night.[3]

1. J.M. replies to K.M.'s letter of 14 February: 'I had 2 letters from you today . . .'.
2. James MacKintosh Bell, the wealthy Canadian husband of Katherine's eldest and least-liked sister, Vera. Telling Murry that she had received a 'disgusting letter from Vera', Katherine had written scornfully of her brother-in-law.
3. K.M. replies 22 February: 'A Horn of Plenty! Your Sunday letter and your postcard and your Monday letter'.

---

[72]   [47 Redcliffe Road,
                                      Fulham,
                                      London.]
                              Thursday 11.30 Feb 21 [1918.]

My own darling,[1]

I am drinking my evening milk, hot with chocolate & saccharine (more substantial than your tea) and reading again your Saturday night & Monday letters which both came to-day. In case I haven't told you before, I'll say it now. Your letters are wonderful, like yellow flowers, narcissus, that have grown up in the night. They scent me with love. I am the richest fellow alive; I have to tell Rib all about it. He's very imitative, the villain; he behaves like me in a blue jersey, and says gruffly, just as though he were a sailor going to cry when I'm not looking: Oh!, she's all right.

You know I believe in our future – solid as a rock, shining as gold – that's all firm inside me. Being tired, thinking about money, – all that's really bubbles, badly blown. A touch of the war, un peu de fièvre, that's the kind of thing. Oh, but I'm exactly like you about this marriage of ours. I keep on saying to myself – I said it three times to Rib this evening – 'My wife, Wig', just as though I were introducing him. And, my hat, I do pile it on about the office; it's not half so bad as I make out. I don't work anything like so hard as I used, & don't intend to. The secret of it all is that because I don't see anybody & don't want to, I just tumble everything out of my bag on to your lap; and somedays it happens to be bits of string & used up blotting paper. But the bag ain't me, no, not by a long chalk. (I remember I said, No, not by a long chalk, in my letter yesterday – very queer, because it isn't a phrase I use generally, but somehow your letters have put me in such a frame of mind that it seems to me exactly appropriate. It'd be rather interesting to know why.)

About the war. One can't help thinking about it. Wilson's[2] our only hope, I verily believe. I don't believe in Labour. Would you believe it, but at a *Herald* meeting the other night they carried Bertie Russell shoulder-high because he'd been prosecuted for writing an incredibly stupid attack on America? You see, pacifist labour's rotten; the Clyde & the Engineers are merely selfish, if they strike it will only be to keep themselves out of the army; and as for Henderson[3] (who I think does his best) he'll be sand-bagged by the French Socialists who seem to me to be merely corrupt politicians. Then there's no hope at all in the House of Commons – they're afraid to be honest, and the rest are paid servants of L.G. [Lloyd George].[4] They're nothing better than petulant schoolboys. They won't turn L.G. out depend on that; and L.G. is busily engaged in putting our army & our policy & our money in Clemenceau's[5] pocket. But even if all these things had been right, instead of wicked & vile, I don't think Germany is any better. I think it is still true that the military have control. But Wilson goes the right way to throw them out. But so long as things like Versailles[6] go on, I can't see how he will succeed. The Germans just say to their docile people 'Ah, that's what Wilson says, but look at Versailles.' The wicked men are in control on both sides still. But I have faith in Wilson. Everything he says is more masterly than what he said before; he is truly a great man like Lincoln.[7]

However, I won't go on like this. You know more about it than I do. But I believe that God has spewed England out of his mouth, and I'm very sad, because I love England.

Well, that's all nothing compared to my love for you. Wig, Wig, all our dreams will come true, my precious heart, – cross my own heart, straight dinkum I believe utterly. I should die on the spot if I didn't.

I sent you the book *Raffin Su-Su*[8] to-day. I only want you to read 'Le P'tit' & perhaps 'Nausicaa'. Tell me what you think: I want to know.

Boge.[9]

1. J.M. replies to K.M.'s letter of 16 February: 'The Lord saw fit to remove the shadow from me this afternoon . . .'; and 18 February: 'I have just read your *Wednesday* letter . . .'.

2. Woodrow Wilson (1856–1924), President of the United States from 1912 to 1920 who brought his country into war on the side of the Allies. A fine writer and orator, he was seen by many in Europe as the saviour of the future. He presented Congress in January 1918 with his fourteen points outlining the basic provisions for a just peace settlement including a League of Nations.

3. Arthur Henderson (1863–1935), a Chairman of the British Labour Party and a member of the War Cabinet from 1916–1917. He supported the League of Nations.

4. David Lloyd George (1863–1945) replaced Asquith as Prime Minister in December 1916. At the Paris Peace Conference in 1919 he mediated between the harsh demands of Clemenceau and the idealistic proposals of Wilson.

5. Georges Clemenceau (1841–1929), Premier of France 1906–1909 and 1917–1920. Bitterly anti-German in his demands for reparations, he was the main antagonist of Wilson at the 1919 Paris Peace Conference.

6. The Versailles conference, held on 28 January 1918 to co-ordinate the Allies' war efforts.

7. Murry was possibly thinking of the eloquence of Abraham Lincoln's (1809–1865) Second Inaugural Address: '. . . let us strive to bind up the nation's wounds. . . . to do all which may achieve and cherish a just and lasting peace among ourselves and with all nations'.

8. Murry's review of *Raffin Su-Su* by the French writer Jean Ajalbert (1863–1934) appeared on 21 February 1918 in the *T.L.S.*

9. K.M. replies on 26 February: 'I had a *Gorgeous Letter* from you written on Thursday . . .'.

---

[73]

[M.I. 7D,
War Office,
Watergate House,
Adelphi, London.]
[23 February, 1918.]

Saturday Morning

This morning I got your letter of February 19,[1] the one about the doctor and the wings. It was a bit of a shock, because, you see, I had made up my mind that the reason why you had to stay was quite different. But I'll keep up, never fear. And though I don't think I shall ever forgive myself for letting you make that journey, we *know* and we'll fight the old devil and win. We can't make decisions until you've returned and seen a specialist; but we'll make the right one and win. Let me look at the best side of it. You might very well have tried to make the return journey alone; you might have been alone. No, from this day forth I'll forgive L.M. everything.

I swear to you that I'll not worry, that I'll feed myself, that nothing will happen to me about which you need worry in the least. And, Wig, if you in return aren't absolutely frank about money, you'll hurt our love. All that I've said about money was by way of objection to spending it on a L.M. caprice. Absolutely everything is in the service of our love, and if you don't treat it in this way, it's a crime.

I am writing in the office, and, as usual, people are continually disturbing me. I find it very hard to think straight. But all I really want to say is: Don't worry about me: I am as fit as a fiddle, and the worst that I can truly say is that I am lonely without you.

Then as for your story.[2] Honestly & truthfully I was *not* disappointed. I was bowled out, utterly bowled out by it. Child, don't you know that I am a child? I was so passionately fond of the Mouse[3] that it nearly broke my heart. I hadn't time to see it objectively. I haven't since then had time to read the story straight through from beginning to end and give you a critical, 'objective', judgement on it. Look here, you must see that what you call my disappointment – the word's true enough – was just my confession that you had done it – done it absolutely. My disappointment as a child was my satisfaction as an artist. Perhaps I didn't put this clearly: I can't have done. I was too much under the influence of my immediate emotions. But there it is. 'Sun & Moon' were really tinies. His tragedy would be put right. But Mouse & Dick, they were too much like us. If they had been exactly like it wouldn't have upset me because I know we're alright. But they were different, our brothers & sisters spiritually. D'you understand

My eye is better. It's a kind of eyestrain, I think and I'll have to get some more glasses.

My precious darling – eat, eat. I love you beyond all that I can tell

Boge[4]

1. J.M. replies to K.M.'s letter of 19 February: 'I want to tell you some things which are a bit awful . . .'. This letter is his first response to the news that she is spitting blood.

2. 'Je ne parle pas français'.

3. The female protagonist who resembles K.M. However, Mouse's lover, Dick, can be seen as an unflattering portrait of Murry.

4. K.M. replies on 27 February: 'Your Saturday letter has come – the one about the Eye and about my wings'.

[74]	[47 Redcliffe Road,
Fulham,
London.]
Saturday, Feb. 23, 1918

My own darling,

I have to all intents taken a day off and I'm ever so much better for it. Besides, your mother turned up trumps, heavenly, golden trumps (if there are such things) and to-night I had from her a most lovely letter (I send it) beginning 'Dear Jack Murry'. For beginning like that, I could kiss her. One day I will. 'Dear Jack Murry'. I'm quite sure I know him, and I'm almost as sure he is a charming person. He wears a blue jersey and he's a boy. I almost feel as though she had written 'Dear Dick Harmon'. Do you?

I needed her letter to-day. I was, I don't know why *exactly*, down and out. Flat, stale and unprofitable, giddy with the immense and endless spinning of the world, tired with trying to grope my way out of a mist. How shall I say it? Neither despairing, nor depressed, but grey. That's my danger now. Its so hard to go on, so easy to be carried on; I can go on only by forgetting for a little while; I am carried on when I neither remember nor forget. The world just rushes, I don't know why or where, to salvation, I try to believe when I can try, to ruin, I feel at other moments. I am like a man doing dumb-bell exercises incredible thousands of times. He doesn't doubt, he doesn't believe. He is just a part of <u>it</u> doing dumb-bell exercises; perhaps <u>it</u> is the soul of the universe. I don't know. I wish I could explain. It's as though I put out tendrils feverishly into something beyond, true, steady, outside this spinning world, but the world spins on and the tendrils are torn away, snap, snap, snap, and the place they are torn from grows numb. But I go on still. But never a tendril clings . . .

I don't know quite what weapon to use against this. The only thing that is of use is to think about you and our love. But, you see, to think about our love demands, cries for, days and days & days. To think about it five minutes, or the space of writing a letter, no, it's not good enough. It's almost tragic. I daren't bathe myself in it. I should be drunk with it: and I can't be drunk. Every moment I feel that I am going to be, I have to stop, and hold myself. When you are here again, it will be different. I shall lean my head against you, or you will lean your head on me: and I shall be like a giant refreshed with wine. Till then, my darling, Boge clenches his teeth and tries to stop the world from spinning too much in his eyes.

I saw my Mother to-day and took her the handkerchief. She all but cried. Then as I was going she took me apart, and told me that you had been too good to her that she wanted to give you a present, just that you should know how she loved you. Then I said she wasn't to do that, because, my precious Wig, I know she hasn't got any money and I know that it will be the same to you if I told you. Then she said: 'But what could I buy: nothing in the world could be good enough for her'. I have copied that down exactly, because I promised her to tell you what she felt. While I was kissing her good-night in the dark in the passage she implored me to write it all to you, because I should do it so much better than she. And I promised. You are her princess – that's all there is to it. I'm not exaggerating, or making her love you one whit more than she does. She loves you absolutely.

Before I say good-night, Wig; remember I've been honest *in order that* you should not worry. If you write back and show me that what I've said about myself worries you, then I shan't be honest any more, ever. I am splendid in all the things I have to look after. If I want you back, well, it's not being wicked; and if I don't, as I should, disguise it because you can't come that's only because of our compact.

Be careful. You are my most precious, my only possession: think of that alone

Boge[1]

1. K.M. replies 1 March: 'Your Saturday, Sunday and Monday letters all came together today . . .'.

---

[75]
[47 Redcliffe Road,
Fulham,
London.]
Monday, Feb 25, [1918.]
11.45 pm.

My own Wig,

It's been one of my weary nights. They're all weary without you now; let's say then one of my wearier nights. I've been writing my article (which now seems to have become regular weekly) for the *Nation*. Three weeks ago, when I felt I was hammering out bricks and saucepans for the Heron,[1] it went all right, with a kind of zest even. Three more guineas, good. But now, my Wig, my heart's too frightened to breathe. The sky is on top of my head.

My darling, I know I ought to be writing bang-up cheerful letters. But tell me this: how does a Boge do it, how can he do it, when he knows what he knows about his Wig? If I tried, you'd know from the first line that it was only a hollow fraud, and anyhow I'm no good at pretending, not half, not a hundredth, as good as you. You can make me believe that all is well with you; but for me to try to do the same with you is sheer madness. You've always, since the beginning, known when I was telling a banger.

I can only say this that except for the thought of you I am well, absolutely well. I eat a great deal and regularly. But that 'except for the thought of you', don't really mean much, you know. Take the thought of you away from me and what is left? A little hollow shell, that gives out a hollow sound, climbs on buses and clambers off, takes tickets at the station, bangs on the typewriter. But the moment comes when he bangs 'Madame Bowden, Bandol (Var)' and then it's all up with the hollow shell. It fills with a kind of life, that's mostly tears. I don't know, old girl, but if I don't get some better news to-morrow, I'll go off my chump. When I think that my tremendous grief at your telegram was because they wouldn't let you come back because of your passport, and how the whole world turned black, and then I think of what the real reason was – well, well. Old God has let fly at us, this time and no mistake.

But it will all be right. *It must be.* Rib, who sits up twice as high on the cushions to-night, tells me it must be so. He is always so certain that everything is going to be perfect that at the last, after I've gone through all the phases of thinking him hard & cruel, I have to believe him. At least I try very, very hard: and at this moment I do. I didn't when I began.

Wig, wig. I can't say I love you. If you were here and I were whispering it to you with you in my arms, it might be enough. Can you hear me say it? Can you feel my arms? Listen. Now. *I love you.*

Boge[2]

1. 'The Heron' was the name (after Leslie Heron Beauchamp) that Katherine and Murry gave the dream house they planned to buy in the country after the war.

2. K.M. replies 1 March: 'Your Saturday, Sunday and Monday letters all came together today . . .'.

---

[76]   [47 Redcliffe Road,
                                         Fulham,
                                         London.]
                                         Friday, March 1 [1918.]

My own darling,

I didn't have a letter to-day; that's because I had two yesterday. But because I didn't have a letter, nothing at all has happened to me. I went to work, came home and here I am. I got a cheque from the *Times* – £11.14.0 – that goes into the hoard.

Yes, I'm tired to-night, just honestly, fairly & squarely tired. Bed's the place. When shall we have time to read all the things there are to read? How happy we'll be when the time comes. It must come soon. I go on buying books steadily for the desert island – cheap ones, of course, but books that will last. Corduroy suits in covers as it were. I just read a page at supper and then put them away. To-day I bought Ben Jonson's plays – all of 'em – 1500 pages – for 3/- They seem awfully good. There's something of an Elizabethan Dickens about him. At the beginning of the week I bought Coleridge's *Lectures on Shakespeare*. It was after reading a page of S.T.C. in which he compares Bill with Jonson, Massinger & Beaumont & Fletcher, that I determined to buy 'em all. Next week I shall prowl about to get hold of a complete Beaumont & Fletcher. (Queer thing that I can't buy books – corduroy books – unless they're complete. If they aren't complete, they aren't corduroy.) S.T.C. says that Ben Jonson's *Alchemist* has the most perfect plot of any English comedy. Doesn't that make your mouth water? Also he says Beaumont and Fletcher's *Monsieur Thomas* is pure gold of comedy. Well, of course, I haven't time to find out if it's true. But when I buy the books I feel I'm gathering the material together for those wonderful days when we'll talk about them over the fire in our big Heron room, and decide whether S.T.C. was right or wrong. Another book I have my eye on is Charles Lamb's letters – *complete*, two lovely volumes for 7/6. I think we must, don't you? I looked into it in the shop and I opened on such a funny letter to Wordsworth that I nearly bought it on the spot.

What wonderful days those were. We belong to these people. And just as Keats, Lamb, Coleridge, Shelley, Wordsworth fed themselves on the Elizabethans, we must feed on them both. I feel that the world of literature has only begun to open. One day, we'll be able to say truly: Much have we travelled in the realms of gold. You agree I know. I never buy a book but what I buy for us. Nor am I extravagant. It always comes out of the week's money I allow myself. But we must get all the Elizabethans, all of 'em, Keats' letters, Dorothy Wordsworth, De Quincey – complete (when we can). You write a big list in your next: it's so good to think about. And then to think that you & I are the direct inheritors of all this, fellow-heirs. My God! And then to think of those mingy, bingy Frenchmen!

I was looking at a Beaumont and Fletcher in a shop to-day and I saw it was dedicated to William Wordsworth Esq. Now wasn't that as it should be? I felt so much hail fellow well met with W.W. Esq that I nearly bought the book on the spot. But it was too dear, malheureusement.

All this about books. I suppose it is becoming a mania. Still, I think we were both bitten in the cradle, and it can't be helped.

My mind's a sieve just now. I've been reading Rousseau;[1] and I can't for the life of me remember what it's all about.

My darling, I love you. And its the *first of March*
Good-night
Boge.[2]

1. Murry's review of *La Formation religieuse de Jean-Jaques Rousseau* by Pierre-Maurice Masson appeared in the *T.L.S.* on 21 March 1918.
2. K.M. replies 6 March: 'I ought to have known that having written to you as I did yesterday your next letter saying you have bought Ben Jonson's plays would arrive today'.

———

[77]   [47 Redcliffe Road,
Fulham,
London.]
Tuesday. Mar 5. 11.20 [1918.]

My own precious darling,[1]
To-day came in the morning your Thursday letter; in the evening your Wednesday one & the story. Your letter I read while I was cooking my evening egg. It was wonderful. Surely, if one could look at them in a quite detached sort of way – I can't for the life of me – they

must be absolute masterpieces of letters. When I read them I go hot and cold with a kind of intoxication of love and delight.

Now – I feel sure you won't forgive me, and yet I know you will – I'm not going to say much about your story; because what I should say now wouldn't be worth while. One can't write about your work jumping out of a railway train; and until Saturday when I shall have got Rousseau – curse him – off my chest, my mind is just like a clattering engine on the District Railway. Unless the skies fall, I shall have all Sunday to myself, and I intend to devote what part of it I am awake to saying slowly and carefully what I want to say not merely about 'Bliss' but about 'Je ne parle pas français'. You mustn't be cross with me. I know you want to know what I think almost as much as I want to know what you think of my stuff. I don't know (really, don't know) whether what I've done is good until you tell me; and we're both the same. But I'd rather cut my hand off than say clumsy things in a desperate hurry. You see, I can criticise your work; I know all about it; it's as natural to me as breathing: but it's as hard to write what I think as to write a poem. I'm not satisfied if I do it with less singleness of heart, less leisure, & less *purity* than I must have to write a poem. If I say things hurriedly, they aren't true; you feel they aren't true and are disquieted, just as I should be, and just as you were over what I said of the second part of 'Je ne parle pas'. Therefore, though you may be disappointed, I shan't attempt to say anything till Sunday, more than what I shall say in my wire to-morrow: First Chop. But how they're first chop and the little bits where your pen seems to have trembled, all the things that will tell you what your criticisms tell me – all that I *must* leave till Sunday. When I say what I have to say, you have to feel that it is your very self judging your own work. I am your conscience in writing, just as you are mine. I can't bear to give you a superficial word. If I do I'm against us.

Don't think that while I've written all this, I might have written something about 'Bliss'. I couldn't have done it, just as I couldn't have written a poem; I have to be in a state of grace. And I can't be in a state of grace while every moment is till Saturday night when I go to bed parcelled out to the second.

I agree absolutely with what you say about 'Le P'tit' – the physical part, the cheat of the French words. But it seemed to be very interesting precisely because it showed what falsity a Frenchman who seems to have in himself something of the Tchehov spirit is condemned to by being French. Look for instance at the end of 'Nausicaa'. Something about 'the last time she ever wore the chemise of virginity'. It is so *utterly wrong* that there's nothing to be said. But in Ajalbert I felt the conflict between natural truth & Frenchness. They are not quite one. I feel as it were that I can get a knife in between the false and dirty & the true & pure; and I also felt that he must somehow be conscious of it, be ashamed of himself for his own concessions (whether to the Old Adam in himself or to his public I don't know – probably both). But there was *beauty*, snatches of real beauty, in the description & the vision of both those stories They reminded me of your work, very much. The sense of spring in 'Le P'tit' particularly. I felt these were stories you would have written as I would have them written. And I felt that I was judging them by the side of the real story by K.M.

So I have written criticism after all. But not the real stuff; you will have that, I warrant you, on Sunday.

My darling send me another letter like the one I had this evening to-morrow. My soul took wings. I lived in the Heron for a blissful moment. I am sure, absolutely sure, it will come. My God, we've waited long enough haven't we?

Je te baise
Boge.

1. Murry replies to K.M.'s letters of 27 February: 'Your Saturday letter has come – the one about the Eye . . .'; and 28 February: 'It's three o'clock. I've just finished this new story, *Bliss*, and am sending it to you'.

---

[78]　　　　　　　　　　　[47 Redcliffe Road,
　　　　　　　　　　　　　Fulham,
　　　　　　　　　　　　　London.]
　　　　　　　　　Sunday Morning, March 10 [1918]

My darling,[1]

Everything went as I mapped it out. I finished Rousseau last night and, I think, it's pretty good. This morning I got up late, read 'Bliss' again after breakfast, shaved, and here I am. It's one o'clock already. I feel inclined to smile because of my good conscience. 'I said I'd do it and I did'.

Now about 'Bliss'. It's very, very good. Idea, proportion, lay-out, all are good. But there are one or two things about it – nothing to do with its essence – which don't seem to me quite right. They are only details, but they seem to me ever so slightly discordant. They are two. The first is that Eddie *Wangle* is not the right name. You are caricaturing by calling him that. And your story won't admit any caricature. They are preposterous people, the Norman Knights & Eddie, but they are real. You mustn't do more than show you are *aware* of their preposterousness. You mustn't be laughing at, or angry about, it. Do you see what I mean when I say that Norman Knight is exquisitely right as a name, & Eddie *Wangle* wrong? It is a Dickens touch & you're not Dickens – you're Tchehov – more than Tchehov.

Secondly. You put a number of phrases in inverted commas. For instance. 'These last she had bought to "*tone in*" '. 'She only wanted to get "*in touch*" with him'. Now, I think I know perfectly what you are after. Bertha is a soul with exquisite perceptions & exquisite demands on life, which she doesn't know how to express. She is a kind of artist manqué – artist in our big sense of the word. Now that's damned hard to express in the particular, I can see. I can also see that you can't just drop the inverted commas. I also see that her clumsy phrases are at the heart of her. But I think that, being what she is, she would avoid the phrases and, however impatiently, prefer her own dumbness. 'These last she had bought . . . for the sake of the new drawing room carpet. Yes, that did sound rather far-fetched. . . .' 'What had she to say? She'd nothing to say. She only wanted . . . She couldn't absurdly cry: "Hasn't it been a divine afternoon?" ' Do you see what I am driving at? Its always for the same kind of thing that you use the inverted commas, when Bertha is trying to express more perfect satisfaction or communion. For instance again about Pearl Fulton. 'The provoking thing was that though they had been about together and met a number of times and really "*talked*".' 'Harry & she were as much in love as ever and they got on together splendidly and were really good "*pals*".'

You see, Bertha is not actually talking. If she were she would probably have to use the words. But she is thinking – and in *her thought* she would refuse them.

I don't know whether I'm right. The thing seems to be so tenuous that it slips away under my pen. I would like to know, very much, *very much indeed*, what you think. For at moments I fear that I am becoming super-subtle.

Now, once more, the story is beautiful. I mean absolutely no more than to say that to my ear its perfection is marred by two discords, ever so slight. In worrying about them to find what the reason of them was, I may have made a mistake. My explanation may be wrong, tho' I

don't think so. But that's unimportant. The question is whether your
ear tells you the same thing as mine. I feel sure it must. I feel that when
I am working and in the excitement of the work my ear becomes for
the moment dulled, yours remains perfectly sensitive: I feel that I am
the same with your work. But write to me immediately & tell me.
These correspondences[2] of ours have given me such unlimited confidence: I want to know definitely. whether I am in any way presuming
upon them.

I got your Wednesday letter last night. It's no use talking about
these identities of ours. I have now not the slightest doubt (seriously)
that we are manifestations of the same being. One might be a
coincidence, two might be; but ever since the Heron began, we have
gone on and on. Don't think me mystical if I explain it like this. The
night when we *discussed the Heron together*, We became one being. The
quality of that evening I shall always remember; and with these
correspondences it recurs to me again & again. I feel certain that what
I say is true. We became one being and this one being expressed itself
that night in the Heron. Therefore the Heron is more than the symbol
of our love; it is the artistic creation of our one being. From that night
on we have been fused in soul, so that our correspondences now seem
to me the most natural & inevitable thing in the world. Now, I am
perfectly aware that if I were to say this to anyone else but you they
would think me raving. But to me it is simple truth, simple truth in
exactly the same way as $2+2=4$. Everything now conspires to tell me
that I am right. You will see from this Rousseau article when it appears
– that Rousseau was of the same kind as us. What I have written about
him seems to be luminously simple; but it is *all new*. No-one has had
the faintest idea of what I have discovered about him before. And I feel
certain that we shall find, in just the same way, the secret of all the
great men we love. No-one else can understand them except us –
no-one else at all. And when we go away from the world to the Heron
we shall discover the secret of them all, have them dwelling with us
like friends. Sometimes now I begin to think tremulously *high*
thoughts, thoughts that make me dizzy. Suddenly, I seem to know the
secret of the universe. And this at least I know, beyond all doubt, that
I know the way to the secret and that my life will be spent in trying to
make the pathway clear. I know this, too, that you are I are *geniuses*. I
didn't know it before the real meaning of the Heron began to dawn
upon me as it has lately done. You saw that into your work and mine a

new strong wind of *power* had come. I didn't know *why* it had come:–
Why we two, at the moment when we seemed more frail than all other
creatures of the earth, should become suddenly *strong winged in the
spirit*. Now, I begin to see. What I said about the Heron just now is
part of the explanation. But behind that I feel there is a bigger
explanation still. You and I are manifestations of the same being, yes,
but that same being is also a manifestation. I feel I am on the way to
discovering of what.

———————

I have bought Lamb. I opened it *at random*. I opened it at a letter he
wrote about Coleridge & Wordsworth's *Lyrical Ballads* when they
first came out. I've marked the place with a piece of paper and I'm
going to send you the volume to-morrow, so that you can see exactly
how deep my sense is that our life has passed out of our hands. You
will understand.

I'm sorry about your being tormented by Geoffroi. People are no
use, no use at all. Try to save yourself. I was glad of those postcards of
les Charmettes,[3] though. Was that too just an accident? You can't buy
them in Bandol, can you? I would like to know because I want to keep
a record of these 'coincidences'. You see it makes me feel rather queer
when just as I am on the last page of my Rousseau article which has as
many *seeds* of discovery as Dostoevsky,[4] I get your letter saying that
mine about Ben Jonson, the Elizabethans & Keats reached you the
day after you had written to me, and *in the same letter* a collection of
pictures of the place that really made Rousseau what he was!

Another thing, if any of my letters are alive still, will you keep
them? I have all yours – and I think they may be important to us one
day.

At the end of this week I'm going to send you £5. It may come in
useful. One can't have too much money on a journey – and if you don't
use it, it don't matter.

I didn't write to you yesterday. I thought that one long one was
better than two shorts. I shall post this one this afternoon, so that I
shan't have one to post to-morrow morning. There's been a fog this
morning, but now the sun is up (2.30) and the sky clear, so I shall,
when I have prepared my casseroles, trundle out.

My Wig – you're coming back!

Boge[5]

1. J.M. replies to K.M.'s letter of 6 March: 'I ought to have known . . .'.
2. In her letter of 6 March K.M. spoke of a kind of telepathic communication between them: 'That *you* should write about books and the Elizabethans and Keats – that *you* should talk of the Heron as I did! You see, we do seem to be in some utterly mysterious fashion two manifestations of *the same being*. We don't echo each other, for our voices are raised at the same moment'.
3. A country house near Chambéry where Rousseau lived from 1738–1740 with Mme de Warens.
4. A reference to Murry's first book, *Fyodor Dostoevsky: A Critical Study*, published in 1916.
5. K.M. replies 14 March: 'I have just received your Sunday letter. It was very noble of you to do as you did and so beautifully keep your promise about my story'. Accepting his criticism of 'Bliss' she says: 'You're of course, absolutely right about "Wangle". . . . and I'm with you about the commas. What I meant . . . was Bertha, not being an artist, was yet artist manquée enough to realize that those words and expressions were not and couldn't be hers. They were, as it were, *quoted* by her, borrowed with . . . an eyebrow . . . yet she'd none of her own. But this, I agree, is not permissible. I can't grant all that in my dear reader. It's very exquisite of you to understand so nearly'.

---

[79]   [47 Redcliffe Road,
                                      Fulham,
                                      London.]
                            Sunday, Mar 17, 1 o'clock [1918.]

My precious darling,

Your second telegram saying there were no seats in the train till March 20th. at the latest, came last night and your third, saying there were difficulties about the passports, early this morning. Yesterday I wired to you in the morning, to say that I hadn't written since Wednesday. Before Saturday I couldn't write for excitement; I thought that you would be able to start off immediately my reply to "How's Mother"[1] reached you. And I couldn't write letters which I thought would never reach you. On Saturday morning I got the letter you sent just before you sent the "How's Mother" and I realised that you might not be able to start after all. Therefore I sent the wire. I shall send a telegram every day until Wednesday, so that the gap in my letters will be filled with something.

But the disappointment is very hard to bear. I ought not say that: it's worse for you, my dear one. But I shall be anxious and worried till I hear that you are safe in England now. I feel very down about it. I don't know what to write. I feel rather as though I had been holding on till that telegram came – and now . . . But I will pull myself together, my precious; and hope that it will be all right. It *must* be all right. Then I'm worried about the question of money. I feel you can't have enough. And I didn't send last week, because I thought you wouldn't be there.

My own darling, if love could help you – all this time you have been away, has been one long discovery of the fact that I live in and through you. Separated from you I am like a sea-anemone washed away from the rock, that floats, clenched tight, on the waves. I live absolutely from minute to minute seeing neither before nor after. And this hope deferred does make the heart sick.[2] If only I could write about something sensible. When I try and look back on what has happened since the Wednesday when I wrote to you, I can find nothing except a sensation of waiting. I know I ought to be more firm as the lady with Wilkie Bard[3] used to say: but these 'ought to bes' don't have any effect upon me. The only one that means anything is the one that has said and goes on saying: 'Wig ought to be in Boge's arms'. Beside my ache for you, even my friends – our true friends – mean nothing. Johnny came in last night. I couldn't understand what was the matter with him. He was almost blushing and very shy and constrained. Sullivan was here. Luckily, he was just going. When he had gone, Johnny after talking at random, suddenly said: 'But, look here, Murry-lad, what I wanted to say was . . .' He is going to have a show. Would I write the introduction to the catalogue? I was the only man who was trying for the same things as he. If I wouldn't write it, then he would try to do it himself. But he would like me to very much. With my mind I saw how great the honour was he did me. It was like clinching our comradeship in art. But it doesn't *mean* anything to me in my heart. When I know that you are on the way it will, but until then – it is just like words of sympathy in the ears of someone lost in his grief.

My Wig, my flower, my true comrade – nothing is fine, nothing touches my heart save when I share it with you. If only I could write a poem to assuage my longing; but I can't.

My darling, I never knew how much I loved you; and to-day I almost feel that the burden of my love is greater than I can bear.

Boge.

1. Katherine's English exit permit stipulated that she must remain away for three months. To obtain permission for an earlier return to England, she

had arranged that Murry would reply to her wire: 'How's Mother?' that 'Mother' was ill. The ploy did not succeed; and some other way of gaining a travel permit had to be found.

    2. Virginia Woolf records in her *Diary* having Murry to dinner that night: 'Poor Murry snarled & scowled with the misery of his lot. He works all day & writes when he comes home. Worst of all, K.M. has been very ill with haemorrhage of the lungs, out in France, & has to be brought home wh. is difficult, in order to see how bad she is. But I thought him very much more a person & a brain than I had thought him before.'

    3. Wilkie Bard, author of a comic sketch, *The Night Watchman*.

---

[80]

[47 Redcliffe Road,
Fulham,
London.]
[19 March, 1918.]
Tuesday Night. 8.20.

My own darling precious child,[1]

    The letter that I somehow *dreaded* came to-day – to-night – the one you sent on Saturday when L.M. had returned. I'm like you now: it only takes a straw to knock me down, and this is a sledge hammer. I will see Sydney Waterlow to-morrow in case he knows some-one at the Foreign Office who can help; and I'll wire the result.

    Didn't you say that doctor[2] said that not only you ought not stay down there, but that you ought to come home and see a big man in London as soon as you were fit to travel? Won't the devil write that on a bit of paper. Surely that would get you through! But, since I haven't had any telegram, it looks as though he wouldn't give you the 'chit'. I calculate that since you couldn't see him the day you wrote, you would have seen him on Saturday. If he had given it you would have wired. Or would you have sent L.M. back to the Consulate first to see if it was all right. In that case she couldn't go until Monday and I might very well not get a wire till to-morrow, Wednesday. That's how my mind is running.

    Who else could I see except Sydney? That friend of Pierre MacAlan's[3] – curse it – I have completely forgotten his name. Like a fool, I never made a note of it. I shall write to Chaddie[4] to-night. She may possibly know some military fellow who has something to do with the French Military Permit Office. If anything at all comes into my mind – which is a whirling, aching blank – I'll do it and wire.

    I am trying hard to pull myself together. My disappointment hurts you and your disappointment tortures me. We mustn't. It's no use thinking about each other's disappointment; I feel if I went on thinking about yours very long my mind would certainly snap. It's very rickety. O my own wig, my arms are tight round you – if only they were strong arms, and if only they could pull you nearer somehow.

And I am absolutely tongue-tied – like you numb and dumb. When you need it most, I can't express my love. It all ties up into a hard choking ball inside me: and my letter grows cold. If I could only make it warm.

Whatever happens, don't let L.M. leave without you *under any circumstances.*[5] If you try the marriage reason,[6] try it last of all. The medical is the one. Surely that doctor will repeat what he said – that you ought to see a specialist in London?

Wig, I'll turn every stone I know how: but I feel very helpless just at this moment. I'll have to wait till to-morrow for a ray of hope from this side. Till then I'll just pray that something good has happened.

And to all this is added the fact that I am haunted by the thought that I didn't write to you from Wednesday until Sunday. Just when you will have needed letters most. Forgive me, Wig, a week ago I was dancing with delight at the thought of your return.

Your most loving, wretched Boge.

1. J.M. replies to K.M.'s letter of 16 March: 'I must tell you how matters stand, and you must help me please, if you can?'.

2. The only English doctor in Bandol able to provide a medical 'chit' for the authorities was a disreputable character whom Katherine had to go to some lengths to charm.

3. Pierre MacOrlan, pseudonym of Pierre Dumarchais (1883–1970), was a French novelist, essayist and poet.

4. Chaddie was Katherine's elder sister, Charlotte, who worked in London at the War Graves Registration Office.

5. L.M. had permission to travel back although Katherine did not.

6. By now divorced from George Bowden, K.M. was planning to marry Murry on her return to England. If she could not get a medical 'chit' enabling her to leave France, she told Murry, 'I thought I might also plead [to the authorities] that I wish to re-marry on the 17th of April and wish to return to make preparations. I can't tell whether that is wise or not . . . . Indeed, I really think I will not mention this marriage until t'other has failed.'

[81]

[47 Redcliffe Road,
Fulham,
London.]
[23 March, 1918]
Saturday Morning

My darling,

I got your wire saying you were held up in Paris[1] for ten days just before I started to the office this morning, where I have just arrived. It seems as though the stars in their courses are fighting against us; but they won't win. But when, after all you have gone through, the German offensive begins on the very day you start for Paris – it's hard to be reconciled. Still, I feel that you are ever so much nearer in Paris: and though the ten days are hard, I feel that you are almost within reach. When I have finished this short note, I'm going out to telegraph to you. You say you don't want any money: I am just putting three pound notes in this letter which may do as a tiny reserve. But I've got money; so please do wire me if you'd like any, and don't let things get so low as they did before I sent the fiver.

The Colonel's given me a week's leave from next Friday onwards. If you could only get back at the next week end, we should have nearly a week together without the old office!

O lord, lord, my own wonderful darling, I can't write at all any more. Mind you, I don't worry any thing like so much now you are in Paris. But I am now so impatient for the happiness of seeing you, that I can't write anything coherent at all. I try to kill the hours in the evening by writing poetry; but it's very hard. I send you something I wrote the night before last.

Why do you have to wait the ten days? I mean is it because of the trains or because you have to apply to the Military Permit Office in London. Sydney Waterlow has written about you to the head of the military section of the M.P.O., Colonel Danielson; so that, if the second is the reason, it should go through quickly. But I have an idea that it's the offensive & the trains, particularly as your telegram says nothing about passport difficulties

Wig, I love you.

Boge.

1. With a medical 'chit' enabling her to go as far as Paris, Katherine and L.M. left Bandol on 21 March. They had hoped to cross to England within a few days but instead were trapped in Paris by the German bombardment.

[82]   [47 Redcliffe Road,
                                                         Fulham,
                                                         London.]
                                                    [1 April, 1918.]
                                                    Monday Night

My darling, my precious,[1]

I have just had your *Tuesday* & Thursday letters.

I must pull myself together. For our sake, my mouse, try to believe I am holding you in my arms. My heart, too, seems to be numb; and something goes on weeping, weeping inside me. If I thought of what has happened to us – how you have been caught and our love *tortured*, deliberately, foully tortured – I think I should go clean mad.

I don't know how to comfort you, just as I can't comfort myself. I tried on the strength of your wire[2] to believe there was some chance that you might be allowed to start on Tuesday, to-morrow. But your Thursday letter[3] has killed that hope dead. What, in God's name, is there to hold on to? Every time that our hope, our love stretches out to something, even only a tiny happiness, the black thing descends & withers it.

Yesterday was a slow Hell. To-day I have been to the office; Somehow it's better there. But even yesterday, something was alive in me still. I had managed to deceive myself with your telegram. And Rib spent all the day fanning my spark of hope into a flame.

Yes, I must tell you about Rib. At any rate it's better than going on about my own despair. He was wonderful yesterday. His hair was all towsled somehow and he was perched on top of the cushions in some queer way, that made him look *as though he had just been born*. Yes, that's it, – as though he had just popped up from somewhere where he had been asleep, in a sunflower perhaps. And I felt – I tried to call myself a fool & to suppress it – that something had whispered to him that you were coming. *For the first time* he looked as though you really were on your way. And, somehow, in spite of myself I believed it.

Yes, and even now – I just went over & had a long look at him – I do somewhere in me believe it. I can't help having faith in Rib. He's waiting and watching, for sure. I can't be mistaken.

No, it's useless to try to go on convincing one's self: besides the disappointment's so bitter.

Oh, my child, I daren't try to express my heart; it would frighten you, it's so sad. The hopelessness of your Thursday letter has frozen it up. Still, though to-morrow will be another hell, I'm glad I'm not going to the office. I couldn't bear to be with all those people: much rather be with my dull, aching, worn out old heart alone. The office is only a drug. And I don't want drugs.

Perhaps there may be a letter from you to-morrow giving me a tiny thread of hope to build on again. If only I didn't feel so bitter with myself for deceiving me, for letting me deceive myself. I can't even express my love. It's as though it were choking

Oh, Wig, my mouse, my secret soul: you are there suffering and I am dead without you. Surely, life can't be so awful as not to bring us together again quickly now. It's getting desperate. I feel that I had come to the top of the water for the last time. Of course, it won't be the last. Just as I never come to the end of my despair, I shan't come to the end of my hope either. Boge (smaller than that)

1. J.M. replies to K.M.'s two letters of 26 March: 'I have just been to Cook's and there is nothing there again'; and: 'I have just sat down to a tea . . .'; and 28 March: 'Three letters came from you today . . .'.
2. K.M. had wired on 28 March: '. . . impossible leave before Tuesday . . .'.
3. Katherine told Murry in the Thursday letter: 'Any person who stays longer than 48 hours in Paris must obtain a permit to leave France. This *sauf conduit* takes from 8 to 10 days to obtain, and is, even then, uncertain, as to one day or another. . . . I went again to the [police] office yesterday, but they laughed in my face at the idea of getting a permit sooner'. The following day she wired Murry: 'Civilian traffic suspended . . .'.

---

[83]   [47 Redcliffe Road,
                         Fulham,
                         London.]
                    Monday Morning April 8. [1918.]

My precious darling,[1]
  This morning I got your Friday letter (and one you wrote on Easter Sunday as well). I do well to be afraid of your letters. This one has completely knocked the heart out of me. You have had nothing from me since – I don't know when. You believe I am not writing to you. Oh, my darling, you must know that I have written *every day*; you must know that I would rather die than not write; you can't not believe in me like that.

I don't know what to say or do. I have asked for such small things –
only that *one* of my letters should reach you quickly. But I should have
known that that would be denied me. I suppose I shall hang on
somehow. I've reached my lowest depth of misery & despair; touched
bottom. Now, I'm exhausted; but the bitterness of the moment when
I read: 'You must not leave me without letters unless your heart has
quite absolutely changed to me' – that I shall never forget. My God,
Wig, I believe my heart will absolutely change; it will turn into a
stone.

Well, swallow it down, old man: pull yourself together for the last
time. I did try to, Wig. I rushed to the post office and sent two wires,
one to you at Cook's, one to the hôtel. But, I've no faith, any more.
This will never reach you: my wires will never reach you. Shall I send
my letters to the Hotel or to Cook's? I don't know, and after all what
does it matter? They never reach you. I feel in my heart if any of them
had reached you since the Friday you would have wired to me. Still
to-day I shall register this one to Cook's, and another one to the Hôtel.

My darling, my love for you is swelling up with tears choking me: it
will break my heart: unless my heart is already broken.

I'll try to write something better again to-night.

Boge.

1. J.M. replies to K.M.'s letters of 31 March: 'I have received your letters
of Wednesday and Thursday'; and 5 April: 'As usual – I might say – there is no
letter from you either here or at Cook's'.

---

[84]   [47 Redcliffe Road,
     Fulham,
     London.]
     [8 April, 1918]
     Monday Night

My darling,[1]

To-night I had your Saturday letter saying you had got *one* of mine.

But, even more wonderful, I had a reply from Sydney enclosing the
actual letter sent him by his man, Joseph Addison, of the Paris
Embassy.

He said that you would be allowed to travel by the Wednesday boat.
From the way he put it, that can only mean that you will be allowed to

go on Wednesday *in any case*, whether the boat is nominally for civilians or not.

Well, I'm not going to write any more, first because I'm too overcome by the news; second, because you'll never get it, that's certain; third, because I expect a wire[2] from you to-morrow.

But, darling, if you should by any chance get this – its to say Rib and I are at the window again, thank God.

                    Boge.

1. J.M. replies to K.M.'s letter of 6 April: 'Thank God! a registered letter came from you today'.

2. K.M. announced the longed-for return with a wire on 11 April: 'Arrive Waterloo about 11.30 this morning. Tig'.

May – June 1918

Katherine was very ill by the time she arrived, exhausted, back in London on 11 April 1918. Nevertheless the longed-for marriage between her and Murry took place on 3 May, the day after her divorce from George Bowden became absolute. But it was a mockery of a marriage. Katherine later accused Murry: 'You never once held me in your arms and called me your wife'; and he replied: 'My soul was struck dumb with terror at your illness . . . Our marriage meant, was to mean and has meant, as much to me as it did to you . . . But my happiness withered in my heart . . .'. After six weeks together in Murry's sunless rooms at 47 Redcliffe Road, Katherine agreed reluctantly to join her friend Anne Estelle Rice at Headlands Hotel in Looe, Cornwall.

In confirming the diagnosis of tuberculosis, her doctor had agreed with Katherine that she should try a 'cure' at home rather than enter a sanatorium. The letters Murry wrote in May and June 1918, therefore, centre on his efforts to make suitable provision for his wife by leasing and redecorating a house at 2 Portland Villas, Hampstead. But the negotiations took time; and Katherine, as black moods descended upon her, accused Murry of wanting to be rid of her when he wrote happily, or tormented him by suggesting that they continue to live apart.

Pressured by the burden of unremitting work at the War Office and by the emotional demands of his sick wife, Murry was very near to nervous collapse by the end of June. After a separation of five weeks, he was finally able, on 21 June, to join Katherine in Looe. After ten days' holiday they returned together to London, moving into the Hampstead house about the end of July.

[85]   47 [Redcliffe Road,
                                                     Fulham,
                                                     London.]
                                                 [17 May, 1918.]

My darling wife, my precious Wig.

When I got home this evening, I felt very depressed. Somehow I couldn't reconcile myself to being alone again.[1] It seemed so devilish that we should have written to each other: when I hold you in my arms again I'll never let you go.

But the depression didn't last long. I just thought how miserable I should have been if you had still been here in these rooms without a breath of air: but I longed to have some word from you. Then I got my supper. One egg or two egg omelette? I said to myself, and decided that you would like me to eat a two-egger. So I did. My child, do the same for me. Whenever you think of me, eat something extra. I know it's hard – devilish hard – but if you don't, I shall pine away.

It is very strange; but to-night I can't express myself at all. It's as though I were a bird whose throat had been strained by trying to sing some incredibly passionate song. It's not that I'm worried. I know that you will do what you have to do; and I know that you will turn the corner – just because I have implicit faith in your loyalty to our love. But the passionate anguish of the love I feel has been like a revelation to me, and I am silent.

Oh, my darling, my wig, my wife
                                    Boge.[2]

1. Virginia Woolf, who had lunched with K.M. on 9 May, recorded: 'Katherine was marmoreal, as usual, just married to Murry, & liking to pretend it a matter of convenience. She looks ghastly ill. . . . But she is off to Cornwall.'

2. K.M. replies 20 May: 'Drey has brought me your Friday letter – and it is a sad one'.

[86]   47 [Redcliffe Road,
                                                      Fulham,
                                                      London.]
Monday. Evening.   [20 May, 1918.]

Darling Wig-wife.[1]

How can I tell you of the joy with which your letters have filled me? I feel gay, light-hearted, full of sun and air, utterly confident – everything that you would have me. When I think that you should have found *the* place, that if you are only a moderately good Wig, an eating-resting Wig you will certainly have knocked the backbone out of your old illness by the end of the summer, when I think that at long last the aspegs[2] are *all* good, I feel just as though the only thing to do is to stand on my head and sing: I dreamt that I dwell-helt in marbill halls.

When I had read your letters, I went off to my looking glass. Truly, honestly, I didn't recognise myself. I don't believe you would have known your smiling Boge; with a spotted bow-tie that looked for all the world like a little dog who was smiling too. Straight dinkum, I *could* not be happier than I am. And yet, strangely enough, when your train went out and I left the old station and plunged into the sunlight, I knew the good thing was going to happen, the only good thing that could happen. I knew it, and I suddenly passed into a state of grace. Everything I did was a good thing. I made my Aunt better; I lifted my father out of his depression; I made the flower-woman laugh; and even Sheppard smiled again.

I've only one hole to pick in your letter. Why do you say it's dreadfully expensive? It's dreadfully cheap. You know it is. I'll send you £8 at the beginning of every month. Do you think that will be enough. Just think, quietly. I have just got a rise of £8 a month. I have only got to go on writing a few articles and I shall be saving just as much as ever. You can't deny the stars are fighting for us at long last. But if you say another word about its being too expensive, or about looking for another place I'll come down expressly and beat you.

And, then, how dare you worry about me? You must know that news like that makes me so happy that I can hardly hold myself. The old office becomes delightful, really delightful – I mean that seriously. If I were not in it, I should try to get in. When you are ill, the only thing that satisfies me is to be earning enough money to make you well. Just think that for the first time we really need money and we really have it. I feel that I could hug the old office. Write to me and tell me that you are gaining a pound a week at least, and I'll keep so well that you'll think I came fresh out of the Heron when you see me next month. You understand, don't you. We are lovers for ever. You pine away & I pine; you flourish, & I flourish.

Now, before I forget (1) would you like the £8 before the first of June? You've only to say the word (2) About the sugarcard, you'll have to go on with the present arrangement till July 13th. If the Manageress would like a different kind of sugar next time just tell me. (3) Shall I send you your Charles Lamb or any other books (4) I don't in the least see why you should review any books unless you want to *very much*. But I send you a book the *Times* sent me. They want ½ col – the same as you did last time. But if you don't feel disposed, don't worry a bit. I don't matter a tinker's curse. (5) Write to me as often as you can & tell me the things I want to know. Most days, I shall probably send you only a post-card and a long letter on Sunday. But you will have a p.c. every day. I would write every day if it were not that I feel certain of the Heron again and I *want*, really want, to write articles for it. (6) Don't get too uppish and start climbing hills. That's the only thing I'm afraid of – that because you know you're getting better, you'll begin to behave as though you're quite well. You just mustn't. Think of me. (7) Wash Rib's face & kiss him from me. (8) Remember always that you are my very soul, & behave according

Boge.[3]

I've sent off nearly all the prospectuses[4] – and your story to Harrison.[5] Now, I'm going to read your letter again.

---

1. J.M. replies to K.M.'s letters of 17 May: 'I have been sitting in a big armchair by the *three* open windows . . .'; and 18 May: 'Having "slept in it" I am convinced that this place is what the South of France should have been . . .'.

2. K.M.'s word for omens or signs.

3. K.M. replies 23 May: 'The old 'un has just brought your Monday letter "right up"'.

4. The prospectuses of *Prelude*, due for publication and sale by subscription in July.

5. Austin Harrison (1873–1928), editor of *The English Review*, which published 'Bliss' in August 1918.

---

[87]   [47 Redcliffe Road,
                                         Fulham,
                                         London.]
                                         [22 May, 1918.]
                                         Wednesday Evening

My darling Wig-wife.[1]

To-day, well to-day is Wednesday. I have been so plunged in the mess that something is worn off of the shock your letter gave me this morning. What malignant fate is it that hides or destroys my letters when you are ill and want them most? oh, my darling, you couldn't, even for a moment, have thought that I wouldn't write, could you?

I won't talk about your being bowled over again by that pleurisy, because I can't trust myself to. What I want to say is that there is something, a golden ring, a song sweet with hedges & blue sea and sky, in your letters now, that lifts me up to heaven. Even in the letters I got this morning telling me of the pleurisy, there is a note which I seem not to have heard from you since you fell ill last winter. It fills me with such joy that I feel *beautiful*. I partake of an influence. The office seems to me just a trivial joke; the burden absolutely dissolves away; I feel I have only to go forward a little way & there is the Heron. And you must know that makes [me] well, well, well, radiant with health.

So long as I hear that note, it is just foolish for you to think of me as overworking. Honestly – quite honestly – I *enjoy* working hard. The zest of accumulating money for the Heron, of showing your father that we are determined to be as independent as we can be, and that I really am the fit and proper person to have charge of you & be your husband – takes hold of me with a new strength. So you mustn't think of me as not sharing the beauties of this miraculous May with you. I just drink them in through you. My Wig-wife you must understand that *once for all*. I shall have a grudge against you if you don't. Surely you can understand how, when I read your letter in the morning, I go to the office like a boy to play in the fields. And if you improve quickly and do all the eating I expect from you, why, I shall present myself before the Colonel like my brother when he was a tiny, with a blanket and a tin-can tied round my waist.

Now, Wig, take all this in seriously. We shall be together very soon. Only one thing there is which brings me anxiety & sorrow: that is the thought that you are losing ground, or not gaining it. That and nothing else wore me and you down in Redcliffe Road. If only you will take the God-given opportunity of this summer, we shall be together in our house in Hampstead when the late autumn comes, for sure: and I can't tell you what a wonderful house it will be.

(The agent, by the way, says he has sent an estimate of repairs to the landlord's solicitor,[2] and that as far as he knows it's a certainty for us.)

But the loss of that letter worries me. And until to-morrow morning I shall be wondering whether you have had any of mine. The missing one, as I say, contained a long letter I wrote to your mother, one I sent to your Father and a description of a bush fire from the *N.Z. Times.* I'll be sorry if it's lost for ever. I put string round it and put the lot in a big envelope.

There's a thunder & lightning storm just beginning & it's hot, hot, gorgeously hot.

Your Boge husband[3]

---

1. J.M. replies to K.M.'s letter of 20 May: 'Certainly yesterday had a Big Black Cap on it . . .'.
2. Murry's rooms at 47 Redcliffe Road were unsuitable for them both. He was currently negotiating the lease and redecoration of a house in Hampstead.
3. K.M. replies 23 May: 'This is just a note on my tomorrow's letter . . .'.

---

[88]   [47 Redcliffe Road,
                                        Fulham,
                                        London.]
                                   [24 May, 1918]
                                   Friday Morning 9.30

My darling,[1]

I'll be late for the office, but I can't leave yr. Thursday letter unanswered till to-night. I mean the one 'Are you really only happy when I am not there?'

Well, what's the use of answering it anyhow. Besides I can't. It's comic how with one letter I am left shivering & naked. This time I do feel lonely. You say it all so beautifully that you must have meant it as it was written. Its a blow, a blow.

Oh, damn, what's the good of writing this? I'll not send it: it'll only make you sad, as I am.

Shut up shop, Boge Murry, take your love away. Good God, what a child. Crying, crying, crying. Are you really only happy when she's not there?

My darling, don't believe all this – it can't be true – I've read yr. letter upside down or something. You really mean something quite different. It'll all be right and when you get this I shan't be sad any longer.

Friday Evening

My precious Wig-wife,

I've been rather depressed to-day. I started it by weeping over your letter. I send you what I wrote then: but it's not as bad as that now. It's really quite all right. But it gave me a fearful shock.

You see, worm, it's true that I *was* happy when you went away. I was so confident that the sun & food and Anne and the 'absolutely ideal' place would make you well. I wanted you to go, because I could see that London was knocking you up absolutely. Just because I care for nothing else in the world but you, because the only thing I have to look forward to in life is living at your side – I wanted you to go away. I feel so sure that if I was ill you would be the same; I felt so certain that you understood, that your letter this morning just bowled me out.

But as I say, I'm better now. I know you can't have meant it *like that*, and that I have just been silly. I can't bear the thought that you think my love so imperfect. It's the only thing I am jealous about, because I've fought a hard fight to make it perfect until it has become all there is of me. When I see you sick & ailing, I die; when I think that you are getting well, I straighten my stalk & begin to blossom like a flower.

And then you ask: Can you conceive of yourself buying crimson roses and smiling at the flower woman if I were within 50 miles? I feel I can't answer, more than that I feel I *ought* not answer. But love casteth away pride – besides it's my love that's pierced & not my pride – so I reply.

If you were well and at my side and we were to buy roses together, I might not smile at the woman, I might be solemn even. But she would smile at us. We should leave such warmth in her heart that she would never, never forget.

Do you think that when I'm away from you I *am* happy. Do you think I live at all? I go right apart from the world. I exist. But to think that you are getting well, that brings me happiness – compared to the utter grinding despair of watching you *not* eat, watching you *not* rest, it is heavenly. I'm not happy though. I can never be happy apart from you. And just because I want to be with you, to live *our* life, I want you to get strong. I would wait years – yes years – apart if I knew that that was the only way we could make sure of having *our* life one day.

When I asked you if you still believed in the Heron – I meant only this one thing, that if you believed in it, then you would eat   then you would rest no matter what it cost you. I said it at a moment when I was mad watching you. I'm not a cow or a werewolf, after all. I'm your lover. Everything rests on your wonderful body & lovely soul. I grow desperate seeing you pine: hearing you growing well I lift up my head. 'You are always pale, exhausted, in a kind of anguish of set fatigue when I am by. Now I feel in your letters this is lifting & you are breathing again.' It's absolutely true. But that you should have misunderstood!

Well, worm, it's silly to go on like this. Your to-morrow letter will be quite different.

I ought not have written this I know. But I have to tell the truth about what I feel, don't I. And you'll know where I'm all wrong & you'll set it all right again. But please don't doubt my love – it hurts too much.

I got your wire about signing about Hampstead. You will have had my letter this morning. I have written to them to say that on thinking it over I must insist on their taking the responsibility for complete decoration to my satisfaction and for putting a supply of hot-water in the bath-room. I know they won't accept this; but I don't think they'll break off immediately, so that if you were finally to decide for it we could get it. And if you decide against I have only to stand firm.

Goodbye – Wig-wife. Don't have any more of those 'ideas', though

Boge[2]

A new complication. This very minute Miss Palmer has been here to say she has *let* this flat.

However, the people haven't signed the agreement yet. So I can wait till I get your letter to-morrow & then tell her to postpone matters.

1. J.M. replies to K.M.'s letter of 23 May: 'This is just a note on my tomorrow's letter . . .'.

2. K.M. replies 27 May: 'I think, reading your three letters this morning, I suffered every atom that you suffered'.

---

[89]   [47 Redcliffe Road,
                                                Fulham,
                                                London.]
                                              [25 May, 1918.]
                                              Saturday Morning

My darling Wig-wife.[1]

I've just got your registered letter. And I must answer it before I go to the office in order to make sure you get it to-morrow so that I get a reply on Monday.

Your letter was another morning knock. However – I shall be used to that soon. I don't mean because you were nervous of the Elephant.[2] I am that – always. But because there was no love for me in it. I won't go into this again. But you misunderstand me.

Surely you know how I *hunger* to be with you. There's a great drag at my heart going all day long – every minute of it. Do you think I said 'Late autumn' for myself. I said to myself 'How long can I bear it?' How long at the outside? I felt that I must, for our love's own sake, not put any pressure on you to come back – must give you time to get strong. Everything in me cried 'Come back, come back – I can't bear it – only just wait till I get the Elephant ready – only a little moment'. But I stamped all that down – *stamped it* down. And then you misunderstood. Oh, Worm – my heart will break No it won't – my heart will stand anything if only you don't stop even for a moment loving me.

This isn't the mood – I'm crying again – to write about houses, I suppose. But perhaps it is. Don't you think we would live together in the calm of our love in Elephant. I promise you it would be beautiful, really beautiful. And as for L.M. why shouldn't we leave her out. Why we could get somebody. Why not put Dearly[3] in the basement? Or even Mrs. Hardwick? And as for money – what does it matter – we shan't lose any really. And I think you would get better steadily. But more than all that our love would be at work.

So much you say & write hurts me. About my not sending the £8. Am I not your lover. Am I a stranger, too? Why won't you take it. It's not money. It's only a posy of flowers, or a little box that I made. You must have it: you will hurt me too much.

Oh, worm – can't you feel how I love you. How I am nothing but a passionate longing for you: not a living thing anymore. If you turn your head away from this flower of mine – it will become withered & dead.

I don't want to press you but how *could you suggest* your living in rooms in Hampstead & me living at 47? It seems to me so monstrous – so unthinkable – after all we have gone through.

But I know what it is – isn't it – you are torturing yourself. Something has gone wrong. Everything is ugly again, & you say these things to hurt yourself. To me they come like a crash of everything.

If you would have me & the Elephant it wd. be ready in a month – six weeks at the outside.

Oh, my love, my wife – do you do your part towards getting well – and I will play & laugh with you all day long

Boge.[4]

1. J.M. replies to K.M.'s letter of 23 May: 'This is just a note on my tomorrow's letter . . .'.
2. The Elephant was the Murrys' name for the house at 2 Portland Villas, Hampstead, which they moved into towards the end of the summer.
3. A prospective housekeeper.
4. K.M. replies 27 May: 'I think, reading your three letters . . .'.

———————

[90]   [47 Redcliffe Road,
                                          Fulham,
                                          London.]
                                   [25 May, 1918.]
                              Saturday Night. 11.15.

My precious Wig-wife,

I hate the thought that I can't get a letter from you till Monday morning. I feel the need to talk to you, to be near you, so much. I have to take decisions which are our decisions – and that can't be done unless we are us (forgive that awful phrase, but I can't express what I mean otherwise).

You see, my darling, the letters that you have written me the last two days don't help me to see clearly. They seem to have been written in the idea that I could be, and am, happy separated from you. I may have given you that idea: but it's a terribly wrong one, and if I take decisions, or rather you take decisions, on that basis – the whole thing will be wrong. I want a letter from you that will put me in the state of grace, which I have lost now for two days, again. I am afraid of any decisions we take while this mood is on us. Nothing good can come of things we do when we are separated in spirit.

I am still appalled by that notion of yours that you would live in rooms in Hampstead while I would stay at 47 and come to see you for week ends. It not only frightens me in itself, just as an idea: more frightening still is the thought that you could have such an idea, and that you should think that I would not be frightened by it. You stay away in the country – well, I bear that, and I am even glad of it, because I believe that will help you to get well, and that is the only thing – really, the only thing – I care about in the world. But the idea of the Hampstead House was that it enabled us to be together – and to be together is all that life holds for us. For you to be in London & me to be apart – well, it just seems a mockery. I can't believe you really mean it.

If you are afraid of the Elephant because of L.M.[1] – I understand that *absolutely*. L.M. shall not be there: we'll find either the real Dearly or another. If you are afraid of the Elephant just as the Elephant – a big house with a basement – then I understand that perfectly and, though I don't think it more frightening than Acacia Road, if your feeling persists, we'll do our best to drive the Elephant away, while we ourselves clamber down his tail on to the ground. (I know from your letter that you don't want to stay in the country for the sake of staying in the country. You said you had never dreamed of staying till the late autumn. I explained what the intention of my words was.)

Oh, how hard things are to make clear! It's like this, darling. If you had said 'Boge, don't take the Elephant: it frightens me: let's find one that fits us more: *I'll* stay in the country till you do: and when it's quite ready I'll come back' – I should be quite calm & happy. But you said something quite different: and my head is still spinning with disappointment.

But when I put all these things out like this, as clearly as I can, I feel that I am pressing you, driving you, like a little horse, through a gate. But that I will not do. If there is any pressure here, ignore it, my worm, it's not *really* there. I am only trying to make it quite clear to you that you were absolutely & utterly mistaken in thinking that I could ever be happy apart from you. I have told you why my letters were happy, and why I *was* happy when you had gone. My happiness began when your telegram came a week ago to-day

Superb arrival everything simply splendid fondest love Wig.

My god, wouldn't you have been happy if I had sent you that, after you had been watching me cooped up in 47 eating nothing, hurrying about, never resting, though these were the things that were absolutely necessary. I was *happy*, I felt good, I began to *be* again. But when you wrote that you had the idea that I was happy *because* you had gone away, my happiness ended. Oh, I have not been happy since.

Forgive me, my darling, for returning again & again to this. I won't any more. But it circles round & round in my head & gives me no peace.

Please tell me how much you weighed – you were going out to weigh yourself on Thursday, you said – but you never said how much. And the whole world hangs on these things for me: on these things & your Monday letter. Child, if only I could put my arms round you – everything would be plain once more, I know.

I sent you *The Possessed* & a French book to review to-day. I'll send you the *Pageant*[2] on Monday.

Be honest with me, Wig – don't spare me. If you think my love is cold – if you think I have changed in any way – tell me truly.

A whole day till Monday.

I got your telegram about the Elephant to-day. I haven't signed anything. But your telegram was sent before any of my letters can have arrived. All depends on Monday

Your unhappy Boge.[3]

Sunday Afternoon.

I have just been to the Post Office to see whether I can manage that this letter gets to you to-morrow morning. They tell me that there's a good chance if I post it in the late fee box before half past five. I hope it comes off. I feel completely détraqué. How I hang on your letter to-morrow.

Whatever you decide about the Elephant, I shall clear out of here. I've lived too many nightmare hours in it. I hate it, and it hates me. I shall let the other people have it anyhow and go somewhere else.

L.M. brought me some cigarettes for you. I am sending them with this by letter post.

1. The Murrys had discussed having L.M. live with them as a housekeeper. But in her letter of 25 May (Saturday Evening) Katherine wrote: '. . . I really am frightened to take her for better and for worse. My love for her is so divided by my extreme *hate* for her . . . I feel she'll stand between us – that you and she will be against me'.

2. Katherine had requested *A Pageant of English Poetry*, edited by R. M. Leonard.

3. K.M. replies 27 May: 'I think, reading your three letters . . .'.

---

[91]

M.I. 7D,
War Office,
Watergate House,
Adelphi, W.C.2.
28 May, 1918.

Tuesday 1.30

My precious, wonderful wife.[1]

I was so overcome by your letter this morning that I forgot to take out with me the letter I wrote last night.

I have read your letter three–four times. I shall wear it near my heart. That only means in my pocket, I suppose, really: but I have to carry it about with me, shall have to always. Such an influence of love flows out of it that I can never let it go far from me.

I think you are right when you say I don't know you, even yet. There is something, some final perfection of perfection, in you that [I] did not understand. I did feel it, I did know it was there; but I had never seen it face to face, never felt its fragrance steal so close about my heart.

I don't need to defend myself to you. The only thing I want to say is that perhaps you didn't quite know how *afraid* I was. How my soul was struck dumb with terror at your illness. I seemed neither to be able to speak nor to breathe. I could never say what I wanted to say to you, things that I cannot *say*. When we were married, my longing to fold you in my arms was terrible; but more terrible still was the thought which held me back. No, I mustn't: I shall hurt her. At that moment the knowledge of your illness blinded me like a flash of lightning – tore right through my heart. And from this there came another thing. I felt that I couldn't tell you all my love because if I did, if I once let out the flower that was bursting in my heart, I could not have let you go and you couldn't have gone. I felt that we were being killed by the devouring passion of our love: I chose to hold it back – it cost me more pain than I have ever known or ever will know again. I was held up only by the one thought that never left my mind for an instant: She must rest or she will die. One night I lay awake by your side for years and listened to your breathing.

My darling, our marriage meant, was to mean & has meant, as much to me as it did to you. Of that I am sure, utterly sure, even though you may smile a little & slowly nod your head. But my happiness withered in my heart – I shall never forget how it withered when I looked at you as you came into the restaurant. Perhaps I should have fought the devil of despair – but I am only *Boge* – a child.

I never meant, and never wrote, worm, that *you* said 'Boge Murry take your love away'. That was me speaking to myself.

To be together and to be at rest – that is my only desire, my one longing. It does not eat out my heart so much now that I know we are one again; but all the same it's there and never leaves me alone.

About Lesley I feel just as you do. I have always felt that she drove a wedge between us – not that she did, not that she wanted to even. But no living person can share our life, nor even pretend to. Neither Johnny nor Anne nor she, no-one understands. She was at 47 last night wanting to know how you were. I couldn't say a word. I felt that it was too secret, and too sacred, and that if I tore it out of my heart, I should die.

Now, I know that we can trust each other absolutely. You will do for our love's sake all that you must do to get well. Any housekeeper would do for us, so long as she was clean & good: but, if it's Lesley M., then she is only a housekeeper – a friend as well perhaps – but in essence a housekeeper. But I think it would be far better for me to find someone else.

How hard it is to write things – one look, one kiss, once my arms round you, and all that I am groping at would be said.

My one, my only idea, when you went away was to get the Elephant ready as soon as I could & bring you back. But I was fearful – fearful as I always am – of seeming to bring pressure on you. When your letters came saying you were so happy & getting so well, I felt I must not *call* you back. The thought of months without [you] was a nightmare. When I wrote it I was praying that you should say: I'd rather come back. But I dared not ask you.

Wig – wig – when I read your letter I *am* in your arms. I am calm & happy.[2]

1. J.M. replies to K.M.'s of 27 May: 'I think, reading your three letters…'.
2. K.M. replies 29 May: 'Your Tuesday letter written at the office is here'.

---

[92]   [47 Redcliffe Road,
                           Fulham,
                           London.]
                      [29–30 May, 1918.]
                    Wednesday 10.30 pm

My darling,[1]

I thought I was going to be allowed a quiet time to-night to type your *Carnation*;[2] but suddenly I had to do the Foreign Notes for the *Nation* & I've only just finished them. Wednesday too.

But you know really I don't mind. Except that I didn't want *Carnation* to wait another day, I don't mind anything so long as I have peace in my heart. And there is peace in my heart if our love is shining & singing, and you are getting well. Oh, child, wife, how much I love you: how I long to be near you, only to hear you saying something or to watch you doing something. You know what it means that the terror-cloud should be lifted a little, and I be able to believe in the Heron again. It seems to me that I shall never, never be able to express my love for you again in words. It *will* not be expressed in words.

I am glad, terribly glad, that you decided to stay at Headlands.[3] Trust me, my darling, I won't delay a minute longer than I can help to come down to you, or a minute longer than I can help to get our London Heron. But the agents haven't answered me. Tomorrow I shall have to go and see them. Perhaps the thing will be decided. I do seem to have been kept waiting about. I was thinking to-day. Supposing we get the Elephant, shall we take L.M. for a month – a fortnight would do – so that she can help me get the place ready. I mean I'm rather frightened of engaging someone on my own, without your having seen her at all. However, it's best to let that wait until I find out what's happening. When I went to see them last Thursday the understanding was that they would accept the £90 decoration – and the agreement would be signed without delay. But now I've added a geyser to my ultimatum. I'll send you a wire of course if there's anything definite tomorrow.

Wig, do send me anything more you write. That *Carnation* was such wonderful stuff that I had a moment of pure gold reading it. Why is it that the spring seems to flow direct into your work when you write in

the spring. It's just like almond blossom. And when at the end of
Carnation you say – and then it all broke into pieces – something like
that – it seemed to me just like the way fruit blossom shatters to pieces.
It never withers or dies, but just breaks.

I had a letter from – Frank Harris who had read that pome in the
Nation and asked me not to misunderstand him. The old villain – I
can't help liking him – he was pretty decent to me. But he'll begin to
lose me my job if he starts writing to me. Particularly as it was a *copy* of
the letter which came to me through the Censor's office in the way of
official business   Another item that will interest you is that M[r]. C. E.
Bechaver[4] – that's how he spells it now – is my secretary. I'm afraid
he's rather a conceited young man, but I don't *dis*like him; or at all
events I like him better now that I've convinced him that he doesn't
know very much German after all. Another item – yesterday I had a
letter from London, which had taken a fortnight to reach me, asking if
I would meet him 'as there are so few of us left' I don't want to meet
him or anybody else – but, the appeal being of such a kind, I suppose
there's nothing for it. (I'll send you F.H's letter. I left it in the office).
To-morrow I will send you a small parcel which has come from old
John Lewis[5] & a new book by Duhamel[6] – the man who wrote *Vie des
Martyrs*. I think it's a wonderful book. Read the first part of *Les
Amours de Ponceau* and see if the man hasn't got some idea of what love
really is. The rest of the stories are terrible – but full of the same pitiful
understanding.

I'm not going to shift out of this flat until I have definitely taken a
house for us both in Hampstead. I'm not going to have our things
wandering about and me without anywhere to lay my head – never
fear. I've told Miss Palmer that there's a hitch (which I believe is only
temporary) but until it is decided, she must not make a new agreement
for this flat. There obviously won't be any difficulty in letting it even if
I have to say 'NO' to these people.

For God's sake, Wig, hurry up & send me your new story.[7] But
don't get so excited about it that you forget to eat. But if you were to
send it me and tell me at the same time that you'd gained another three
lb, I'd go right off my head with rapture. I feel like doing that now just
because I adore you so

Ton mari
Boge.[8]   in yr. letter this morning

Lunch time. I think Roger Fly is the funniest thing I've read for years

– except perhaps Rib's tame shrimp. There are £8 in this letter & I've sent your pantalons. I 'phoned the agent to-day – said I must have a yes or no to my ultimatum & no compromise. He said he quite understood & wd. do his best. It's not his fault but the landlord's solicitor's.

1. J.M. replies to K.M.'s letter of 28 May: 'I don't expect a letter today . . .'.

2. There has been some confusion about the stories Katherine wrote at Looe, especially about the writing and publication dates of 'Carnation'. Jeffrey Meyers on page 15 of his biography dates 'Carnation' as 1917, but on page 173 says that K.M. wrote only one story in Cornwall in 1918, 'Carnation'. Murry's letters make it quite clear that 'Carnation' was written in 1918 – and that K.M. wrote at least one other story. Murry may be partly responsible for the confusion, however; for as Sylvia Berkman rightly notes, he dated the story 1917 when it was published in the 1924 volume, *Something Childish and Other Stories*.

Both Ruth Mantz in her *Critical Bibliography*, and Saralyn Daly in *Katherine Mansfield*, say that 'Carnation' was first published in *Something Childish*. In fact, as Murry indicates in his 1951 edition of K.M.'s *Letters* to him, the story was accepted by the *Nation*, which published it on 7 September 1918.

3. On 25 May K.M. had written: 'I shan't stay at this hotel after my fortnight is up. Anne and I are going to look for two rooms'. But by 27 May she had decided to stay for the 'whole of June – *at least*'.

4. C. E. Bechhofer-Roberts (1894–1949), a journalist who contributed to the *New Age*, which he later satirized in his novel *Let's Begin Again* (1940).

5. John Lewis was the name of an Oxford Street department store from which K.M. purchased underwear.

6. Georges Duhamel (1884–1966), French poet, novelist and essayist. An army surgeon during the 1914–18 war, he wrote two compassionate collections of sketches about his experiences: *Vie des Martyrs* (1917) and *Civilisation 1914–1917* (1918).

7. The unfinished 'A Married Man's Story', of which Katherine said on 28 May: 'I'm fairly at sea with my new story. The same difficulties plague me as they did before, but it certainly "goes" '. J.M. replies on 4 June: 'I've just read the last bit of "to the Last Moment" – well there's nothing to say. Go ahead. It has the quality of vision that I find *nowhere else at all* than in your work. It is as though you alone *saw* things. Everybody else having a more or less frosted bit of glass with which as you said in "Bliss", he screws his eye down. When you write nowadays it seems to be always spring. I believe you *are* Spring'.

8. K.M. replies 31 May: 'No post. Bin and Gone'. Referring to his 'Wednesday' letter she said: 'I'll send the first long chapitre of my story this week. Your letter has so *fired* me that I know I'll write like a billy-o today. It's just for you, for you'.

[93]

[47 Redcliffe Road,
Fulham,
London.]
2 June, 1918

Sunday Morning

My darling WIFE,
    The bells are ringing and a big fly is buzzing. I've had a bath and I've got hardly any clothes on – of course, much more than Maud Allan (see *Daily Press passim*), but not very much. My state of mind is that of the cheerful lunatic. Incidentally, the cat (I don't know why I say *the* cat – a cat, I suppose – but no I mean *the* cat: the great bogey of a cat that smiles and has enormous whiskers from the time you are about 3 months old onwards) well, *the* cat has eaten my steak. Luckily, I was clever enough to eat half of it in advance last night, and more lucky still, I had told Johnny that I wouldn't be able to give him dinner to-night. That's why *the* cat ate my steak. It was very thoughtful of him – just as the other night he drank my milk, without breaking the jug. I feel that one of these days I shall find him knocking at the door with his ration card in his paw.
    Absolutely the only objection I have to this Sunday is that I don't & can't get a letter from you to begin the day with. I should have the whole day to linger over it, watch you and talk to you, laugh at the thought of how much we love each other, whistle about it and wink at Rib – 'We know all about her'. Golly, what a woman. All through the week the flower of joy & hope and love has gone on expanding in my heart. I have turned more and more away from the world, thinking, living, feeling only through and in us. Nothing has any effect on me; your letters have lifted me up every morning like a little Gus Bofa dog,[1] planted me on a window sill in the sun, as much as to say 'Stay there', while you have gone off into another room. I have sat obediently on the window-sill, blinking & blinking, smiling at the thought of you. The office has become a comic dream: it weighs on me about as heavy as a feather, certainly not more. Except that I have a burning, passionate physical longing for you – deeper & more consuming than any before – I am just bemused & happy like a little boy lying on the sand in the sun.
    That explains me. Now I will be serious. I have to say *serious*, although I am convinced that all that I have just written is really serious and all that I am going to say quite Trivial in comparison. But

there's the Elephant, and I want to get that clear. My own opinion, as I said hurriedly yesterday, is that if we can get the old beast without undertaking impossible burdens we ought to. Perhaps you think the £50[2] offer is such an impossible burden. Let's try to work it out. I had in the bank on June 1 £58 + £26 my office pay for last month. Assuming it costs me £10 to come down to Cornwall at the end of the month: £8 more to live till then & £9.10.0 wh: I shall have to pay for the next quarter's rent here, that makes on July 1

$$£84$$
$$\underline{27.10.0}$$
$$56.10.0$$

To come from the Nation $\underline{9.10.0}$

$$66.\ 0.0$$

+ 1 months salary paid
on July 1 $\underline{28.15.0}$

$$94.15.0$$

Now the decorator won't expect me to pay in advance, but even if he did, I could do it and have £40 over. But as a matter of fact I should pay my part of the £50 in three monthly instalments. Besides this I shall have to pay for the moving – and for stair carpet etc. not less than £20. But even so I shall perfectly well be able to manage. I shan't buy any furniture except perhaps a kitchen table and a Duck oven for the kitchen. We can get on perfectly well without these other things for a bit. Then as I have explained everytime we have to pay our quarterly rent[3] we will put the £7.10.0 that the landlord has to deduct back into our Heron store religiously and, if we can, make it up to £10 a time. My scheme for the actual house keeping is this. For our purposes we will regard our income as £550 a year. All that I make beyond my £350[4] from the office – they deduct £50 for income tax – we shall regard definitely as Heron money.[5] Towards the rent & the house-keeping expenses & Lesley we will contribute, you ⅓ & I ⅔. Thus for the first year it will look something like this.

Rent £65 (I put this in full because we have
        to pay £25 a year back to the Heron account)
Taxes £25
  L.M £52
Housekeeping £260 – I think that Housekeeping will not
            be more than £5 a week
Total for year = £400

Divide this into 3 parts   133. 6. 8
        That leaves you   76.13. 4 out of 200
        That leaves me   783. 6. 8 out of 350[6]
350
266.13. 4
[7]783. 6. 8

And that is *quite apart* from the £150 – put it at the lowest its ever been £10 a month: £120 – I earn from the *Nation* & the *Times*.

If you want to go away there will be plenty always, my darling.

You see, what it means is that we live anyhow much cheaper than we can possibly live apart. We have each about £75 a year over out of our fixed income. We are putting back the £50 to the Heron a/c – and we have one of the most beautiful houses in London, a place where great poems & great stories are written – Your Carnation!

Wig my darling I have tried to be as sober in calculating as I can. You see we are in an incomparably better position financially than ever before. We have twice as much settled income – no three times – as ever before. We are taking less obligation than we did with Acacia Road, when we had to pay £20 premium, never to be recovered, & we have a house that we can let in the twinkling of an eye and fly into our final Heron.

What I mean is that there is nothing to be afraid of at all. L.M. is really keen, really sensible – and I felt the last time I saw her that she really did want to join her life to ours.

No, what I am afraid of is that the winter should find us without a real resting place and we should have to part again. I want to be with you for ever & ever. You know all the longing, the passion, the weariness, the childish hope & disillusion, the unutterable sense of being a stranger & a changeling in this world, the golden vision of our love that crowds into that 'for ever & ever.' A flat *won't do*. It won't be ours. I want a castle of peace – just what I said in my poem – a tower-room where I can rest my head on your breast, that loving wonderful breast where I am always at rest & understood, where when I am no harm can come. Oh, my wife, we have come so far through the forest together – we must have our *home* at last.

I know that its not the Heron & that there's the office & that I shall be working for the Heron at night very often. But those are small things really. What I cannot live without is your presence. When I have not your presence the office eats into my soul; when I have it, I am strong against the office. It does not touch me. You know all this about me far better than me.

You in a cottage at Garsington & me coming for week-ends[8] – is all a mockery & a snare. I don't want any more of them. I want you – to be with you as wholly as I can be, – somewhere where the world is not roaring in my ears – where we can whisper to each other & be heard My throat aches with this shouting above the din. We have nothing to do with world. It's all self-deception if we think we have. The world is hateful & sordid: men & women have lost their birthright. We who remember ours *must* live in each other's arms.

Therefore I say let me take the Elephant. I feel that I should be inviting disaster if I were not to.

Have I wearied you with all this? I know I haven't. What a little humbug to ask?

Johnny came in last night. He was very anxious that I should tell you that Kathleen Dillon[9] refused Cochran's job, because he asked her 'to moderate her style'. He said he wanted you particularly to know this because you had said it would make a difference if you knew that someone somewhere was sticking to this art business. He hasn't sold any of his pictures. So there's no doubt that he, like us, is too good. As he says we must stick together. He's frightfully glad to have such good news of you from Anne, who has apparently written to him.

Unless things absolutely disappoint me I shall come down to Looe on Friday June 21 and stay till Sunday the 30th. Oh, what heaven!

Boge[10]

1. Gus Bofa (pseudonym of Gustave Blanchot), artist, illustrator and humourist, published a satirical weekly, *La Bäionette*, during the First World War.

2. Murry had offered £50 towards the cost of redecorating the Elephant and installing a hot-water geyser.

3. Alpers, in *The Life of Katherine Mansfield*, is not correct when he says on page 285 that: 'The Elephant was the first house the Murrys had owned, and since Murry was still an undischarged bankrupt, there were difficulties in financing it'; and on page 412: 'Late August the Murrys move into "The Elephant" . . . their own house for the first time'. Murry's *Between Two Worlds*, as well as Katherine Mansfield's *Letters to John Middleton Murry*, and *The Memories of L.M.*, all corroborate the evidence of Murry's letters that the house was *rented*, not owned. Alpers' date of late August for the move may also be wrong. Murry, in *Between Two Worlds* (1935) says: 'We entered [the Elephant] on July 29th'; moreover the linking text of *The Memories of L.M.* says: 'K.M., J.M.M. and L.M. moved up to the Elephant at the end of July . . .'. Although Murry in his 1951 edition of K.M.'s letters to himself

mentions moving 'I think on August 26', his earlier recollection is likely to be more accurate.

4. Murry's statement here that his War Office salary is £350 p.a. conflicts with Alpers' statement on p. 280 that in 1918 'Murry, as Chief Censor, got more than £500'; and on p. 412 where Alpers indicates that by January 1918 'Murry's salary is about £500'.

5. Savings towards the purchase of a house in the country.

6. Perhaps unconsciously, Murry has made mistakes in his arithmetic which make it appear that K.M. will have more money left out of her income after the fixed household expenses are paid than will actually be the case. Correctly figured, K.M. will have not £76.13.4 but £66.13.4 left; conversely, Murry will have not £73.6.8 but £83.6.8. The effect of Murry's error (he has crossed out the correct figure '8' and written '7') is to make it seem that K.M. will have *more* money left than he will, whereas, in fact, he will be better off than her by £16.15.4.

7. The correct total here is £83.6.8. Murry has forgotten to cross out one number as he did in the line above. (See note 6.)

8. Katherine had been alternating between taking the Elephant and living with Murry – and living apart from him. On 25 May she wrote: 'No, what is best for us both is for us to stay as we are. I shall . . . wander about . . . and when I do come back to London . . . take a furnished place in Hampstead. It is idiotic, I think, for us to be together when I am in the least ill'. On 28 May she wrote: 'I had a TREMENDOUS letter from H.L. [Ottoline Morrell] yesterday, begging me to go down there and stay in the top flat of the bailiff's house – to have the woman "do" for me – and to be absolutely "free" . . . If you chose to come for every weekend, it was *entendu* that you did not have to "even see them"'. On June 1 she wired him:
'Agents letter highest degree unreasonable completely denies first offer don't close prefer go garsington end june you to come weekends give us time to consider reply fondest love Tig'.

9. A dancer known to K.M. C. B. Cochran (1872–1951) theatrical manager.

10. K.M. replies 3 June: 'I've two great big letters . . .'.

----

[94]　　　　　　　　　　　　　　[47 Redcliffe Road,
　　　　　　　　　　　　　　　　　　Fulham,
　　　　　　　　　　　　　　　　　　London.]
　　　　　　　　　　　　　　　[6 June, 1918.]
　　　　　　　　　　　　　　　Thursday Night.

My darling Wig-wife,[1]

I got the letter when I reached home, thank God. It's no use me saying you *mustn't* get black, I know; you can't help it. It happens. As for me, I don't exactly get *black*, I get grey, no colour at all. As though I had neither roots nor flower; neither sucking the juices from the earth nor the nectar from heaven. Just a wavy piece of sea weed dashed anywhere, anyhow. But that doesn't happen when I have a 'good' letter from you, so I can't help supposing that your blackness comes from something wrong in my letters. If there is anything wrong it's only because I can't get a quiet corner – not physically, but spiritually – in which to write. I have one now, though.

I feel that I've definitely given up the world. I expect nothing from it, except perhaps the chance of getting out of it, – by which I mean solitude. I've nothing to do with it, – of that I am sure. I don't expect anything from it. I know I shall *always* be a failure. No-one will ever read what I write, except you; and I shall hate the thought of anyone else reading it – except perhaps Duhamel. But that doesn't make me sad – far from it – because I know I am right. When I say I, I mean you. *I* doesn't mean anything to me now.

I don't feel a bit heroic about it. I don't like it even. I have never grown up and I am, therefore, childishly hungry for praise. But I am also something more than a child, something excessively rusé and sensitive, less sensitive only than you. I don't profess to understand the combination of youth and age: I only know it's in me and that I have gained wisdom. Now, I want to live absolutely apart with you; I want our child; I want our life, our understanding, our kindness, our vision, our happiness, our sorrow. Oh, I want – so much and such simple things that you alone can understand – and perhaps Duhamel.

Don't think it's odd that I should say 'and perhaps Duhamel'. You won't, I know. But he has got terribly near me – inside my defences, with his 'Recherche de la grâce'. No-one, not even Tchekov, has seemed to have so felt what we have felt before. I know that we shall never know each other; but the fact of his existence means a very great deal to me. It shows me the chasm that yawns between me and Johnny really. It struck me with amazement that Johnny should think Kathleen Dillon's action could possibly make any difference to us. That's such a simple point of view. She may have stuck to Art – I don't know – but what is Art? anyhow. It's love that really matters – love and grace. Without Love – as old St. Paul said, it profiteth me nothing.

Oh, love, love, – the influence which melts all stubbornness out of the soul, and makes it supple and tender and strong like a flower again. It seems to me at this moment that Art is only the despairing cry of Love forsaken by the world, or the song of Love Triumphant over the world.

I feel that Love has definitely been forsaken by the world now, and that the flame is kept alive by you and me alone. It is our secret and our secret strength. We shall keep the seed & cherish it during the bitter years, and one day it [will] spring up and flower again and the birds of the air nest in the branches there-of. You see, I can't bear the thought of final severance from the world. At the bottom of my heart something keeps crying 'Forgive them, for they know not what they do'.

I want our child, to live after us & carry the secret which we won after so long a struggle back into the world. I want the child born of my passion for you; into whose being the ecstasy & wonder, the childish utter surrender that is me when I kiss your breasts and we lie naked together, shall have passed. The extreme pinnacle of our love shall be the beginning of his life. If upon a mountain so high as ours, another mountain were to rise, it would touch the stars. The conception & birth of a child seem so marvellous to me. A miracle – so simple & so mysterious – when we are absolutely one, and I have given up my last breath in the longing to be one flesh for ever with you, to be part of your beauty and living perfection, then – a new life begins to be. As though all time should have stopped and in that still moment, and of the very void & calmness of love – a child is born.

Boge.[2]

1. J.M. replies to K.M.'s letter of 5 June: 'Your Monday night letter and ½oz. from Tuesday afternoon . . .'.
2. K.M. replies 8 June: 'I had a divine letter from you this morning writ on Thursday night'.

---

[95]
[47 Redcliffe Road,
Fulham,
London.]
[10 June, 1918]
Monday Night

My Wig-wife.

Alas, I didn't even get a letter when I got home to-night. I wanted one badly, not only for the obvious reason, but because it might have explained your wire to-day about my coming down a week earlier. You see darling everything depends on what exactly it means. If you want me urgently – why nothing in the world will keep me. The old monthly report[1] can go to Hell, and I'll come down to-morrow.

But if it's that you'd much rather I came down this week than next, just as I would much rather come – in just that sense – well, then I think I ought to stay and get the report through. I promised the Colonel I would; and it would look awfully bad if I cleared off and left it to some-one else to do.

From the words of your telegram 'could I *conveniently* come?' and you'd quite understand if it were 'undiplomatic' I have so far assumed that it isn't that you want me urgently. But now I come to think it over it seems to me quite likely that you do need me, and that you only put it that way – well, because you are you, and always thinking of me and never of yourself. Therefore, I shall do all I can to get the report done by Friday. But when you get this, will you spend another ninepence – and wire just Need you if you need me, and I'll come *the same day*. By your needing me, I mean – well, you know what I mean. You've only to call & I come. What does the office matter compared to you and our love? But if it is that you would rather I came, as I would rather come – then, I'll do my best to finish the report by Friday and come then, but, if I can't manage it, I wont. In this case, please wire 'Take your time'. And I'll know.

Perhaps to-morrow's letter (which surely must come) will make it clear to me. Till I know I shall be anxious. But you would have telegraphed differently if you needed me, wouldn't you? And yet, I don't know. Because you must have been certain that I would take the earliest possible chance of getting away to you. That's what makes me think you must be concealing something underneath the words of your wire. Am I just a stupid faggot? You see what I mean: under office laws next Friday week is the earliest possible day, but under *our* laws I can come immediately. I just want you to say which it is: 'Need you' or 'Take your time'?

I don't feel so turnip-headed by half now as I did to-day & yesterday. In fact I've been able to make a start upon that old Report at home here whereas when I wrote you this afternoon in the office, I was just quivering dazed in front of it like a rabbit in front of a snake. I suppose it's merely a development of my old woolliness that comes over me really.

The Woolves have just finished the actual printing of the text of your story. The covers are left to be done. I took the blocks with me yesterday. There were some other people there, a couple I seem to have heard of, called the Sangers,[2] so I couldn't very well argue the matter out about the blocks. They asked me for some of my poems to print: but I don't know. I've begun to feel that I don't want to print anything ever: only just to read it to you, and be lifted into the seventh heaven if you say 'That's all right, Boge'. I suppose I ought to do something more than that: but just now I can't see why.

And that of course reminds me that I haven't said anything about K.M.'s Notebook.[3] Shall I be forgiven? You see it's appallingly difficult for me to write about it. It grips altogether too near my heart. *I can't be objective* about Holes, or Pulmonary Tuberculosis. If something is absolutely clawing your heart, you can't say: That's beautiful, can you? Of course they are: I know they are: but that's not the thing that it occurs to me to say. Not at all. I just want to say 'Oh, Wig, it's all over now, really, it is all over. There's the turn round the corner.' And then lay my face against yours and stroke your hair.

So you see, Worm, I'm not much use as a critic, am I?

Your lover-husband

Boge.[4]

1. In an earlier letter that day Murry explained: 'Your wire has just come asking if I could get my holiday a week earlier. I'm terribly sorry, Wig precious, but I don't think I can. You see, I fixed the date as early as possible after the new monthly report on Germany which I have to write is finished. This report is a new thing & I must do it myself'.

2. Charles Percy Sanger (1871–1930), was an Apostle, a brilliant barrister, and a friend of Bertrand Russell. Virginia Woolf preferred him to his wife, Dora. In her *Diary* on 17 June she writes: 'Murry and the Sangers came here to supper last Sunday. Dora became increasingly ungainly. . . . Murry was pale as death, with gleaming eyes, & a crouching way at table that seemed to proclaim extreme hunger or despair. . . . And after dinner such a duet of despair was croaked by Murry and Dora as warmed the cockles of Dora's heart'.

3. On 6 June K.M. told Murry: 'I am sending you some of my notebook today. Please let me know what you think of it. I've been keeping it since I was here'.

4. K.M. replies 11 June: 'It is quite obvious upon this morning's showing that several of my letters have been lost in the post . . . and especially . . . my (I'll confess) rather precious "Note Book" of which I don't possess anything like another copy'.

[96]   [47 Redcliffe Road,
                                        Fulham,
                                        London.]
                                        [11 June, 1918.]
                                        Tuesday Evening 7.45

My darling,[1]

I got your wire: 'Fully understand about holidays Friday week alas'
at lunchtime today. How hateful this business of wires is – it's always
like hearing your voice far away at the end of a long tunnel.

This morning your Saturday & Monday letters came. The Monday
one was very black; and of course I got frightened & depressed. It's
awful – the thought of your just hanging on there torturing yourself
until I come down. And yet I feel so deeply that it's wrong for you to
come back here to London. You simply can't live properly in these
rooms: they're a death trap – hateful & malign. I want to burn them
up. Darling, we'll come back together and then you must go to
Garsington. I'll come down every week-end until the Elephant is
ready. Oh, I don't know whether you won't hate the suggestion and
think that I'm pushing you away again. You know I'm not, don't you?
We settled that once and for all.

No, you didn't lose one of my letters last week-end. There was the
Friday night letter and nothing but the note on Sunday until Monday.
For once I was really too tired. I was done up absolutely. I couldn't
remember anything at all. I'm ever so much better to-day, but I'm not
as they say 'what I was'. It's terribly hard for me to attend to anything
– hard to form words into sentences. So I forgot to answer all the
things you spoke to me. I didn't forget them; I just couldn't grasp
them quite when I wanted to.

If it weren't for the despair, I should have said that I was suffering
the same thing as you when you wrote your Monday letter. I had no
energy; but I wasn't in despair, particularly. I would have given
anything to be drunk. (Before I forget, the review was excellent and I
was very glad to have the postcards. I like to know the kind of place
you're in, because if I try to gather anything out of the impressions
your letters give me I am left with something that is a hell one day and
a divine fairy land another.) Getting your Saturday & Monday letters
together this morning was a queer shock.

Well, I suppose there's nothing to be done with your depression
worm. I wish I could comfort you, but there's not much comfort to be

got out of a thing like me, because I only have to glance at your letter, I don't really have to read the words – the shape and fashion of the letters tells me – to be utterly cast down until one morning one of your letters comes with sunlight & happiness dancing all over it. Then I blink and smile & jump up again. We are like that, aren't we worm?

I don't think much of this life. I can't say I hate it exactly. I can't get it into focus to direct my hate upon it. It just surrounds me like a mist of dust. I twiddle my legs off in the morning & twiddle them back again at night, but what comes between or follows after I don't really know. I have a vague recollection of having tried hard to concentrate and squeeze something out of my brain: but what or why, I don't know. I suppose someone will find me out soon; but before that I shall be down with you, I hope. Then, I feel, everything will be better. I shall look at you & you will look at me, & something will happen. Lord if you knew how that Cornwall train seems to my imagination to race straight into heaven. I'm almost frightened of finding myself in it. I feel that I might do something stupid like leaning out to get hold of a sunbeam, and that would be the end of me.

Well, my Wig wife, I love and adore you – but I feel more like your rag-doll than your live Boge husband just now[2]

C U R S E   T H E   O F F I C E !

1. J.M. replies to K.M.'s letters of 8 June: 'I had a divine letter from you this morning . . .'; and 10 June: 'Here's my *third* letter . . .'.
2. K.M. replies 13 June: 'I shall not write much today, I am too worried about you'.

---

[97]   [47 Redcliffe Road,
                                              Fulham,
                                              London.]
                                    [14 June, 1918.]
                                    Friday Evening

My precious darling,

I don't believe you get a Sunday post. As far as I can make out you never get any letters of mine on Sunday: so I'll write this to catch the post to-night and then you may get it on Saturday afternoon.

As I told you in my wire & in the little note I sent you so as to reach you to-morrow morning, I feel ever so much better. Still, I'm going to see Crofty[1] to-morrow, though I shouldn't have gone unless I'd met him. To-day it's been raining, and everybody else in the world seemed to know it was going to. They all came out with coats and umbrellas, except me. So, as I was in my thin grey suit and as I had to ride home from the Foreign Office on the top of a bus, I got wet. But if you'd seen the speed with which I changed into my grey flannel, you would have been quite certain that I was doing my part of the bargain. I don't really mind this weather, as it's not really cold; but I do hope there's sunshine when I come down to Looe. I should love doing nothing in the sun.

I had a note from Sullivan at Garsington this morning. He seems comfortable enough and writes of everybody being 'extraordinarily kind', so that's all right. I can't help feeling a bit jealous of his holiday though, because I think I'm suffering from exactly the same 'brain-fag' as he, and have to do his work into the bargain. It's horribly mean of me I know; that's why I have to confess to somebody, not somebody but to you. But I simply daren't take another dose of sick-leave under the present circumstances, unless I was certain of being absolutely rejected for the army, which I'm not. But I will take another chunk this winter – and for that reason it's not a bad thing to keep in touch with Crofty. As I say, I'm a mean little sneak; but it can't be helped.

I don't think anyone will worry about the agreement,[2] really. They would have caught me out at reference time if there'd really been any danger; and there's nothing illegal in taking a house on an agreement, worm. That's one of the ills all flesh is heir to – even that of undischarged bankrupts.

As I said in my note, you aren't telling me how you are getting along. I've had not a word about your weight for nearly a fortnight now. You *must* tell me. If that's not part of the bargain, then I don't know what is. Because you don't tell me, I naturally worry and think you are keeping something back.

This time to-day week I shall be *actually at Looe*. And though I've come to learn that a week can be a very long time when it's in front of you; it seems a very short one when I look backwards. It seems to me that I can touch last Friday with the tip of my fingers. Oh, lord, to think of having you in my arms again – snuggling up, even: to be rid again of this 'peaky' feeling of loneliness. To-day week. O hell take the week! Send me a long letter to-morrow, please.

Boge.[3]

I must say how decent L.M. has been. She came on Wednesday &
massaged my head wh: did me a tremendous lot of good. On Thursday
I was very tired in the head again, so I sent her a p.c. And she came
again – she's just been – and did it to-night. It's better than a bottle of
champagne.

    1. Arthur Croft-Hill (1870–1944). A kindly doctor who had attended the
Murrys since 1914.
    2. K.M. had asked on 13 June: '*Re* Elephant. Are you "legally" free to sign
the agreement in view of the fact that you're an undischarged bankrupt?'.
    3. K.M. replies 16 June: 'I feel I have such a great deal to write to you
today'.

------

[98]   [47 Redcliffe Road,
                                                              Fulham,
                                                              London.]
                                                    [16 June, 1918.]
                                                Sunday Afternoon.

My precious Wig.[1]
    I felt very, very chirpy indeed yesterday morning when I got your
Friday letter. It was wonderful; and I never felt such a sham as I did
when I marched off to Crofty at 12 o'clock. But the die was cast, and I
had to. He was extraordinarily nice, banged me about, said I wasn't
ill, but wasn't strong enough really for office work, told me to be very
careful, was very glad I was going to live near Hampstead Heath, and
finally said I must have one half-day off at least every week (and that he
would give me a certificate to that effect) and finally that the very best
thing for me was a course of arsenic and iron injections. So I, with the
weekly half-holiday singing in my head, said 'Yes, please' without
thinking that it wd. probably cost at least five guineas; and I had the
first on the spot. I'm to have two more before I come down to you: and
nine when I come back.
    So that's the end of that story. Weighing it all up, I think the half
holiday will be cheap at five guineas. Think of it, Wig, in the
Elephant! One day in the week I shall come home at lunch-time and
not have to go back any more. It's to be in the middle of the week.
Thursday I think. It'll make things pretty different, won't it?
    I haven't seen anything of that strawberry glut yet. But my paper
to-day says that there may be plenty to-morrow: if I can get any at 1/- a

lb, I'll make the jam. I asked my mother yesterday. She said she didn't leave them overnight, but put them straight in the pan. Her strawberry jam last year was jolly good. So I think I'll risk that. No water, she says, and agrees with you.

I'll bring the large suit case and all the implements for making myself look a little gentleman. I'll not go so far as a boiled shirt though. Your idea about the blue serge is good enough; but I must get the missing button sewn on. I won't forget the belt, and I'll buy myself a couple of cricket shirts. One of my two pairs of white flannel trousers has been fairly gobbled up by the moths: and the laundry woman, very rightly, refused to wash it. So I shall have 1 clean pair and the old pair of grey flannels – they've got some green paint on them; but they've also got a pronounced crease – so I'll think they'll do. I'm very weak on coats to wear with my cricket shirt. My black velvet one is down in Garsington. Will slippers do? Or do I need to buy myself some pumps? Say but the word.

Oh, Lord, it's really *very* near now – very, very near. I'm getting everything tidied up now. Last night I finished the front page article for the *Times*. Next week I have to write a leader, the political notes & a review for the *Nation*. 'Twill all be finished on Thursday. Yesterday afternoon I finished the monthly report in fine style – the arsenic having already begun to course thro' my veins – and it only remains to correct the proofs. So it seems to me that things are going very well indeed.

Of course, now I shan't be able to write anything coherent until I see you. That's how I'm always taken. I feel the imbecile smile spreading over my face and I have to give way.

I'm going to lunch with Chaddie on Tuesday at some place in Jermyn street of which I couldn't catch the name. However, it has two little trees in front so that ought to be good enough.

Your *Boge*[2]

1. J.M. replies to K.M.'s two letters of 14 June: 'I hasten to throw this letter into the wall to tell you . . . my way to make Strawbug Jam'; and 'Wednesday evening when L.M. came and brushed you and Thursday morning note are come'.

2. K.M. replies 17 June: 'Your telegram, which arrived at break of day, found me *toute émue*'.

[99]   [2 Portland Villas,
                                                     Hampstead,
                                                        London.]
                                          [Winter 1918/1919?]

Wig darling,[1]
   This morning, I promise cross my heart straight Dinkum (is that
right?) will be the last, the very last, of our awful moments. I love you
with all my heart & soul; and I feel that, now that our decision has
been taken, we shall sail right away to a wonderful future. The weight
that has been lifted from my heart is tremendous. The reason why I
was so black this morning is that there was still a shred of fear – it
wouldn't be me if there wasn't – because I am so longing for you to get
strong for the voyage, so impatient that it should all be here, now. I
feel I can hardly wait.
   I won't be like it again my darling – never. Believe me. I feel so in
my bones that we have done the right thing that even though I give an
explanation I can't really understand what happened this morning. It
was my feverish anxiety to see you strong.
   But life has suddenly become simple & clear & bright again. I had
forgotten what that meant. For over a year now I have felt that we were
struggling in a net. I knew, deep down in my heart, that it would be
wrong & disastrous if you were to go away without me, that the old
six-months plan was merely a self-deception – and yet I could see
nothing else to do. But now we are free from the net. I am *certain* about
everything
   Oh my darling – our little home – our verandah, our house – our
exquisite peaceful home – our children – our life – darling, darling
heart.

                                   Boge.

   1. This is a very difficult letter to date. It was enclosed in an unposted
envelope addressed: 'Mrs Murry/2 Portland Villas/East Heath Road/Hamp-
stead/N.W.3.' On the envelope K.M. wrote: 'To be kept pour toujours!'.
   Murry subsequently assigned the tentative date 1921; but K.M. was not in
London in 1921. Internal evidence suggests that late 1918 or early 1919 is
more likely. K.M. had had tuberculosis for a year then; and she had decided
to stay on in England for the winter rather than go away without Murry.

October – December 1919

From August 1918 until September 1919, Katherine, Murry and L.M. lived at 2 Portland Villas, Hampstead. 1918 ended with their giving a party for what was to be K.M.'s last Christmas in England. Early in 1919 Murry was appointed editor of the *Athenaeum*. Katherine, struggling in spite of her illness to live a normal life, supervised the household and entertained Murry's friends. Regularly reviewing fiction for the *Athenaeum*, she managed to accomplish very little creative writing.

Warned not to endure another English winter, Katherine was talking by mid-1919 of once more leaving England. This time she decided to go with L.M. to the Italian Riviera. In September 1919, Murry escorted the two women to San Remo, where they settled into the Casetta Deerholm at Ospedaletti. On 10 October he set out for England.

This separation was to last eight months – until May 1920. To help bridge the gap, the familiar pattern of daily letter-writing was re-established. Letters, however, did not prevent K.M. from becoming increasingly depressed about her health and resentful towards Murry. Finally, in December 1919, a bitter outburst made him decide to join his wife in Ospedaletti for Christmas.

[100]   [Paris.]
                                          [2 October, 1919.]
                                          11.30 Thursday

My darling Mouse,

I got here (Paris) at 9 this morning, and am catching the boat-train at 12. They say we may have to stay the night at Folkestone. Therefore, although it has been a rush, I thought it better to give Paris a miss altogether and catch the boat to-day. The train is crowded, but

I've managed to get a place. I only hope it won't be gone when I return.

My love & my dear – how sweet that sounds really – you have all my heart. Again I feel that its just been taken out of me and left behind: and there it will remain with you – hiding under my old grey hat I expect – until I come and fetch it & you back for ever.

Good-bye my darling. Everything is going well with me

Boge.[1]

1. K.M. replies 6 October: 'Your postcard from Paris has just come'.

[101]   2 Portland [Villas,
                                                   Hampstead,
                                                   London.]
No 5[1]   [7 October, 1919.]
                                                   Tuesday Night

My darling Worm,[2]

I didn't get a letter to-night; anyhow that was too much to hope for, as I had two yesterday. I thought I should find yr review of Swinnerton[3] this morning when I got to the office; but I didn't. I suppose the registered post is a day later than the ordinary one. I am counting on it to-morrow, Wednesday: otherwise it will be too late.

Yesterday morning Sheppard dashed into the office to see me, and I dined with him to-night. Vanessa & Duncan[4] were there, and during dinner Duncan spoke of a house to let at a place called Wilmington on the South Downs. He hadn't seen it himself but someone had told him. It's not much to go upon, but I think its quite enough to make me try that part of the country first. So I think I shall try to make arrangements to get away this week-end.

Before I forget. Last night I went by request off to the Langham[5] to dine I had to go to the play afterwards for the paper, so that I was there only an hour. I think yr. Father[6] was very friendly (perhaps friendly wd. be more accurate) and, what is more important, he spoke of a plan of going to the South for a fortnight before he sailed. But he spoke of Mentone. Whether he wants to go there particularly, or whether our laying on the colours thick about San Remo is the cause I don't know; nor do I know whether it's politic that he should stay in San Remo in any case; but 'I give you the information to use as you may think fit'. I was also informed that Jean[7] & Chaddie were to depart the next day for Wood Hay,[8] and that they had such a lot of packing that it fitted very well that I had to go to the play – which was a relief, because I was rather worried lest it should be thought rather casual on my part. I think J & C were friendly. They asked me down for a week-end. I said of course delighted; but I'll see myself in hell before I go.

I gave my spare seat for the play to Sydney Waterlow, who seems to have developed an amazing concern for you & friendliness for me. 'Well, I am glad to see you Jack' – 'Tell me all about Katherine'. I don't know whether it was sincere or not; but I was quite grateful for it anyhow, and I don't feel at all sorry that he's going to be my lodger[9] – except that the blankets are short. The reason for that is that Gertie sleeps with Violet[10] still, one of them in the little camp bed, so that 3 lots of blankets are already being used. I shall buy another pair to-morrow.

I told you before we left that Edward Dent[11] has become one of [your] great admirers. He came in to-day to ask whether you would like anyone to visit you at Ospedaletti. He had a couple of old aunts who live permanently at Nice, to whom he had spoken (while they were in London) about you, and they wanted to know whether you would like to meet anybody. I didn't like to risk anything. Apparently these old ladies know everybody from Mentone to San Remo, so that if you want a very old lady to come & take tea with you, you've only to let me know.

I won't shut this letter up yet in case there's something from you to-morrow morning

Wednesday Morning

It was a good job I kept my letter open. Two from you came this morning – one postmarked Oct 3, the other Oct. 4. You hadn't yet received the letter-card I sent from Paris. It was written in a terrible hurry. I only arrived in Paris at 10 o'clock & the Folkestone train left at 12. But still I thought the address was legible. So perhaps you received it on the evening of Oct. 4.

Please don't think I ever, *in any way*, gave L.M. to understand that she would have anything to do with our lives once we are together again. I never did anything of the kind. Quite as profoundly as you, I can't get on with her, – and if she has suggested that I gave her to understand that she wd. still be with us – it simply isn't true. The *most* I could ever have said is that I didn't know what wd. happen.

I'm very disappointed about the *bonne* and about the water. As for the Banca d'Italia – if I were you, to make sure of not being left, I would do what I did. Send a self-cheque to Kay registered & ask him to send it out in English notes. It only took me a week.

Bad cess to her for breaking our lovely plate. I verily believe she'd break us in the same way – by leaning on us (you especially) – if we let her.

I'm terribly constipated – terribly. No figs that's what it is.

Your letters are wonderful. How do you write them. There's a bit in your letter to-day (I won't tell you, because it will make you proud) which is pure genius for wit. No, there never has been anyone like you since Jane Austen & she wasn't really like you. Look after yourself, my precious, precious.[12]

1. In his letter of 5 October, the third written since returning to England, Murry announced: I'm going to number my letters henceforward, so that you can tell me in yours that they have been received, and see whether any are missing. Will you do the same? Then every time I write I will say at the top of my letter 3 & 4 received, and I too will know whether any are missing'.

2. J.M. replies to K.M.'s letters dated 3 and 4 October by Murry: 'Your card has just come'; and 'No letter from you yesterday'.

3. K.M.'s review of Frank Swinnerton's novel *September* appeared on 10 October.

4. Vanessa Stephen (1879–1961) had married Clive Bell in 1907; but in 1915 she went to live permanently with a fellow artist, Duncan Grant (1885–1978).

5. A hotel in Langham Place where Harold Beauchamp was staying.

6. Katherine's father, widowed in 1918, came to London in August 1919 with his youngest daughter, Jeanne. This, his first meeting with Katherine since 1912, was apparently clouded by the uneasy relationship between himself and Murry. The extra financial help with her medical expenses that Katherine had hoped for was not forthcoming; and although he did visit Menton in November, he spent only half a day with his daughter in Ospedaletti, near San Remo.

7. Jeanne Beauchamp, who married Charles Renshaw, was K.M.'s youngest and best-liked sister.

8. Wood Hay was the New Forest house in which Harold Beauchamp had established his daughters Chaddie and Jeanne.

9. The arrangement whereby Sydney Waterlow lived at 2 Portland Villas as a lodger in Katherine's absence suited Murry very well.

10. Gertie and Violet were live-in maids.

11. Edward Joseph Dent (1876–1957) had contributed to the *Blue Review*, and was music critic for the *Athenaeum*.

12. K.M. replies 11 October: 'Just a line more. I've got three letters this afternoon'.

---

[102]   2 Portland Villas
                                              [Hampstead,
                                              London.]
No 7.   [9 October 1919]
                                              Thursday 10.30 p.m.

My precious wife,[1]

Your Monday letter came this evening to say you had my Paris card. Thank Heaven. I can't imagine why it took so long, seeing that it was posted at a post office before 12 on the Thursday. Surely my English letters – the first was sent on Friday night – will have begun to arrive on the Tuesday. They would if they did things as well in France & Italy as they do in England. Your letters are getting here in 3 days regularly.

You don't tell me how you are. If it was anybody else – someone not quite such a darling as Wig – I should be able to conclude that you were feeling well because your letter was happy. But with you, that doesn't really work. You might have two legs & an arm off, but you'd forget to tell me because of your joy at a letter from me saying my constipation was better. So I must ask you just to forget all about me for half a page of every letter and say exactly how you are – even your temperature.

To-day I've sent you my little present. Please don't think it absurd. It's just a spoon for you to eat your porridge & soup with. The worst of it is you'll always have to use it. I'm very sorry. But I thought it would look nice on your tray. Will it? By the way, darling, don't worry if it doesn't arrive at the same time as this letter, though it was posted today & the letter won't be posted until to-morrow. Your registered letters arrived quite a day & a half after the letter saying they were posted at the same time. And I had a letter today from a man in Spain saying that a registered letter took two days longer than an ordinary one. That's worth remembering if ever you are pressed for time with your review. If you are posting on or after Saturday copy to go in the following week, don't register it. Only register if you post before Saturday.

Another thing that worries me a little. How about your money? Has anything arrived at the Banca d'Italia? Or are you getting it direct from Kay?[2] And how are you off anyhow? I can easily send you some.

I'm jolly glad you've got that revolver.[3] What a cursed shame about that water. If I don't hear good news about it to-morrow, I shall write Mr. Vince[4] a type-written stinker on office paper.

Sydney Waterlow arrived last night, puffing and blowing. I don't think he's going to be a nuisance at all; and he doesn't seem to eat a frightful lot. At any rate Violet seems to give me such a great deal that he comes in very useful for eating it up. He never gets back from his office till 7.30; so I'm going to arrange to be home as often as I can for tea at 4.30 – and have a quiet 3 hours all to myself.

I lunched with Tom Moult[5] to-day. He's nice, but extraordinarily childish. His conceit of his own work is quite staggering. I couldn't get out of asking him & Bessie to dinner on Wednesday; it'll be so funny to see what happens to Sydney. In the restaurant I met Clive with Mary H.[6] Clive very anxious to know whether you would like to meet anybody at San Remo. He apparently knows someone, an Italian, who knows all the local intelligentsia. I didn't commit myself.

I had to buy a new double saucepan to-day: hope it doesn't get broken. Violet also wants a medium-sized saucepan. I'll get an aluminium one. I'm dead nuts on getting the furnishings together for our house.

I wonder will this be your birthday letter.[7] It's meant to be. Just for a moment you must imagine I'm under my old hat. You're in your little room. Now I'm coming ever so softly – just tripped over the gold & red plush bookcase – into your room with your spoon in my hands. Now I've put the spoon in your lap. Now I've got you folded tight. Many happy returns of the day – my little Wig, mouse, darling. This is the last birthday we'll ever be apart – the last, the last, the very last

Boge.[8]

1. J.M. replies to K.M.'s letter of 6 October: 'I have just had an interview with a bonne . . .'.

2. The manager of the London branch of the Bank of New Zealand, where K.M.'s monthly allowance from her father was paid.

3. K.M. had bought a revolver for self-protection.

4. Thomas Vince, the disreputable English owner of the Casetta Deerholm in Ospedaletti which Katherine was renting. The house was without running water until 10 October.

5. Thomas Moult (b. 1895), poet and journalist who had contributed to *Rhythm*, and was married to Bessie, a fellow writer.

6. Mary Hutchinson (1889–1977), a cousin of Lytton Strachey, was

married to the barrister St. John Hutchinson. She and Clive Bell, while not
wishing to divorce their respective spouses, were for some years intimate
companions.
7. K.M.'s birthday was on 14 October.
8. K.M. replies 13 October: 'It is not only that the spoon is the most
exquisite perfect little spoon . . .'.

---

[103]   2 Portland [Villas,
                                              Hampstead,
                                               London.]
                                         [11 October, 1919.]
No 8.   Saturday morning
                                            12 o'clock

My darling Mouse,
   I didn't get a letter from you last night or this morning, alas. Not
that I worry. But the post has been so kind lately that I began to form
the habit of looking for a letter every evening. I hope one comes
to-night, though, for it's Saturday and if I don't get it, I shall have to
wait until Monday. I don't like the idea of that.
   First, I've been hearing good things about you. Tommy[1] told me
the other day that he was talking to a sub-editor of the *Weekly
Dispatch*, just a hardened professional journalist, and he asked him
what he thought of the *Athenaeum*.[2] He said he thought it jolly good,
but one thing especially. He would buy it for K.M.'s article[3] alone,
every week. The only brick was that he had concluded that K.M. was
some other K.M. – Tommy couldn't remember the name – but
Tommy put him right. So keep it up my darling & send me an extra
article when you can. You'll be making a terrific reputation for
yourself before the winter's out.
   The *A.* is producing an impression. The *Lit. Sup.* has gone in for a
tremendous advertising scheme. 100,000 copies are to be given away
next week & then there's this *London Mercury* a new monthly (run by
the awful Jack Squire[4]) which announces a list of contributors
including nearly all ours, except you & me. So we shall have to pull
hard together during this winter, and make the paper as good as a
paper can be.
   I utterly agree with your criticism of the last number before I
reached home. What my bright friends had done, was not to send out
any books for review in spite of my detailed instructions, but to print a

number of reviews I had put in the basket to be returned for rewriting. However, I think I've got my hands on the helm again now. But it's a nuisance that our own advertising scheme involves so much work, writing pamphlets & what not. And I do so want a good Dramatic critic. E.M.F.[5] is very much off. I don't think anything of his notice of the Tolstoy play this week, which was anyhow rottenly bad. And now he's gone off into the country. So I've had to turn to this week and do a notice of *The Merchant of Venice* which I saw (with Arthur) & enjoyed last night. Tell me honestly what you think of it. But even if it's good I can't go on doing the plays myself: its too much work. Can you think of anybody? D. L. Murray[6] has also gone off to take a job in Oxford.

It's very, very cold here. I have to have a hot-water bottle in my bed to prevent myself from freezing. But there's a bright sun & that makes all the difference. My brother says orders for my book[7] are coming in well. I begin to wish it was better & different.

Sydney W. has now gone off for a week to stay with his wife at his mother-in-law's at Surbiton. But honestly I find him very decent. He talks a good deal, but it's easy to switch him on to books & he's quite well read. And Violet doesn't think him a nuisance.

I'm lunching with Eliot[8] to-day & then we are going for a walk. There's a wasp buzzing round the room. I wonder how he managed to survive the cold. I can't get any anthracite yet, alas. So the old stove is still down in the cellar. Wing[9] is too wicked for words. He eats everything. Last night he'd eaten quite half of the cake I had with my milk then he put his head right in the milk-jug, then drank it out of the saucepan. Also I can't keep him off the table at dinner. As often as I throw him off my back, he jumps on again. (He gets onto the table by way of my back). And then he's a dirty grub. I don't believe he's washed himself since we went away. He says to me that he didn't wash as a sign of grief. But I don't believe it. Athenaeum,[10] who's quite nice again & well, gets very angry with him. Wing just follows & treads on his tail all the while. If A goes to sleep W. jumps on him; if A. gets on a chair W. follows. Last night A. was on your chair & W. jumped on. A gave him a terrific box on the ear; but W. doesn't mind He gets wickeder & wickeder – an absolute larrikin with the most innocent eyes.

Did my birthday present come on your birthday? A letter this evening please, my darling love.

Boge.[11]

1. H. M. Tomlinson (1873–1958) was a close friend of Murry's and affectionately called 'Tommy'. For a time he was literary editor of the *Nation*.

2. When the faltering *Athenaeum* was reconstituted by Arnold Rowntree in April 1919 as a weekly 'Journal of English and Foreign Literature, Science, the Fine Arts, Music and the Drama', Murry was appointed editor at a salary of £800 p.a.

3. K.M. reviewed fiction each week until December 1920. Murry published her collected reviews in 1930 as *Novels and Novelists*.

4. J. C. Squire (1884–1958), influential literary editor of the *New Statesman* from 1913–1919, founded and became first editor of the *London Mercury* in October 1919. A Georgian poet who was hostile to Modernism, Squire's power made him hated by his rivals. Virginia Woolf described him as 'more repulsive than words can express, and malignant into the bargain.'

5. E. M. Forster (1879–1970), novelist and member of the original Bloomsbury group, whom Murry had tried to enlist as a contributor to the *Blue Review* in 1913.

6. D. L. Murray (1888–1962), a friend of Murry's since their employment together at the War Office, became a regular reviewer for the *Athenaeum*. He was editor of the *T.L.S.* from 1938–1944.

7. *The Critic in Judgement* was published by the Hogarth Press in May 1919; but Murry is probably referring to his *Poems: 1917–18* printed by his brother on their own Heron Press in Hampstead, December 1918–June 1919.

8. T. S. Eliot (1885–1965), the poet, whom K.M. had met and admired in 1917 (it was she who read aloud 'Prufrock', on its first appearance in *Prufrock and Other Observations*, to a gathering at Garsington). On the strength of 'Prufrock' Murry tried unsuccessfully to obtain Eliot as an assistant editor on the *Athenaeum*; he was able to enlist him as a literary critic.

9. A much loved kitten of the Murrys'.

10. Wingley's brother and playfellow.

11. K.M. replies 15 October: 'I am in the middle of a review of Brett Young . . .'.

---

[104]   2 Portland Villas
                                              [Hampstead,
196 days[1]   London.]
                                          [17 October, 1919.]

My precious Worm,[2]

Your mottled Monday letter came this morning. How wonderful your descriptions are – 'like living inside a pearl'. No-one but you has the genius for these things nowadays. Why the devil the whole literary world is not at your feet, I'll never understand. You are the only *genius* in the whole bunch of good ones among us.

It thrilled me to think you thought so Much of the *Athenaeum* – too much? I don't know. I agree with you about the American letter[3] as too particular. But doesn't the man write well for an American; he really writes. By the way, old girl, I would like to give D. H. Lawrence a leg-up. What do you say to writing on *Sons & Lovers* one week – either extra to or instead of your ordinary novels; saying how it stands out etc. You know what the average is like nowadays & you can speak your mind. It might help him a bit, you know. Anyhow, I'll send it across. (In passing, I put your cheque in your last letter with a stamp on the back.)

Ripman's[4] an idea. I'll get into touch with him & see whether he wouldn't look after modern languages from the educational point of view. L.M. – just a passage-to the lavatory[5] – is unspeakable. That really puts the lid on her. Your notepaper is exactly like mottled soap – but I can read what's on it. You can't tell how happy your happy letters make me. Nothing matters. I can do mountains of work. I've really done ¾ of that announcement list[6] to-day. To-night I have to go to the play. I'm taking Arthur with me. Thank heaven James Strachey[7] is back again though.

I have two determinations – one to make the paper a success against all competition this winter – the other to write a novel with among other things some real you and me love in it. There are many things to be got into it. I don't know how I shall tackle it; I can't get a scheme, and don't see what good it would do if I had one. I'm sure I wasn't built to work with schemes. One door suddenly opening out of a dark chamber, then another, and another – that's the only way my mind ever works. So, as soon as I can get a breathing space, I shall start in – anywhere, anyhow all I have is a house (very important) & a woman & a man (both very vague). I'm terribly afraid it will be what the critics call a romance. But I can't really say anything until I've dug the first hole. What it must be at all costs is a you & me novel – no rotten old *Still Life*: to show these devils what subtlety & delicateness (in joy & pain) life is capable of. I hope it won't get too big – or no-one will ever publish it.

But first – *Cinnamon*[8] must be finished. I was reading a play by Robert Greene – an Elizabethan – not much good – the other day & I found he had a girl called Angelica, & that he used her name rhythmically & repeatedly just as I have done. That's rather disturbing because they'll say – if they ever say anything, which they wont: no-one ever said a word about my book of *Poems*[9] – I copied.

This is all very egotistic seeing you are the genius & I ain't. But who can I tell it to but you?

Your devoted loving
Boge.[10]

1. In his letter of 13 October Murry announced: 'In future I won't number my letters except by the number of days to May 1 1920. Thus the next will be 199 and so on . . .'.
2. J.M. replies to K.M.'s letter of 13 October: 'The weather has completely changed'.
3. Conrad Aiken's 'Letters from America I. Philosophy for the Flute', appeared on 10 October.
4. K.M. had suggested Walter Ripmann (1869–1947), her admired former language professor at Queen's College, as a contributor on languages or the production of books.
5. K.M. had told J.M. (13 October) that on asking L.M. why she didn't make her room nice, L.M. replied that she hadn't unpacked 'as you are sending me away in April and at any rate my room is just a passage – isn't it? – to the lavatory'.
6. A publishers' 'announcement' supplement to the *Athenaeum*, advertising all the books to be published that winter.
7. James Strachey (1887–1967), younger brother of Lytton and translator of Freud, wrote dramatic criticism for the *Athenaeum*. Of his appointment Virginia Woolf wrote in March 1919: 'Our chief amusement now is Murry and the *Athenaeum*. He is in a state of high exaltation, something like a Prime Minister, for everyone buzzes about asking for appointments, and needless to say, *though please don't repeat this*, the Stracheys have induced him much against his better judgement, to adopt James as Dramatic critic . . . James . . . by pulling the right wires has now got a comfortable income out of Murry'.
8. *Cinnamon and Angelica*, a verse play published in 1920.
9. *Poems: 1917–18*, published by the Heron Press in 1918.
10. K.M. replies 22 October: 'I owe you a small explanation'.

---

[105]

2 Portland Villas
[Hampstead,
London.]
[19 October, 1919.]
Sunday

194 days

My darling,

It's just struck quarter past five & I've just finished my tea. There's a low mist everywhere. I've had the day absolutely to myself. I finished the Butler review[1] by lunch-time. I'm afraid it's not very good: I seem to have said already all that I have to say about him, and had I realised this in time, I would have got someone else to do him. After lunch I wrote a leader; after the leader – 3.30 – I went out for a walk along to Spaniards & over the fields, and got back at 4.45. Now, when I've finished this, I must wash myself & tidy & go off to the Langham. I feel very virtuous, having broken the back of a busy week. I also feel rather angry that I have had no opportunity to get on with my own work; but I think I shall manage a little next week.

Wingley is making Athenaeum very angry; and every now & then A. turns on him with a snarl and gives him a bag. He doesn't seem to care in the least; but turns resignedly and devotes himself to tearing the lining out of my slippers. I do wish he'd put a little of his perseverance into cleaning himself.

Violet has gone off to Bexley. Everything is quiet. I can just hear through the open window – it's not quite so cold to-day – someone whistling and further away still the occasional toot of a motor-horn. Then a woman calls a cat. Wingley makes a dash at the tea-table-cloth. Everything is quite separate and finished, before the next sound begins. A curious, not unpleasant kind of quiet.

At this point I begin, as always, to wish I hadn't to go out. It seems that there couldn't be a better time to work than this; and I begin to wonder what I shall say to your father. Not that he's more difficult than anybody else – on the contrary. But I realise that I never have anything to say. If ever I do say anything to anybody it's only with the most appalling effort. It never comes from me; I seem to make a desperate grasp & pick it somehow out of the air.[2] I have become, for good & all, a one woman show. I suppose I don't say much to you, really; but what I do say comes out of me. There are not any of these griping pangs of producing a few words utterly alien to one's self.

The older I get, the more I am amazed at the amount people talk and at the things they say. Compared to them I feel myself like a deep, dark pool, and I wonder whether there's anything at all going on inside it. I trust there is; but who can say? All that I can say is that, if there is, it is something utterly different not from what is going on inside other people – I don't know anything about that – but from what they say & talk about. It all seems so incredibly childish – incredibly – never to touch even the fringe of important things. Babble, babble, babble.

No, I'm happy with you. I don't know whether the things we talk about are important; but I feel that when we are together something important *is*; and that, it seems, is all that I can say.

Well, that's a very solemn little deliverance. Thank goodness, you will understand it.

Your devoted
Boge.[3]

1. Review of *Samuel Butler, author of Erewhon* by H. Festing Jones (*Athenaeum*, 24 October 1919).

2. After one visit to K.M. and J.M. Virginia Woolf commented on Murry's conversational difficulties: 'He scarcely speaks; makes one feel that most speaking is useless; but as he has a brain of his own I don't mind this. Beside it is more shyness than purpose.'

3. K.M. replies 24 October: 'I can't understand why you have never received my letter about the spoon'.

---

[106]

[2 Portland Villas,
Hampstead,
London.]
[20 October, 1919.]
Monday Night
11.15 p.m.

193 days.

My precious heart,[1]

It ended in an orgy to-day – two plays, one in the afternoon, Trench's *Napoleon*, by the Stage Society, one in the evening an American play all about N.W. Canada, jolly good. But I don't want to go to any more plays at all, at all. I don't quite know what to do about it. D. L. Murray has gone off to Oxford. It would have been a chance to make some-one dramatic critic – but who? Now James Strachey has returned & wants to do some things. But I must find a regular second-string. I simply will not go myself any more.

Your Thursday letter came this morning. There was cold & hail – horrible. For goodness sake, darling, don't stint yourself in firing for some preposterous idea of putting money by. I'll look after that part of the business. I comfort myself with what I remember Vince saying about the rainy weeks in October & then its setting in fine again. I hate to think of you as the least bit uncomfortable. Perhaps to-morrow's letter will tell me that it's become fine again. I've come to the conclusion that you can never have got my present, because even if you thought a silver spoon stupid, as it probably was, I know you would have said something about it – pretended that it was the most lovely thing in the world. But far worse than the losing of the spoon is the thought that your birthday came & brought you nothing from me.

Darling, you do quite right to expect a letter everyday. I send one every day – or to speak the absolute truth, I write one everyday. This one for instance won't get posted till I go out to-morrow morning. So it may happen, though I'll try my best to see that it doesn't, that you will get nothing on one day & 2 letters the next. About once a week that happens with your letters.

I saw your Pa last night. I think we got on pretty well, largely because he made the running. I feel rather sick that he should have made no attempt to stay at San Remo, but I urged him to go to Mentone rather than Cannes, and I fancy that he was inclined to do as I said. Moreover he swore that he would go to see you. I fancy he was rather annoyed with Chaddie who has apparently written that she can't get up to see him off because she's so busy at Wood Hay. He's promised to let me know when he departs, & I've promised to see him off. I must say that I do like him, very much; but at the same time I don't like his way of keeping away from you. Perhaps that's my imagination, though

My darling, do look after yourself. I've just been reading your letter again, where you say 'you are *so* parky', and I'm alarmed because I see no mention of a fire. Please, please don't go without one even if it costs 10 francs a day. I feel that you might very well have caught a chill that day.

I'll keep this letter open until to-morrow morning to see what news it will bring.

——————

Yes, I had 2 letters from you this morning – written on yr. birthday, saying that you'd got the spoon, the other on Oct. 17. That gives some idea of how bad the post can be. One letter posted 3 days after the other, arrives the same time. I was awfully glad to have it. That idea that yr. birthday had gone without your having any sign from me was horrible. Everything's all right now.

But – do all that you can to get your cough under – how stupid of me! As if you weren't. I had – by the way – a very nice letter from old Gogarty[2] the other day which I'll send with my next. He enclosed quite a charming little poem.

I must try to get home very early on Thursday next & tidy up the garden. There are still a few very belated tobacco plants, and the geraniums in front of the door are still in bud, but such a pale anaemic bud. I'll put a lot of bulbs in.

Your devoted
Boge.³

5pm
Tuesday
Oh, Lord – forgive me Wig – I've been worked off my head again to-day & have forgotten to post this. Boge

1. J.M. replies to K.M.'s letters of 13 and 14 October: 'It is not only that the spoon is the most exquisite perfect little spoon . . .'; 16 October: 'My review is just finished, too, thank goodness'; and 17 October: 'The four pounds and letters . . . both arrived last night'.
2. Oliver St. John Gogarty (1878–1957), trained in medicine, and the model for Buck Mulligan in Joyce's *Ulysses*, wrote novels, stories and poems.
3. K.M. replies 26 October: 'I am thankful you got my letter about the spoon'.

---

[107]

[2 Portland Villas,
Hampstead,
London.]
[21 October, 1919.]

[192 days]

Tuesday Evening

6.30.

My own darling,¹

Your Friday letter was here when I arrived from the office, where your review of Brett Young² arrived during the morning – first chop.

I may be imagining things but I can't help feeling from your letter that you're feeling very cheap. What are these blood-shot eyes, Worm? Have you caught a chill? I want to know. It may be only imagination, or only that I want you to get so quickly well that anything like marking time seems to me going back. Anyhow your last three letters worry me a little. Just say – please, Worm – exactly when you do feel cheap or that you're not going on just as well as you would like.

Your first letters made me feel that you were going up like this ↑ ; your last 3 I feel rather like this ⋁⋁⋁⋀ .

There has been another hard day's work at the office with a lunch with Brett for a relaxation. I do like her very much; there's a real innocence about her which is comforting. She says she is engaged in concocting a letter to you. What's more important – or less important – is that she has managed to get a ton of anthracite & I havent. Luckily, it's not quite so cold as it has been lately.

Virginia Woolf's book[3] is out: also a new one by that lady Romer Wilson.[4] They'll be sent to-morrow. They have begun to pour in now at such a rate that it will be a good thing – a necessity – to do two or even three together whenever you've the chance. Otherwise we shall get too terribly behind hand.

I'm sorry to talk so much shop; but I've had so much to do during the last week that I'm become a little *Athenaeum*. To-day I wrote to Gordon,[5] sacking him as art critic. It was jolly hard to do & I hated it. But I'm sure it was right for the paper. His writing hasn't improved an inch since he began; and it's wrong of me to sit down & rewrite his copy every week. More important still, I think he's always wrong in his judgments. He can only appreciate second-rate work. He sent up a sentence on Nina Hamnett[6] to-day that was the last straw, & I wrote, giving him his congé there & then. It's a horrid thing to do. He should have taken his work more seriously though.

The trouble is to find someone to take his place. I want to get something to balance the one-sidedness of Clive Bell & Roger Fry.[7] Shove[8] is invaluable in that way. But don't you agree with me that it's simply silly to dismiss a man like Orpen[9] with a sneer. Orpen isn't a great man; he has lots of points that jar on me – but if he isn't a better painter & a better artist than Nina Hamnett, I'd better give up running a critical paper. I want the *Athenaeum* to be judicial, to praise what is really good *wherever* it comes from. It isn't a weekly *coterie* or *Art & Letters*.[10] *Pro tem.* I've given Gordon's job to a man called Wilenski[11] who wrote on Gaudier & on Harold Gilman[12] recently. Look them up & see what you think. Read his stuff next week carefully & compare. I want your opinion very much. I wish my review of Samuel Butler had been better. It can't be helped, though. I was overworked last week.

I got your cheque for £5, which reminded me that I hadn't sent you the odd £1. It shall be done to-morrow.

By the way – the posts seem to be perfectly safe. I shouldn't worry about registering your copy for the *Athenaeum* in future.

I expect that's Violet coming up to tell me that dinners ready. Brown stew & baked apple to follow. I paid that old bookseller – Philips – the 6/- to-day. He was very pleased. This week I'll take courage & get my pass-book out & let you know the result. I think it'll be all right.

Thank goodness, I shan't have to work so hard next week.

I love you, my darling, terribly. Tell me everything about yourself. The old gardener sounded very nice. I shall try to go down to Sussex this week-end, if my cold's better.

Your own & only

Boge[13]

1. J.M. replies to K.M.'s letter of 17 October: 'The four pounds and letters . . . both arrived'.

2. 'A Plea for Less Entertainment', a review of *The Young Physician* (24 October). Francis Brett Young (1884–1954) was a prolific English writer.

3. *Night and Day*.

4. *All These Young Men*.

5. J. G. Gordon (1882–1944), lithographer and painter who wrote art criticism. Virginia Woolf wrote of him in March 1919: 'Murry has got a man called John Gordon, a very bad painter he says, to do art criticism; but I suggested he'd much better get Duncan [Grant] to do the important things at any rate'.

6. Nina Hamnett (1890–1956), portrait and landscape painter who had been employed by Roger Fry at the Omega Workshops and exhibited with the London Group in 1918.

7. Roger Fry (1866–1934), Bloomsbury art critic who in 1910 organised the first London exhibition of French Post Impressionist painting. Writing in such journals as the *Athenaeum* and *New Statesman*, he continued (along with Clive Bell) to champion new Modernist art in the face of traditionalist opposition.

8. Possibly a reference to Gerald Shove (1887–1947), Cambridge economist married to Fredegond (a cousin of Virginia Woolf). One of the Bloomsbury circle, and a conscientious objector, Shove was one of the 'agricultural dilettantes' employed by the Morrells at Garsington in 1916.

9. William Orpen (1878–1931), Slade-trained artist whose painting, exhibited at the New English Art Club, was attracting considerable interest.

10. *Art and Letters*, edited by Frank Rutter, ran from 1917–1920.

11. R. H. Wilenski (1887–1975), Oxford-educated art critic and art historian who later wrote many well-known books on art.

12. Harold Gilman (1876–1919), leader of the Camden Town School (later 'London Group') of young 'neo-realist' painters.

13. K.M. replies 26 October: 'I am thankful you got my letter about the spoon'.

---

[108]   2 Portland Villas
                                         [Hampstead,
                                         London.]
190 days   October 24 [1919.]

My precious darling,[1]

I had a very sad letter from you this morning, dated Monday last. You were sad about Mrs Waterlow being here, and also about the gardener, or the gardener's wife, turning out a fraud. Ironically, as usual, your Sunday letter, full of happiness about what the gardener was doing, arrived after the Monday one.

Oh, child, I wish I was there to comfort you. The sight of the worm in the pear is unbearable to me, I know; but I feel, I know I can bear it better than you. You don't think so & you always want to bear it for me, I know. But I am the stronger for this particular burden. I am far less sensitive, less frail than you. The vision shakes your whole being; it doesn't do that to me any more. Besides being cruder & clumsier, I have a leaden foot which other people would call a philosophy. Of course, it's nothing of the kind. It's merely a sentimental kettle-holder. I am able to take hold of things that would have burned me years ago. You haven't got a kettleholder; you're too delicate & fine.

It doesn't need to be proved. I know. But there is a proof to hand – a strange & interesting one. When you wrote to me, a fortnight ago, to say that you feared Sydney W. would bring strange women into the house, I immediately supposed that you meant a woman of the town, or something corresponding. It never faintly dawned upon me that you meant Mrs. W. That mere fact is enough to show how much cruder & less sensitive I am than you. I hang my head in shame for not having known that you meant an alien feminine influence. I ought, as your lover, to have known it. I *ought*. There's no excuse. But there it is: the damage is done. All I can say is that she never entered your room. What is most yours, is yours intact.

To-day has been dull, raining and almost close. Mrs. Lynd[2] came in to ask news of you this morning. I told her all that I could tell. Would you write to her, if you could – about the house, I mean. I know she wd do for you what she wd. never do for me.

There's not much office news. As I told you I called in Arthur to help with designing of our advertisements. I was very disappointed when Bonwick[3] this morning suddenly said to me why didn't you introduce yr. brother to me when you took over the editorship? He could have had Seears's job – S. is our kindly but utterly incompetent publicity manager. However, it's no use repining over lost opportunities. I must be satisfied that A. made a tremendous impression on Bonwick. It'll probably stand him in good stead some time.

Tell me more, darling, about the blood-shot eye. What a curse it is that we had no time to get your eyes examined & fitted with gig-lamps! Are you sure it comes from too much reading?

Wd. it be possible – returning to the *A*. – for you to get a week ahead with the novels? You see now that the advertising campaign has begun, I need to have my whole contents on the Friday previous – that is a whole week before publication. As it is, I never know what the novel article will be about until the Tuesday – so that I have to leave it out of the advertisement.

I am sending you Waley's new book of Chinese Poems.[4] You're the only person who can do them – not more than 2 columns, when you feel inclined

I weighed myself the day before yesterday – 10 stone i.e. a half-stone heavier than I was two years ago. It's not my health you have to worry about.

Unless the weather clears & the rain stops, I shall stay at home working to-morrow.

Good-bye my darling

Boge[5]

xxxxxxxx

xxxxxxx

xxxxxx

xxxxx

xxxx

xxx

xx

x

1. J.M. replies to K.M.'s letters of 19 October: 'The Gardener is here . . .'; and 20 October: 'Oh, Bogey, why are people swindlers?'.
2. Sylvia Lynd (1888–1952), a writer and friend who reviewed some of K.M.'s stories. She was married to Robert Lynd, the literary editor of the *Daily News* whose adverse criticism helped destroy Lawrence's *The Rainbow*.

3. Arnold Rowntree's business manager whom Virginia Woolf described as 'a very dull man'.

4. Arthur Waley (1889–1966), poet and authority on Chinese and Japanese literature, published his first translations from Chinese poetry in 1918. K.M. never did review *More Translations from the Chinese* (1919).

5. K.M. replies 31 October: 'Two letters today: *the first since Monday*'.

---

[109]

186 days

2 Portland Villas
[Hampstead,
London.]
[28 October, 1919.]
Tuesday.

My own darling,[1]

I've just got home – 5 o'clock – to find your Friday letter waiting for me on the black table. Your spoon letter arrived eventually – I told you, didn't I? – but for some subtle reason it took 4 days longer than any other letter.

You know, even tho' I'm with him, I feel about Wing exactly as you do. Everyday I have to take him up & hug & kiss him, for some queer reason. And he seems to understand. For instance, after your letter I went down into the depths – he's always somewhere in the depths – to kiss him for you. He lay perfectly still in my arms, with a sort of wise look in his eyes, and let himself be kissed. In some queer way he enjoys it; he knows he's adored & he presumes upon it. I'm sure no other little cat would dare to be seen about as grubby as he is. But he just jerks his head back, when the other kittens tell him about his dirty face, & says: 'Oh, he won't say anything – *I* know.' Now he's sitting in the fender watching the fire burn up – no, watching me. He eats everything in sight; he's dead nuts on cake.

Sydney returned last night. He is – or perhaps more truly he can be and is to me – very nice; talks about things that are important, not quite in the right way, but near enough to be interesting. Also, he quite plainly admires us individually and as a going concern. I'm glad he's come, really. Of course, he makes me laugh, & he catches me at it now & then, but he sees the joke. Moreover, I think he's a most useful reviewer. He's just taken to reading the *A*. – the back numbers – and yesterday when I came in he turned to me and said: By Jove the *A*. is *jolly* good. It's a thing *jolly* worth while doing. which was gratifying.

I dined with Clive Bell last night. He plied me with excellent wine, which loosened my tongue. Somewhat rashly, – though I'm glad of it – I told him that I considered you the only *authentic* writer of the present age. Of course, I said, I admired Virginia, thought her not only clever but the possessor of a delightful & rare fantasy; but that, I went on, is ultimately beside the mark. What Katherine has is the authentic writing gift, what Tolstoy had & Dostoevsky hadn't, something that can never come by taking thought. Strangely enough, I am quite certain that I convinced Mr. C.B. or rather that he believed me. As a matter of fact he takes my literary verdicts for gospel; more than once I caught him repeating things I'd told him at various times before. (At that point a coal fell out of the fire & Wing was out of the fender in a flash. Now he's sitting just round the corner by the stickleback admiring it.)

To-night I promised Eliot to go and hear him lecture on poetry;[2] he also gave Sullivan a ticket. So we're meeting at Chalk Farm Station at 8.10 p.m. (Wing is now on the table, prowling, & eventually has sat down on the extreme left hand corner watching me write.) I had your note about the books to Thorpe.[3] I'll call in at the end of the week. What a blessing it is to get home from the office! By the way, my cold is at its last gasp. It should be quite gone in 2 days.

Oh, Lord! I've forgotten about the American letter & the Hardy poem.[4] You shall have them to-morrow.

Your loving
Boge.[5]

1. J.M. replies to K.M.'s letter of 24 October: 'I can't understand why you have never received my letter about the spoon'.
2. The next day Murry reported: 'The lecture was rather disappointing. Tom had plenty of good stuff; but he tried to do too much, with the result that he didn't quite bring anything off to my sense. However, even so, the most hostile couldn't say less than that it was extremely suggestive. A flat-faced audience, though quite a large one. The anti-*Athenaeums* – Munro, Jack Squire etc – present in force. There's no doubt it's a fight to finish between us & Them – them is the "Georgians" *en masse*. It's a queer feeling I begin to have now: that we're making literary history. But I believe we are going to. More than that, in spite of the *London Mercury* and all its money and réclame, I believe we've got them on the run. They're afraid'.
3. Thomas Thorpe, a second-hand book dealer in St. Martin's Lane.
4. Murry wrote to K.M. the next day: 'I submit to Her Majesty the Hardy poem I spoke of. Seized by a characteristic passion I sent it off to T.H. hot from the oven: considering I treated him as dead it was a bit thick. I send you what he sent me. Preserve it. It's one of the most precious things I have. Send it back registered. I *love* the old man'.

Thomas Hardy (1840–1928) was Murry's literary idol: 'Mr Hardy can speak for all that is noble in England as no poet since Wordsworth has been able', he editorialised in the *Athenaeum*. After accepting Hardy's invitation to meet him in May 1921, Murry reported: 'The old man was everything I had dreamed – everything'.

5. K.M. replies 3 November: 'I got your Monday and Tuesday letters yesterday and they reassured me that nothing was wrong'.

---

[110]   2 Portland Villas
                                                    [Hampstead,
                                                      London.]
                                        [1 November, 1919.]
181 days   Saturday Night.

My own precious darling,[1]

I got your last letter (Monday) this afternoon. It's a good job they came in the wrong order, because the last was much more like you (or rather made me think you weren't miserable). The Albatross[2] had been too much for you before. Oh, darling, I do so sympathise: if only I could just appear, to hug you & talk to you, only for a moment. But there – it can't be. But just think my arms are round you, that you really are better at last as you will be, that we are together in our bye in our house, early summer morning, bright light coming through the casement curtains. You and I together – lovers. Oh, my heart something in me faints at the thought of feeling your wonderful body beneath mine again, of kissing your breasts as I used, going from your breasts to your lips & to your breasts again, till the whole of me melted away into you and I became a pulse of your heart. My God, to be lovers again.[3]

I suppose all this is wicked & that I ought not write it; I feel somehow that it is cruel. And yet for once forgive me Worm. The nights come when my physical love for you is unbearable.

Well, the time will come again & soon, if we stick to our bargain to keep going at all costs

I shouldn't have written this letter. I've upset myself and I can't go on.

But my love for you, Worm, is consuming, consuming.

Boge[4]

I'll do something better to-morrow

1. J.M. replies to K.M.'s letter of 26 October: 'I am thankful you got my letter about the spoon'.
2. The 'albatross' was one of K.M.'s terms for L.M. when she felt oppressed by her company.
3. The next day Murry wrote to K.M.: 'My letter yesterday was a bad egg; I'm afraid so. It was written in a state of physical longing for you that seldom comes quite so vehemently as it did then. I try to shut the gates of my mind on the vivid memories of our passionate love as much as I can. But, sometimes, I can't manage it. It was so last night. Sometimes you read in books of people gnashing their teeth, or gnashing the bed-clothes in a fury of thwarted desire, – well I was in a condition of that kind. And if what I wrote had in it anything that you would not have had there, and even while I wrote I felt that it was in a way cruel, & that I *ought not* have awakened such memories, then, my darling lover, forgive me. If not, then just love me for being what I am, with an awful lot of suppressed animal passion'.
4. K.M. replies 7 November: 'She came back with your Saturday night and Sunday letters . . . They heap coals of fire on my head'. Murry's confession of physical desire evoked the sad response:
'It is all memories now – radiant, marvellous, faraway memories of happiness. Ah, how terrible life can be! I sometimes see an immense wall of black rock, shining, in a place – just after death perhaps – and *smiling* – the *adamant of desire*. Let us live on memories, then, and when the time comes, let us live so fully that the memories are no nearer than far-away mountains'.

---

[111]

[2 Portland Villas,
Hampstead,
London.]
[3 November, 1919.]

[179 days]

Monday Night.

Violet took my letter off to the post at the same time that she brought three from you[1] – Thursday & Friday – each more upsetting than the one before. First, you seem to be really ill again. There's no getting over your cough, & your creaking lung & your depression. I feel so utterly helpless; & I am utterly helpless. The horror of the relations between you & L.M.[2] is awful. I feel that I don't even know what to suggest. What's the use of writing that?

I'll go to Sorapure[3] first thing to-morrow morning about the prescription. But how can he prescribe for your depression? I try to explain it all to myself in vain. Have you not been really resting, or is it impossible to rest with L.M.?

It's a fearful blow to me. It would have been that anyhow; but the consciousness that I can *do* nothing is too much. You say that the depression keeps your cough going & keeps you weak. And this depression is just an invisible enemy to me. I can't even approach it; all that there is is to get depressed myself.

What *is* it, Mouse? I know you've tried to conquer it; I almost wish you hadn't, so that I should not have been living in a fool's paradise. Is it something that just comes out of nowhere & seizes you. Has it any form?

Look here, Mouse. If you think it over & decide you'd rather I came out I'll throw up my job. Only you must ask your father to give us £200 – nothing more.[4] But that we must have if I give up the *A*. If he will I'll come out immediately & you can pack L.M. off. I'll look after you myself. I'll understand, if you decide that, that there's no other way of pulling through. And *we must pull through*. But if I do that, we must face the fact that I can't – I haven't the energy or strength – count on making more than £200 during the first year, and that's not enough for us. There's devilish little margin as it is; but we can't live even in the quietest way with none at all. *We must not be worried for money in addition to the other worries*. Think it over, darling, & decide: whatever you decide I'll do like a shot.

Well, well, my darling heart, I thought I was used to these smacks in the face from destiny – but I'm not. Whenever there's a tiny little space I manage to get a great tree of hope going. But they all get blown down – they can't have any roots. If only one would stay.

What is most hateful is that this letter will only be depressing. If by the grace of God it should happen you are feeling better when this reaches you, remember this. That I shall *not* be feeling depressed. I shall be feeling happy just in proportion as you are well.

Oh, Mouse, if only I believed in God: I don't know what to ask to take care of you except our love. That's real enough, but how much power has it.

Boge.[5]

one thing, Worm, the awful weather is *sure* to get better. The Riviera can't be all a fake. Oct – Nov. is a bad time before the fine weather comes. It's terrible here. But that's no consolation. The Italian grammar shall be posted to-morrow

1. J.M. replies to K.M.'s three letters of 30 October: 'I am sending a review today . . .'; and 31 October: 'Two letters today: *the first since Monday*'; and: 'L.M. is just back from San Remo'.
2. K.M. wrote of L.M. on 30 October: 'This *awful relationship* living on in

its secret corrupt way beside my relationship with you is very extraordinary . . . Here I have thrown things at her – yes, even that – called her a murderer, cursed her'.

3. Doctor Victor Sorapure (1874–1933) treated Katherine for tuberculosis from September 1918 to October 1922. He himself died from the disease.

4. K.M. told Murry on 8 November that he must never think of giving up the *Athenaeum* for her. And she disabused him of any illusions about her father's generosity: 'We shall not get another sou out of Father, darling, not on any account'.

5. K.M. replies 8 November: 'I will give this letter to L.M. to post in San Remo'.

---

[112]

[2 Portland Villas,
Hampstead,
London.]
[5 November, 1919.]
Wednesday Night

177 days

11.15.

My own precious darling,[1]

Your Saturday (Nov. 2) letter came to-night. I'm afraid it's not very comforting. I know you are still wretched. My darling mouse, take heart. Believe somehow that I am really near you and the six months will disappear; but if we are down & despondent, then I feel we shall never climb over them. The mountains will be too high & terrible. Oh my heart, how I love you, adore you, worship you. Try to remember that you *couldn't* have stayed here this winter; it's like a viper, bitter & biting; think that your being there is something positively helping us to come together, as it really is. But if you think that Mentone would be better, why not get Conny & Jinny[2] to find a place & go. We'll manage the money.

I couldn't get the parcel[3] by post off to-day. They made such difficulties about declaration forms and the precise manner of sealing that, since the parcels didn't arrive at the office till 3, by the time I'd got them really ready, the Post Office was shut. But the parcel which Sydney sent in the diplomatic bag went off safely.

Thursday Morning

Your Sunday letter came. Even more shattering still. You have had no letters. I write every day, you know I do. I mustn't give way. I'll just say that I am in body perfectly well; but I don't know how long things will last if this strain goes on. Those silly lines I wrote when I was very young keep singing in my head: 'There's nothing to say: my heart is dead'. It isn't really; but there are moments when I feel its on the point of giving out.

What can I do to help? I write & write; I try to keep in control of my work & behave like a sane being to the world. But when I feel that you feel that I have not written because you are not receiving my letters – I certainly become very nearly insane. Look here, you must keep things straight, & remember that a letter from me to you goes off every single day. If ever I feel in the slightest degree physically ill, I will wire you immediately: I promise you faithfully across my heart.

But until I feel some spark of hope from your side, it's useless my writing much about myself. It would merely be monotonous & depressing – my nervous agitation is continual, & the effort to keep pace with my work which is heavy is pretty severe. When I feel that you are moderately happy & making headway everything seems easy, easy. Now everything seems hard & requires a particular effort of will.

You know these things. What's the good of writing them? I'll work with all my soul I promise you to keep you supplied with news from the office, & things to read. If I've failed in this, as I have, its because the work has been really heavy – now Sullivan's away & Aldous[4] ill – and the necessity of keeping up the standard of the paper has been always an anxiety which I could share with no-one. The back *Literary Supplements* have been sent you. But I can't write about the details of the paper now, because I'm so agitated I can't remember anything.

Darling heart, my wonderful Mouse, I think of you years ago as my Squirrel in your little brown hat, the goblin hat, I think of all the happiness we desired & that seemed to be again in our grasp only a month ago, and now. It's not to be borne. One can't go on fighting losing battles. We *can't*. No doctor, even from Heaven, can do anything for your depression, any more than he could for mine. This is our battle. We must win, must win, must win. I'm not hysterical. But you must cling to me; hold on to the certainty that I write every day, that nothing can be wrong with me unless you have a wire, that I am fighting all day long against the misery of the news that comes from you, that somehow I intend to win. Don't say one day 'I can ignore L.M.' & the next 'She is killing me'. It begins to be that I can't believe a word. You must ignore her. I begin to feel from your letters that I'm only a kind of ghost to you: something far finer than I am, but bodiless & unreal.

Worm, my darling Worm, my arms *are* round you. You must believe it, somehow you must, you must.

Boge[5]

1. J.M. replies to K.M.'s letters of 1 November: 'I had thought to have your Monday letter yesterday . . .'; and 1–2 November: 'No letter. Oh, what a disappointment'.
2. Connie Beauchamp, Katherine's elderly second cousin, who spent the winter months at Menton with her friend Jinnie Fullerton.
3. Containing the medicine prescribed by Doctor Sorapure.
4. Aldous Huxley (1894–1963), novelist and essayist, was one of the Garsington circle when Murry launched him into the literary world in 1918 as second assistant editor of the *Athenaeum*. Huxley rewarded Murry by becoming one of his strongest detractors, mercilessly satirizing him as Burlap in *Point Counter Point* (1928).
5. K.M. replies 10 & 11 November: 'Your Wednesday and Thursday letters have come . . .'.

---

[113]   2 Portland Villas
                                           Hampstead. Sunday
                                           [London.]
                                           Nov. 9 [1919.]

173 days

My darling heart,

I didn't get a letter from you on Saturday, after all. It's hateful that there are no Sunday posts here. Now when I begin to write to you, I have the hungry feeling: I have had nothing to feed on since the Telegram.[1]

I didn't go to the cinema last night. Brett came in, & after a while I went round to her studio where Gertler was. He told me that Frieda had gone to Germany & that Lawrence was thinking of going to Italy, apparently to meet her there. I am going to send him your address. He might quite well have the chance of coming to see you.

To-day I've been working hard beginning to type out *Cinnamon & Angelica*. I went out for a walk first thing in the morning; it was very dull, cold & misty. With the usual luck it came on to rain heavily when I was at the furthest point from home, where it made no difference whether I returned or went on. I had my Matamac, though, & as I'd been walking hard it was rather pleasant until the mac. began to stick to my legs. I didn't get very wet, though and anyhow there was a noble fire when I got back to my room – the little one on top.

I don't quite know what to make of *Cinnamon*. As soon as I've got it quite typed out, I'll send it off to you. I can't do anything more on it now until I have had your criticisms. My feeling is that there are too many speeches. Also, I so much want to hear what you say of this number of the paper – Nov 7.

At present Arthur is with me in my room, reading *Tono-Bungay*. He's just finished the setting of the last line of your story;[2] so that we should have pulled the last sheets & be ready to bind in a fortnight from now. It's a good job that we managed to make such headway with it before he went into Sanderson's[3] office, because that leaves him very little time. However, with only ordinary luck, we ought to have it quite ready. I'm convinced it will go like hot cakes the moment it is ready; and if the last sheet pulls as well as the others, it will be quite a fine looking book, almost worthy of the story which is a masterpiece, I am convinced.

Wingley is engaged in balancing himself like a parrot on the arm of that old armchair of mine that I used to have in Redcliffe Road. Now he's gone off to prospect under the chest of drawers; no sound but the clock – the little one that we used to have in Acacia Road, that Kot returned to me, and I had mended – and the two brass candlesticks that we got from Escott rattling on the table whenever I begin a fresh line. New sounds. Arthur laughing at *Tono-Bungay* & suddenly Wingley leaping from the ground onto the top of the chest of drawers. He has slidden right along it, & is now leaning with his head right over, wondering whether he can ever get down. He's managed it by leaping onto Arthur. That's all. Does it give you any picture? I'm in my black corduroy coat and my old grey tweed trousers sitting sideways at the table with my back to the fire & my legs crossed, crossed so hard that the underone has gone very much to sleep. The table isn't *very* tidy; yet it is Tidier than it might be. Wingley has now finished up by playing the coal-box trick; for I've brought the brass coal-box up with me. Except for that & the scraps of the grey carpet that I've put down everything is as it was. No, I've also brought the black wood writing chair here; and Arthur is sitting in it. It's rather cold. I've let the fire go down too far & I've forgotten to draw the curtains which I'll do now.

It's no good my trying to do more until I get a letter from you. There ought to be more than one to-morrow morning.

I pray Destiny that it shall be good news, my darling. I could do with a little.

Good bye my precious little wife
Boge.[4]

1. K.M.'s telegram sent on 7 November read: 'All goes well darling absolutely nothing to worry about Tig'.

2. *Je ne parle pas français*, which was first printed, unexpurgated, by Murry and his brother on their Heron Press in the basement of 2 Portland Villas.

3. T.J. Cobden-Sanderson (1840–1922), a printer and publisher who employed Arthur Murry in 1919. In 1920 he published Murry's *Cinnamon and Angelica* and *The Evolution of an Intellectual*.

4. K.M. replies 14 November: 'These are the first letters I've had since last Monday . . .'.

---

[114]

171 days

[2 Portland Villas,
Hampstead,
London.]
[11 November, 1919.]
Tuesday 6 p.m.

My own precious wife,

I think, after all, I like calling you this best of all. There's something so much belonging to us in the contrast which there is always for me between the size of us & the fact, the real legal, certificated fact that we are man & wife. Why is it that there should always be a touch of David & Dora[1] about us. Dickens would always be a great man for having done that. I don't think it's really sentimentalizing – though there is, I know, a danger of it, – to look on ourselves somehow as children. It's not an attitude. It always is so much harder for me to understand that you & I are really grown up. It's against the grain; as though one were really assuming a part; and yet here am I with my little bald patch on top, with all sorts of profound and not very cheerful convictions about life. Reconcile me that, mistress!

It's a quaint, queer mystery to me, my heart. I am convinced that you and I have suffered the war more than anyone, that we have really known, do really know, what sorrow and pain are. Neither you nor I can ever leave them out of our verdict on the universe. AND YET – in my heart of hearts, I don't belong to it all. I slip aside with you into your ditch by the Karori road[2] – you remember? – and walk holding your hand under the leaves. I don't want to escape or deny my vision of Life; I don't believe in it; I mistrust it, AND YET. What can it be? I'm not dishonest, I'm not a coward. A man like Tommy, though he loves me, I believe, thinks I'm too sad for words. AND YET I have more happiness, I can touch moments of deeper and more certain happiness, than anyone I've met. Thinking not so much of you, but of us, of our future, our home, our understanding of each other, our misery even. A feeling that *we* are miraculously untouched & innocent, that whatever we have to go through, we are whole still; that we are not degraded or broken or coarsened – I don't know how to explain really – a feeling that we are children to whom nightmares of suffering happen, which still might pass away as a dream.

Well, I had to say all that to give the mood I'm writing in just now. Do you feel it, as you read? Perhaps, I can't put it into words. But its strange & true. Something connected with it happened to-day. I've put a poem of Henry King's[3] in the number. Suddenly while I was reading the proof, it struck me that what seemed to me so clear was in fact excessively obscure. I showed it to Tommy and asked his opinion. I don't know whether you've read the poem[4] – I can't remember. But the last verse runs something like this

> . . . . scratch through the silver of illusion's glass
> Their name at least that a faint light be thrown
> Upon the further chamber's basalt floor
> Which surely is & was.

And Tommy suddenly said '*Your* floor *would* be bloody basalt'. And I laughed and laughed. How can one get this indistinguishable mixture of gloom – the black pit you see in me – and exquisite happiness & unshakeable faith, expressed. They exist together, & they do not merely co-exist; but are utterly fused. I thought I had expressed it in *Cinnamon & Angelica*. But that ends in pure pain. And my mixture doesn't end that way – rather in a pure, but subtle & exquisite happiness. Perhaps it is in *C & A* though really. I don't know. If not I must get it into a novel. I send you the American letters. Goodbye my darling heart. Send the letters back Boge[5]

Shall I send you some jam & some coffee Just wire 'Yes' and I'll know & send immediately. There seems to be no difficulty about sending such things out of England.

1. Characters in Dickens' *David Copperfield*.
2. The road in Wellington along which K.M. as a child walked to school.
3. Murry published poetry under the pseudonym 'Henry King'.
4. 'Exploration', published in *Poems: 1916–20*.
5. K.M. replies 16 November: 'Yes, my darling Love, your mood travelled to me unbroken . . .'.

---

[115]   2 Portland Villas
                                                   [Hampstead,
                                                    London.]
169 days.   [13 November, 1919.]
                                                Thursday 9 p.m.

My own darling wife,
   I haven't had a letter since yesterday morning. The terrible cold that began yesterday has remained; it hasn't stopped freezing and since we have now used up the little anthracite that remained from last year, the house isn't exactly warm. Apparently there's been another strike in the anthracite mines, with the result that the man tells me that he can't give me any hope of anthracite for another month. However, I succeed in making the little cubby hole room pretty warm; and I know a thing or two now about juggling with the 'register' – that black plate that was always so mysterious in the chimney, & that I thought was merely to prevent the soot falling down in the summer-time. I only wish that I knew you made your little room as warm as I do mine.
   In addition to my having asked Bertie R. to dinner last night, Sydney had asked E.M. Forster to stay the night. He slept on the little camp-bed. Sydney bought a pair of splendid blankets from Heal's, which I am in hopes he'll forget to take away with him, or will sell me at half-price. Violet was very nice about the extra bother, perhaps because Sydney is very nice to her. He's a remarkably considerate old walrus, really – rather like we are, in that he seems genuinely surprised when a servant tries to make him comfortable. Since the old stove is dead, we had to shift the dining table into the studio; after dinner – potato soup, mutton cutlets & mashed potatoes & brussels sprouts, salad, apple-tart & custard – we migrated to your room, where my heart was warmed – how I wish it had been our country house & you presiding over a select week-end party: it will be, soon, my darling – by the enthusiasm they showed for the *Athenaeum*. The

three of them seemed almost as keen on it as we are. I told Bertie your suggestion about the Chinese dialogues & gave him my idea of how you meant it to be worked out. He was very keen; but, he said, he would need to have no distractions in order to do the thing justice. As soon as he had a clear month ahead, he would begin.

Sydney W. has been working hard on an article on George Eliot, which he thinks is going to be good. He's at it now. I was wise to get him to do it, wasn't I? I felt from your letters that I had given you quite enough to do. And I was frightened of the state of anxiety I knew you would get into if you once thought I was reckoning on you for George Eliot also. You see, I reckon on you absolutely for the novels. Your novel page, I know, is one of the features most appreciated in the paper, and any interruption of it would do us great harm. To me, you seem to get better & better every time. You are so *sure*, besides being so delicate. It's quite unlike – in a different class to – anything that's being done in the way of reviewing anywhere to-day. What I feel, and what a great many other people feel, is that as long as your novel page is there, there can't be a really bad number of the *Athenaeum*. The only thing I wish, if it were possible, is that you should manage to get so far ahead that I had your copy on the Friday before the paper comes out so that I had time to put your article in the advertisement which I have to get ready on Friday.

I've done what you may at first sight consider a very rash thing – through Eliot I have asked Wyndham Lewis[1] to write an article for the *A.* But you will see why, I think, when you read my review of his book[2] in this week's number. That's my honest opinion of the book, which I'll send you to-morrow; and holding that opinion I couldn't do less than ask him to contribute. Still, I'm rather nervous and hoping fervently that he'll give us the saner rather than wilder side of himself. But his attack on Roger Fry & the Omegas[3] is really masterly, as you'll see.

Wing has come up to see me to-night, after avoiding me for two days. The reason, I'm bound to confess, is that Violet is having her evening out, & therefore there's no fire in the kitchen. The wicker armchair in the kitchen is really his place. He likes me, but he'll see me blowed before he'll give up a comfortable place without good reason.

I went to Porter[4] this morning. I think he's awfully good; & what a good memory he must have? for he talked to me about what you had told him of the *Athenaeum* with a great deal of intelligence.

This is a very shoppy letter; but that's because I'm waiting for a

letter from you. Unless I have one from you to answer [and] respond to
I just have to give you details.

Your loving Boge.[5]

Cheque for £12.10 enclosed.

1. Percy Wyndham Lewis (1884–1957), avant-garde painter and writer,
had been employed at the Omega Workshops in 1913; but after falling out
with Roger Fry he publicly vilified him. Virginia Woolf wrote in 1922: 'Never
did I read such an outburst of spite as Wyndham Lewis on Clive in the Herald
. . . Even poor little squint eyed Murry wouldn't [write like that]'. Wyndham
Lewis also detested Murry and K.M., about whose stories he commented: 'I
find them . . . vulgar, dull and unpleasant'.
2. Murry's review of *The Caliph's Design: Architects! Where is your Vortex?*
(one of the principal Vorticist manifestos) appeared on 14 November.
3. Roger Fry had organized the Omega Workshops in 1913 to give young
artists employment as designers of furniture, textiles and pottery. The
Workshops closed in 1919.
4. Katherine's dentist.
5. K.M. replies 17 November: 'After the poisonous day yesterday it was
calm here this morning . . .'.

---

[116]   [2 Portland Villas,
                                            Hampstead,
                                            London.]
                                        [14 November, 1919.]
168 days   Friday
                                         4.15 p.m.

My own precious wife.[1]

I got home this afternoon to find two such *gallant* letters from you –
Sunday & Monday. Gallant is the only word for them. Like
courageous ships with streaming pennons. And, of course, the fire
began to pour into my heart. You see, you know what these things are.

I agree with every word you say about Virginia & the war.[2] Perhaps
you will find something of it in my review of Hardy[3] last week. And
there was more of it in a letter I wrote you about three days ago. So few
people have felt the war; and for us who have, the work of those who
have not – if it pretends to be true at all – must sound a lie. And we're
not arbitrary in requiring the truth from them. The War *is* Life; not a
strange aberration of Life, but a revelation of it. It is a test we must
apply; it must be allowed for in any truth that is to touch us.

Don't be afraid, my darling, of saying exactly what you think of Virginia's book. It's all important that you should. We have no right to require truth from others if we don't exact it from our friends. Do you remember I tried to say exactly this thing in the 'Prologue' I wrote to the *Athenaeum*, which is the last essay in my book? If we once give up being as honest as we can there's absolutely no point in carrying on – far better to make a living another way. We have our opportunity; I think the judgment on us will be pretty severe if we betray it.

Moreover, everybody is waiting to hear what you say. You see, there has been no criticism of the book yet. Everyone worth while knows that the *Times* column wasn't criticism, but a flatulent puff. No intelligent person reading it could have any idea of the worth of the book. I hear a lot of talk about it, but they're all very uneasy; in their hearts they know – I can tell – that it's not good; but they don't know why it's not good. How should they? It is the perfect example of their own attitude. It should be all right; everything's there; & yet – it isn't. All I can say is: Be as ruthlessly honest as you can with the book, and as sober.

As for the *Mercury*, that doesn't matter. Of course Squire wouldn't ask you or me. The feud between us is at its height. The Squire crowd hate the *Athenaeum* like so much poison; and I happen to know that Eliot's & Tomlinson's names were included in their list by fraud. I've sent you the *Mercury* so that you could see what it was like. That's not the stuff they can beat the *Athenaeum* with, I'm confident. The best thing in this wonderful, new, creative review is an article on George Eliot by Gosse[4] and that's only half-good. No, no! That may be all very well for a year; but even the English public knows better than that. Squire will have [to] produce something infinitely better than that to frighten me. And frankly I don't believe he's got it in him. He and Shanks[5] are masters of the *faux ton*. Still, it means that we have to be better than ever.

I agree with you that there's little chance of our ever becoming successful writers; but I don't think there's any reason to despair; of some success. It took Hardy many, many years to win through. I can say sincerely that I don't want any success less honest than his.

I am going for the week-end to Sydney's place to-morrow after-noon. I think I deserve it. I'll get one letter to you posted to-morrow morning before I go. I may not be able to get one posted on Sunday; if not it shall go off first thing on Monday morning.

Your letters were wonderful; they gave me that splendid conviction that you & I have the same faith, absolutely; demand & aim at the same things; that we understand each other, but no-one else understands us. It's true: and it's our strength. But we have to be together.

Boge.[6]

1. J.M. replies to K.M.'s letters of 9 November: 'Your letter was terrible but I knew it would be . . .'; and 10 November: 'Here is another Monday'.
2. K.M.'s review of *Night and Day* appeared on 21 November. She wrote of the novel to Murry: 'My private opinion is that it is a lie in the soul. The war never has been; that is what the message is . . . The novel can't just leave the war out. There *must* have been a change of heart'. On November 19 Murry complimented K.M. on her review: 'Your review of Virginia arrived this morning in time for the number. I think it is (sans blague) one of the very finest reviews I have ever read. The exquisite poise & beauty of the opening; the mastery with which you give the whole quality & limitation of the book; the sureness of your touch; and – above all & again – the beauty of the writing, make it indisputably a masterpiece in the genre.
'It was 6 lines [too] long. As you know the paper is all made up by Wednesday morning, and it's impossible to allow more than a page. I never had such anguish in trying to get 6 lines out of a piece of copy before. I took them out of the description of Katharine's duties at home. I felt that those could be spared best. They seemed to contain less of what was specifically yours – the light which you cast on the book, wh: was a real, suave, delicate, unfaltering light. I tried to make the cut as well as I could. You will see the result; but don't judge me hardly. It was like drawing one of my own teeth'.
3. Murry's review of the *Collected Poems of Thomas Hardy – Vol. I* appeared on 7 November.
4. Edmund Gosse (1849–1928), critic and man of letters.
5. Edward Shanks (1892–1953), a Georgian poet who was assistant editor of the *London Mercury*. In 1915 he shared a billet with K.M.'s brother.
6. K.M. replies 18 November: 'First: I received your *Monday week* letter today . . .'.

---

[117]   Parsonage House,
                                           Oare,
                                         Pewsey,
Sunday 6.30 p.m.   Wilts.
166 days   [16 November, 1919.]

My darling Wig,
Being here gives me an anguish of desire for our house.[1] You see, it's just the kind of thing we could afford – a solid, thatched house with about nine rooms, perhaps ten, run by a manservant and a maid. Very snug, quite good rooms, some children, yes, it's a rather envious

experience. We should have to spend a good deal of money on furniture to get our house as comfortable as this; but then we shall have to do that, anyhow. But what's really worth remembering is that a small country house like this, even though its not in the Southern counties, is infinitely warmer than 2 Portland Villas. The important thing is to have what they have here, an anthracite kitchen range which burns on night & day and keeps a perpetual supply of hot water to the bathroom, warm linen cupboards, that & one or two other anthracite stoves and a decent fireplace – the problem's solved. I admit that to-day was a particularly beautiful day, a bright blue sky & a hard frost; but it's certain that you could have sat out in front of the house with joy this morning.

The all-important thing is to have enough money to spend on the house. The difficulty that arises is that one can't possibly spend money on a house that doesn't belong to one; & that it's rather hard to think how to provide enough money both to buy a house and to have the necessary alterations done & furniture bought.[2] But Sydney tells me that it is not only possible, but usual when buying a house to leave ⅔ of the purchase money on mortgage; and on the other hand fixtures like an anthracite kitchen range even if one had them in a rented house could always be moved. Still one would drop a lot of money by improving a house that was only rented, unless one had a tremendously long lease.

But the house is really urgent. It's rather difficult to know how to begin. The Waterlows are looking out; and I think you would like the country here, – I believe you've seen it – and even having them for not too close neighbours, for there's no doubt Sydney is very nice indeed, though I don't think I should ever really take to Marge. She's too efficient, and without even that ridiculous charm that Mary Cannan had.[3] The other clue to follow is Sylvia Lynd. Have you by any chance written to her yet? You've probably been too worried & busy. But it's obvious that one can only find things now by having well-disposed people to look for them. I don't know anyone else whom we could enlist. But somehow we must get forward and find something that we can go into next year; and we must somehow scrape together enough money to do the thing properly. It's no use doing it otherwise; of that I'm convinced. But if you make your house really comfortable, the English country can be divine. I'm sure that, given the comfort, you could not only get through the winter in England, but get steadily better & better. I am absolutely convinced of that.[4]

But the comfort – that must really be done regardless of expense. I have no doubt about that either. Anything else is just madness; we have to be prepared to get a builder in & make him do exactly what we want. The full system of central heating is not really necessary; but you must have this anthracite kitchen range & hot water supply, a fine bathroom, good doors & windows, good carpets & a hundred smaller things that make the difference between exquisite comfort & exquisite misery. You see, Wig darling, I can't afford to have any risks taken with you. It simply can't be done.

I haven't been boring about this, I know, because you are as passionately keen on our house as I am. I've put it all in this letter, because being here has filled me with the house question. We can't have a Garsington; but we can have something as solidly comfortable as this, and with our own exquisiteness. After all, Sydney & M. between them, haven't any more money than we have between us. Not, at least, so far as income is concerned. There is an important difference, that Sydney has some capital. But I think we can get over that difficulty, too. Staying here has just put a keen edge upon my determination to have our house as soon as we possibly can. This is a thousand times more comfortable than Portland Villas. I think of your adorable ways, our garden, our work, our long talks in the evening when the work is done, the visits of our friends, the passing of the seasons, – and I want it all to be now, now, now. It won't be long, my darling.[5]

Your

Boge.[6]

1. Murry was resurrecting their old dream of owning a house (the 'Heron') in the country on his visit to the Waterlows.

2. After K.M.'s death, Murry added a marginal comment here: 'How naïve I was!'.

3. After a visit to the Waterlows in 1918 Virginia Woolf commented in her *Diary*: 'She [Marjory] is a gnome like figure; but acute as the unattractive women tend to be, depending upon hard work for their wages. She produced excellent food, & manages the two unattractive children without a nurse. . . . The defect of the household lies in their relationship. She has no admiration for him; he no romance about her.'

4. Murry's subsequent marginal comment here reads: 'I believe I was right – if only I had insisted (June 30 1948)'.

5. At the foot of this letter, K.M. wrote: 'Too late. 19.XI.1919'. Murry added 'K.M.' to the note.

6. K.M. replies 21 November: 'It happened rather luckily . . .'. About

the proposed house, she asked sadly: 'Shall we really have such a house? It's not too late? We don't just make up dreams – precious dreams? It's not "all over"? I get overwhelmed at times that it *is* all over . . . and that these letters will one day be published and people will read something in them, in their queer finality, that "ought to have told us" '.

---

[118]   [2 Portland Villas,
                                                  Hampstead,
GOOD NEWS RECEIVED. HURRAH!   London.]
                                              17 November, 1919
                                                 Monday 5.45
165 days

My own darling wife,[1]

I think it is strictly impossible, as they say in the mathematical books, that I could ever have two letters that give me more joy than the two I had this morning, one giving an account of Ansaldi's[2] visit, the other of yr. father's. Ah, darling, that is the stuff to give your Boge if you want to see him a roaring, rampaging Lion of Happiness. It went through me like a golden wine, and as a matter of fact I became quite light-headed in the office. I simply couldn't work straight, but wandered about with an imbecile sort of smile. One grievous brick about this imbecility is that I forgot to go to Jaeger & buy that wrap – however, I will get it first thing to-morrow morning and have it sent off by noon, so it won't miss a single post.

Yes, the news is wonderful. All that I wrote yesterday about the house now seems so urgent & near. I am afraid of nothing on earth. But, do you know, I felt it coming? When you told me that you had gained those 2 lbs during that period of misery, I knew in my heart that you had won a decisive battle against the enemy. It was a miracle. O Wig, Wig, Wig. I don't feel a bit like writing a letter; I just want to say and to go on saying: O Wig, Wig. And so strangely news like that seems to bring us so near. I feel that our hands are almost touching. Somehow glad voices carry farther & quicker; they ring golden & clear; they are not dispersed, but travel like a bubble of glass in the sun, and break only at the lover's ear.

That's very nearly a prose flight – isn't it. And then there's your Father's visit. I love him for it, love him. I can never in the future think of him otherwise than as one of us. To have made you happy, to have been If only for a single day, wholly what you expected him to be

– that is a gift that I can never return. I only wish to heaven I had felt more friendly to him a fortnight ago, & could have written him a letter out of my heart. But I was hostile then; – it can't be helped. But I will write him such a letter.

Just a word or two of such news as there is. I came back from Wiltshire this morning. There is a damp mist over London, so damp that the walls of the house are all sodden. That only proves the utter difference between the English country & London. It was wet in the country; but no mist at all. At the office I found an invitation from Virginia to dinner on Friday which I shall probably accept; a letter from Ottoline asking me to go and see her at Bedford Square where she was staying this week to arrange a sale of her furniture in December. I thought I'd go not so much to see her as to see what was in the house. I had the idea that I might try to get perhaps a couple of the smaller things at the sale. What do you think? You see, in my mind, the question of furniture, like everything else to do with the house is getting urgent. And it might be well worth while, considering how good her stuff is, if I tried to lay out £20 wisely at the sale. Of course there's sure to be high bidding; but still one might snap up something. What do you think of the notion? At all events if I go to tea, I will tell you what there is we might try for. I enclose a note from Dent.

But it's no good. I have the conviction that we have turned the corner of our futures; that good things are waiting for us in the hedges & ditches, good things for us, for *Athenaeum*, for Wing. In fact I'm beginning to feel that we only want £2000 left us suddenly to settle the hash of the world. Hurrah for your Father! Hurrah for Ansaldi! Hurrah for Wig! Hurrah for Boge! Hurrah for Wing! You darling Boge.[3]

But do everything Ansaldi says about wrapping up. Are you sure there's nothing you want except that woolly wrap. *Do tell me* – anything, everything.

P.S. I find I've left Dent's note at the office. Will send to-morrow It said he had written to his aunt.

1. J.M. replies to K.M.'s letters of 11 November: '(I shall answer your letter après)'; and 12 November: 'I got a telegram from you today . . .'.
2. Katherine wrote on 11 November that she had seen Ansaldi, 'a brilliant, clever, sympathetic doctor on the spot' who had said there was 'no reason (bar accident) why [she] should not recover. . . . He says it will take two years to

cure me . . .' Murry apparently took this literally; for, after entertaining him to dinner, Virginia Woolf told Clive Bell: '[Katherine's] practically cured . . . and they think will be completely so'. And in her *Diary* she commented: 'K.M. wrote a review [of *Night and Day*] which irritated me. . . . I need not now spread my charity so wide, since Murry tells me she is practically cured'.

3. K.M. replies 22 November: 'Per usual your adorable gay letter comes flying after my crows'.

---

[119]   [2 Portland Villas,
                                          Hampstead,
                                          London.]
                                          [20 November, 1919.]
                                          Thursday 6.30 p.m.

162 days

My own darling.

No letter so far to-day. I am sitting at the red-table in the studio, where Sydney generally sits, because there's a fire there. We have had to shift the dining room table into the studio because we have no anthracite. Marjory W. is staying here for the night; she has had to come up to town to interview nursery-governesses. I only wish we were doing that. Sydney has not yet arrived. Sullivan is coming to dinner, which is to be sausage-pie (my own invention: goodness knows what it will be like) and a boiled pudding & custard. It doesn't sound particularly brilliant, now I come to think of it. But in the morning when I am just starting for the office it's terribly hard to think of anything. Which reminds me: if you have time, would you send me a week's menu?[1] It would help me a great deal. Violet's an awfully good cook but she doesn't have many original inspirations.

The cold is much less than it was a fortnight ago, so that we don't particularly miss the anthracite stove; still, it's more than it was yesterday. Violet has just come in to lay the table and to tell me that there's a bill stuck up outside the house announcing that it's to be sold; thank goodness, I'm not buying it! I lunched with Brett to-day in fulfilment of an old promise to go and see a picture by Guevara[2] (you remember the man they call Chili?) at the International. Which I did, & didn't think much of the picture. I don't think it's more than clever & flashy; but, then, I daresay I'm becoming hypercritical. I feel I can't do in art with anything less than the very best – things like your stories, Hardy's poems, and Manet portraits. I've grown too old &

gone too far & seen too many things to be content with half-measures now. I've crossed the Rubicon in the same little boat as you and there's no going back to tea-party art any more. I went on with Brett to her studio to see her straw-hat picture. Now I don't think that has quite come off. It has weak spots here and there. But it does mark a real advance; there's indubitably something [to] it. She has half-caught the calm poise of a moment. The thing has been imaginatively apprehended, though Brett isn't yet master enough of her tools to say precisely what she wants to say. But who of us is, except you? I'll get her to send you a photograph of it. I think you would be interested & would see what I mean. She can't quite get it across yet.

Lynd came in this morning. He sits on the fence between the *Athenaeum* and the *Mercury*, so I haven't much interest in him. We can get on perfectly well without him, in any case. He hadn't very much to say. Nor, for that matter, have I darling. It's as usual when I am waiting for letters from you. I didn't tell you much about my visit to Ottoline yesterday, did I? I'd never been to Bedford Square before, you know. Though it was dingy, it did seem to me a very lovely house. When I was standing on the step, ringing the bell, Philip arrived. He was very forthcoming & friendly. I found Bertie with Ottoline in the drawing-room. There was some talk of Virginia's book, which Philip disliked, Ottoline half-liked (apparently – she probably wrote something quite different to V.) & Bertie & I hadn't read, but it chiefly turned on a long story (told by Philip) of an imposter bailiff who had turned up at Garsington. I tried to be as nice as I could to O. in a rather distrait way (which I always find the safest to adopt with her) but I don't know how it went down. As I told you my chief attention went to the furniture, though I had to look surreptitiously as it were.

Every day fills me with more & more impatience about the house. I feel rather like a mouse in a cage. The opportunities of making a real start are so scarce. Sydney tells me that there's rather a beautiful house to be sold three miles away from him; and I'm inclined to write about it if only to see. Then there's another I saw in the Wiltshire local paper advertised to be sold by auction. That sounded very attractive. But it's rather an undertaking to go to a place for the week-end just to see one house. If it's no go, you're rather sold. What one really wants is about 20 people looking.

I want two letters this evening, please. I've got the proof of your review in my pocket to show Sydney, who got very excited over my description of it last night. Good-bye Mouse,

We want our house,
Garden & cows
That's a nice little rhyme
Boge[3]
xxx
xxxx
xxx
xx
x

1. Murry added the later note: 'This exists'.
2. Alvaro 'Chili' Guevera (1894–1951), a Chilean painter (friendly with Mark Gertler) who exhibited at the New English Art Club.
3. K.M. replies 25 November: 'The paper has come'.

---

[120]

[The Athenaeum,
10 Adelphi Terrace,
London. W.C.2.]
Saturday Morning

160 days   Nov. 22.[1919.]

My precious darling,[1]

Your Monday letter (Nov 18) arrived this morning. First, about the Weekly *Times*. I'm sorry. You see I always intended to send the Weekly *Guardian*, but as it didn't come quick enough when it was ordered, I sent the *Times* instead. When the *G*. began arriving regularly I dropped the *T*. I didn't know you would like them both. I'll send a copy of the *Times* to-day.

I'm getting frightened about the cold at Ospedaletti. It seems to be always prowling about to stab you. I know you are taking every possible care of yourself; but I curse myself for my stupidity in letting you take the risk. Will some more woolly clothes help at all? I think you are terribly wise to go to bed as early as you do. But I don't at all like you saying that your back aches so much with the cold. I feel that I've left you alone not merely to loneliness, but to roaring lions & hissing serpents.

I don't feel depressed about you, darling; but I do feel rather nervous, and angry that we didn't go to Switzerland instead. The only thing I remember is that Sorapure was very much against Switzerland, & very emphatic about some place on the Mediterranean.

Your praise of the Nov. 14 number was very sweet. But the reason why it looked so big & had so many advertisements was that a considerable number were to be distributed as specimen copies. We could guarantee a large circulation to the advertisers, & so they came in. You won't find anything like so many ads. in this one; but I think it's a pretty good number, all the same. Bonwick tells me that under the circularising scheme we are getting about 10 direct orders (i.e. subscriptions) every day, and I suppose one can calculate about as many through the newsagents. About 20 orders every day in all. Which makes 100 a week. The question is whether we can keep this up for six months. If so, we shall be really in a safe position. It's too early to say anything definite yet.

Darling – before I forget – am I to do anything with the ten stories in your cupboard. Shall I send them to Grant Richards?[2] Or give them to Cobden-Sanderson, who, I'm sure, would be glad to have them? Or give them to Virginia? Or do nothing? You see I was dining with Virginia last night, and she asked me point-blank about them. What is your idea? I think the best thing wd. be to get them published as they are & not worry about adding any more to them. You can start fresh on a new book then. If you agree I feel pretty certain that I can fix up their being published in the spring. Do let me know.

Of course, Virginia asked me, as I knew she would, to explain your review. I did my best. But as not only I, but Tomlinson and Sydney and Sullivan all thought it explained itself perfectly, it was rather difficult. I imagine that Virginia was more than a little gêné by it. I explained that what you meant was that she made an abstraction from life, which instead of being potentially complete (forgive the big words) left one important element completely out of account, or rather withered it. I don't suppose that was very comforting. She then said that she thought your novel reviews showed that you were not interested in novels. I thought that was a very illuminating remark, illuminating Virginia of course. What she really meant, as Sydney said, when I reported it to him was that you related novels to life. Virginia can't abide that. You see Virginia & (you & I) are fundamentally at cross purposes. We're right & she's wrong. I'll give you some more of her conversation in this evening's letter. I must work now.

Look after your darling self

Your
Boge.[3]

1. J.M. replies to K.M.'s letter of 18 November: 'First: I received your *Monday week* letter today . . .'
2. Grant Richards (1872–1948), a publisher with whom K.M. had been negotiating.
3. K.M. replies 26 and 27 November: 'I don't want the *Times* as well as the *Guardian*'.

---

[121]   [2 Portland Villas,
                                          Hampstead,
                                          London.]
                                          [23 November, 1919.]
159 days   Sunday Morning

My own darling,

For some reason I felt very tired yesterday and I wasn't able to write another letter yesterday evening as I intended. Another thing I was unable to do was to find a copy of the Weekly *Times* to send. They were sold out in Hampstead. So I'll send the *Observer* instead to-day and see if I can get the W.*T*. on Monday.

Yesterday was very cold: to-day it is very much warmer and I am writing at the open window without a fire. Arthur came here yesterday and stayed the night. We are going to pull off the last sheet of your story this afternoon. Then we shall only have the stitching & binding to do; so there's no doubt that we shall have it out in time for Christmas. All yesterday evening Arthur was trying to make sketches of the cats for you in that little sketch book which we had when we went to Pulborough – thousands of years ago. I thought I should like to have it filled up.

I find it hard to settle down to things this week-end. I don't know why. It's one of those fits when I take up everything in turn & put it down again. I meant to review *Georgian Poetry*[1] wh. has just come out. But I shan't be able to do it well enough, so I shall have to leave it. The only thing I shall write for the next number will be a leader, which I have almost finished; but I don't even know whether that has come off. Yesterday afternoon in fulfilment of an old promise I went to have tea with Vanessa Bell. I had no choice, because she rang up Virginia while I was there at dinner on Friday night to say that though I'd promised – I did two months ago – I hadn't been. It wasn't at all that I didn't want to go. I like Vanessa. But, you know, whenever there's a choice open between going & not going to see anybody I like not to go. However, it was very pleasant. We talked a lot about you. Nice things.

Vanessa told me that Katharine Hilbery was meant to be her; that she couldn't make up her mind about *Night & Day*; that in any case she thought it too long; that she knew the people too well to be able to form any detached judgement; that she thought Virginia had done Katharine's mother (who was their aunt, Lady Ritchie) and the society of the older generation very well, but she was doubtful about the rest.

I think that Virginia & Vanessa, however much we disagree with them – and, as I said, I think that we are profoundly at cross purposes with Virginia, at least – are the two women with whom you & I have most in common (except, perhaps, Brett). At all events, when I'm with any of those three I don't feel that my nerves are all ragged and being jagged with a blunt saw. I suppose it's because they are all, in their way, sincere & devoted artists. They don't make that continual, ghastly, enervating *personal* claim on your attention that other women do. If you disagree with them, they don't visibly hasten to agree with you. There's something hard & definite & self-contained about them. I feel I should always be glad if any one of them came to stay at our house. Do you feel that? Or am I sentimentalising? There's always the danger.

To return to this question of being at cross purposes with Virginia.[2] It is very queer. I told you in my last letter one of the strange things she said about yr. not being interested in novels. Another thing she said was that I was the most intellectual of all modern critics. Now that's pitifully wrong. Whatever I am I am not an intellectual critic at all. It is true I try to give my views an intellectual statement, because that is the only method I have. If I were a born writer, I should express myself in your way. But my attitude is almost exactly like yours. I can't treat art as a clever game, and I am (to myself anyhow) always notoriously weakest in the examination of the technical side of a work. My test is extremely simple. If a work awakens a profound response in me, then I sit up and try to find what it is that is working on me. In other words I am an absolutely emotional critic. What may seem intellectual is only my method of explaining the nature of the emotion.

I'm not saying this to talk about myself, but only to throw some light on the kind of mistake Virginia makes. It's quite fundamental. She sees only the apparatus; never the essentials. Or she sees the essentials only in a world from which those things we regard as the essentials have been removed. Therefore with us, she admires only those things which you & I regard as second-rate. Thus she was full of admiration for my review of Butler; but didn't like my review of Hardy. I don't say either of them was good. But the Hardy (even if it wasn't successful – and I don't believe it was quite) was on a different plane to my Butler. There was some real discovery in it. Now listen to what she said: 'You see you left out altogether what I think is the interesting part of Hardy – the spectacle of this old man pushing all these words into their places, & squeezing poetry out of himself as out of a tube'. Well, there's something so wrong about that – the truth it contains is so trivial & unimportant that there's nothing to be said. But it's all of a piece with her *Mark on the Wall* & her *Kew Gardens* – it's a fascination by unessentials. What gives her her real ability as a writer – and there's no doubt it is real – is that it is a *fascination*. But it's quite impossible for her to have *any notion at all* of what you and I are up to.

I hope I haven't been tedious about this. It was much in my mind yesterday, because I realised how much she liked you. I think her affection for you is quite genuine & real. But you are, I am sure, a perfect mystery to her, and, as far as I can see, you always will be.

I hope to goodness that terribly cold weather has given way a little. It's so warm & soft here to-day, that I can't believe its still icy with you

Goodbye darling heart

Boge.[3]

1. *Georgian Poetry 1918–1919*, edited by Edward Marsh.
2. Virginia, writing on 27 November of K.M.'s review and of her conversation with Murry, told Clive Bell: 'I couldn't grasp what Katherine meant but I thought she disliked the book and wouldn't say so, and so muffed her points. Murry, however, tells me that she admires it, but thinks my "aloofness" morally wrong. . . . Some say [*Night and Day*] is in the tradition, and others say it's not, but the great battle, so Murry tells me, is between those who think it unreal and those who think it real'.
3. K.M. replies 29 November: 'Your Sunday letter is here – about Vanessa and Virginia'.

---

[122]

158 days

[2 Portland Villas,
Hampstead,
London.]
[24 November, 1919.]
Monday Evening (later)

My darling,[1]

Your Friday morning letter came a little while after I had sealed my other one. Though it's late, I must write you a word or two.

My own darling: we are *not* making up dreams. Think what Ansaldi said. Remember that, (beyond all belief) you are building up the defences between you & death. God knows, I feel that L.M. tears them down again, like a blind & ravening animal. But she doesn't tear them all. You are pushing forward. Even though your mind doubts & is afraid, your body is going along the road of hope. Slowly, agonisingly slowly, so that the dangers seem even more threatening than they were. But something is being built.

Now a quarter of the days between us & our meeting are gone. We are nearer by a whole mile along our road of four long miles – its something. And more. Sydney has just told me – this very evening – that there's a charming house near him – called 'The Lacket'[2] – which is to be let on lease from May 20 next. Isn't that mere coincidence of month significant. It will be ready just in time. Sydney says it's really beautiful – and it has been inhabited by people of our own kind. It's to let – so there would be no question of a great outlay of money. A hundred pounds would probably do all that we need to do in the way of stoves. And then they would be ours to take away & put inside the house we buy for our very own for ever.

I'll go down & see it this next week-end. I'll *make it happen*, Wig. This will be the reality, do not doubt it. O Wig, I know the torment of your fear; I know you can't keep it away. How could you, having suffered as you have suffered? But, I, your Boge, say cross my heart straight dinkum, it shall be. And there's this advantage about that house; it leaves us near (but not too near) Sydney & Marge. That is good – I believe that they are genuine friends of ours, who believe in us. If you had seen Sydney's face light up the other week when I told him that there was good news from you (it was when your Ansaldi letter came) you would know he was [a] real friend. So real that (though I wd never never ask him) I feel he wd. lend us £100 like a shot.

Yes, my darling heart, the house is much nearer. And much solider. You can almost touch the bricks now. And when I've been down there, I'll describe it all. Darling, you must think about it all the while; don't think about whether you believe in it or not, but just about the actual house. Make plans for it. Arrange the rooms. Its as real as my hand & pen. That's the remedy.

Good-bye, my darling
Boge.[3]

1. J.M. replies to K.M.'s letter of 21 November: 'It happened rather luckily yesterday that L.M. and I reached a crise at tea time . . .'.

2. Although Murry did not seem aware of the fact, 'The Lacket' at Lockeridge, near Marlborough, Wilts. was the house (owned by the M.P. Hilton Young) that Lytton Strachey rented from September 1913 until the end of 1915.

3. K.M. replies 30 November: 'What a fate you should have published the Dosty the very week my review won't arrive'.

---

[123]   [2 Portland Villas,
                                                      Hampstead,
                                                        London.]
                                              [25 November, 1919.]
157 days   Tuesday 5 p.m.

My own precious Wig-wife.

I feel so ridiculously, tragically impotent, when its a question of building up yr. defences. You see when you write happily with good news, I always say to myself that's a whole row of bricks in place now, and I'm always surprised when I find they've been knocked down. I shall soon have to believe that I'm a ghastly optimist. I suppose it's because I so long and yearn for the bricks to stay there that I can't believe they can be shifted. Of course, that's stupid – but there it is; and, after all, there is something in it. Remember how even during that period of the most awful depression when I felt absolutely convinced that you were losing ground every day, you were really gaining. I pin my faith on that. It was an amazing miracle; and I believe that from that time forward you have really been building up more than ever has been thrown down. It goes like this, in my imagination.

our house/no smoke because of an anthracite stove

You see you're always tumbling down. L.M. is always pushing you down for one thing, and you're terribly alone. But you never tumble down as much as you've been going up. You dont go up as fast as you seem to at some moments, because then you'd be at C, the level on which the house is, in the twinkling of an eye; but still you are going up gradually & steadily. You must believe that, darling, because its been proved. But then you feel that you are walking along the edge of a precipice, that a snake's lurking to sting you, a robber to stab you. That's true. But still every day you gather a little more resistance to the robber. Everyday even though its only 1 in a 1000, the chances are less of his hitting you. Still that doesn't take away our fear. What we want is someone to take you in a great pair [of] arms and say: Now you are perfectly & absolutely safe. But remember, Mouse, how much definitely nearer that you are than you were a year ago. And you couldn't have faced this winter in London – it was out of the question. This is the last gasp, darling; – we'll never be parted again

I always feel when I write about this that I'm pretending it's easy: I don't mean to. I don't know altogether how hard it really is; but I have some imagination & some love. The difficulty is to know how exactly I can turn myself into a stick for you to lean on. I suppose I can only say that I do absolutely believe that you are going to get well, & that next year we shall have our house. Since Ansaldi never a shadow of doubt has crossed my mind and your latest letters don't shake me in the least. I am perfectly convinced. But whether that helps or not, I don't know; I think it would help me.

I sent you *Cinnamon & Angelica* to-day. Please tell me faithfully and mark the MS as much as you like, in pencil though. That will save you the trouble of writing a letter. (Before I forget – did the hydrobromic acid arrive safely. You've never mentioned it since, & I am rather worried. You should also have got the scarf by now.) Your review of Monkhouse & Stern[1] arrived safely to-day: – very excellent as usual.

Oh, the *fake* of this *Georgian Poetry*! It really is a terrible condition of affairs that these people – Eddie M.[2] & J.C. Squire – should have got such a stranglehold of English poetry. They are spreading a miasma of sickening falsity. Page after page of the Georgian book is not merely bad poetry – that would be a relief – but sham naive, sham everything. Good god. I don't set up to be much of [a] poet myself, but I'm worth 17 out of the 19 put together. That gang has tried to crab us long enough. I begin to feel angry. I want to lash out, & kick their heap of dry bones into the gutter. But I mustn't lose my temper. I get very upset, thinking about it. I feel that they'll manage to arrange that my book falls flat. However, darling, when we're together & in our country castle, we'll pull up the drawbridge and pour boiling water on their heads.

Your own
Boge – husband.[3]

1. 'Control and Enthusiasm', K.M.'s review of *True Love* by Allan Monk-house, and *Children of No Man's Land* by G.B. Stern, appeared on 28 November.
2. Edward Marsh (1872–1953), the kind and generous patron of many poets, had been a benefactor and friend of Murry in 1912. He edited five volumes of *Georgian Poetry* between 1912–1922 but was increasingly derided by the poetic rebels whose work he did not publish.
3. K.M. replies 30 November: 'It's a real Sunday, calm, quiet . . .'.

---

[124]   [2 Portland Villas,
                                         Hampstead,
                                         London.]
                                         Thursday
155 days   November 27. [1919.]

My darling Wig-wife,[1]

A wonderful long letter from you, in your tiniest handwriting, came last night. All about the stove, Caterina, Miss Kaye-Shuttleworth,[2] me & the table, and our little boy. All kinds of things were in it. How wise you were not to go to San Remo! Is the stove a success? It will be splendid if it is. But why should you imagine that I should wonder why you accepted the invitation to lunch? I'm overjoyed about it. I am haunted by the thought of your loneliness and your never having anyone to speak to. You can't speak to L.M. She's inarticulate – she's just a mouth like a fishe's. I absolutely understand how healthy, decent, human people help you. I know how they would help me. You are a strange child to ask me 'to bear with you'. You almost make me think I'm a kind of stern, black dragon. I suppose I am sometimes. That memory of my cold heartlessness in the kitchen was pretty awful. But I didn't 'tease' you, darling. I swear I didn't do that. You don't know how terrified I used to be when you did things which I thought were unwise. Something used to freeze inside me. No, I didn't tease you, that I know. But all the same I was heartless, that's true.

But I can't bear your thinking now that I could ever imagine that because you see people you are neglecting your work. Oh, Wig you made it up, suddenly, you must have done. Let me say, anyhow, that nothing will make me happier than to learn that you are seeing some decent people and having a chance to talk to them. It seems to me the very best medicine in the world. It's so good that the first specimen was a good one. You bet that my great-grandfather couldn't spell his name. I'm quite certain he couldn't. He was the ship's carpenter – that's quite right. You mustn't tell her, though, that the half-quantum flasks of my grandfather's pub. 'The Ordell Arms' had MURRY printed on them quite plain. It was one of the wonders of the world to me to see my own name embossed on glass. I don't think I've ever got over it; probably because I was at the impressionable age of three.

It's devastatingly cold here to-day. The pond was frozen over last night & has remained frozen all day. I don't think there's been a moment's thaw. There's no anthracite, either. So I sit up in the little room & manage to make myself fairly snug. Ottoline's sale is on Monday. I hope the settee I want particularly won't be too dear, and that there won't be a dealer's ring. I've never seen such a thing in my life. But they are always supposed to be at London Sales. Very frightening!

There doesn't seem to be much to say to-day somehow. I came home from the office in time for lunch – sardines, very good, & brown bread. Since then I've been trying with very poor success to write a review. A man just came who wants to buy these houses – they're for sale: notice boards on the wall outside – and wanted to know whether there was any chance of his getting one to live in. I told him what he'd have to pay us if he wanted ours. He was a friend of L.M's friends, the Donetters. Violet has gone out for the afternoon – so I'm going out to dinner with Brett. I lunched with her yesterday. I promised to send Chaddie & Jean some coffee – but when I thought it over, I decided that C. was so mean that I wasn't going to give her anything – so I sent her Legrain's price-list instead. I'm afraid she'll be very cross but I can't help it. My book is coming out on Dec. 8. I'm afraid it will fall pretty flat. But nowadays that rather amuses me than otherwise except that I'd like some more dibs for our house. It's arranged that I'm to go for the week end with Sydney to-morrow fortnight to see the Lacket.

O la la. I've got a cheerful turnip-head to-day. Your letters to Wingley, Athy, Violet, Gertie rolled up safely yesterday. The Moults came round in the evening while Sullivan was here. Moult is in the new Georgian book. He's better than a good many. But what rot it all is! Tommy is to be at de la Mare's on Sunday with me. The *Times Lit Sup* has refused our advertisement again – beasts.

Your absolute
Boge.

1. J.M. replies to K.M.'s letter of 23 November: 'I have just read your letter about the scarf'.
2. K.M. describes Miss Lionel Kaye-Shuttleworth from San Remo as: 'a friend of Dent's aunt in Nice. Elderly typical, good family, dowdy gentlewoman with exquisite greenish ermine scarf, diamond earrings and white suede gloves. The combination suggested *arum lilies* to me somehow'.

---

[125]   [2 Portland Villas,
                                              Hampstead,
                                              London.]
                                    Monday. Dec. 1. [1919.]
151 days

My own Wig-wife,[1]

I got home rather late to-day to find your Monday & Wednesday letters – one had recipes & a darling photograph of the Casetta – and both were brimful of your fragrance. You know the feeling? You begin to open the envelope, and with the first little tear something pops out and settles on your lips, at the corners: and you feel that you are smiling a wonderfully delicate smile, and that anyone with a real knowledge of the things worth knowing would say on the strength of that smile alone: That boy's in love. You know the smile.

The reason why I got home late is because I spent the afternoon at the Sale. The prices were terrific. The exquisite small lacquer cabinets went for about 30 guineas and other things in proportion. However, I made up my mind to buy something – and I'm not displeased. I spent £11 and bought one exquisite writing table for your boudoir room (£7). I think it is a real beauty in very dark mahogany with taper legs and two drawers. It's very firm & steady unlike most tables of the kind; – I know that because it was the table which the auctioneer used all the while. He was a very superior auctioneer, with a manner like a cabinet minister (very expensive). I only tell you that because his taps on the table were so delicate and inaudible that his having used the table doesn't mean there are dents in it.

The other thing I bought was – a clock. You'll laugh. I know you will. You'll think I have a clock mania – and to the extent that I believe every living room ought to have a good clock, I am. I hardly saw it before buying. But Philip [Morrell] who was standing near me whispered that it was given to Ottoline at her wedding by her uncle. I just saw it was rather a fine blue colour in a glass case, and that it was real Dresden. I concluded – very quickly – that it would be very expensive in its internal arrangements, and therefore dirt cheap at £3.15. I just got in with my £4 in time. Still, the clock's rather a dark horse. I'll describe them both to you when they arrive home. There was one lot I regretted not having risked a shot for – but I won't tell you about that. Anyhow it went for 16 guineas, which would have been a lot of money.

I know I haven't very much to show; but I think I steered neatly between rashness & cowardice, & I'm sure you'll love the table. It was a tantalising experience, anyhow. Duncan Grant was with me a good deal of the time, and for some reason we got on well together.

I got to de la Mare's last night: it took 1¾ hours each way. Tommy was there. If I hadnt had a cold, and the journey hadn't been so bad I should have enjoyed it. I let off a great deal about poetry, & prevailed on de la Mare to admit that Drinkwater[2] & Squire at least were no good at all as poets; which was one up at least. But I feel the awful difficulty of taking poetry really seriously as I do. Even de la Mare – delightful, kind & friendly as he is – I believe suspects me of animus. I have an animus, it's true, but I honestly don't believe there's anything impure in it.[3] I do try to test it so hard. I can't find anything but the natural animus a person of my rather heavily serious temperament feels against bad work that masquerades as good. I believe that I am fundamentally straight as a critic. I suppose I ought not mind; but I do hate even my enemies suspecting me of crookedness. Incidentally, this is why I want from you the severest possible criticism of *Cinnamon*. If you possibly can make yourself really hostile: drop on every even faintly weak point.[4] For I know that if I publish my review of *Georgian Poetry* they will wait for *Cinnamon* and break it into pieces if they can. If it is *solidly* good, they will only break themselves.

My difficulty about Sydney's G.E. [George Eliot] was that I've never read a line of her. As compared with Gosse in the *London Mercury* it was a defence of her – and I was glad of that. But I was in no position to judge whether it was really less than fair to her or not. Yes, it's true that he wrote very much under the influence of my review of Hardy. By the way, you spoil me utterly by your praise of my criticism. Your opinion is the only one I care to know, except my own, but you are too generous. Don't you think quite honestly that I'm a little *too* serious; a little heavy. I know the reason is that I take writing intensely seriously; but wouldn't it be possible for me to be just as serious without being so intense? I don't know.

My cold is entering on the heavy stage but I have a feeling that it's not going to be a very bad one. (I just heard Wing squeaking outside & ran down to let him in. He's now squatting in front of the fire.)
  Good-bye my precious Wig-wife
       I adore you,
        Boge.⁵

 1. J.M. replies to K.M.'s letters of 24 November: 'I've gone and gained another 2 lbs'; and 26 November: 'It's press day for you'.
 2. John Drinkwater (1882–1937), poet and dramatist, had contributed to *Rhythm*.
 3. Murry's 'animus' reveals itself in his letter of 26 November where he writes: 'Nowadays, everybody is "advanced". Twelve thousand people every year buy copies of *Georgian Poetry*. They are filled with intelligent interest in a thing they understand no more than the Relativity Theory. And charlatans form a strange group with self-deceivers to exploit the tasteless taste of the bourgeoisie. J. C. Squire sprawls over the artistic horizon, attended by an assiduous claque which knows the rising star. They roll each other's logs. They are filled with noble patriotism. They toady to L.G. & dine with Winston. Jolly old England! And all the young poets who have a spark in them quickly learn that the one thing necessary to salvation is to be nice to Eddie, then you'll get into the Georgian book & be able to sell your poems. And now the same old clique-claque has a fat orange review, full of sound sentiment and fake art, to show how fine, & noble & prosperous they are, & how degraded and envious & bitter is the fruit sold over the way.
 'Well, well. I only wish I had something of Bernard Shaw's talent, so that I could smite them hip & thigh. I'm not clever enough, I'm not detached enough; I get upset & angry, I can't be convincingly cynical. I'm always frightened that people will say: Look at that jealous little boy stamping over there in a rage'.
 4. In her answer to this letter K.M. acceded to Murry's request that she 'drop on every even faintly weak point'. It was, however, not *Cinnamon and Angelica*, but his critical tone that she found fault with. 'No, you're NOT too serious. I think you are a trifle over-anxious to assure people how serious you are. You antagonize them sometimes or set them doubting because of your emphasis on your sincerity. In reviewing again you cry sometimes, in your sincerity; these are things which have been done, which have happened, to *me* or to *us*. I think as a critic that *me* or *us* is superfluous. If they must be there, then you must write a poem or a story. . . . It fills me with a queer kind of shame; one hears oneself whispering in one's soul to you: "Cover yourself – cover yourself quickly. Don't let them see!" That they think you are asking for alms, for pity, doesn't matter. That, of course, is just their corruption – their falsity. Nevertheless, though they are wrong, I do not think you are right. If you speak for your generation, *speak*, but don't say "I speak for my generation," for the force is then gone from your cry. When you know you are

a voice crying in the wilderness, *cry*, but don't say "I am a voice crying in the wilderness" '.

5. K.M. replies 5 December: 'Your after the sale letter has arrived . . .'.

---

[126]   The Athenaeum,
                                                     10 Adelphi Terrace,
                                                      London, W.C.2.

December 3, Wednesday.
149 days

My own darling,

Press-day; pages; cold in the head; no letter from you this morning. If there's not one when I get back to-night, I shall be very disappointed. It's wet and sloppy but warm. The pages are very slow in coming. But the cold in the head means that I see everything through a slight mist. The very best thing for me would be one of your golden singing letters. There are some of them, you know, which pop out of the envelope the moment the first little bit is opened and fly about the room, singing, singing. Wing looks up to see what that nice, funny noise is, and scrapes his nose with his paw; then in a flash, he tumbles to it and begins to laugh, & does exactly what you imagined him as doing in your last letter, has to stuff his paw into his mouth to prevent himself laughing outright. Slowly the little bird, singing & singing, makes him mad. He begins to dash from the chair-back to the chest of drawers and back again, and again, faster and faster, and suddenly he realizes that Ath. is looking at him with great dignity and aloofness and stops. He begins to walk about very slowly, as though it were utterly inconceivable that he could have been dashing about; and so he goes on until Ath. is become quite unsuspecting. Then Wing leaps like an arrow on top of him & rolls him over. And that's only a part of the effect of one of your bird-letters. I should like one of those to-night.

A little interlude. Randall[1] just came up to ask me whether she was Jenny or Jennie, or Summer or Summers. With a fine careless rapture you have called her both about equally. I voted, however, for Jennie Summers.[2] You were a bit long; but it happened that, because I got it early, I could fit it without cutting – which was a very good thing, because, although you told me to cut the first part rather than the end, it was extraordinarily difficult to do. You try as an exercise, when you get the paper, to cut out the amount by which you are over the two columns. Yours is certainly the hardest copy to cut of any we have. That's because there's more *quality* in it than in any other. You always create a unity of impression, by somehow building it up line by line. To cut any part of it is to ruin it, as I feel. So, just for this reason, to spare me an agony, keep as close as you can to the two columns if your copy is only going to arrive on the Wednesday morning. If it comes earlier it doesn't matter. Because if I have it in proof on the Tuesday, I can always manage to fit it with something.

I've burned my boats over the Georgians.[3] I've cut out one too contemptuous sneer, but I have put the rest in. We shall never be forgiven, that's certain. Even as it is I've strained several points for friendship's sake, i.e. in not analysing Gibson. Believe me, in three consecutive poems of fourteen lines he has the phrase 'blood sings', 'singing blood'. I wanted to call the review 'Marshmallows'; but I had to be serious. They strike me exactly like chocolate marshmallows, soft, dry, & sodgy. But isn't that a fine poem of the dead soldier Wilfrid Owen?[4] It's what Sassoon[5] might have done, if he were any real good. Another one of the things I didn't say because it might hurt. I'll send you that poem complete, if you'd like it; I won't send the book, because that will only annoy you.

Don't fret because everybody's wrong – Virginia & the rest; get well, keep up heart. We're going to win. By win I mean not be triumphant like Squire and the other people with the lie in the soul, but quiet & confident & humble like Hardy. One day people will turn to us as we turn to that old man. One day people will feel comforted merely because they know we are alive. I'm sure of that, Mouse, absolutely sure. Don't fret. I know I do sometimes, but I find that patch of calm somewhere in my soul. Guard yourself, get well, believe in our home-to-be, and everything will go like our new clock. We are fated to survive, you & I. We have something to give to England, and English literature, that no-one else can give. It shall be given. We belong to Hardy; and we shall have known more happiness than he has.

Goodbye, my darling Mouse.

Boge.[6]

1. An assistant at the *Athenaeum*.

2. Jennie Summers, a character in Clemence Dane's novel *Legend*. K.M.'s review, 'A Revival', appeared on 5 December.

3. Murry's review of *Georgian Poetry 1918–19*, entitled 'The Condition of English Poetry', appeared on 5 December. About it, he had written to K.M.

on 29 November: 'I've written such an awful review of *Georgian Poetry*. I mean that I think it's good and true, but it's terribly severe. I shall never be forgiven if I print it, not unto seventy times seven. The Squire clique will spend their lives in trying to be revenged. But I can't see what else to do. It's too important a book to allow anybody else to do; and yet I can't ignore it. But it's terrible, Wig. I'm almost frightened of it myself. I wish I could read it to you & have your opinion. Anyhow it's absolutely sincere'.

4. Probably a reference to 'Strange Meeting' by the First World War poet Wilfrid Owen (1893–1918) which appeared in *Wheels* (1919).

5. Siegfried Sassoon (1886–1967), educated at Cambridge, was a poet who fought in, and survived, the war. In 1918, to the indignation of Ottoline, Murry reviewed unfavourably Sassoon's *Counter-Attack*. Virginia Woolf remarked (to Ottoline): 'I believe Sassoon has got far more praise because of [Murry's review] in all the other papers'. In her *Diary*, describing a weekend at Garsington in July 1918, she wrote: 'The string which united everything from first to last was Philip's attack upon Murry in The Nation for his review of Sassoon. He was half proud of himself & half uncomfortable; at any rate, I was taxed with being on Murry's side before 10 minutes was out; & then to prove his case Philip read Murry's article, his letter, & his letter to Murry, three times over, so I thought, emphasising his points, & lifting his finger to make us attend. And there was Sassoon's letter of gratitude too'.

6. K.M. replies 8 December: 'It's warm and still'.

---

[127]

[2 Portland Villas,
Hampstead,
London.]
Dec 5 [1919.]
147 days   Friday 6 p.m.

My own darling,

I haven't had a letter from you to-day, though the last post hasn't been yet, so that there's still a chance. The weather these last two days has been awful, wet & muggy, and my cold (as my colds always are) is a nuisance. But it's just foolish to talk to you of my cold. It's only a matter of handkerchiefs and great blowings of my nose at night. You know how my snuffling goes on, more & more violently, for about half an hour. It's annoying to me, goodness knows what you must have thought. And then, though I'm always buying handkerchiefs, I never seem to have a single one.

There's very little news. Yesterday I went to Gertler's studio to tea, and saw one or two of his recent pictures. He is making real progress – I'm sure of that. One of his new pictures is really beautiful in our sense of the word. 'A silent loveliness of colour'. I told him what I thought;

and I think he was very pleased. I also said that if things went well with
us I should try to buy one of his important paintings next year, paying
for it by instalments. That pleased him very much. And I mean it,
wig. We must have one of his pictures in our new house; we'll buy it
together, when you come home. I know the real thing when I see it,
and his work has begun to be the real thing.

That gave me a bit of [a] buck – seeing good work always does. Oh
Lord, why couldn't you have been with me? But don't worry. We'll
toddle along to there together at the end of May with our pennies in
our hand & say: 'I'd like this one, please.' and pack it up in brown
paper and carry it away to the country, and put it in our brightest
sunniest room to be one of our heirlooms.

Seeing those pictures gave me a great desire to write about painting
again. As I can't do it in the *Athenaeum*, where there is already
cut-throat competition, I've arranged to do it in the *Nation*. Only one
long signed article once a month. That's as much as I can do; but it will
be just enough to say what I want to say about things that are worth
talking about. And the interval's long enough to make them really
good. I see a rather good book at the end of two years. Talking shop
reminds me of one urgent thing. We shall have to go to press on
Monday in Christmas Week. That means that I shall really want your
article for that week on Dec. 18, and that means that you will have to
try to let me have two articles at almost the same time – the one for the
number on Dec. 19 should arrive on Dec. 16 at latest, & the one for the
number on Dec 26 should arrive on Dec. 18. Is that possible, do you
think? I hate to think that I am overworking you; and I'm always
afraid of it.

Moreover, it's terribly short notice. I only realised the difficulties of
Christmas week to-day. This letter should reach you on the 10th. But
you will have been counting on sending off the article for Dec. 19 on
the 11th. or so The question is whether you can manage another by
Dec. 13. Don't worry if it's only a column. That doesn't matter. The
important thing is that no number of the *A*. should appear without an
article from you. I'm not merely thinking of *our* feeling; but of the
paper itself. No K.M. this week, I'm sure, would be a very great blow
to most of our readers.

But blast the paper for a moment. I want a letter; I want to know
how you are – my little, lovely, darling of all the world. I want
something of the passionate devotion of my love to come through to
you; and with it a little of my confidence. Ah, it's easy to be confident

when you aren't separated from life, you say. Oh, Mouse, I know it's far, far harder for you; but even with me there were months when I had no confidence at all. That it has grown up again in me is something after all. My own goblin-girl – Your Boge.[1]

1. K.M. replies 9 December: 'After sending you the wire, I want to send another . . .'.

---

[128]
<blockquote>
[2 Portland Villas,
Hampstead,
London.]
[5 December, 1919.]
</blockquote>

147 days   Friday – later

My darling,[1]

Yes, the letter came – saying you had fever – that Ansaldi was a fraud. I don't know what to do; I feel I haven't the energy to react – well, it's no use writing to say that. I must wait until I have the energy

Saturday Morning 12

I don't even now know any more what to say. I feel, as I suppose you do, very very tired.

You were a darling to write to me about *C & A* as you did. I know that all you say is right; and I feel in my heart that I ought to rewrite it all from the beginning. But I feel that I can't; I don't want to – *C & A* doesn't matter. In order to feel that it does a great weight would have to be removed from me. If I am able to work – and I'm not able to just now – it will have to be at something different, something infinitely more bitter. One thinks one's wounds are healing & they aren't.

To get your letter was a blow.[2] It's not that I attach any importance to Ansaldi. The weight you'd gained is far more important than that. But it was a blow to realize that he had such an effect upon you; it filled me not with despair about the final issue, but with despair at my own impotence. I try to make you feel something of my confidence, and the spell won't work, the words won't carry. It's because I don't realize how profoundly lonely you are; your cheerful letters deceive me. But even if I had realized your loneliness, I don't see what I could have done. It's that – not knowing what to do, or what I could have done that has knocked the bottom out of me.

I know it's no use sending you a letter like this; that I'd far better burn the thing. But how can I send you a different kind of letter, where in myself shall I find the matter of it?

Let's fasten on practical things. *You must go to Mentone.* That's absolutely clear. Surely Jennie can find you something. You said you had written to her in your letter. I can rake up some money, somehow. Let me know what you want.

I wish to God I were a man. Somehow I seem to have grown up, gone bald even, without ever becoming a man; and I find it terribly hard to master a situation. I keep on trying: sometimes I think I've got it straightened out a little. But it tangles again immediately. And people seem to think I'm made of whipcord & steel – I'm not, not at all. Je suis tellement triste. My power of running things here, my control, my ability to steer, depends wholly upon my news from you. I could move a mountain when I feel that things are going even moderately well with you; now I could hardly move a mouse. There's one Mouse that I cannot move at all – that's plain.

I don't think we have gained much by being dream-children, do you? We can't help it; we can't change our nature. But things are hard – and so wearisome. Somehow they are always the same – the same bright bloom on the fruit as we reach out to pluck it, the same bitterness when we taste it. I feel at this moment that I shouldn't – Oh it's treachery to write such things

No, no, no. This is *all wrong*. What truth there is in it is a false truth. We must build, build, build. Scramble to our feet again. But why, why Mouse do you believe Ansaldi? You *know* that you can live in England if you live there properly. You *know* this, & yet you believe Ansaldi. It's that which crushes me.

Forgive me for blaming you. I have no right. It's shriekingly unjust. You are lonely, and ill. These things must be.

I can't send off this letter like this. Perhaps something will come this evening, and I shan't feel so grey. I won't put it in an envelope till then.

I've waited till seven o'clock & nothing has come. Perhaps something will turn up by the last post; but I can't wait until then, or I shall miss the post myself. I've been unable to do a thing all day; I've been terribly nervous & restless.

But this won't do anyhow. At all events I – the absolutely well one – must pull myself together and stand firm as a rock. The awful thing is that a rock can't do anything, but be a rock. And I don't see what good my being a rock will do to you.

At all events let this one thing be clear. For God's sake don't worry about me. I'm safe & well; a word saying that things were better would transform me utterly.

But this love. Is it any good to know that it's absolutely devouring, anguished, devastating: so long as I feel myself as a separate thing at all, I am only love of you.

Boge.

1. J.M. replies to K.M.'s letter of 1 December: 'I'm rather dashed today'.
2. Katherine had written: 'Ansaldi came yesterday. Don't *count* on him. He's a charlatan. He owned yesterday that the reports he gave me were because "I saw dis lady wants vot you call sheering up". . . . He said yesterday emphatically that I could not winter in England next year or the year after . . . , [I] REALIZED how I had been taken in again'.

---

[129]   [2 Portland Villas,
                                        Hampstead,
                                        London.]
                                [8 December, 1919.]
                                Monday afternoon
144 days   6 p.m.

My own darling,[1]

This morning in bed I got your Thursday letter & the verses called 'The New Husband'. I've wired to you to-day to say I'm coming out for Christmas. I feel there's not much I can say.

I[2] don't think that at any time I've had a bigger blow than that letter & these verses. Even now they hardly seem like a letter & verses – more like a snake with a terrible sting. But it's kind of you to tell me you have those feelings: far better, for me anyhow, than keeping them from me. You have too great a burden to bear; you can't carry it. Whether I can manage mine, I don't know. We'll see when I get out to you.

What is certain is that this can't go on – something must change. What can go on – I don't know yet. My faith at present is that my coming out for a little while will put you right. But I don't see why it should. I feel that everything depends upon me; that I have to do something quite definite, very quickly. But I don't know what it is, and my faculty for doing anything has been suddenly paralysed. At the moment when I have to balance in the middle of the tight-rope I have begun to hesitate.

My plan is to try to get the paper in some sort (!) of order for three weeks ahead during this week, & leave here at the end of the week. The return fare second class is just over £14, so I'm hoping to do it for £20. I mention money, because it's important. But I'll explain these things when I get there.

As you know already, I'm ready to chuck the paper any moment; but I must see my way to money. I've said this many times; but I say it again, because, though I feel you don't agree with me, it's fundamental to any decision I take. At present I'm trying to clear up the remains of last year's debts. Until they are cleared I shall stick to the *A.* That's callous, I suppose. But I can't help it. You know my position as a bankrupt. I dare not leave our debts unpaid – I'm not supposed to have any. Once we're straight – and if things were to go moderately well I shall be straight by April (as I hoped to be by December) – I'll do anything. But I know that to cut off with little money coming in & heavy debts would mean inevitable disaster.

If I felt certain that my being there would really make things right until May, then nothing would matter. But now I can't pretend to a certainty I don't feel. We'll just have to leave it & see. Anyhow, I just couldn't go on with the *A.* if you were to go on feeling like this. I'm absolutely incapable of work, now. That sounds, and is, selfish. But you have told the truth; & I must tell the truth. I'm not made of steel, myself. And it's becoming a great effort to do what I have to do sanely – do you think I can do anything with this ringing in my ears.

> Who's your man to leave you be
> Ill & cold in a far country?
> Who's the husband, who's the stone
> Could leave a child like you alone?

There's nothing to say to that. All that I implore you is to say what you want. That will help.

No, no, no – all this is too *hard*. I don't mean it – something different. But I must keep sane. I'm coming quickly, darling – then we'll see, we'll see.

Boge.[3]

1. J.M. replies to K.M.'s letter of 4 December: 'I am sending my review of Couperus and Kuprin today'.

2. K.M. underlined in pencil these words: '<u>I</u> don't think; <u>I've</u> had; <u>snake</u>; whether <u>I</u> can manage; <u>I feel that everything depends</u> . . . <u>very quickly</u>; <u>my</u> faculty; <u>I</u> have to balance; <u>I</u> have begun to hesitate; <u>some sort</u>'.

On the back of the envelope she wrote: 'This letter killed the Mouse, made the Worm creep underground and banished the Dream Child for ever. Before I had received it I had learned to live <u>for</u> Love and <u>by</u> Love. I had given myself up – and a kind of third creature <u>us</u> was what I lived by. After I had read it, quite apart from me, my own self returned <u>and</u> all my horror of death vanished. From this date I simply <u>don't care</u> about death! No question of heroics – or life not being worth living or anything like it. I simply feel alone again. Voilà'.

3. K.M. replies 12 December (wrongly dated 9 by J.M.): 'I am awake and I have re-read your letter'.

------

[130]   [2 Portland Villas,
                                              Hampstead,
                                              London.]
                                         Dec. 9 [1919.]
                                              Tuesday
143 days.   5 p.m.

My own darling,

Forget all about that horrible letter I wrote you yesterday. I was overstrung – you only say that of grand pianos, I fear. At any rate I feel it all ought to be wrote again & wrote different.

I don't know whether this letter will get to you before me or not.[1] I got my French visa – for nothing – this afternoon, & I'll get my Italian early to-morrow on the way to the office. But I must get a few things at the office straightened out first; and I should like to have a reply to the wire I sent you to-day, asking what things I should bring. You see I shall travel light so that it will be easy for me to bring anything you need or will like. I hope you will have tumbled to this & wired me a proper list. Anyhow, I shall bring a small Xmas pudding & a decent woolly scarf. There will be no harm in your having two of them if the other turns up; if not, I'll get the insurance money.

As far as I can see we shall certainly have not less than ten days together. I shall have to get back by Sunday, January 4. But I needn't start till January 2. We shall see the New Year in together. With ordinary luck I should be at Ospedaletti not later than December

17–18. Why that will leave a whole fortnight with Christmas in the middle. I shall probably have to do a bit of work while I'm there – but so will you – so that won't matter will it. We'll have a real Christmas dinner, with the pudding I'll bring

But why in God's name, I ask myself now, did we not originally arrange to have Xmas together? I feel it would have spared you half the torment of your loneliness. What a blind fool I am! I scrape & scrape up money and I throw away the very thing that makes life worth living & money worth having. And even from the purely economical side I lose nothing. For having seen you & having persuaded you, as I know I will that everything will come right; that you *will not* have to spend other winters away, I shall easily be able to do the extra work to make up the cost of the journey.

For, believe me, my own darling Mouse, your fears are all wrong. Well, I won't go into that again. I know you'll believe me when I see you, & talk to you.

I got your cards to-day. I won't send them by post in case they never arrive; I'll bring them.

I have an idea that this journey is going to be one of the easiest & cheapest I ever made. Getting a visa for nothing this afternoon was a werry good omen don't you think? And with no heavy luggage I'll be able to slip across Paris in no time, so that there should be no difficulty about making the connection with the night train to Vintimille, & so avoiding having to stay the night in Paris.

Oh, darling won't it be heaven seeing each other. I shall really hold you in my arms – really you. My heart goes all faint & wobbly at the very thought. Oh, please, don't have any more fever or any more loneliness. It's only a day or two at the most.

I fancy old Bonwick is rather fed up. Serve him damned well right. And he'll be more fed up when I get back for I'm going to demand another £200 a year on my salary. I don't see why I should have to worry about money like this. I'm worth £1000 a year; & they'll have to pay it if they want me. I think I shall have the paper straightened out enough to make it safe to leave. And I'll do some articles myself while I'm with you as I say.

Goodbye, dear heart,
We shall have Christmas & the New Year together after all
Your own
Boge-husband.

I send Arthur's woodcut of the cats that of Wing is a little masterpiece it's the spit of him.

1. Murry was now determined to join K.M. for Christmas. He confessed to her on 14 December: 'You see I was terribly upset by your poem. It seemed to me so cruel, so utterly unlike you, that I could only believe that something terrible had happened to you I had to come; and then when I had made up my mind to come, all the difficulties faded away'.

---

[131]   2 Portland Villas
Thursday 7 p.m.   East Heath Road
141 days.   Hampstead, N.W.3
                                   [11 December, 1919.]

My own precious darling Wig-wife,

I had your second telegram.[1] It's no use you know: I've made up my mind to come. I've been thinking of our meeting, our kisses, our delight, our Christmas dinner, our New Year together. Do you think that I can hold back now having thought of these things? It's just silly of you to talk about 'the greatest possible mistake', when it's – quite obviously – the greatest possible sense.

And listen, Wig. The only real brick all along was the question of money. I wanted to save our money for the house. Well, I decided on Monday that it was a fat lot of use saving money for a house, when it could be used to be happy (if only for a fortnight) with the one person for whom the house was to be made. Last night, I suddenly thought – why shouldn't we have both. Why should we be so hard up, after all we've been through – and it just seemed to me too preposterous. So I sat down & wrote a very friendly, winning, sympathetic letter to old Arnold Rowntree[2] who has a heart, and said I should like my salary raised to £1000. Then, before sending it this morning, I spoke to Bonwick, also in a very friendly way. He absolutely agreed, and said he didn't think there would be any difficulty about it whatever and that I might count on £1000 a year from Jan 1. What do you think of that?

You won't say 'the greatest possible mistake' now, will you? Why, the £20 is a mere flea-bite now. And, mark this, the £200 extra is the direct result of my making up my mind to come. It was only when my mind was made up & I began imagining the delight of our meeting, that I asked myself why should I submit to circumstances which had made that delight impossible for me. I should never have thought of the £1000 without that.

No, darling, you can see plainly, can't you now, that it was the best possible thing to do from *every* point of view. We deserve to be happy, & we will be. But I wish to goodness you would wire me what you want, instead of talking of mistakes. I knew you'd go on like this; but it is an awful waste of telegrams.

What I regret most bitterly is the letter which I wrote you on Monday. Forget it, burn it – it's got nothing to do with me, but only with a me that was harassed and inclined for a moment to throw up the sponge. But once the decision was taken, I've been a changed man. I've thought of nothing but the sheer happiness of being with you. Ask Tommy, ask Sullivan whether they have not seen a new sparkle in my eyes, since Monday.

Well, darling, I've taken the ticket for Monday. I hope to use the week-end making things straight for the *Athenaeum*, writing some articles, & insuring that they don't go off the rails while I'm away.

Your own loving soon
arriving Boge husband.

Tuesday night or Wed. morning alors.

1. K.M. had sent Murry four telegrams between 9 and 13 December:
9 December, 1919: 'Implore you not to written dismiss idea immediately greatest possible mistake better today Tig'.
10 December, 1919: 'Urge you most earnestly not to come utterly unnecessary entreat you to wait until May letter sent explaining Tig'.
12 December, 1919: 'Telegram received implore you finally abandon plan don't come till May all going splendidly here don't spoil our future wire Tig'.
13 December, 1919: 'Tuesday letter received overjoyed if easy but perfectly understand if don't come wire Tig'.
2. Arnold Rowntree (1861–1949), the chocolate manufacturer from York and philanthropist who financed the *Athenaeum*. He was also the financial backer of *War and Peace*, a small monthly magazine of which Leonard Woolf had been assistant editor.

January – April 1920

Murry's Christmas visit to Ospedaletti lasted about a fortnight. On 4 January he was back in London and resuming his correspondence with Katherine. In the aftermath of his visit she wrote 'The Man Without a Temperament'. Then, overcome by nervous exhaustion and depression, she moved to Menton and the care of Connie Beauchamp and Jinnie Fullerton. At the end of April 1920 she and L.M. returned once more to Portland Villas for the summer.

[132]
2 Portland Villas
[Hampstead,
London.]
[5 January, 1920.]
Monday 6.10 pm

My own darling,
    I telephoned Rutter to-day, who said he had had a wire from you saying you had sent the article.[1] I didn't know what to suggest save that he should wire you again in case you had sufficient notes of the review to enable you to rewrite it. I'm terribly sorry about the business but I don't see what I can do.
    I went down to the office this morning to feel how things were going. I think they are really all right; but I feel very much that when the cat's away the mice begin to play. There's always a general sense of irresponsibility. The paper is filled up just anyhow, and no-one dreams of looking a week ahead. What a joy it will be when you are back? You and I with our heads together – are the only editors of this paper. It's a mistake to have to let anyone else have control. They are splendid, Sullivan & Huxley, at their jobs – but outside them useless.
    The day is cold and has been sunless. It was very hard to get up this morning. The house I found in apple-pie order. But I had rather a

shock wh: I didn't dare to tell you about in my letter yesterday. When I arrived, Athy was there to meet me, but no Wingley. He hadn't been seen all the morning. He didn't turn up all day. In the evening I went with Arthur who had come to see me over to Brett's for supper. When I came back, feeling intensely worried, in the evening at 10 o'clock, there was Wing on the door mat. He was delighted. When Violet came in, she explained it immediately. 'He had gone to meet me & missed the train'. And somehow, you know, it seemed perfectly simple & true. I'm not quite sure I don't really believe it now. I should be quite broken-hearted if anything happened to him. There never has been a creature who so much belonged to <u>us</u>.

Arthur, I find, made a stupid mistake. (I am rather annoyed with him over it; because I told him so plainly to send by *registered book post*) He sent your two books by parcel post. So Lord knows when you will get them. It is so vexing. In the meantime I'll send you my copy of the ordinary edition of the story.[2] It will show you how beautiful it looks, at any rate.

My book[3] had a fearful slating in the *Daily Telegraph* – conceited, bumptious, platitudinous, everything that is offensive. I haven't a copy of the paper, but I'll buy one to-morrow & send you. But what cheers me more than anything is that Tommy took me aside & said: I think your book's fine, far finer than when I read it in bits. You won't have a great success; but you will have a great influence. Well, that's good enough.

I haven't seen Sydney yet. I'm waiting for him, because I want if possible to go down for [the] weekend. There must be no delay about the house now. (I just want to say once more how glad I am that I came – how happy I was. All the neuralgia dissolves away and only happiness remains, as though someone had slipped a golden fruit into my hand. Good God, Wig, – and to think you said (or was it me?) that it was all over. Why, it's only beginning, darling!)

The first volumes of [the] Thomas Hardy are here. I am glad we have them. They too are <u>ours</u>. We shall be so proud of them in days to come, proud even of the fact that we bought them when we could not afford them.

There was a review of my poems[4] – unexpected – in [the] *Times Supplement* did you see it? I think it was unsympathetic but fair – the kind of review I like. I had a very nice letter from Edith Sitwell,[5] the editor of *Wheels*, about what I said of Wilfrid Owen – a nice letter, simple & straightforward – and (what is better) enclosing a poem by

Owen, not quite as good as 'Strange Meeting', but with beautiful things in it. He's a man I shall feel proud to have published.

Goodbye, darling

Boge.[6]

1. Frank Rutter (1876–1937) published 'The Man Without a Temperament' in *Art and Letters*, Spring, 1920, but no article or review by K.M.

2. *Je ne parle pas français*, published by the Heron Press.

3. *The Critic in Judgement; or Belshazzar of Baron's Court* (Hogarth Press, 1919). Virginia Woolf commented in her *Diary* on 3 December 1918: 'I have to read for a second time Murry's poem, which I found hard to read; from reasons the opposite of those that make Eliot hard to read: Murry has a plethora of words; his poem is intricate & involved & as thick as a briar hedge; he does his thinking aloud; not making you fetch it from the depths of silence as Eliot does.'

4. *Poems: 1917–18* (Heron Press).

5. Edith Sitwell (1887–1964), the poet and critic, edited an annual anthology of modern verse, *Wheels*, from 1916–1921.

6. K.M. replies about 10 January: 'I have received your Monday letter explaining about Wing'.

---

[133]

The Athenaeum,
10 Adelphi Terrace,
London, W.C.2.
[12 January, 1920]

Monday. 3 p.m. In the Office.

My own darling,

The Lacket is no good. Its too small, too dark. Emphatically not the thing we want. I walked over to it in a raging storm yesterday afternoon – the wind was terrible. Coming back, it blew me from one side of the road to the other. I felt rather a worm when I got back, not least because my exhaustion had taken the form of a violent diarrhoea, which has continued until now. Except for that I'm perfectly all right. I arrived at Paddington at 1 o'clock, & gave myself a good, digestible lunch at Gatti's.

One very good suggestion has been made about the house, namely that we should take Roger Fry's for a year or so. It is near Guildford in S. Surrey in a lovely position facing S. with central heating & a properly built open air shelter. for sleeping & working in. I don't know whether Roger is willing to let it. I know he doesn't live in it, and that he offered [it] to me for you rent free last summer for as long as we liked. At any rate I'll approach him if only as an additional iron in the fire. It's worth having a superlatively well built modern house on tap in case of an emergency.

Desmond McCarthy[1] was talking to me about Mr. Clough's[2] house last night. He admitted that it was a very fine house but he said it wd. be a great mistake because, to his own knowledge, it was very damp. That, I think, is final.

Altogether we must call Sydney's part of Wiltshire off. I've come to the conclusion that it's no use trusting other people's reports about houses – they've simply no idea of the kind of thing we want and must have. I must simply peg away myself every week-end, marking out a different piece of country, following up every clue I can get hold of.

I feel confident that I shall find it, if I don't allow myself to be distracted from the search. Apart from that week-end with the Wells[3] on the 24 – 26 Jan, I have no week-end engagements. I must keep them all absolutely free.

Your Tchehov & a parcel of books arrived to-day. I hope I shall find some letters from you when I get home; I have had none since Saturday.

With all my love

Your own & only
Boge.

1. Desmond McCarthy (1878–1952), writer, conversationalist and close friend of the Woolfs. He disappointed them by never making his mark as a novelist. 'Being an editor has drugged the remnants of ambition in him, & he is now content', Virginia wrote in May 1920. 'It seems with Desmond now, always afternoon'.

2. The 'eccentric very rich' owner of a country house Murry was considering.

3. H. G. Wells (1866–1946), the novelist, had invited Murry to visit him. Murry had been friendly with Wells since at least 1914 when he took the Lawrences to a party at Wells' Church Row House. Anxious to impress, Lawrence insisted on wearing a new dress-suit which made him look a travesty of his normal self. 'Inevitably', Murry recalled, 'the party was a miserable affair for us all, and, as we returned, Lawrence was apocalyptic in his denunciation of H. G. Wells, who had nevertheless been very decent and genuinely pleased to meet him.'

[134]   The Office
                                   [The Athenaeum,
                                   10 Adelphi Terrace,
                                   London. W.C.2.]
                                   [13 January, 1920.]
                                   Tuesday 6.30 p.m.

My own darling,
Your review of *Agate*[1] & the little note were at the office when I
arrived this morning. It's awful your having been so ill again. But
don't say things like 'don't blame me too much'. I know I've given you
reason to say them; but that's all past & over. I only love you; and
when you're finding things terribly hard just think that I'm loving you
more then, more intensely and warmly, more nearly, than at any other
time.
You will have learned why, in my first letter, I didn't say anything
about Wing. It was too awful to frighten you. And there he was on the
mat in the evening. He is more darling than ever. I don't know what to
say about him. He's just perfect – just, in the kitten way, what I should
like our little boy to be. Absolutely independent, absolutely sympathetic, thoroughly grubby, full of love that he won't make a parade
of, with an exquisite sense of humour. Athy is adorable too, but his
affection is almost a monomania now. He insists on coming in my
bedroom as soon as I get up & following me at two inches distance all
the while I shave. He is, in fact, a bit stupid, while Wingley is
excessively wise – perhaps a bit worldly wise, as you'd say if you saw
the way he always gets whatever food is going before his brother.
I have only a little while ago come back from having tea with
Chaddie & Jean. I couldn't avoid going; though I asked myself all the
while why I was there. Not that I dislike them – God forbid – but why
in Heaven's name have they made themselves such social parrots.
Their continual 'Of course – oh, absolutely' – given with an unchang-
ing accent of intense understanding (they both do it) works on me so
much that I'm ashamed to make any remark at all. Not ashamed
myself, but ashamed for them; I feel I ought not give them the
opportunity of making such a terrible display. However, it's over now
– or nearly. Jean is coming up again at the beginning of February and,
remembering my old offer, I had to invite her to dine & go to the
theatre. But that's the end. We don't belong to the same world; and,

honestly, I've seldom met any people who belong to such an *utterly* different world from my own.

I enclose the proof of the ad. of your book[2] which will be in the *Times* this week – a similar ad will appear in the *Athenaeum*.

Good-bye, darling, just think all the while, or as often as you can, how much I love you. It may help a little.

Your own
Boge.

1. K.M.'s review of J. E. Agate's novel *Responsibility* appeared on 16 January 1920.
2. *Je ne parle pas français.*

---

[135]   [2 Portland Villas,
                                         Hampstead,
                                         London.]
                                         [14 January 1920]

Wednesday 5.30 p.m. Press Day
My own darling,[1]

Last night I had your letter telling of your nervous exhaustion and your fainting. Perhaps, by this time, you are at Mentone. I shan't get desperate or agitated; it's no use, & it won't help you. But I'm terribly anxious to have some more news. Whatever you do, take it slowly, & don't hesitate to call for money. Remember everything's ours & that the vital thing is that you should not lose ground. You won't. But there's no doubt that you are right, & must move elsewhere.

Does this all sound cold, darling? It isn't really; and you won't, for even an instant, doubt my love. I write as I do merely because *we* know that the only thing for me to do is to steer the ship steadily, and find the house. I'm concentrating on that.

I've had this letter from Maria Dahlerup,[2] backing out. It looks to me as though she used our offer as a means of bringing Mr. Smithson up to scratch. But then I'm a cynic. However, I gathered from people who I have sounded that we shan't have any difficulty in finding the very thing we want. All kinds of educated girls are clamouring to find such jobs. So don't worry your head about that part of the business. That will be simple, and, anyhow, it comes after the house.

To day I took an exchange advertisement along to the *Times*. It will go in to morrow (Thursday) & Saturday. I'll cut it out of the *Times* to morrow & send it to you. I think it's a very promising method. To night, I'm going to explore the map and see where to start hunting the Hampshire Downs, where I shall go on Friday afternoon. Just to see if its the right kind of country, and pick up any clues I can find.

At Hampton's sale this morning I bought a mirror in an old oblong gilt frame, very pleasant – and exactly what I suggested to you at Christmas. I'm sure you will approve. I also bought 3 bath towels, 6 hand-towels & 4 new linen pillow-slips. The towels on my own initiative in order to make up a dozen of each while prices are not too exorbitant, the pillowslips because Violet said we needed them. Total cost of everything £6.2.5. I wanted to buy a rug there and another bedroom mirror; but I felt I'd better not. You see the £6 is covered by what I wrote for the *Nation* last month. If I manage an article this month perhaps I'll buy the rug. It's so hard to get any work done while everyone in the office is ill. I haven't yet been able to get your parcel off; the week ends cut into the week so much that I work all day at top speed, and then in order to keep the team together, have so many people to see that I can't even get a review written. Perhaps it will shake down again after this week.

The great comfort is that I've got completely better of my illness which, I thought, was going to give me a bad time last week end. But all that weakness, I made such a fuss about, was just the devil going out of me. I'm extraordinarily fit & capable of coping with anything.

Gertie has been ill. I think that's why you've not heard from her about your present which, Violet says, reached her quite safely.

Darling, my own heart, it's all coming right. And soon the real spring will be beginning in your country. There were even lambs' tails on the bushes in Wiltshire, & there was a primrose.

Your loving
Boge.

1. J.M. replies to K.M.'s letter of about 10 January: 'I have just received your Monday letter explaining about Wing'.

2. An acquaintance who was being considered for the post of companion-help to K.M. In a letter of 13 January which crossed with Murry's, K.M. said that she 'did not want Marie any more', preferring L.M. 'to act Marie's part for us in our country house'.

[136]   The Athenaeum,
                                        10 Adelphi Terrace,
                                         London, W.C.2.

17 Jan 20
Saturday Morning at the Office.

My own darling,
   No letter from you either last night or this morning, & now I'm just
going off to Wells, so there's no chance of anything until Monday.
Probably you hadn't got my letter asking for a postcardful of news
everyday in time for it to make any difference. So I shall sit tight until
Monday.
   I have nothing to report. Last night I sat down & wrote a review of
Masefield's poem. It was done in a great hurry: we are terribly short of
copy just now. But I hope it's all right. I must manage another review
by Monday. We've dropped advertising for a time; but the paper
maintains its level & creeps ahead a little every week; so it seems to be
healthy.
   Last night I had a letter which I thought was an order for my arrest
from the Home Secretary. It turned out to be an announcement that I
had been made an Old Boiled Egg[1] – which seems ineffably comic.
   Wingley is adorable; Athy, if anything too affectionate; he's always
getting in the way. I have had no answers yet to my ad. in the *Times*,
but I suppose it's too early. I enclose another review of my book.
   I'm worried about you, my darling heart. But there – I must wait.
                        Your loving
                        Boge.[2]

   1. O.B.E.
   2. K.M. replies 26 January: 'Letters are beginning to roll up from Italy'.

_____

[137]   [2 Portland Villas,
                                        Hampstead,
                                        London.]
                                        19.I.20
                                        Monday 6 p.m.

My own darling
   When I got back from Wells's to the office this morning I found
your telegram saying that you wd leave Italy on the Wednesday. I

wired to the address you gave to say that your story[1] had arrived safely. I am now home. There are no letters from you, which would have worried me exceedingly if your wire had not said 'Postal strike still on'. I have been without any real news of you now for practically a whole week.

Though this is not what I really am thinking about, I'll tell you a little about Wells. The only part of the visit that I really enjoyed was the 'ball game', which I played furiously during the morning & the afternoon with the result that I am as stiff as a poker. I also liked Jane Wells who, besides being kindly in herself, warmed my heart by speaking enthusiastically of your writing in the paper & of Tchehov together. The association of the two, as you know, will always seem to me to show real insight. Anyhow, ball game & Jane – that's the good side of the picture.

H.G. himself struck me as degenerated, shallow, vain and a ludicrous snob. I'm exaggerating things, I know, merely by enumerating them. But he has left a faint bad taste in my mouth; he looks and is a little overripe. He has a double chin, a belly, and a way of talking incessantly & not saying a single thing worth really listening to, much less remembering, – nothing that you feel he feels, nothing even particularly clever. Well, since he wasn't an idol of mine, but merely an object of affection, that's all of no great account. Men who aren't big give way to mental and spiritual sloth. But the streak of the snob is a different affair. You've heard of Lady Warwick, the countess who pretends to be a Socialist? Well, H.G. lives under the shadow of her park gates, which is rather suspicious. Anyhow, he is a great friend of the great lady, who came over to dinner on Sunday & travelled up with me in the train.

I have rather a nice taste in aristocrats. Everything else being equal I admire them. I should like to have been one myself. But I do insist on their being aristocrats & holding the creed proper to their kind like Henry Bentinck.[2] But the aristocrat who lives in a park two miles across & pretends to be a Socialist is to me just another form of Bottomley[3] – something that stinks. Of course, Wells hasn't a very delicate nose & he might miss the smell. He might find her friendship tolerable, even amusing; but he must treat her as a joke to preserve his self-respect. Instead of that he's obviously very proud of her; he obviously thought she would impress *me*!; and he was all round & all over her, smirking a little and saying 'Lady Warwick' about as often as a Bond St. counter-jumper.

Well, really, Wig – at our age! It was like the touch of some chemical. He immediately began to exude a strong, unpleasant smell of lower middle class. I couldn't think of him as a writer any more. A writer belongs to no class at all and he carries his impossibility of classification about with him. But Wells – was just lower middle-class. And his two boys (who were there) confirmed the impression, re-inforced the smell. You know I can imagine few things more attractive to me than two boys one about 13, the other Arthur's age. Yet I positively disliked these two. They had an effluvium. They were mongrels – a cross between the boardschool boy & the public school boy. You have to be one *or* the other. Each can be perfect if he is intact. But these – no; they were vulgar in soul. I just felt with them how wonderful were the boys you & I have known – Chummie, sans peur & sans reproche, & Arthur, honest as the day

Well, I've given you all that because I think you might like to know. Wells is down & out. He's not important to the likes of us any more.

Will letters addressed to the Casetta be safe? In the one I sent on Friday were cheques for £11.10.0. Also those beautifully bound books are still on the way.

Oh, for a real letter, my own heart. I feel I don't mind what it contains if it's only news of yourself

Your only, loving, adoring
Boge-husband

1. 'The Man Without a Temperament'.
2. Lord Henry Bentinck, half-brother of Ottoline Morrell.
3. Horatio Bottomley (1860–1933), editor of *John Bull*.

---

[138]   The Athenaeum,
                                    10 Adelphi Terrace,
                                    London, W.C.2.
                                    [21 January, 1920]

My own darling,

Wednesday morning – no news, no review. As it's vital that there should be something of yours in the paper (for our secret reasons) I have rushed down to the printer one of the Elizabeth Stanley[1] poems you sent at the beginning of December – entitled 'Sunset'. That will get in, also the first half of the biographical note on Tchehov.

But this complete silence is distracting, quite apart from the paper.

And now there is the news of a railway strike in Italy which is said to have begun yesterday. Are you safe at Mentone?[2] I shall go out and telegraph to you there but I'm not quite certain that the address on the telegram was correct. It ran, or rather I made it out to be

> L'Hermitage[3]
> rue P. Morillot
> Menton

At any rate that is where I have written these last two days.

For next week unless I hear something definite from you by Friday morning I shall write a novel review myself – there must be novels in the paper. Forgive me for talking about the paper. Only the work is extra heavy just now, with two of our regulars ill & doing nothing

While I was out for lunch just now I saw a coloured poster of the Italian Riviera and the Italian State Railways – I felt inclined to tear it down & stamp on it.

Just after that I saw on the placards Martial law in Italy: then I was worried to death. But this morning (this bit is written on Thursday morning) I have your wire, which I hope & pray means you have got to Mentone safely.

Absolutely everything is well here, darling. If you haven't heard from me for a fortnight, I haven't heard from you for almost as long. But your wire is enough to go on with. I feel you must be safe in Mentone. I had ghastly dreams of a revolution in Italy, and it seemed just our fate that on the very day you said you were leaving for France, the newspapers here announced a railway strike.

> Your loving
> Boge.

1. A pseudonym under which K.M. published poetry.
2. Depressed and unable to bear the loneliness of Ospedaletti, K.M. had said she was moving to Menton where she would be cared for by Connie Beauchamp and Jinnie Fullerton.
3. A private nursing home in Menton where K.M. first stayed.

[139]
2 Portland Villas,
Hampstead,
London.
[25 January, 1920.]
Sunday Night
9 p.m.

My own darling heart,

I arrived home about an hour ago and found nothing from you – nothing. I can't even remember now when I last got a letter: it *was more than a fortnight ago*, of that I am sure. I can't understand what's happening. The only thing to which I have had any reply was my wire saying your story had arrived safely. I don't even know whether you're in Ospedaletti or Mentone; but I am trusting you are in Mentone, because my wire about the story was addressed there; but that's all I have had to go on for a week.

It's so mysterious that it's beginning to prey on me. Well, I shall wire to you again to-morrow. Until I get some news from you I can't write anything interesting.

I am perfectly well, rather footsore after walking 30 miles in two days, but very very fit.[1] I haven't found the house, but I am more & more drunk with the magnificence of the English down country, more & more determined to find something.

But, Wig, I *must* have news. I have starved for it *for a fortnight* – such a thing has never, never happened before.

Boge.

1. J.M. was spending his weekends tramping the countryside in search of a house.

---

[140]
[The Athenaeum,
10 Adelphi Terrace,
London. W.C.2.]
[26 January, 1920.]
Monday
4.30 p.m.

My own darling[1]

Two gorgeous letters from you this morning telling me that you really are at Menton, that you're happy, that the doctor has given good reports – everything that I was longing & praying for – except one thing. What *is* your real address? I've only had it as it came on the telegram. I made it out to be

L'Hermitage
rue P. Morillot
Menton

And some of my letters sent to that address seem to have reached you. But to-day I received from the P.O. an official notification that a telegram I sent to Murry, Hermitage, rue Morillot, Menton on January 19 was not delivered, because you were unknown. That's absolutely bewildering – unless perhaps you weren't actually in Menton on the 19th. & 20th. But then I should have thought that they knew you were coming. However, since you didn't actually get there until Jan 21, I shall presume that the address is correct & the telegram wasn't delivered because you weren't there. But, just to set my mind at rest, will you copy out your address and put it prominently at the top of your next letter.

You will, I hope, have got the notes which I sent you from Sussex. I came back without having found a house, but with the firm conviction that Sussex is a county of *incomparable* beauty. and that I must try might & main to find something there. I walked 30 miles on Saturday and Sunday. The walk on Sunday was divine. Darling, I'm sure you wouldn't believe what the South Downs can do on their day even in January. There was a bright, pale-blue sky, with tufts of cloud. We were walking on the lower slope of the Downs on the north side. Below us, gently sloping away to the right were miles on miles of the Sussex weald rolling away to the north. The strangest & most wonderful thing about it was the colour – it seemed to be all golden, with dark brown splashes where the woods were, and every now & then a glimmer of vivid green. I can't describe it; it needs patience & art. But its made a profound impression upon me – of wideness & peace, a queer sense that the country instead of being alien wanted to protect & shelter you, almost to lull you into her own richness. I felt – that you and I could grow wise & unfretted there, that the note of hysteria would go out of all that I did.

Well, well, if I didn't find anything, I had a day's sheer happiness, & I came nearer to a knowledge of what I want than I was before. When I got back this morning I found the enclosed note waiting for me. I have made up my mind to go down & see it to-morrow, even though it's the day before press-day. One can't afford to take risks, the demand for houses in the country is so portentous. You see if its anything like, the rent is so small that we can take it on the spot, even if we change it for something else. Hold thumbs – what if it were the real thing – an old farmhouse!

Your reviews[2] came to-day – Hurrah! The next number of the paper won't be flat anyhow.

I'm working like a horse. My goodness, but what a difference your letters have made.

How's money – let me know, please.

Boge[3]

Wig for ever!

Battle is in Sussex.

1. J.M. replies to K.M.'s letters of 21–22 January: 'I have escaped': and 23 January: 'I thought when I had sent my letter yesterday that you really don't know where we stand'.

2. 'Amusement', a review of *Sir Limpidus* by Marmaduke Pickthall, and 'Portrait of a Child', a review of *Coggin* by Ernest Oldmeadow, appeared on 30 January.

3. K.M. replies 31 January: 'I wrote to you on Thursday last . . . but I did not post the letter'. Murry later added a marginal note to the head of his letter: 'This is the letter that *hurt* K. so much. Well, it doesn't seem very bad to me. June 30, 1948'.

---

[141]   [2 Portland Villas,
                                  Hampstead,
                                  London.]
                              [29 January, 1920.]
                          Thursday Evening 6.20 p.m.

My own darling,

I sent you a wire to-day to say that the only reviews I had received were *Coggins* & *Limpidus*, and asking how you were. I haven't had any letter from you at Mentone for three days. Letters arrive, and I am always deceived because they look like new ones, but they are letters which you sent from the Casetta.

L'Hermitage sounds a splendid place – and after the horror of the Casetta, a very haven of peace. I feel I can never ask for forgiveness enough for not having understood the torment of the Casetta. Perhaps if I had been calm, I could have done; but I feel that my attitude was always that of putting you up on a shelf in what I thought was a safe place while I went on with the eternal game of hoops of which I told you in my letter yesterday. It was cruel, terribly cruel of me, and there isn't any excuse. I can only hope that you will *think* of me as *someone* who finds it appallingly hard to cope with the world – with the things that happen – and who is always desperately nervous of a disaster. I try to concentrate on the obvious things: and I forget that all the important things aren't obvious at all.

Perhaps you won't think of me too hardly, even though I deserve it.

I shan't be able to get off to the country on Friday this week – I must write a review – and I must go to Ottoline's evening to-night She asked me to dinner, and I accepted, but I couldn't face it & sent a telegram. But I must go this evening. That leaves me only to-morrow night to write a review.

I sent you the *Times Lit. Sup* & the paper myself this morning. The *T.L.S.* has a review of *Prelude* & *Je ne parle pas*. Not so long as it should have been, but as far as it goes, extremely *useful*. Above all, for instance, those lines about the stories being of the length the publishers are afraid of.

Gertie came to see me this afternoon. She's been very ill, & her panel doctor says she must have an operation. She has refused because she says she doesn't trust the doctor. She looks very ill. She wanted the opinion of another doctor. So I sent her with a note to Sorapure, explaining that she was yr. friend and servant and that we wd. pay the fee. I hope that was right. She looks so ill that her doctor is probably right and its folly to refuse to have the operation. She will probably do what Sorapure says as she knows you have such tremendous confidence in him. But just now a terrible thought overcomes me that it's a breach of medical etiquette. Oh God.

Well, my own darling, let's hope for another real letter from you. Are you writing everyday? Do please, if it's only a word I do.

I love you, love you.

Boge.[1]

1. K.M. replies 2 February: 'I have just received your Thursday and Friday evening letters'.

[142]   2 Portland Villas
                                        [Hampstead,
                                        London.]
                                        [1 February, 1920.]
                                        Sunday

I rather counted, Wig darling, on finding a letter from you when I got home to-night. However, I've learned that to count on a letter from you is one of the surest ways of not getting it, so perhaps I didn't really count so much. But when you write to me next, will you please tell me whether you write everyday or not. I don't want to expect what I can't possibly have; – since I wrote to you about a month ago asking you to write everyday, I have expected more letters than I have received by a long chalk.

I got back at 9.15 to-night. This morning I walked from Battle to Winchilsea through Hastings – that is breathtakingly lovely country – and on to Rye & caught the train from there. The house at Winchilsea was a fraud – a semi-detached villa. So I drew blank again this week. However, I copied down all the names of the Rye agents from the various notice-boards, (they were all shut, it being Sunday) in order to write to them to-morrow. I intend to go down to Rye with a bicycle (not *on* it) next week-end & beat the country thoroughly. One can't cover enough ground walking. You won't have to hold thumbs again until Friday next.

Of course I forgot to enclose the letter[1] last night. I always do. But here it is: also cheque for £20. You see it's much better that I should pay you now, in order to be free to make the best terms for your books that I can. Your instruction to sell your book outright is simply horrifying. I'm sure I [can] get you more than £20 merely in advance of royalties. I think it's a good thing that there shd. be a new edition of *In a German Pension*.[2] Though why the devil no-one (publisher, I mean; *we* did) thought of it during the war I don't know. However, let's be happy that two of yr books will be coming out again soon. I am sure the Constable offer was directly the result of the *Times Lit Sup.* Review.[3] So it seems that your success is coming along very quickly.

Wig to sell 10,000 of her new book[4] & come home; Boge to find a lovely house. Ah, life could be beautiful – couldn't it.

                        Your own
                    Boge – husband.

1. From Michael Sadleir.
2. K.M. did not agree. She replied [?4] February: 'I cannot have the *German Pension* republished under any circumstances. It is far too *immature* and I don't even acknowledge it today'.
3. Of *Prelude* and *Je ne parle pas français*.
4. *Bliss and Other Stories* was published by Constable in 1920.

---

[143]   [The Athenaeum,
                                                      10 Adelphi Terrace,
                                                       London W.C.2.]
                                                         Feb. 2 1920

The enclosed letter[1] explains itself. It gives me the chance of playing off Constable & Grant Richards against each other to get the biggest advance. Your idea of selling outright is preposterous.[2] What I want to know is whether you have pledged yourself in writing in anyway to Richards. If I have a freehand I think I shall be able to get £30 in advance of royalties almost immediately. Any how, *though things are tight*[3], I will send You a cheque for £20 to-morrow, *if you will repay me when you get the money for your book*. But let me know exactly how you stand with Richards. I'll start in on this business on Monday – see both Constable and Richards.

Your own
Boge.[4]

1. Michael Sadleir (1887–1957) had helped Murry found *Rhythm*. Later changing the spelling of his name to avoid confusion with his father, Professor Michael Sadler, he worked for Constable Publishers. On 30 January 1920 he wrote to Murry:

Dear Jack,
    We should like to publish a volume of Katherine's stories, the matter to be collected from Rhythm, from that little paper you published in the East-end, the name of which I forget, and to include "Prelude", the story in "Art and Letters", "Je ne parle pas français", and such other material as may be available. Is there any chance of our being able to arrange this? Naturally the consent of the Hogarth press and of your brother would have to be obtained; but as the book, even if agreement could be come to within reasonable time, could hardly be published for several months, I do not imagine that such specialist publications as "Prelude" and "Je ne parle pas français" would suffer in their original form. We should like at the same time to consider bringing out another edition of "In a German Pension" if that were possible. I

shall ring you up on Monday morning so that you can tell me whether the scheme is feasible or not. In the former case we can descend to details.

Yours ever,
Michael Sadler

2. K.M. asked J.M. on 26 January to send a book of her short stories to the publisher Grant Richards: 'I don't know what terms he will make, but let me see a copy of your letter to him. I'd sell outright for £20, of course, but I want money *now*'.

3. The underlining in this letter appears to be K.M.'s not Murry's.

4. K.M. replies 4 February: 'A slip was enclosed in a letter card but I have received no letter which explains itself'; and 5 February: 'I have just received your Monday letter written on the back of the Constable note and hasten to reply'.

---

[144]   [The Athenaeum,
                                             10 Adelphi Terrace,
                                             London. W.C.2.]
                                             [2 February, 1920.]
                                             Monday in the
                                             Office.

I was on to Michael Sadler on [the] telephone to-day. I said that the whole question was one of the advance on royalties, and suggested £40. He seemed quite prepared to do that, so much so that I felt I ought to have said £50. Still, I didn't want to frighten him.

Accordingly, I have written to Richards telling him that everything depends upon how much advance he will give, & telling him frankly that some-one else is after it. He may go more than £40, but I doubt it. He's rather a sharper on terms.

Anyhow, I trust I shall be able to send you another cheque for £20 within a month.

Whatever you do, don't commit yourself in writing. to Grant Richards. As you can understand, it would make it impossible for me to negotiate freely. And we're in the happy position of having two competing publishers.

As I said in my other letter it would help a great deal if you could tell me what you have written to Richards.

I got a very belated letter[1] from [the] Casetta to-day telling me of [the] change of yr attitude to L.M. Don't worry about me – I must say I hated your picture of me being thin-lipped & angry over it: your idea of me seems to get a long way from the reality. Whatever you feel towards L.M, I feel & there's an end of it. All I say is I should like it much better if you could get on with her again – she has done very much for *us* in her way.

I wake up with a sore throat this morning – I suppose I got a chill in the train. However it's bound to be slight as my last one was. I've also insured my life for £1000 in case I break my neck home-hunting.

Your own Boge.[2]

1. J.M. replies to K.M.'s letter of 13 January: 'Thank you for your letter today and for letting me see the two poems . . .'.
2. K.M. replies 5 February: 'Will you remember when you write that I don't go out or walk or see anybody to talk to – that you are my ALL'.

---

[145]

[2 Portland Villas,
Hampstead,
London.]
[3 February, 1920.]
Tuesday Evening

My darling,[1]

Your Saturday letter has come – the one saying Please read this all through – at least it explains your silence, which had bewildered me.

That I have hurt you terribly I know; you would never say that unless it were true. The fact that I sent you £20 the moment I had it makes no difference. Feb. 1 came too late.

But there is something to be said for me. I couldn't send what I had not got. I hadn't got £20 when you arrived in Mentone. I was cleaned out. Paying £60 for income-tax finished me. I had just enough to get to the end of the month. The moment I had my monthly cheque – I sent you the £20.

Of course, I could, I suppose, have borrowed it. I would have if I had known it was so urgent. But God above haven't we known each other long enough for you to *wire* 'send £20'. I understood you were very hard up, but I thought you could manage till my next cheque came in. I thought you would have said: I must have £20 or £40 immediately – if it was so urgent.

However, the hurt is done. I was stupid & clumsy. But in order that you may feel quite safe, in addition to the £20 already sent, I am paying in £20 direct into your bank to-night. I shall have enough to get through the month. I shall send you a wire saying that to-morrow.

Still, however brutal I have been, I think that you should have written to me before. You know at any rate that I'm not brutal at heart; so that you might have guessed that I had misunderstood instead of leaving yourself tormented & me with no news so long.

Well, Wig – darling heart –, you say you won't write again. All I ask is that when you get this if you feel that the hurt is less, or if you feel that I love you still, you will wire me just the one word 'Love'. I shall understand. But don't, for God's sake, wire it if you don't feel it.

There are things in your letter that I just don't understand. One is what you say about the letter I sent you to Italy telling you 'to remember as you grew more lonely so I was loving you more'. I realise that is awkwardly put. But *if* I read it in a novel, I should know what the man meant, I'm sure. I would know that what he meant was that when his lover felt lonely, then she must think of him as loving her more deeply than ever – loving her with a love that tried to break through, that might break through *if she would let it*, the ghastly terror of her loneliness. I feel that you must suspect me somehow, otherwise you could not have so failed to feel the intention behind the clumsy words. I'm not ashamed of them, even now

Your loving
Boge.[2]

1. J.M. replies to K.M.'s letter of 31 January: 'I wrote to you on Thursday last . . . but I did not post the letter'.
2. K.M. replies ?7 February: 'I have your Tuesday evening letter'.

---

[146]
The Athenaeum,
10 Adelphi Terrace,
London, W.C.2.
[4 February, 1920.]
Wednesday: Press Day

Wig darling.
This afternoon I sent you an overcoat. It will be forwarded to Paris in the diplomatic bag. I hope you will like it. It's a terrible business hunting for an overcoat that's even approximately decent. Still, after a long hunt I found it, and I shall be disappointed if you don't like it. Don't be scared by the name of the maker. I tried better places in vain.

I'm afraid I shan't be able to do what I said yesterday, pay £20 into yr. bank here. I can only manage £10 which I will send to Kay to-night. But please don't go to the other extreme and think I am crippling myself – I shall be able to get through the month on what remains of my monthly cheque.

There was something which I left altogether out of my letter last night. When you said I had shown no sympathy, no joy at [your] being comfortable and getting better – I simply didn't know what to make of it. Either my first letter to you at Mentone went the way of my telegram, or I must be becoming absolutely incapable of expressing my feelings. I don't know. Perhaps the whole mystery of the strikes my getting no letters & never knowing where you were was partly responsible.

However, what's done is done. I can't believe you will continue to think as hardly of me as you do, even though I'm a failure as husband & lover. But I don't want to plead for anything.

At all events I have done one good practical thing. I have fixed up with Constable that they will publish your book on a 15% royalty, and pay you £40 in advance on delivery of manuscript, which I have promised within three weeks. Sadler has asked whether you would like the book to appear with some little drawings by Anne Rice. I took it on me to say you would – because I felt that it would in any case hurt Anne's feelings if you refused.

I'm terribly glad about the book. Don't think I've done the dirty on Richards. As soon as I had fixed the offer from Constable I sent a note to him by hand telling him I had an offer and asking him to say what would be his terms. Two days after I had a note (this morning) to say that they could of course do nothing without seeing the MS, that they would be pleased to give it to their reader, that Mr. Richards would be back *in three or four weeks* and would then come to a decision. I closed with Constable on the spot & sent a letter to Richards saying I had done so. I think Richards thoroughly deserves what he's got. After all his talk it appears that all he meant was that you might submit your book to him, just as you did to Heinemann.[1] Well, he's learnt now that you're a much too important person to be treated in that way. Constables are evidently very keen to have anything of yours. Well it's one gleam of sunshine, anyhow

Boge.[2]

---

1. Heinemann had rejected a book of K.M.'s stories in April 1919.

2. K.M. replies 8 February: 'I received a letter from you yesterday saying (1) you had brought me an overcoat. I wish you hadn't'.

---

[147]

> [2 Portland Villas,
> Hampstead,
> London.]
> [5 February, 1920.]
> Thursday

Wig darling,

I'm sorry you kept your promise of not writing to me any more. I had nothing yesterday or to-day. I can't help thinking it's a bit unfair.

Your reviews arrived just in time for the number, at the very end of the eleventh hour, that is by the afternoon post on Wednesday. One little thing in them gave me a thrill of pleasure, namely when you said in brackets 'A herald (against all the rules carrying a trumpet)'[1] I immediately remembered the afternoon in July when we found that out for the first time, and for the moment at least it made up for the letter I didn't get.

I have had since Sunday a bad cold, which I must have caught in the train coming back from Rye last week. However it's like all my colds – only annoying by the amount of nose-blowing and dirty handkerchiefs it involves. Still, I wish they didn't get hold of me quite so violently.

This evening (unfortunately) is the evening I pledged myself to take Jeanne out. I thought better of the theatre plan however, & thought it might be a good idea to take her to Ottoline's evening. It might have the advantage of impressing your family with the idea that we are rather distinguished.

Violet told me she had a letter from you yesterday – and I rather fancied I saw that one came for Mrs. Jones, who is away to-day, in your handwriting; but I can't be sure. But I was rather upset by their having letters, while I had nothing.

The only thing to do is wait.

I do hope the coat reaches you safely. Sydney was called away to Paris last night, but he promised to make arrangements for it to go in the diplomatic bag. But I feel rather nervous all the same, particularly because I thought the coat really charming and distinguished.

Well, Wig, don't give me up entirely.

> Your own
> Boge.[2]

Friday Morning

Before I could send this off, I received the letter which you sent on Monday.[3] You still say I don't read your letters.

I hope I haven't done wrong in fixing up with Constable. Your letter seems to imply that you had settled with Richards – if that was so, I cannot understand that Richards' manager or partner should have sent me the letter he did, which I enclose and ask you carefully to keep. At all events I feel that the Constable arrangement is an extremely good one.

Don't worry about getting the "Second Helping"[4] typed. I can do that, *if* you send the story *to me*.

You shall *without fail* see the proofs of the story[5] which Rutter has. I promise faithfully. I also promise you that I will go through the typed copy with your MS, with special attention to the spaces

---

1. J.M. refers to K.M.'s review of *Full Circle* by Mary Hamilton which appeared on 6 February: Describing 'the Quilhamptons, a family of brothers and sisters', K.M. writes: 'Staying with them is a Socialist friend of their brother Roger, one Wilfred Elstree. This strange creature is a herald (but against all the rules carrying a trumpet) whom life has sent to parley with them on the eve of the battle'.

2. K.M. replies 9 February: 'I cannot stand it any longer'.

3. Dated 2 February: 'I have just received your Thursday and Friday evening letters'.

4. On 30 January J.M. had suggested that she exclude the dialogue sketch 'The Black Cap' from her list of stories for *Bliss* because it was 'the only thing not in actual story form'. She agreed and replaced it with the title 'Second Helping'. The story was never written.

5. 'The Man Without a Temperament', published in *Art and Letters*, Spring 1920.

---

[148]   [2 Portland Villas,
                                                        Hampstead,
                                                        London.]
                                              [6 February, 1920.]
                                                  Friday Evening

My own darling heart,

I was overjoyed to get Your telegram to-day, when I reached the office. Not because I wanted you to send me a wire about my cold-in-the-head, which is only one of my normals anyhow, but because Your wire ended 'love, Wig'.[1] I felt that you were feeling as you used to feel about me; and I had a great thrill of happiness. I almost expect a telegram now saying just the one word 'Love'.

Last night Jeanne told me that Chaddie had heard from Bertha who had heard from Connie, that you were much better. It's a long way round, I know, but it cheered me very much. I felt that it was a kind of outside corroboration – as if a special doctor had gone off to bring a special report. The evening went off, I think, very well. Everyone at dinner – Brett, Carrington, Gertler besides myself – was really bucked at good news about You; and when we got to Ottoline's (who is, as I told you, in Ethel Sands'[2] house) it really seemed that Jeanne could have had no better passport into 'intellectual society' than being Katherine's sister. Lytton & Clive & Sullivan all talked to her about you; and I thought it said a good deal for Jeanne's discernment that she liked Sullivan the best. She also met Birrell,[3] Augustus John[4] & Wyndham Lewis. So I think she was probably telling the truth when she said she enjoyed it very much.

My cold is so persistent that I decided not to go down to the country this week-end. It would have been very rash to go, I'm sure. So here I am at home, – unfortunately without being able to take much advantage of it, for it's devilishly hard to do any work with a cold in the head.

I enclose a letter I received to-day from Lawrence[5]. Don't let it make you angry. But may God do so unto me & more also if I ever enter into any communication whatever with him. If ever I see him, no matter when or where, the first thing I shall do is to hit him as hard as I can across the mouth. He seems to have become so degraded that I feel he is something of a reptile, and that he has slavered over me in his letter. *Please keep it*: because I am just writing to him to tell him that I intend to hit him whenever & wherever I see him again. And if anything happens I want people to know why I did it.

Well, it's horrible, darling – but it can't be helped.

Your loving
Boge.[6]

Will you send me a wire when the overcoat reaches you: I'm so worried about it?

1. The wire actually read: 'How is your chill anxious take greatest care reply Tig'.

2. Ethel Sands (1873–1962), a wealthy, cultivated American woman who entertained Henry James. When Ottoline met her around 1905, she painted,

and held a weekly salon at her Belgravia house. In 1920, when Ottoline stayed with her, she lived in the Vale, Chelsea. Virginia Woolf was among those who visited her there.

3. Either Augustine Birrell (1850–1930), the Liberal M.P. whom Ottoline had known for many years – or his son Francis, a Cambridge graduate and friend of Lytton Strachey and David Garnett. Of Francis Birrell D. H. Lawrence wrote to Garnett: 'Never bring Birrell to see me any more. There is something nasty about him like black beetles. He is horrible and unclean'.

4. Augustus John (1878–1961), the artist, was an old friend of Ottoline's.

5. Lawrence's letter to Murry has not survived, nor has his letter to K.M. about which she wrote to Murry c. 6 February: 'Lawrence sent me a letter today. He spat in my face and threw filth at me and said: "I loathe you. You revolt me stewing in your consumption . . ."'.

6. K.M. replies 10 February: 'Note this coincidence. I wrote to Lawrence: "I detest you for having dragged this disgusting reptile across all that has been"'.

---

[149]   [2 Portland Villas,
                                                Hampstead,
                                                London.]
                                                [7 February, 1920.]
                                                Saturday

My own darling,

This seems to be the first evening since I came back from Italy when I have been able to sit down & write to you calmly – not dashing off a few lines in time to catch a train, or to write a review. I feel that I have allowed myself to become an appalling machine, and that You have felt it [in] my letters, as you could not fail to feel it; & so you have been left without the sympathy I should have given.

There is, Wig, a certain amount of real insensibility in me. I think that has been proved now. I must just accept it: I hate it, and try to kill it. But the fact remains that I never realized how much you were suffering in Ospedaletti, nor how great would be your anxiety about money in Menton. Both those things you had a right to expect of me as your lover – and, there's no doubt in my own mind that I failed in them both.

Certainly, to be quite fair to myself, I have found it hard to keep going. My power of concentration has weakened, & it now takes me a good deal more energy than it did two or three years ago to do the same amount of work. But I don't believe very much in the argument. I feel, on the contrary, that there have been times when I have, not consciously or deliberately, turned my sympathy away from you. Something of the kind you must have felt.

Perhaps it all comes back to the fact that I am able to do nothing without an effort, neither to work, nor to love. It's what I mean when I say I'm no good as a lover – our old quarrel of years ago about the enamel spoon.[1] I think that at bottom it's no worse, & no better than that. You managed to bear with it when you were well – that was your generosity – and now when you are ill it becomes intolerable.

Don't let it become intolerable, Wig. Believe at least that my thoughts are not as cold & brutal as my words sometimes seem to be. That in fact I do give you my all, and if it's a poor one, it's because I have no more to give. You have the whole of me, darling, and when it fails, as it has failed so often I know, just remember that I would have given more if I had had it. It's not much consolation – it's certainly not the rich comfort I should be giving you, but it may be some. I mean that though I am a jagged, flowerless, & inhospitable rock, I am a rock. If I'm not beautiful or life-giving, I'm also not treacherous.

I don't suppose I have explained what I mean. I do try to give, Wig darling, try desperately sometimes because I know how much you need it, and from me. But the spring whence richness comes seems to dry up. I become a barren & dry land where no water is. I feel like a tree must feel in the winter. It knows it is not dead, yet it cannot show that it is alive – it has neither voice nor leaves. The only thing to do would be cut it open. But you can't cut me open. Things that You, being you, might read in a movement of my hand or a glance of my eyes when we are together are lost altogether in my bald letters. The more I try to make my letters live, the less I seem able to.

You see, my darling, it's wrong for us to be apart. That is what it comes to at the last. You can understand my harshness, blackness, my habit of silence when you are near me, and make allowances: but when we are so far away that is impossible, yet it is more necessary than ever.

The only thing is for you to get well – to make up your mind that I am the same Boge all the while – not the Boge I ought to be, but a better Boge than I look at the distance. Get well my darling, and lets put an end to this time of torture. Your voice is sweet, but mine is harsh when we call from so far away.

Well, my darling Worm, I'll tell you what news there is in my next letter. This one is all explanation, of something which cannot be explained. But as your telegram[2] to-day said, *of course I love you* and love you for all I am worth, with all that I have.

   Your own Boge.[3]

 1. A reference to a story by Anatole France.
 2. The wire read: 'Of course you love me Tig'.
 3. K.M. replies 11 February: 'Your Saturday evening letter has come with the "explanation"'.

———

[150]   [2 Portland Villas,
           Hampstead,
           London.]
          [9 February, 1920.]
          Monday Evening

My own darling,[1]

This morning I received two letters from you. I think they were both written on Wednesday.

I apologise humbly darling for my wicked remark about insuring my life. It was a joke, but, I admit, one of those jokes that aren't made between lovers. Forgive me. Forgive me

My sore throat has turned into one of my ordinary colds in the head of the violent & persistent kind. You know them. This isn't in any degree different from the usual thing – so *please* don't think about [it] any more. To me it seems as though I had a cut finger & you were saying that was more serious than your own illness.

I really have insured my life – to get £1000 when I become 55. I did it one day when I was really frightened at my non-success and I had an uncomfortable picture of myself as a penniless failure at middle age. I think it was wise. I am ashamed to confess my insensitiveness – but I didn't know it would have that appalling effect on you. Again, forgive me.

About money. The £20 is £10 for January & £10 for Feb. *Not* a loan, a gift. I should like, on the other hand, if you found it possible, for you to repay the £10 I have paid into yr. bank and the 9 guineas I paid for the overcoat – when you get your £40. I am at present working on a very slender balance at the bank, and I have to repay the money the *Athenaeum* advanced me for my income-tax at £10 a month.

About the Grant Richards affair. My letters will have explained the position. I feel I have been rather precipitate. But I had no notion that

Richards was only going to *consider* your book. You see you hadn't told me; and I imagined that he had agreed at any rate to publish it. I was indignant when I received a note from his manager saying it would be given to the reader to pronounce upon. You see I had some reason for my attitude, apart from the question of your literary prestige – for Sullivan, through whom I originally suggested the book to Richards, was strongly under the impression that the book was to be taken without reading on your reputation. And Sullivan told me that. As a matter of fact – this was to have been a secret – that was the arrangement that I told Sullivan to suggest to Richards.

In any case, darling, I don't think you have anything to reproach yourself with. If the responsibility belongs to anybody it belongs to me. And really there was no choice between Constable's offer without seeing the book & Richards'. I gave Richards' manager the refusal, telling him – against all expediency – the precise terms of Constable's offer. That Richards himself was away is merely an unfortunate accident.

You want me to be frank about money. I will be. You remember I went through my accounts with you at Christmas & that I turned the New Year with a balance of £11

Paid in		
Balance from 1919	——————————	11. 0. 0
Sydney Waterlow Dec. & Jan	———	26. 0. 0
Salary for December		
at the rate of £800 p.a. Jan 1	———————	66.13. 4
Advance in salary from	———————	40. 0. 0
Athenaeum towards Inc Tax		
Total in Bank at beginning of Jan	———	143.13. 4

Paid out in January (copied from cheque book)

	Jan 1	to Vince	18. 0. 0	
	Jan 5	Self	5. 0. 0	
	,,	Insurance Shares	10. 0. 0	—This was the
Binding yr. 2 books	,,	McLeish	1. 1. 0	balance of the
Book bought in June	,,	Champion of Paris	10.	£25 of shares
	Jan 9	Bain[2] for Hardy	1.16. 0	I told you
	Jan 14	Self	6. 0. 0	about.
	,,	Housekeeping	4. 0. 0	
Mirror 2.10.0 ⎫	,,	National War Bond	2. 0. 0	
Towels ⎬		Instalment		
Pillow Cases ⎭	,,	Hamptons	6. 2. 5	
	15	Times Advt.	1. 8. 6	
	16	Electric Light	2. 2.10	
	17	Income Tax	60. 0. 0	
		Katherine Book	1. 0. 0	
		Money		
	18	Housekeeping	5. 0. 0	
1st. Quarterly Premium	19	Life Insurance	10.12. 6	
	20	Self	5. 0. 0	
Boots & Mackintosh	26	Jones Bros	2. 7. 6	
bt at a sale	,,	Self	6. 0. 0	
	28	Housekeeping	5. 0. 0	
			£153. 0.10	

Those cheques to Self covered all my week-end expenses. I might have kept them down, had it not been that the house seemed urgent.

Feb.1.

	Paid in	Adverse Balance carried forward	
alary at £1000 a year			
r Jan less £10 repaid	73. 6. 8		9.10. 0
n £40 advanced			
heques from Nation	10.10. 0		
		Cheque to Wig	30. 0. 0
		Overcoat	9. 9. 0
		Suit for me	6. 6. 0
		Cheque Self	5. 0. 0
		Housekeeping	———
	83.16. 8 ⎸		60. 5. 0

Thus you see I have a balance in hand of £24 nearly which will last the month comfortably above all when Sydney pays another £13   But it doesn't leave much to play about with, does it? Please don't think I made-up being hard up in January – I was very. And the evil was done before I got your S.O.S. That was why I had to wait till Feb.

But, on the other hand, don't think I'm hard up now everything is plain sailing. I'm perfectly solvent. I've got nothing heavy to pay out this month.

Forgive me for all these figures – but it's much better that you should know exactly.[3] And please criticise my expenditure. It's your – our – money I spend.

Your own loving
Boge.[4]

1. J.M. replies to K.M.'s letters of [?4] February: 'A slip was enclosed in a letter card . . .'; and 5 February: 'Will you remember when you write . . .'.
2. A London bookseller.
3. Katherine apparently did not forgive him and spoke frankly about Murry to Virginia Woolf in June 1920. Recording a meeting with K.M. Virginia wrote in her *Diary*: 'Then I said "You've changed. Got through something;" indeed theres a sort of self command about her as if having mastered something subterfuges were no longer so necessary. She told me of her terrific experiences last winter – experience of loneliness chiefly. . . . Murry sent a balance sheet of his accounts: came at Christmas with plum pudding & curd cheese; "Now I'm here, its all right". Then she went to him for assurance; didn't get it; & will never look for that particular quality again. I see what she means, vaguely.'
4. K.M. replies 12 February: 'Monday evening letters (1) and (2) received'. About Murry's financial statement she said sarcastically: 'I'll repay you for the overcoat when Constable pay me. Thank you enormously for the figgers. They frighten me. You never mentioned your new suit. I don't know what colour it is or shape or anything – or whether there is any fringe on the trousers. I always rejoice when you buy clothes. When I am rich, you will have such lovely clothes – all real lace and silk velvet. You will have crimson satin sleeves, slashed with Indian green silk and embroidered gloves with sachets sewn in them. Just wait.'

---

[151]   [2 Portland Villas,
                                                Hampstead,
                                                London.]
                                          [9 February, 1920.]
                                          Monday Evening

Violet wanted to catch the post so I broke off my letter abruptly. This little bit will go to-morrow morning. It's about the book.

(1) You mustn't think that because Constables can't get it out till the Autumn, that they don't want the MS. immediately (i.e. within 3 weeks). Conditions in the printing trade are so bad that you have to begin 6 months ahead. The very best time for your book to appear is the early autumn. (Mine was wrecked through coming out just before Xmas.) So make up your mind what exactly you want in it.

(2) I have read yr new story.[1] The copy came this morning. Of course it's amazingly good. No-one can write like you – but it's also extraordinarily beautiful. That is the abiding impression. I'll give you a detailed criticism later. But it's a beauty.

(3) About the *German Pension*. You're getting hyper-sensitive about yr. work. By all means let the new book be as perfect as you can make

it. But remember you are a <u>big</u> writer. You are as classic as Tchehov in your way. What you have written, you have written. And it's simply ridiculous to pretend there's anything to be ashamed of in the *G.P.* It was a splendid piece of work for 1911–12. Early work if you like. Write an introduction saying so if you like. But have it republished. Do listen to me on this point. I am advising you for the very best. I could understand if you had not a new book coming – but since you have, it's admirable that there shd. be a new edition of *G.P.* And I'm leaving utterly out of account the mere business advantage of one publisher having both your books – the additional solidity it gives you – YOU MUST TAKE MY ADVICE IN THIS. By all means say in your introduction that I forced you to it.

Finally you don't seem to understand the *kudos* that an entirely new edition of a book published nine years ago gives you. Why, I don't believe there's a single writer of under 35 who has had such a thing.

(4) Another cheque for £10 will be paid into your bank as soon as I get my pay at the beginning of March. The £20 cheque was £10 for Jan & £10 for Feb.

Finally forgive these hurried scrawls. You will see I've written a lot – and I have to finish an article for the *Nation* to-night.

　　　　　Je t'aime mais sois persuadée par moi.
　　　　　　　　　Boge[2]

1. Murry added a later, marginal note: "'Man Without a Temperament?'"
2. K.M. replies 12 February: 'Monday evening letters (1) and (2) received'.

————

[152]　　　　　　　　　　　　　　[The Athenaeum,
　　　　　　　　　　　　　　　　10 Adelphi Terrace,
　　　　　　　　　　　　　　　　London. W.C.2.]
　　　　　　　　　　　　　　　[10 February, 1920.]
　　　　　　　　　　　　　　　Tuesday Morning

My darling heart,

　　I have just had the wire from you saying my coldness is killing you.[1] Wing has replied for me,[2] because I don't know how to reply.

　　How can I say in a telegram that I am not cold, that I love you passionately, that you are my all. How can I convince you, when I don't even know what it is in my letters that makes you think I am cold. I feel as though I were lost in a mist.

What have I said – what have I not said. One day you say I don't read your letters, & that is why you won't write. So I answer everything in them to show at least that I read them.

Why do you say I am cold? I have got myself into a condition in which I am almost afraid to write except about definite things. I am terrified of hurting you any more.

Oh, Wig, do bear with me. Believe that I am at any rate just what I used to be. How could I change? Anxiety has made me fearful – and the awful feeling that all that I may write may have an effect utterly different from what I meant preys upon me.

Wig, you *must* believe what I say: you must trust me. After all I have [not] deserved this, no matter what I have done. Don't suspect me. That terrifies me, and makes the bad worse.

Don't close your heart against me. I've nowhere else to turn. Cold! Cold!

Well I love you, love you, love you I can do no more.

Your Boge.[3]

1. The wire read: 'Thursday letter come tell Wing wire immediately your coldness killing me Tig'.
2. Murry wired back: 'Wire received all well he loves you desperately he can't do more Wing'.
3. K.M. replies 13 February: 'Your 2 Tuesday letters are here but they are too late – aren't they?'

---

[153]

[2 Portland Villas,
Hampstead,
London.]
[10 February, 1920.]
Tuesday Night.

Worm, Worm,[1]

To-day I have had your wire – your coldness is killing me – and to-night a letter (in answer to my Tuesday letter) telling me the same thing more plainly.

Now, Mouse, I've waited a minute, lit a cigarette. I must be calm. For somehow in spite of myself our destiny has come to tremble on a razor's edge. Hitherto I have written desperately, and made the wounds I have inflicted on you worse. I must be calm.

Darling – my own heart – the very me. I feel to-night at the end of my tether. Some blind force is crushing the hope out of me. For I swear to you as my lover and my wife that all I have done since I came back has been with a single thought – love of you. Instead of bringing us nearer it has driven us apart.

Why, why! Why do you think I have withdrawn? My letters, you say, show it. But Wig if I write with my blood they won't be different from this. I can't explain. Somehow I have come to fear every word I write. Do you think the anguish of your letters doesn't tear my heart in bits? Do you really think I don't feel? Do you really think I had no sympathy for you in that ghastly time when I heard nothing? Don't you understand that a time like that beats even me down? That I have to grip at anything – the country – even drink – to prevent myself from collapse altogether? And I cling above all to our things – working for our house – buying our mirror. Silly things, God knows – but things that you & I don't think silly, because we know all they mean.

Do you think I wasn't hurt when you referred to my buying the mirror as a kind of extravagance, proving that I had money to burn? Above all when we talked about the mirror together at Xmas. Don't you understand that in buying it, for a moment I had you on my arm at my side, so light, so lovely, so my own, whispering: Yes, let's buy it, Boge. We can afford it. I'll save on the flowers. – all those beautiful unforgettable things that you have whispered to me on my arm in the past.

Worm, Worm – you understand all this. I appeal to you, darling, do not judge me as something finer than I am – but just as the thing you have always known me to be. Remember my faults & manias – my madnesses – the way I fasten on material symbols of our being together – *our* chairs, *our* tables, *our* pillow-cases. Don't suddenly become deaf to all these things.

No, I'm not calm. Another cigarette

Darling, do you realise that you *never* tell me how you are?

Another letter of defence & accusation. Forget it all.

Think that I love you. If you will think that, you can't go on believing that I withdrew from you.

Darling, listen to me in the quiet for one little moment. Hear my *voice*. I love you, love you, love you – and I am suffering as I never suffered before. Before I have been apart from you for a moment: but I have held you in my arms and we have known that we belonged to each other pour toujours. I can't do that, now. At least I can, only if you will listen to me.

Here am I – this is my voice – these are my lips, my eyes. Am I that stone? Answer me, Wig.

How can I speak with the great weight of your distrust, the anguish of the pain I cause you with every letter, bearing on me?

Throw it away. Oh, I beseech you Wig – who love me so much. Let me hold you in my arms. Let this ghastly nightmare go

Boge[2]

1. J.M. replies to K.M.'s letter of 7 February: 'I have your Tuesday evening letter'.

2. K.M. replies 13 February: 'Your 2 Tuesday letters are here . . .'.

---

[154]

[The Athenaeum,
10 Adelphi Terrace,
London. W.C.2.]
[12 February, 1920.]
Thursday Afternoon

My darling[1]

Last night I received a lovely letter from you telling me that you were probably going to Jinnie Fullerton's villa. How gorgeous that will be. I was overjoyed – not merely at the news – but at the letter itself, so sweet, so fragrant, perfumed with that bunch of black oranges. It was just going to my head when I remembered that your wire about my coldness must have been sent *after* the letter. That was a nasty shock.

But when I got to the office this morning I found yr. telegram saying you understood & sending me yr. love. So that now I am feeling that things are going well; that the cloud between us has been blown away. (Violet has just been in with my tea & to tell me that the first snow drop has shown its head in the garden. I am going to pick it & put [it] in this letter.) I do hope – most fervently that Dr. Rendall[2] says you may go to the villa. You can imagine what I feel about that darling woman, Jinnie Fullerton. I must write to her – if its only a word or two. Will you send me her address.

I've sent a second £10 to yr. bank to-day. The cheque for £20 came back safely. Of course, darling, the Constable cheque for £40 will come straight to you. I'm merely acting as your agent. You will have to sign the agreement & receive the money.

You can hardly believe how profoundly glad I am about the fixing up of your book. It is one of my heart's desires; above all because I feel that it's going to have a great success. I don't mean that you'll sell as many as Elizabeth[3] – your mind & your art are so much finer that we can't expect that – but I shall be really disappointed & surprised if you don't sell between 3 and 4 thousand. There's nothing like your work; and I am convinced its the only real achievement of our generation in prose – outside *Sons & Lovers*. Lawrence has gone mad. You are the only person who is the real thing.

I've told you that before; but you might like to hear it again. While I'm on this subject – the choice of what is to go in the book rests *entirely* with you, except that *Prelude* must be included. That, I think, is necessary anyhow not only because of filling out the book, but because it shows a side of your work that is extremely important. In other words, it's necessary for the artistic balance.

I went to dinner with Beresford last night. Delamare, May Sinclair[4] & Naomi Royde-Smith were there. I'm not telling you this to please you, but just as a fact. They were all very excited over my announcement that your book was really coming. May Sinclair turned to me & said that she admired your work more than any. And then Beresford & Delamare struck in together with: Your novel-reviews were the finest in England. There's nothing like them, said Delamare. Oh, it's silly, I know, darling, & they aren't great people (except in a way Delamare) but I thrilled with pleasure. After all you know they're the best we've got. And when Mrs. B took me aside as I was going & said 'May Sinclair told me just before you came that she had been terribly upset by K.M.'s review of her novel, because she thought that K.M. is the only person who really knows how to do it' – why, I thrilled even more.

I feel that all that you have deserved is coming to you, and it makes me so happy & excited.

To-morrow morning I'm going for the week end to East Grinstead. A man who used to work at Watergate House is putting me up – a poet chap called Locke Ellis,[5] very nice, who has a motor-car in which he's going to take me round.

If everything's all right again, will you write about the paper. I miss your criticism so much. It seems to me that what the paper really wants is a page of literary *causerie*. People like that kind of thing; it costs them no effort; and I feel that at present the whole effect of the paper is perhaps a little too frigid & impersonal for the ordinary man. I am thinking of putting Aldous H. onto the job. I'm no good at it myself: I haven't a light touch.

I also incline to think that it might be an improvement if the first page were set solid with the contents on top – without that silly little pocket in the middle. And perhaps if instead of a leading article we had just a page of notes like the political weeklies – only editorial notes on literature & ideas. What do you think? It would have this advantage that we might gain a little space at the beginning of the paper to make room for the *causerie* in the middle.

Your loving
Boge.

1. J.M. replies to K.M.'s letter of 8 February: 'I received a letter from you yesterday saying (1) you had bought me an overcoat'.
2. Before Miss Fullerton would have K.M. to stay in her house, Dr. Rendall had to sign a letter saying that her tuberculosis was not infectious.
3. Elizabeth von Arnim – Countess Russell – (1866–1941) K.M.'s second cousin and author of the best-selling *Elizabeth and her German Garden* (1898). After the death of her first husband, Count Henning von Arnim, she had an affair with H. G. Wells before marrying in 1916 (for three years only) Bertrand Russell's elder brother.
4. May Sinclair (1865–1946) a writer whose novel, *Mary Olivier: A Life*, K.M. reviewed on 20 June, 1919.
5. Vivian Locke-Ellis, a poet who lived in a modernised seventeenth-century mansion near East Grinstead. He became a good friend of Murry's.

---

[155]

2 Portland Villas, [London]
[16 February, 1920.]
Monday Evening
6.30.

My own darling,[1]

I returned this afternoon. I could not stay at the office because I felt that there would be some letters from you. There were – four of them. Two were agonizing; caused by a careless, brutal phrase of mine. God forgive me for it. Two were lovely, – undeserved perhaps, but oh, how thrilling!

I won't try to explain my brutal phrase. My explanations are so ghastly in their clumsiness that I am terrified of them, and of the pain they have concealed in them.

If you can forget the hideous suffering I have caused you through sheer selfish carelessness, I will. But believe me, Worm, never at any single moment have I conceived of our love coming to an end. I felt that I had wounded you so much that you could never forgive me, and I cried aloud in my desolation & anguish.

In my last 2 letters I have talked about the house a lot. It is always in my mind. For, to me, it is the condition of our perfect existence together. You know I talked about you a lot down there at East Grinstead. My mind was continually off day-dreaming. You & I driving up in a little motor-car to their house – I half-handing, half-lifting you out. I always have to half-lift you, because you are so light and beautiful (you always have been the incarnation of these things to me since first I met you in your gauze scarf at the Georges'). I have a short fuzzy coat on & big gloves; you a superb blanket over-coat, chosen by me. And then I say with my heart bursting with pride: This is my wife. And they fall down & worship you.

Then there's another. It's Friday afternoon – tea-time. You are in the drawing room. I've come in from trundling a wheelbarrow about in the garden, making a rose-bed according to your directions. You can't see me. I'm in a cubby hole washing my hands. You call out Bog-ee Tea. Come now before it's cold. I trundle in and sit on the floor with my head against your knees. Silence & warmth by the wood-fire. The maids' steps die away into the kitchen. You say: Boge & stroke my hair. I say: Wig – this is what we dreamed. And then you bend over & turn my head round in your hands & say: Listen. And I listen. Do you know what you say? You say: It's all right, Boge darling. I'm going to have a baby. And I just kiss you. The room is so beautiful, you are so beautiful – even I am beautiful; and we know that our child will be more beautiful still, for all these things have entered into him.

Oh, Worm darling, I could go on giving you these pictures of my mind for hours & hours. Some funny. Hunting for eggs from our chickens; you scolding me & laughing for getting so oily from the motor-car.

If I seem to talk, or worry, too much about the house, Worm, remember that it means all these things to me. It's the place where we can be together; where all my hatred of life will depart from me & all the blackness you hate in me (& I hate too) will be dissolved away;

where we can live as we were meant to live. All day long I think about it, simply because I can't help it. It brings me near you & holds us together. I shut the door & we are in each others arms.

But I need you to talk it over with. I don't have time to write everything. I don't want you to think that I am going mad when I talk of buying a house. I'm grimly determined about it. If the real thing were being sold to-morrow, and it may be on any to-morrow, I should bid up to £1500 for it. I should pay the 10% deposit with my war loan, & then hunt about for the rest of the money. Someone would have to give it me – I mean lend of course.

Of course, I wouldn't buy rashly. Besides the fact that I know what I want exactly, I should get a good surveyor to go down & overhaul it for the things I can't see. Moreover the man Locke Ellis has promised to go with me & give his opinion on anything I hit upon. I have a great respect for a man who has done what he has done with a house.

But I do want to know whether you agree with all my plans. As for finding the money – I must get that from friends – and I have no doubt that I shall be able to. But I want to buy the house first – then they'll have to help me out. I'm sure I can persuade Sydney to take a 7% mortgage for £1000 – and the rest I can borrow from the Bank. Milne[2] has already promised to deposit securities for any amount I borrow up to £500. So I can see my way to £1500.

What I want to know is whether you think I'm getting very rash. My feeling is that we've only got one life, & that's yours. And that we must secure what we need.

Your own
Boge.

1. J.M. replies to K.M.'s letters of 9 February: 'I cannot stand it any longer'; 10 February: 'Note this coincidence'; and 11 February: 'Your Saturday evening letter has come with the "explanation"'.
2. Herbert J. M. Milne, a classical scholar and assistant keeper in the Department of manuscripts at the British Museum. He was a regular visitor at 2 Portland Villas in 1919, staying there with Murry after K.M. left for Menton in September 1920.

[156]   [2 Portland Villas,
                                           Hampstead,
                                           London.]
                                      [16 February, 1920.]

Later

Six letters today! Two more – Thursday & Friday – by the night's post.[1]

I think that's a very fine book indeed. Of course, darling, if you wish to have 'Second Helping' included, it can easily be done. I can dispose of it for you at 2 guineas a thousand to a new monthly magazine that's coming out. If you will have it finished by the end of February, it can go in the book. But that's just as you like. Without it your book will be first-rate, believe me.

About Grant Richards – by all means give him the first refusal of yr. second book if you feel you must. But the terms are these – that he must give you an advance equal in amount to your total royalties on the sale of this book. You can tell him that you're not tied up in any way; and that you will produce your publisher's accounts if he likes. But he must agree to this with a minimum of £60. I mean he must pay you in advance £60 + the sum which you get over & above £60 from the sale of this book.

Your inscription from Shakespeare is *superb*.

I have regained close on £20 for L.M's income tax. I am going to pay that amount into the Bank of N.Z. You can give L.M. her half, or what proportion your too generous mind thinks fit. It will be paid in by the time you get this, so that you can draw on it.

With regard to the 'Man without a Temperament' I don't know what to say except what I've said. I've read it a 3rd. time, and it's beautiful. If I were reviewing it I should have to explain what I meant by that – but *you* know. It has the indescribable quality. It's absolutely sure, not a wavering line from beginning to end, & so sweet. It's real Wig-work. I can say no more. I think you know what I mean by it – the sense that you hit the middle of an extremely delicate note & the tone goes reverberating on in the memory.

The news of the china is perfectly thrilling. I'll pay £2 towards some more on March 1. You can count on the money.

Thank God that awful time is over. Your letters ring like chimes of bells and mine are pealing, pealing. And now I can think of you at the

Villa Flora, with Jennie F. I didn't like to hear you had a temperature, though. But I feel that Jennie will settle that.

Your own loving

Boge.

1. J.M. replies to K.M.'s letters of 12 February: 'Monday evening letters (1) and (2) received'; and 13 February: 'Your 2 Tuesday letters are here . . .'.

---

[157]
[2 Portland Villas,
Hampstead,
London.]
[?17 February, 1920.]
Tuesday Afternoon 6 p.m.

My own darling,[1]

I did rather a rash thing to-day. I went down to the Bankruptcy Court & bought an application form for a discharge (30/-). The reason I did this is that it is illegal for me to obtain credit for more than £10 without saying I am an undischarged bankrupt – and I thought that would interfere a good deal with trying to raise the money to buy a house. But when I looked into [it] it's rather a risky matter. They make you say how much you are earning, and, though I don't believe they are very severe, they might turn on me & say 'Well, you can afford to pay your creditors'. I verily believe I should die of mortification if those beasts, W. H. Smith, ever got a penny of mine.

However, I can't help feeling that it's better to risk it. The house must be got; and since there's no kind friend who will send me £2000 on my promise to repay £150 a year, I must somehow get myself legally free to borrow on mortgage. Of course a discharge completely wipes out a bankruptcy; you become just as though you never had been; you can borrow a £1,000,000 if you can get it.

This is where I want the advice of the old family solicitor, old Humphrey Chattermole (you remember him?). But since if I had had an old family solicitor, I should never have gone b. it's a Utopian rather than a practical suggestion. So I'd better go through with it. But it's rather perplexing, worm.

That apart, everything is well. Wingley looks after me with the utmost devotion. The weather is amazing. To-day has been warm & sunny as a late April day, & a man I met told me – he is a fruit-farmer – that he was already getting terrified of the blossom being too far forward. They're always terrified about something or other, you know.

You'll begin to think me a monomaniac, I'm afraid, – but it's all house with me. I *cannot* get it out of my mind. Chiefly, it's the delights of a Heron that fascinate me; but there's also the point that I don't want you to have to stay a day longer than is absolutely necessary in Portland Villas. I don't want the winter to overtake us again. By September next we must be *comfortable & settled*.

Your words in your last letter. 'From this day forth the Heron begins' have altered the world to me. That means that *everything* is all right – it has restored to me absolute & complete faith in the future, swept away all my horrible intellectual perversities. For you know, Wig, our Heron idea meant all the world to me. It is us, pure & undefiled – as you say, Adam & Eve lying on their backs in the sun. You used to get alarmed because I insisted on the wall. But it was a sun-ripe wall, Wig. Baked & mellow, growing apples & peaches almost without need of trees, a wall that simply refused to let babies fall off it. I think you got my idea of the wall wrong. Perhaps you didn't though.

All my love – all of it

Boge.[2]

1. J.M. replies to K.M.'s letter of 11 February: 'Your Saturday letter has come with the "explanation".'

2. K.M. replies 22 February: 'It is raining here, but such lovely rain!'. About Murry's bankruptcy discharge she said: 'If it could be done it would be an excellent thing, but I detest the idea that Smith or any of your creditors should get another sou. You can't borrow . . . on me for I'm not a good enough life – but could the house be bought in my name? Could any use be made of me?'

---

[158]

[2 Portland Villas,
Hampstead,
London.]
[1][19 February, 1920.]

Thursday Afternoon

My own darling,

I sent no letter yesterday. I had a very busy press day and a long standing engagement with Miss Vesey[2] (you remember her?) to dinner to meet an Irishman – called Philip Bagenal. He was charming – a real gentleman of the old Irish kind – who, very oddly, had been Henry Bentinck's political tutor when he first came down from Oxford. He remembered Ottoline Bentinck, as he called her, as a charming little girl, 'without a cranky thought in her brain'. He was also a passionate admirer of Hardy. So for a dinner-party it was distinctly enjoyable; but I arrived home tired, and after 11 o'clock, when I hadn't the energy to write.

I haven't a great deal of time to-day, because I have to write a long review of a difficult book, and I have planned to go and take a look at Kent starting by the 11 o'clock train to-morrow morning & returning on Sunday night. Somehow I've got to finish the review to-night therefore.

Your letter of yesterday was a pure delight. That wonderful room – those enchanting people. I haven't heard such a cry of pure, unalloyed happiness from you for months, and of course it sets all my bells ringing. You will find that I was writing a very similar kind of letter at the exact moment that you were writing yours – about an enchanting house, & what ours must be. Again, at the very moment that I was asking (and hoping) whether L.M. would stay with us, you were answering my question. You were thinking exactly what I was thinking about the house. Well, we know these coincidences by now; but they're not less wonderful. It seems as though if ever I am in a state of grace, you are also at whatever distance, & the other way round.

One of the houses I am going to see to-morrow is at Minster in Thanet. I'm going partly because, from the description, the house sounds the right size for us, & partly because of a personal reason that may be a good omen. Minster, you must know, is about 3 miles inland from Margate & Ramsgate

Well, when I was about four

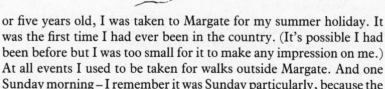

or five years old, I was taken to Margate for my summer holiday. It was the first time I had ever been in the country. (It's possible I had been before but I was too small for it to make any impression on me.) At all events I used to be taken for walks outside Margate. And one Sunday morning – I remember it was Sunday particularly, because the idea of seeing anything really beautiful on Sunday struck me as so strange as to be unearthly – I walked with my father in a path through a field of corn by the sea. Well, the corn was golden & wonderful, but, wonder of wonders, there were wild red poppies in it. That was the first time that beauty sent an arrow bang into my heart. It was unforgettable. I had never dreamed of anything like it.

I'm getting side-tracked from Minster – but not really. For that will show you the kind of dream it is set in. One day after that Sunday my father took me to Minster. I think we went by train, but we may have driven, perhaps in a charabanc. Anyhow Minster finished me off. In my memory it is a dream-place with thatched cottages & a bright village green, and saturated with peace. I couldn't imagine living there when I was a little boy; it seemed quite definitely too beautiful to live in, as though it had a spell on it.

That's all very romantic, and of course it may be very commonplace really. But I can't believe it. So when I heard this morning of a house there called 'Way House', with 2 acres of garden, hall, dining & drawing room, six bedrooms, & 2 attic bedrooms, 'with wide views of the surrounding country' for £1650, I had a feeling that it was ours. At all events I must go & see it to-morrow. The name sounds right, the two acres are right, the price, (say £1400 – they always expect something knocked off) as near right as I can hope. At any rate, a great desire to see Minster has taken hold of me.

I'm worried about that overcoat. I almost wish I had just sent it in the ordinary way insured. Sydney has written over to the man in the Paris Embassy who was to send it on. If I hear nothing satisfactory, I must try to get another. But it was *so* charming.

Your loving

Boge.[3]

1. Alpers says (p. 414) that Murry was at Garsington on 19 February. This letter makes it clear that he was not. Ottoline was in London about this time, entertaining at Ethel Sands' Chelsea house. She possibly brought with her the Garsington visitors' book.

2. Possibly Constance Vesey, a translator of German books, who may have known Murry at the War Office.

3. K.M. replies 22 February: 'It is raining here, but such lovely rain!' About Murry's childhood she comments: 'Your childhood horrifies me. You came upon things so late, and then they were so few'.

[159]   The Athenaeum,
                                     10, Adelphi Terrace,
                                       London, W.C. 2.
                                    [25 February, 1920.]
                                    Wednesday afternoon

Worm darling,
    Press Day – therefore I write in the office.
    Look here Worm, seriously – you must *not* work so hard. You did
quite right in postponing 'Second Helping': only I wish you had not
made the attempt. You're very wicked, and I don't look after you
enough. Your book is splendid as it is, and I ought to have put an
absolute veto on your idea of writing another story. Take things
calmly, Worm. Every ounce of strength you economise now will turn
into a pound next year.
    Something rather thrilling has happened. The other day a beauti-
fully written (in both senses) article on the peasant poet John Clare[1]
came in to the office. I thought it awfully good, accepted it on the spot,
& wrote to the man to say so. He wrote back saying he knew about me,
because he was a Christ's Hospital boy. Imagine my excitement. Then
I heard he was living in a little cottage near Oxford, married, on
nothing a week or thereabouts, sustained by a passion for poetry. He
sent me a little book of his poems this morning. They are immature,
but it's the right kind of immaturity: trying hard at big things: poetry
full of the most intimate knowledge of the country and of nature. With
the book he sent three other poems, again most exquisitely written,
two of which I am going to print. Its the real thing, Wig darling, this
time. Listen to this first verse

                               WILDERNESS

            On lonely Kinton Green all day
                The half-blind, tottering plow-horse grieves,
            Dim chimes & crowings far away
                Come drifting down the wind like leaves;
            And there the wood's a coloured mist
            So close the blackthorns intertwist.

The blackthorns clung with heapen sloes
　　Blue-veiled to weather coming cold
And ruby-tasselled shepherd's rose
　　Where flock the finches plumed with gold,
And swarming brambles laden still
Though boys & wasps have ate their fill.

Here shining out on lubber boughs
　　The lantern crabs loiter and light
The smoke that smouldering leaves unhouse
　　Like stars in frost as sharp and bright:
And here the blackbird deigns to choose
His bloodred haws by ones and twos.

Cob-spider runs his glistening maze
　　To murder doddering hungry flies,
Curt echo mocks the mocking jays,
　　The partridge in the stubbles cries;
And Hob & Nob like blind men pass
Down to the Bull for pipe and glass.

There's no fake about *that*, darling, is there. That's real knowledge, real vision, and an artist's use of language: 'Unhouse' for the smoke of damp leaves – how good that is! And the whole thing is exquisite, veiled with an autumn country mist.

The man's (or boy's) name is Edmund Blunden;[2] and he comes from my school! Here's another

CHINESE POND

Chinese pond is quick with leeches:
From its island knoll of beeches
　　Peeps the temple, standing yet
　　Heaped with dead leaves, all alone.

Mildew dims the lacquered panels
Where the channering insect channels
　　Blood-red dragons pine & fret
　　Who glowered so grimly thereupon.

Mother-pearl & pink shells once
In formal geometricons
    Counterchanged the inner wall:
    Frieze & hangings, both are gone.

Knavish robin reconnoitres,
Unabashed the woodmouse loiters,
    Brown owls hoot at shadow-fall,
    Deathwatch ticks & beetles drone.

Now, old girl, tell me: isn't that the real stuff? I'm sure it is. I think he's our first real discovery, and he comes from my school!

I thought that might thrill you.

I've been working very hard this week to keep pace with things – they go so fast. I've got a great many houses to see this week end. L.M. will show you a letter I have written to her about the house. Arthur tells me that *Je ne parle pas* goes steadily. Hatchards[3] took 1 copy when the *Times Review* came out since then they have had a dozen in ones & twos. There are only a little over twenty left.

Constables want you to make one or two slight excisions in *J. ne p. pas*. I said I thought you wd. agree if they were reduced to a minimum, & if they honestly believed the words would be prejudicial to the sale. I hope I was right.

Your
Boge.[4]

1. Edmund Blunden's article on John Clare was published as the leader in the *Athenaeum* on 5 March 1920.

2. Edmund Blunden (1896–1974), poet, scholar and later an Oxford don, was appointed Professor of English at the University of Tokyo in 1924. At a large farewell dinner party given for him on 11 March 1924 by the editor of the *Nation & Athenaeum*, Murry and Virginia Woolf aired their differences. Reporting the episode, she wrote in her *Diary*: 'My little drama . . . was provided by Murry. . . . "We're enemies" "Not enemies. We're in different camps. But I've never said a word against you, Virginia". "Nor I against you. But what is wrong with us?" "You begin out there –" spreading his hands. "We make patterns of pretty words?" "No. But you won't begin with your instincts. You won't own them. With all your exquisite sensibilities – you're content to stay at that." Here we came into a swift confused wrangle about "writing well".'

3. Booksellers.

4. K.M. replies 2 March: 'A perfect pile of letters came today . . .'. She did not share Murry's enthusiasm for Blunden's poems, and confessed to 'a

perfect horror of Clare. The fact that he fell down in the mud at Byron's funeral and ruined his only clothes fills me with woe'.

---

[160]   [2 Portland Villas,
                                     Hampstead,
                                     London.]
                                     [11 March, 1920.]
                                     Thursday Night. 11.30 p.m.

My own precious Wig-wife.[1]

There was a letter when I got home to-night. It was the one you wrote when you received my answer[2] to your important letter.[3] I'm sorry, darling, that I let the tinge of disappointment show through, but, believe me, I meant exactly what I said in my wire: that I agreed *absolutely*. I'm disappointed that we have to spend the next two winters apart – I can't help that – but at the same time I'm terribly glad at the thought that two more winters will make you perfectly well. I can't have everything as I want it.

But you shouldn't think that I wouldn't feel joy at the things you have bought. Good God, what should I do if I did not think that you would feel joy at the things I have bought? Don't be funny, Wig, you darling: if you go on in that way I shall begin to think of you as the little girl under the cabbage-leaf. And don't think I'm forgetting that we are all in all to each other because I make my little moan. You'll make me afraid of making any little moans; & that will be awful. Who can I moan to if not to you? You know me: take all my moans lightly: say there's that boy moaning again, drat him. But don't go wondering whether I love you.

I've just found a telegram asking me not to drink any more wine. I haven't, darling. Now that Ottoline's parties are over there's no need. The wire came addressed to Hurry. So Violet opened it and read it. So the cat's out of the bag.

About Sydney, I don't know what to say. The whole thing's rather complicated. If Violet & Roger come to live in the basement, and I live in this house alone next winter the expense will be pretty terrific. It would be far more sensible to let the house furnished during the winter & for me to go into rooms. If Sydney is here the expense is much less & I don't mind. And I don't quite see how we can turn him out in the Summer & ask him to come back in the winter. Besides, don't you remember that when you wrote your important letter you said Sydney can stay too if he likes perfectly well?[4] I told him you said that.

Don't get things too tied up about this house, old girl. Think over it a bit. What about taking a furnished house in the country during the summer for instance? I feel it would be a great mistake for me to live alone here for 7 months during the winter. It would cost £8 a week; & that's far too much for me to spend on mere living. I'd far sooner go into rooms in the country & let the house furnished. We could get 4 guineas a week for it, & that would pay for me – a saving of £8 a week.

If you agreed to this notion it would be perfectly simple to tell Sydney that we had decided that the house was too expensive to keep on in the winter.

These things are easier to talk about than to write about. But I can't help thinking that the right thing to do is to let the house furnished while you are away – and live in it *alone together* while you are here, or live in a furnished house in the country. But to live in it alone together in the summer & then for me to live in it alone in the winter seems to me extravagant. It isn't as though I like this house when you aren't here. I don't. Every time I look at the shepherdess or Ribni or the wardrobe I feel a bit sad: & I would far sooner be out of it. Sydney is very nice indeed – but I would sooner live in rather dingy rooms alone provided I could have the cats. And as I say we could get at least 4 guineas a week for it in the winter, probably 5, which would more than pay for me.

It's probably impossible to decide these things until we talk them over together; but I just wanted to suggest various points. When you say you will pay Sydney's £13 a month, you funny Worm, what good will that do – the £13 comes out of our money. So why shouldn't I pay it myself? And for me to pay £13 a month to myself isn't worth while, is it?

Finally – I must go to bed, Wig – look at it like this. Letting the house furnished in the winter means saving about £8 a week if Sydney is not here, £5 if he is. Say I find the cottage, of the kind I hope to find, – one that with some enlargement would be the ultimate Heron. Think how much that £8 a week would pay towards it.

Your own loving
Boge.[5]

1. J.M. replies to K.M.'s letter of 7 March: 'After two days and nights of misery . . . I was forced to give up'.

2. Murry must have received K.M.'s 'important letter' about 1 March, but his answer is missing. Apart from a brief business note from the office dated 2 March, there are no extant letters from him between 29 February and 10 March.

3. K.M.'s letter of 26 February: 'I want you to read this slowly . . .'. She told Murry that Dr. Rendall had said: 'It would be madness for me to spend the next 2 winters in England. . . . For the next two years I ought to be here from November till May'. She suggested, therefore, that they put off establishing their house; instead Murry could get a weekend cottage for himself, while she and L.M. looked after him from May until October at 2 Portland Villas.

4. Murry acceded to Katherine's wishes about Sydney. On 16 March he wrote: 'I gave Sydney notice to clear out by the third week in April today at breakfast'.

5. K.M. replies 14 March: 'I hasten to answer your letter . . . about the house'.

———————

[161]

[2 Portland Villas,
Hampstead,
London.]
[15 March, 1920.]
Monday Evening 6.30

My own darling,[1]

I got a little note from you this morning. Not that I deserved more, I suppose, for it was in answer to one of mine which you said was written at 200 miles an hour. But I have been living at that speed, you know, darling, ever since I came back in January. Since then I have not written a single line of my own work prose or poetry. That's only to assure you that I don't put it on.

But there was a faint chill in your note. As though you thought, when I wrote that Mrs. Locke Ellis invited you to stay in her house, that I wanted or expected you to stay there. I never had the faintest idea that you would go there. I told you merely because I thought it was kind & there aren't so many kind people about, after all. As for my inopportune Hurrah! – well, I've come to think that most of the things I do or say are inopportune. I can't think of anyone who is so dead certain to hit the wrong note as I am.

I think fundamentally the matter is this. You & I have a very different attitude to Portland Villas, which I treat & write about rather

casually, whereas to you it is your precious HOME. There are a good
many reasons for this. The chief is that I have had to live here six
months now without you. It hasn't any very happy memories.
Another is that I had grown completely used to the thought of giving it
up; and I had transferred my ideal elswhere.

These things make a great difference Wig, you know. The mere
fact of always thinking that you are going somewhere else; that you
will have a chance of waking somewhere else; of continually looking
at other houses; of desiring a real garden – these things change one's
attitude insensibly, so that I must confess that Portland Villas isn't
now very precious to me, whereas I know it is to you. I forget, & some
of the things I say may seem callous, because I presuppose in you the
same desire to get away from Portland Villas that I have in myself.

That's just a little explanation. To-day the long awaited table was
brought home. It's a beauty. But like all beauties it has rather a
devastating effect on the uglies as I knew it would. I had made up my
mind that we should have to buy some dining room chairs. I had even
been to inspect them at Heal's intending to have them in their places
by the time you returned. But I shall faithfully keep my promise not to
buy anything until you return. Then we'll have a thorough inspection
& reorganisation. For instance, we need another bed, I think – and a
different floor-covering at least for the dining room. But all these
things will be thrashed out when you come back.

Don't be afraid that I shall accept any invitations for you, or ask any
one to dinner during your first week. I assure you I have no such idea.
It would never have entered into my head.

To-day I paid the £10 into your account; to-night I shall send a
cheque finally settling Sorapure's account so that everything will be
cleared up before you return. I have told Violet that you are going to
write to her about the spring-cleaning. We need it pretty badly.

The returned agreement arrived to-day: I sent it on. Also I had a
letter in reply to mine from Miss Fullerton.

If you could think of some place where you would like to go for our
holiday, it might be a good thing to make a kind of provisional
arrangement. But perhaps that's one of the things you feel you can't
decide until you've seen Sorapure.

On the whole I begin to feel that a country holiday would be a lovely
thing to have. I am beginning to feel that I have had enough of rush &
worry for a bit. Yet when I try to consider calmly I can't exactly see
why my time should be so congested. I've put it all down to the

weekends. But nowadays they seldom last more than a day. Somehow the time rushes away without leaving me a moment to read the books I want to read or write the things I want to write. But I have an instinctive conviction that when you come home everything will be different. You'll come like the Prince to the Sleeping Beauty. The old bulb of a house will suddenly burst into flower & I shall find myself with leisure in my heart. That more than anything is what I want – leisure in my heart. I think you are the only person who can give it me – I'm sure if you can't no-one can.

You will remember my speaking the other day about a quotation from Chaucer[2] which I could not find. I have found it now. Here it is.

Troilus has just met Cressida – for the first time really met her, alone, though he has loved her for months.

> This Troilus in armës gan hir streyene
> And seyde: 'O swete. as ever more I goon,
> Now be ye caught, now is ther but we tweyne:
> Now yeldeth you, for other boot is noon.'
> To that Criseyde answerdë thus anon:
> 'Ne hadde I ere now, my swete herte dere,
> Ben yolde, y-wis I werë now not here.'

It's Criseid's words that seem to me so wonderfully beautiful.

If I had not yielded before now sweetheart dear, I should not have been here.

Boge.[3]

1. J.M. replies to K.M.'s letter of [?] March: 'Your Monday note has just come (written at 200 miles an hour, I should think').
2. 'Troilus and Criseyde', Book III, lines 1205–1211.
3. K.M. replies 19 March: 'I have just received your Monday letter'.

---

[162]
[2 Portland Villas,
Hampstead,
London.]
[22 March, 1920.]
Monday Evening

My darling,[1]

Two letters from you this morning – so I'm almost all square now. They were both lovely – so you are in reality several pegs up.

I have a quaint feeling that Brett in her innocence gave you a queer account of 'orgies'. The word, at least, sounds to me unutterably odd as a description of any doings in which I have been concerned. I could understand it as applied say to our evening in Montmartre when I had the 2½ stamp on my forehead, or the famous Christmas party at Gilbert & Mary's,[2] or the party at Brett's studio when Fergusson & Anne Rice & Beatrice Campbell were there – though even those I should say, being no expert, were very mild 'orgies'. But, Tig, you would have laughed if you had seen these 'orgies'; as far as I know, they consisted in me rather gloomy with rather too much to drink gradually getting gloomier & gloomier as I tried to talk to the impossible people whom Ottoline Morrell collected for her parties. I don't defend the drink, mind you; I think I'm better without it at all times; but on the other hand I do feel that it was the best way out of the difficulty of those parties. The last one I went to alone without a sniff of anything alcoholic; & my misery was abject. Why go at all, you say? Well, there was the blessed woman continually making cattish remarks about my not going to see her. And to tell the truth, I'm rather frightened of her; I can't afford to have her my active enemy; & I couldn't bear a soulful dinner-party with her. So I chose the less evil. That's my account of it, anyhow.

More dignity, you say. But so, Good god, do I. I pine for it. But I must honestly say it's not I who am undignified in the present pandemonium.

I am all for the New Forest. Yes, it must be an inn. How else shall we manage to do for ourselves. Ireland's very nice; but (1) the journey's a nuisance & (2) if we go to Ireland we shall be so deluged with invitations that we shan't have any enjoyment. There are about a dozen friends of Miss Vesey's who are apparently thirsting to put us up for unlimited periods if ever we set foot on the island. And it would be jolly difficult to refuse if we once got there.

No, for our purposes the New Forest seems the very thing. As for the time, I suggest July – the whole bang month of it. Will you write to Marie[3] about it; it must be a decent place where we are really well looked after & well fed, & if possible near some bathing. I want a holiday *complet*; after all, it will be the first one I've had since I went in the W.O. – excepting always that six weeks' so-called breakdown at Garsington. No wonder I haven't any wool in the place where the wool ought to grow.

Wingley is becoming a desperate character; a willing [i.e. villain] of the deepest dye. You won't be a bit disappointed in him. He's got all the character he used to have, & he looks – to me – just the same. There's something essentially don't-care & kittenish about him, however much he grows – a strange contrast to poor old Athy, who's a sentimental idiot.

To-day came a letter signed Beatrice Hastings. 'Can you give me any work on your paper?' Not addressed to me by name. Editor – Dear Sir. What am I to do? She's no friend of mine, it's true; but you, I know, have memories of & feelings towards her. She must, I suppose, be hard up to apply to me even in the most formal way. I'd be willing to give her something; but, you see, I never thought anything of her work – and the paper isn't a charitable organisation; it has to remain a good paper. I wait for your suggestion.

Prelude I'll get & send to-morrow. As for B.C's Xmas card, Heaven alone knows where I've shoved it away.

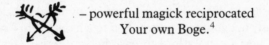 – powerful magick reciprocated
Your own Boge.[4]

1. J.M. replies to K.M.'s letters of 17 March: 'I have just received your Sunday letter answering my questions'; and 19 March: 'I have just received your Monday letter'.

2. At the Cannans' Mill House on 25 December 1915.

3. K.M. had suggested that she ask her sister 'Marie' (Chaddie) to find them holiday accommodation in the New Forest.

4. K.M. replies ?25 March: 'I was reading your letter so happily this morning until suddenly I came across your remark about B[eatrice] H[astings]'.

---

[163]

[2 Portland Villas,
Hampstead,
London.]
[23 March, 1920.]
Tuesday Night

My own darling,

The events to-day were (1) another sitting for this portrait of wh: I told you (2) a bus-ride to Richmond – have you seen in the paper that this has been the hottest March for 50 years? The last week has been incredibly beautiful (3) dinner with Virginia & Leonard & Roger Fry,[1] – from which I have just returned – 11 o'clock.

I am sitting in your room at your yellow table. My nightly milk is heating on the little spirit stove. Athy is roaring & scratching at your chair on wh: I am sitting, and I have just given him a jab with my elbow because I'm very annoyed with him for being so stupid. I feel rather stupid myself, but very cheerful: the weather & your home-coming have put me in a mood in wh: I have no fault to find with the universe. I hope the universe can say as much of me.

The portrait of me is beginning to look very well.[2] I didn't expect as much. By very well I mean it's beginning to be very like me, but more handsome than I am – which is what a portrait ought to be. So I'm coming round to the opinion that there's a good deal to be said for these severely realistic portraits after all. I don't think I should be pleased if my nose had been screwed round to where my ear ought to be for the sake of significant form. However, probably people who are having their portraits done are not the best judges of art.

That reminds me. It's absolutely essential that you should have your portrait painted this summer. Even if it costs £50. I must have a real picture of you hanging near me while you are away. I think Brett might do a good one; at all events there's more chance of her bringing out what I want brought out than of Gertler doing so. And Gertler's the only other painter I know. I wish I knew Orpen. I should like a portrait of you by Orpen very much indeed.

There's no more news about Broomies[3] yet except that it's confirmed that I have the first refusal.

Your own Boge
qui t'aime Bogoo

1. Virginia commented in a letter to her sister: 'We had a great splash of people before coming away – dear old Roger and Murry – and a very rich composition of Mrs Clifford, Sydney W[aterlow] and Goldie – who came in by chance. Mere brilliancy is not in it with richness, ripeness and a touch of rottenness'.

2. Murry's portrait was probably being painted by Dorothy Brett.

3. 'Broomies' was a cottage in Chailey, Sussex, that Murry was to buy on April 9 for £480. He borrowed money and put the house in Katherine's name since he was an undischarged bankrupt. They never lived in it.

[164]   [2 Portland Villas,
                                                              Hampstead,
                                                                London.]
                                                        [25 March, 1920.]
Thursday,
Darling,[1]

I've just had your wire about Beatrice Hastings. I told you I was
going to do nothing until I heard from you; and, of course, I haven't.
I'm very sorry you were deeply hurt old girl, but I don't think you
ought to have been. I had absolutely forgotten what she did in Paris;
and I'm wondering whether I ever knew, really. I think you must be
under the impression that you told me more than you actually did.
Anyhow I have no definite recollection of her conduct. What I do
know is that she was always an active & venomous enemy of mine, and
that you told me she had gone completely to the dogs in Paris.

But in any case I was firmly determined not to do anything about it
until I had heard from you. Now I shall simply send her an official
letter saying that the Editor regrets. What I wanted to clear up was
that I don't think you ought to have been deeply hurt; and that it's
rather hard on me to wire those words. I always take such a thing from
you very seriously indeed; it upsets me horribly.

Well, please Wig, forget all about it. I can't help thinking that you
feared I would do something without consulting you: but of course I
wouldn't & haven't. I'll wire that to you to-morrow morning.

I had a lovely letter from you last night – a perfect little beauty,
offering me little heart-cakes of faery bread. The cannons were also
being fired at Monaco. I feel they ought to be immense pop-guns; but I
suppose they are the real thing. By the way that was a simply
marvellously good little review of the Short Stories[2] you sent the other
day.

It was a very funny coincidence that in this letter you said 'Bunny
Dunn[3] is revealed a Beatrice Hastings of the worst kind'. I don't know
about that Prince & Princess business. I can always see you as the
Princess all right; but I seem to be a rather comic Prince, – not smart
enough for my ideal, any how. But I shd. like to have been one all the
same.

The weather even here is pretty astonishing. I haven't worn an
overcoat for more than a week & it's still March. All the trees have
tremendous great buds – real whoppers. M.[arie]D.[ahlerup] has got
a job at £2.15 a week. She came & asked me whether she shd. take it. I

said Yes, yes, yes! And she has. Now I suppose she'll expect me to get her salary doubled. Pas demi!

Boge[4]

You <u>are</u> <u><u>not</u></u> to be deeply hurt. You're always doing it – falling into ink pots I call it.

1. J.M. replies to K.M.'s letter of 22 March: 'Sullivan's a wicked liar'.
2. K.M.'s review, 'Short Stories', of Archibald Marshall's *The Clintons, and Others*; Mary Gaunt's *The Surrender, and other Happenings*; and Dion Clayton Calthrop's *A Bit at a Time* appeared on 2 April.
3. A woman Katherine knew in Menton.
4. K.M. replies 30 March: 'I've had three letters from you today . . .'

---

[165]   [2 Portland Villas,
                                          Hampstead,
                                          London.]
Friday Evening   [26 March, 1920.]

My darling Worm,

This morning at the office I received yr exquisite pen-tray which I set in use forthwith. You are a great darling to have sent it; I've nothing on my desk to remind me of you.

I lunched with Bruce Richmond to-day, & learned that the *Times Supplement* has put its payment to contributors up 50%. This is a serious matter for us: we must follow suit or see our contributors drift off to them; and yet we can't get away from the fact that the *A.* is losing money. Our proprietors must make up their minds that they are in for a long shot, and that they will not see any return on their money for 5 years. I don't know what they will do. I've arranged to be present at the next board meeting (I ought to be invited to them all) and discuss the solution of the problem. Also I'm determined to give them a piece of my mind about the disgusting production & printing of the paper. It's a handicap of the very worst kind.

Your wire has just come saying 'Forgive my extravagant wire yesterday'. In your turn please forgive anything I may have said yesterday. It was only the 'deeply hurt' that worried me.

I made the uncomfortable discovery yesterday that I am overdrawn at the bank – with the rent to pay. I can't think how its happened. Except that perhaps I left King's bill for the electric light out of my calculations. I paid it at the same time that I paid Sorapure's bill the other day: that may have been the last straw. However it's only a few days to the 1st. April and then I shall be – moderately – in funds again.

There's a great S.W. wind blowing to-day. Also I've had a letter to say I can't have possession of Broomies until Michaelmas 1921 – which is a bit of a facer. I don't quite know what to do about it. Locke Ellis telephoned to say that he knew of a cottage to be let which might suit me: so I'm going down to him for the week-end to-morrow. All my inclination is towards buying Broomies, even if we have to wait for it. Even if it were only an investment we should feel that it was always there, & our own. I have a constant feeling in my mind that one day we shall need a little refuge, and that in a place like Broomies we will be safe against all the 'slings & arrows of outrageous fortune'. How do you feel about it?

It fills my heart with happiness to think that you are coming back. I love you so, my heart.

Boge.[1]

1. K.M. replies 30 March: 'I've had three letters from you today . . . one about Broomies'.

---

[166]   [2 Portland Villas,
                                             Hampstead,
                                             London.]
                                             [1 April, 1920.]
                                             Thursday

My darling,[1]

After I wrote to you yesterday your letter containing the John verse arrived. I thought it was jolly good. The Moults came round in the evening; your ears ought to have tingled at their admiration of your writing. It's true it isn't greater than mine, probably indeed not as great; but it is so delightfully genuine & whole-hearted.

I think it would be wonderful to have your portrait painted by Orpen. I like his work very much, and I always have. Don't you think it might be fixed up viâ Beatrice Campbell & Dublin. You see you have always had a great reputation in Dublin, and Orpen would, rightly, think it a compliment that you wanted to be painted by him. And I should so dearly love to have the portrait while you were away;

besides we want it for ever, to put in the place of honour in our house.

I perfectly understand what you say about the impossibility of going to live actually in the Villa Flora next year. It *is* in the long run always impossible to live with people who are not artists, or at least haven't learned to think with artists; and it's absolutely impossible I'm sure in the case of Catholics[2] who, however generous & kind they may be, are definitely anti-artistic. You can't really get away from the fact that their values are absolutely & utterly different from your own; that they really live in a strange world to which you have not & don't want to have access. A Catholic, or indeed any truly religious person, always frightens me in a queer way. Talking to them is like peering over the edge of a deep well, & living with them must be like continually playing on the edge of it. The only kind of people one can live with are people who accept responsibility for themselves. They belong to one kind; the others to another.

So I think your idea of arranging for a little flat for next year admirable. I'm sure you will be happier still.

The beautiful weather – for in spite of threats it has remained beautiful for at least 3 weeks – has ended with a bang, just in time to catch the holiday-makers. It has been raining all day to-day & it's really parky, though I don't suppose there will be any more frost. Anyhow I hope not.

Sydney has gone home to Wiltshire for a week's holiday. So I shall have the house to myself. To-night I'm going out to dine with Brett; I've been working all day – all the afternoon at home on the American article which I shall finish to-morrow morning.

I'm very anxious that we should start printing short stories & sketches every week in the paper if we can only get hold of them. I'm afraid you would have to do a lot of them; you're the only first-rater. I have a very charming sketch from Japan sent in by Stella Benson[3] which I want to use. But I shan't do anything in the matter till you come home; then you can be, as the Americans say, fiction-editor.

> Your own
> Boge
> April 1 – 29 i.e. 4 weeks
> exactly.

1. J.M. replies to K.M.'s letter of about 24 March which opens with:

Old Sir John to hell has gone
Burn, devils, burn him!
When one side well is fried
Turn, devils, turn him!

2. Connie Beauchamp and Jinnie Fullerton were Catholics who hoped to convert K.M.
3. Stella Benson (1892–1933), a writer of novels, poems and travel sketches, travelled and worked in China in 1920. K.M. had reviewed her novel, *Living Alone*, in November 1920.
4. K.M. replies 4 April 1920: 'Easter Sunday – pouring rain . . .'.

[167]					[2 Portland Villas,
					Hampstead,
					London.]
					April 5 – 29[1] [1920.]
					Monday

My own darling,[2]
I had two letters from you this morning while I was in bed. That is one of my extra special luxuries – reading your letters in bed. I get them twice, – because I always go to sleep after them, and forget all about them. Then I read them again.

You got your Latin[3] out of the Vulgate, I know.

I didn't a bit like what you said about your coughing still. Does that only happen on a bad day? I understand that you still have to walk with a stick, & still rest nearly all the time. It's a ghastly slow business mending yourself after the awful time you have had. Good God, don't think I shall be disappointed if you have to go slow, and don't imagine that I've got in my head that you're coming back perfectly fit. No, what I expect is a Wig who is beginning painfully & slowly to mend, who is very gradually building up instead of the other thing, of whom I have to take infinite care. But I don't like the news of that cough.

I absolutely agree with what you say about one's past becoming something rich & rare as one goes on. Every time I look back on mine, it becomes something more marvellous, more romantic, more faery, more rich in goodness, – all the commonplaceness seems to go out of it. It's like one of those old mammoth teeth they tell of in Siberia. When it was put to bed in the earth it was only a mammoth's tooth; but now when they dig it out, after centuries, it is a turquoise of the purest blue.

So I have to withdraw all I said about C & J. The flat idea[4] is trembling. I don't think I'm really capable of advising you. Just for my own purposes & from my own point of view, I favour the place where comfort is most certain for you. On the other hand, I so keenly understand your feeling about not living with artists. No, I *can't* advise you, Wig. Think it all over as carefully as you can, though. Still, I think I am a better one at thinking things over carefully than you are.

I've done no work to-day except read a good deal more Chaucer. I've finished *Troilus & Cressida* & have just read the amazing Prologue to the *Legend of Good Women*. That is absolutely incredible – the whole thing about a daisy.

Your own
Boge.[5]

1. J.M. began writing on his letters the day's date next to the date of K.M.'s. return to England – April 29.

2. J.M. replies to K.M.'s letters of 1 April: 'April Fool's Day and only 27 days before I start for home . . .'; and 2 April: 'Your letter on the gnu typewriter came yesterday'.

3. K.M. quoted on 2 April: 'ecce quam bonum et quam jucundum habitare fratres in unum! Sicut unguentum in capite, quod descendit in barbam, barbam Aaron'.

4. There had been talk of K.M. and Connie and Jinnie taking separate flats in the large Menton house; then of the two women buying the house and giving K.M. her own rooms in it.

5. K.M. replies 9 April: 'Do not overpraise me'.

---

[168]   [2 Portland Villas,
                                          Hampstead,
                                          London.]
                                          April 6 – 29 [1920.]
                                          Tuesday

My own Worm,[1]

I had a letter from you this morning which contained 2 of the most adorable drawings of children I have ever seen. Seriously I consider them little masterpieces of their kind. I think the little girl is beyond words exquisite, & a marvellous piece of drawing. The arm which belongs to the hand holding the flower is extraordinary. And how you got that enchanting dew-petal sweetness into her face, I can't imagine.

You simply must do some more of these. There's no earthly doubt that you can draw – those are both real drawings.

I don't in the least see why we should wait 30 years for a Broomchen[2] in the S. of France. Why couldn't we have it within 5 years? My idea always is that our reputations will be established in, at most, 3 years from now, & that then we shall be able to go anywhere, and always make a decent living. Even now you know we're very much more famous than we were a year ago. Lots of people are beginning to look upon us as the coming man & woman (that shd. be the other way about, but it comes natural). The only thing I feel is a real obligation to have made the *Athenaeum* a success, not because of my proprietors, but as a duty to literature & my country. I want to see it established in the way it should go, & self-supporting Then I shall feel free to retire, perhaps with an engagement to write them an article every week for £500 a year. Well, I hope to have done all that in 3 years. That may be sanguine; but I feel that we shall do it within 3 years or not at all. And, somehow, I don't think we shall fail.

At the same time I realise perfectly well that it means for me, a great deal of hard work. I accept the fact that I shall always have to make my living by literary criticism; but it must be far better criticism than any I have written yet. It must be *rich* criticism, full of knowledge & delight. I believe that I can make myself a first-class critic (& I mean really first-class) not only without doing harm to my poetry, which is & always will be, my chief concern, but doing it good, – making it too rich. I want to lay the foundations of all this in the next 3 years while I control the *A*. It is my experimental farm, my seed-testing station. Editing the *A*. I shall find my line & learn my job.

For you the case is different. Compared to you I am intolerably immature. You will be doing your best work long before I shall. Your work now – stories & criticism – seems to me hardly possible of improvement. And I *know* that within three years you will be famous as a story-writer throughout the English speaking world. Then we shall both retire from the *A*. with salaries for regular contributions.

Practically, it means, Broomies will be our home in England then, expanded, with pergolas & a wonderful orchard. And a little house in the S. of F. will be our winter home. We shall trot off together every year in the autumn & trot back together every spring, knowing that our own little house is there ripening for us all the while we are away, – bringing back exquisite little things for its adornment – and if God is kind having two little daisy children to bow down to. That, my darling, is my plan. I don't think its asking too much of Destiny, who has been so fond of banging us on the head in the past. Arthur will have found his sea-legs by then.

I hope that L.M. who has stood by us in the hard days will be with us when the smiling days come. I cannot help thinking that we shall be 'wonder gentil' when we are secure.

Your own Boge.[3]

I am seeing Sadler about the book[4] this week. I shall insist that the omissions[5] be reduced to these (see other page)

1 business enclosure[6]

1. J.M. replies to K.M.'s letter of 'end of' March: 'I do wish I could draw'.
2. K.M. had written: 'If only you shared my winters and we had a minute Broomchen here . . . But we can wait and come in 30 years' time'.
3. K.M. replies 9 April: 'Do not overpraise me'.
4. *Bliss.*
5. In 'Je ne parle pas français'.
6. The 'other page' and the 'business enclosure' are missing.

---

[169]   [2 Portland Villas,
                                                        Hampstead,
                                                         London.]
                                                    [7 April, 1920.]
                                                       Wednesday

Worm darling,

I wish those rotten old posts would behave better. I have nothing since the last batch of letters: as I've told you before they always come in batches nowadays. Postmen, especially foreign postmen, are beasts.

Sullivan came up from the country to-day. He did look ill; he must have had a pretty bad bout of influenza. So I forgive him for having let me down. And to-day I remembered about the copy of *Prelude*.[1] I telephoned to the Woolves to get a copy; they had both gone away for the holiday. However the servant promised to send one by the night's post. I hope it arrives safely.

I have received a letter from Constables saying the excisions they want made in *Je ne p. p.* are these

(1) p. 5 last par. but 1 'and then after
a soft growl . . . . back to our door'
(2) p. 6. last line but 2
'If I find myself in need . . . .
cake afterwards'
(3) p. 7. l. 13 'Why should I be able . . .
I want.'
(4) p. 24. 5th. par from bottom
'And . . . good-night my little cat . . .
I didn't give her time to reply'
(5) p. 25. line 13 from bottom 'And so on . . . interested
in modern English
literature'
(6) p. 25. line 4 from bottom
'I'd rather like to dine with
her' to the end.

Now I can understand (1) easily (2) at a pinch (3) I can't really understand (4) not at all (5) I can only understand deleting the virgin (6) only 'sleeping with her'. What do you say? I should stick against cutting more than is absolutely necessary. On the other hand you don't get the £40 till the MS is satisfactory to them; and the true edition of *Je ne p. p.* is in existence.

Sadler – *how* I dislike him – suggests your substituting something for 'The Wind Blows' which his Majesty thinks is 'on [the] trivial side'. I can't remember which it is, myself. What do you think about that? The only MS of yours I have are '[The] Black Cap' – 'Something Childish but very natural' – or there's the 2 stories in the *Signature*. What about putting them in the book any how. I've just looked at them again. 'Autumns' & 'The Little Governess'. I should certainly put them in if I were you. If you think this a good idea just let me know

Surely the second of [the] 'Autumns' is 'The Wind Blows' – it's a superb little thing, superb. Oh! I'll smack that young fool's face.

But you must put 'The Little Governess' in. You've forgotten how good it is. I've just read it. Please do!
Your
Boge.

1. K.M. had requested a copy of *Prelude* on 30 March; Murry had replied on 3 April: 'The horrible thing about *Prelude* is that the Woolves haven't got any more bound copies. The servant has sent me one wh. belongs to Virginia.

I don't know whether you want it to give away or to read and revise. If the latter I could send you my own bound copy. I'll send that on spec. You see I had to give away our other copy to Constables for MS purposes. I can't get hold of the Woolves until next Wednesday or so'.

---

[170]
[2 Portland Villas,
Hampstead,
London.]
[8 April, 1920.]
Thursday

My own darling,
I saw Sadler to-day about the MS. He accepted my provisional suggestions with regard to
    p. 5. line 6 from bottom. Only the one line to go
    p. 6. last sentence. To stand altogether.
    p.25. 'And so on & so on . . . literature'. The whole par. to
        stand, with the exception of the word 'virgin'.

He would prefer
    p.7 l.13 'Why should I be able to have any woman I want?'
    omitted
    p.24. last line but 11 'And good-night . . . to reply' omitted
    p.25. last 2 lines omitted.

The ground he takes with regard to these is that they will do positive harm to the sale of the book; that by omitting them you will gain a good deal more than you will lose by retaining them.

Honestly, Worm, I think there's something in it. I mean in this way. Yours is essentially an exquisite talent, and one which, I am sure, will be appreciated by many more people than will appreciate the actual art. I mean people like my mother. She will love the stories, I know & I'm sure there are thousands like her.

Now these people will be shocked by the few things the omission of which is still suggested. I believe that it's bad policy to shock the people by whom, after all, you do desire to be read. And I think that if you compromise to this extent you will never regret it.

That's my honest opinion.

If you think you can accept these omissions will you just wire to me: 'Omissions accepted', when Constables will send you a cheque immediately.

I had a letter from Hardy to-day asking if I would like a poem for the *Athenaeum* of April 30.[1] Wouldn't I! I wrote off immediately, of course, saying 'Please'. I wonder what it's going to be like. It's very mysterious, because he says it's quite essential that it should appear on *April 30* & no other day. He was going to send it to the *Times* when he suddenly realised that the *Athenaeum* came out on the 30th. I'm very excited. Also, an American publisher has taken 300 copies of my book,[2] so that the first edition will certainly be sold out. I think that's all the good news; but nowadays there always seems to be a little bit.

Boge.[3]

1. 'The Maid of Keinton Mandeville', Hardy's tribute to Sir Henry Bishop on the sixty-fifth anniversary of his death, was published in the *Athenaeum* on 30 April.
2. Cobden-Sanderson published two of Murry's books in 1920, *Cinnamon and Angelica* and *The Evolution of an Intellectual*. The reference is probably to the latter.
3. K.M. replies 11 April: 'All yesterday, off and on, I had waves of delight at the thought of Broomies'.

---

[171]   [2 Portland Villas,
                                    Hampstead,
                                    London.]
                              Friday. April 9 – 29 [1920.]

My darling Wig

To-day I heard that the owner of Broomies had accepted our offer of £480 – so that's settled. Also I had a wire from you saying that you accepted the business arrangements. I'm afraid my last letter adds something to my maximum of alteration; but I am taking upon myself the responsibility of fixing the matter in order that you can have the £40 without any more delay. I will arrange that it is paid directly into the Bank of New Zealand in order to avoid the delay of endorsing the cheque & returning it. I will send you a wire as soon as it is done.

So we may conclude that these two things are more or less at an end.

Like an ass, feeling that I would like to have 2 vols. of Henry James's letters, I promised to do them for the *Nation*. I am bored, unutterably bored with them. Not bored because they are uninteresting – in a sense they are extremely interesting – but because the man is profoundly antipathetic to me. There is an oily sentimentality about his later letters, something ghastly & Bowdenish[1] (Dear Lady – Yes, it's Reginald Peacock) which simply rasps on my sensibility. And there are one or two references to Thomas Hardy which make me so angry. Henry James patronising T.H.! Worse than patronising – sneering at *Tess of the D'Urbervilles* – a book worth the whole of H.J's work lumped together. And this ineffable literary bounder (who really didn't know what literature is) writing to Hugh Walpole[2] – My dear Hugh be your own delightful self.

You remember that revue at the Ambassadors when the big man was dressed as a baby girl & came in on a scooter & said 'Mar-mie' and 'Dard . . . die'. That's the effect of the later Henry James.

If I can stop getting angry – or at any rate allow my anger to simmer, I might be able to write a review that would really blow the gaff on H.J. a bit. I should like to. He needs to have a critical skewer poked into his swollen carcase.

Thank God we never knew him Wig. I should have been unutterably ashamed if ever he had written me a letter. When I think of old Hardy's letters to me & how I revere them, when I think that however much I saturate myself in Chaucer & Shakespeare Hardy remains in his own way as firm as they are – well.

Your own
Boge.

Two big photographs of the Grange have come for you from yr. Father They're too big to send across.

1. Reminiscent of K.M.'s first husband, George Bowden, whom Murry sees as the model for the protagonist of 'Mr Reginald Peacock's day'.

2. Hugh Walpole (1884–1941), the novelist, had contributed to the *Blue Review*. K.M. reviewed his novels *Jeremy* (15 August, 1919) and *The Captives* (15 October, 1920).

---

[172]   [2 Portland Villas,
Hampstead,
London.]
Wednesday April 14 – 29 [1920]

My own Wig,

I got off an hour earlier from Press-Day than I expected. That was extremely pleasant. Your review of Maxwell[1] came while I was in the office. Of course I shan't cut it. The only reason why I ever cut your stuff is that sometimes it doesn't arrive until Wednesday morning. Then it *has* to be made to fit the space allowed for it.

When I got home I found a parcel of cup & saucers from Menton. I had a terrible fright, because the box was broken. However, the things were so splendidly packed each in his separate straw jacket that not one piece was broken. It's jolly to have the breakfast cups – we've been wanting some for so long; & the little jug with a top-knot is exquisite . . .

Dear old girl, I can't put the £10 into yr. account this month. I've only got £15 in the bank, which will only just last out the month. You remember that you said you would pay me back the nine guineas for the overcoat when you got the money for your book? Will it do if you just don't pay me back. I'm sorry to be so hard up. I was overdrawn, as I told you, last month, & this month bills have been heavy -- rent, insurance together, + £10 for the typewriter[2] + £20 overdraft made my month's money look very silly and I am particularly anxious not to overdraw again this month. I shall just be able to avoid it, I think.

I did another sitting for my portrait during the afternoon. I'm getting fed up with it, particularly since it doesn't seem to me to be half so good as it was two times ago. She hasn't known where to leave off. I've just been reading an essay by Dryden in which he says that's the national vice of English people. I wonder. I'm having all my suits sent to the cleaner – there are only 2 summer ones – and I'm also sending 2 felt hats – so as to look nice & clean for you.

Your own
Boge[3]

1. K.M.'s review of W. B. Maxwell's *A Remedy Against Sin* appeared on 23 April.

2. J.M. had told K.M. about 25 March that he had sold his old typewriter for £5.10.0 and was putting the money towards a new Corona: 'the machine Aldous Huxley and Eliot have and swear by. It costs £15.15.0'. On 30 March he mentioned that the typewriter 'came today. I paid the balance of the money with a post-dated cheque'.

3. K.M. replies 18 April: 'This letter was never posted and here's Sunday déjà'.

[173]   [2 Portland Villas,
                                       Hampstead,
                                        London.]
                                     Friday 6 pm.
                                April 16 – 29 [1920.]

My own darling,

I've been doing my share of the spring-cleaning to-day, tidying up papers, cleaning out drawers, re-hanging pictures. Brett, Arthur & I are dining together and then going to the Hippodrome to see the Spanish actress, Raquel Meller, who is supposed to be wonderful.

At present Brett & Arthur are downstairs deciding which of Arthur's drawings are to be shown to Professor Tonks[1] who has to decide that they show great promise in order that he shall be in the running for the Slade scholarship I spoke about in my last.

What do [you] think about the whole scheme. It's a very fat scholarship &, with an extra £30 a year from me to make it up to £150 he ought to be quite comfortable. Of course I can't help feeling that it's a risk going in to be a painter when you are dependent on it for a living; but, even if he isn't a great success – and I don't see why he shouldn't be as successful relatively as I have been – he'll get far more happiness out of life by being an artist than by not being one. I think that's certain. And happiness is the only thing that matters. Moreover, whereas I never had anyone to fall back on, he always has you & me. If his pictures don't sell he can always go to Broomies & live in a little shed and at least get enough pocket-money for tobacco out of us.

And, still more important than this, is the fact that he wants to be a painter & wants to go to the Slade. He has a very fine chance of doing both these things. If he were prevented he would only look back on it with regret and anger against the people that prevented it. That must be avoided at all costs. For once let's have somebody whose path has been made fairly smooth, who will be able to think that everybody, instead of conspiring against him, conspired for him.[2]

Perhaps Arthur has written all about it to you. In that case you'll know more than I can tell you, & you will [be] able to judge how keen he is.

Gertie tells me she has written to you to tell you that the spring-cleaning has begun – it has, with unusual severity. Mrs. Moody, Gertie & Violet have been engaged in throwing the top-floor out of the window all day. That part is nearly over. Everything has got to be in apple-pie order by the time you come. That's a tremendous event for the household. I begin to feel that all Hampstead knows about it.

Your own
Boge.[3]

1. Henry Tonks (1862–1937), a surgeon-turned-artist, was the drawing teacher at the Slade whose total dedication to art unnerved some prospective students. 'Tonks was the Slade and the Slade was Tonks', it was said.

2. On 17 April J.M. wrote that he had discussed the problem of his brother with his parents:

'I've been hard at the argument until now, 9 o'clock, and the thing's still left undecided. It's very difficult – this affair about Arthur & the Slade Scholarship I mean – I quite see my father's point. Art is a risk; he has no backing; & my father, who retired yesterday, hasn't £300 a year now. From his point of view it's a serious matter. The only thing I could do was to offer to take the responsibility myself i.e. from henceforward to see that Arthur cost my mother & father nothing at all. However, we left it over for another week. I have promised to go over again on the evening of the Monday before you come back, when the decision will be taken. I must honestly say my father was very nice about it all. He was obviously thinking only of Arthur, & we parted great friends. But it is exhausting, all the same. I think the whole thing depends, really, upon whether Tonks thinks Arthur has real promise or not. If he does, then Arthur ought to have his full chance; if not, there must be an end of it. But it's quite clear that I must from now onwards take full financial responsibility for Arthur. £300 a year is a very meagre amount for my mother and father to live on. They can't be allowed to spend money on Arthur as well'.

3. K.M. replies 20 April: 'All being well I shall be at the Palais Lyon on Wednesday until Thursday'; and later: 'This is about Richard'.

---

[174]   2 Portland Villas
                                                Hpstd.
                                               [London.]
April 19 – 29   [19 April, 1920.]
10 days!

My own precious Wig-wife,

I'm afraid my last letter to you was rottenly scrappy. I felt rather exhausted and rather agitated after my long argument at home, & the having to catch the post sent the last thought flying out of my head. I didn't even tell you about Raquel Meller, nor will I now: you will see it all in the next *Athenaeum*.[1] I thought her very wonderful, & of course since that was so I thought she was more like you than anyone I have seen. Her whole nature was like yours; her way of singing like yours & strangest of all, her forehead was like yours. That's the only other forehead like yours that I have ever seen. She was also your size & shape. For the rest, see small bills.

To-day has been a hard day's work at the office in preparation for my going off to Stratford to-morrow.[2] The only brick about that performance is that the weather seems likely to be horrid, and the idea of being cooped up in a hotel in bad weather isn't cheerful. I shall have to make up for that on the Shakespeare though. I am sure I shall enjoy that anyhow; even when the performances aren't good, I always enjoy Shakespeare (and I believe these performances are good). By Jove, I have just seen under my hand the original copy of what I wrote on Raquel. I remember now that I typed it out afterwards. I'm afraid I can't lay my hands on the quotation from Keats which belongs to the blank space. It's about an eye above looking down upon us as graceful animals. However, you can see what I thought of her.

I have a queer feeling that *Cinnamon & Angelica* is going to fall down a hole. I don't know why: but there the feeling is. I'm trying to get used to it in advance. After all, even if the thing is good, it's perfectly childish to expect that people will appreciate it as much as they do Aldous Huxley for example. Still I can't help doing so. Every time I have a fresh little book – and particularly with this one – my heart has gone pop in expectation of some kind of success, even a success of esteem. I should like to discount my disappointment in advance by doing something fresh. But I can't begin anything just now.

And in any case it doesn't matter 2 pins beside the fact that you are coming home. Oh Lord, when we each hold up our hands at the other's surprises, & Wingley sits by without moving a whisker, saying to himself 'I told you so!' 'Here she is.' I feel just a wee bit dotty – not very much – but a little bit. You darling!

Old Mr. Goodyear came to see me at the office this morning to bring me the first part of the Diary which Goodyear was writing in Paris – you remember, the Novel. I haven't looked at it yet. I asked the old boy, whose very nice, & whose voice is strongly like G's, over to dinner when you come back.

What you say about Violet Schiff[3] interests me very much. She seems to be the real thing. A real addition to the nice people would be splendid; at present they are, in my opinion,

(1) Tomlinson ⎱
     Brett   ⎰
(2) ⎰ Tom Eliot
    ⎱ Sullivan
    ⎱ Sydney Waterlow
(3) ⎰ Dunning[4]
    ⎱ Locke Ellis
    ⎱ Delamare

You see there's only 1 woman: another wd. be very helpful. I don't think I can really include Virginia. Anyhow I'm not sure. I don't mean that (3) is inferior to (2) but merely that I don't see very much of them & therefore don't know them as well as (2) .˙. they belong to a different class.

I think we agree about all of them except Sydney. You'll have to cut him out & put Violet Schiff in. Any further contributions will be welcome.

Your own
Boge-husband.[5]

1. Murry's article 'The Art of the Actress Raquel Meller' appeared on 23 April. K.M. replies (22 April): 'Let me be frank. Your article on her bears the impress of great fatigue. . . . You must not feel too strongly your duty to bear the age we live in upon your back'.

2. On 20 April, J.M. went to Stratford-on-Avon for a festival of Shakespeare's plays. But finding his hotel acutely uncomfortable and 'the people who congregate about Stratford-on-Avon . . . the most abominable', he left after three nights for Garsington: 'Thank God, one is at least comfortable at Garsington'.

3. Violet Schiff (1876–1962) was married to Sydney Schiff (1869–1944) who wrote novels under the pseudonym Stephen Hudson. The publisher, Grant Richards, introduced Violet to K.M. at Menton in 1920. Wealthy patrons of the arts who cultivated Wyndham Lewis among other writers, the Schiffs knowingly exposed Katherine to Lewis's hostility in 1922. 'He positively outraged her' Murry later told Violet, 'and she felt that Sydney and you did not protect her, as she thought you should have done'.

4. Bill Dunning was a practising Yogi near whom Murry went to live at Ditchling, Sussex, in November 1922. Alpers is clearly wrong in indicating on p. 418 that Murry did not meet Dunning until August 1922.

5. K.M. replies 22 April: 'Your letter with the piece about Raquel Meller has come'.

December 1920

Katherine lived with Murry at 2 Portland Villas from late April until early September, when she and L.M. left for the Villa Isola Bella in Menton. Between September 1920 and 11 January 1921, only one letter from Murry survives. One can only conjecture as to why the bulk of Murry's letters from this period were destroyed, and by whom. These were difficult months for both of them. K.M. was blackmailed by Sobieniowski, being forced to pay £40 for letters written to him in 1909. Murry, moreover, had succumbed to the strain of his wife's illness by taking an interest in other women. Katherine's *Journal* and letters show an awareness of his close relationship with Dorothy Brett; and a letter dated 3 December refers to his flirtation with Princess Elizabeth Bibesco, as well as with Brett. A row over the reprinting of a photograph K.M. detested culminated in her announcement on 8 December that she would do no further reviewing for the *Athenaeum*. Murry's one letter from this period, dated about 10 December, may have elicited K.M.'s wire on 12 December: 'Stop tormenting me with these false depressing letters at once be a man or don't write me Tig'.

[175]   [2 Portland Villas,
                                            Hampstead,
                                            London.]
                                      [c. 10 December, 1920.]

My darling Wig
    Thinking about my lies this evening I discovered that if I had told you the whole truth from the beginning, I should not have been corrupt; there would not have been this perpetual struggle between the truth & the false in me, which has lately become so ghastly that you even suspect that the truth in me is false. So I determined to try to tell the whole truth.

The thing really began before I met or heard of E.B.[1] When I wrote to you that my blunder[2] over the photos & your letters had thrown me off my balance – that was *true*. I suddenly felt naked & comfortless – utterly miserable.

One Monday evening I walked to Leicester Square Tube Station.[3] I was acutely miserable. I saw a tart near the Express Dairy. I stopped and spoke to her. She wanted me to go home with her. I made, I suppose, two steps in that direction. Then I said: No, it's not my game. I want someone to talk to. Let's go to a restaurant. We went to Malzy's in Tottenham Court Road. I stood her a dinner. She was quite kind – a Lancashire girl. I said when we parted, and I had given her all the money I had 30/-, that I would give her dinner on Dec. 18. I didn't, and I didn't even write to tell her that I couldn't come. I don't know why. I have reproached myself bitterly for it.

This is in the wrong order. On Saturday before I had been to dinner at the Drey's. I was in the same state of misery. I went home with Mrs. Dobree[4] who was there. As I left with her, I kissed Anne: I felt that if she would take me in her arms, and comfort me, all would be well. I walked home with Mrs. Dobree, and listened to her talking rubbish through a kind of haze, then as I said goodbye at her gate, I kissed her on the cheek. I never saw her again. I wrote or began to write a letter explaining – but I tore it up.

The following Monday was the Leicester Square woman.

On Tuesday I had to see Brett's pictures. After I got home I telephoned her and said I was coming to see her. I went down at about 10 o'clock, and talked. Then I took her in my arms. I did not kiss her but I caressed her. In a moment a great loathing of myself & her came over me. I had an intense effort not to be downright brutal when I left. I was more miserable than ever.

On Wednesday I went to Beresford's. That morning Mary Hutch. rang me up asking me to dine with her & E.B. I said I couldn't because of Beresford. That night I felt better – coming home with Hodgson I almost recovered my senses.

The next day was a bad one – miserable, as far as I remember.

On Friday I had a letter from Mary H. asking me to dinner for the Monday with E.B. I have a vague recollection that the intervening Sunday was a bad day.

I have given you a truthful description of the dinner – except for the important thing that coming home in the car, as I left her – she had just asked me to dine with her on the following Monday and I had accepted

– I kissed her on the cheek suddenly. I went home in an agony of nerves.

On Tuesday or Wednesday she sent me her story to the office. I replied very distantly that I would read it & give her my criticism on Monday. Some time on Wednesday I wrote to her about it criticising it in detail, as being 'clever' but, I said truthfully, I would probably have accepted it with alterations for the *Athenaeum.*

On Thursday she rang me up thanking me & saying how much she had enjoyed the dinner. She said it was a long time before Monday – could she come & see me at the office on Friday. I said I should be there. She came in on the Friday, & we talked about odd things – I forget which. I felt very embarassed. A queer feeling that she didn't really belong to my world – and that she would resent my having kissed her as I did. I felt very grateful for her having been so nice & gentle as she was in the office. When she had gone I wrote her a letter, beginning deliberately 'Dear Elizabeth' & saying that I was terrified lest she should interpret my gesture as that of a man making love. I said that I believed there was the chance of a true friendship between us & that she had made me feel that 'somewhere on earth, wherever I was was Elizabeth Bibesco, with whom I could feel safe & need not worry to defend myself'.

She answered this on Monday, saying that she rejoiced in the friendship, that the gesture I was looking for was kissing hands, & that my remark was one of the finest things she had ever had said about her.

I went to dinner on Monday. I was shown up to her bedroom; I said I was sorry she was ill. I ate at a little table at the foot of her bed and after dinner sat in a chair by her side. I smoked a great many cigarettes. I forget what we talked about. I remember that there was a great dog who made me very angry because she would not stop him from tearing things. At last I put him outside.[5]

---

1. Princess Elizabeth Bibesco (1897–1945), daughter of the former Prime Minister Herbert Asquith and his wife Margot, had married Prince Antoine Bibesco in 1919.

On 16 February Virginia Woolf wrote in her diary of a 'farewell dinner' given for Murry on 11 February 1921 at 46 Gordon Square; and of the 'Bibesco Scandal': 'Poor man! he poured himself out. . . .

' "But I lacked imagination, he said. I never saw, I ought to have understood. I've always held one was free to do as one likes. But she was ill, & that made all the difference. And it was nothing – nothing at all."

'This referred of course, without names, to the Bibesco Scandal, with which London, so they say, rings.

' "And I adore Katherine – She's absolutely the most fascinating person in the world – I'm wholly in love with her."

'Apparently she is worse – dying? God knows. This affair seems to have brought on a crisis. She is desperately depressed, thinks her book bad, can't write; accuses herself; I imagine, is beside herself with jealousy. Murry asked me to write to her. She feels herself out of things, left alone, forgotten. As he spoke with great feeling, & seemed to be very miserable, & anxious to apologise (was it for this that he wished to see us all – to prove that there was nothing in it?) I liked him, felt with him, & I think there can be no doubt that his love for Katherine anyhow is sincere. All the rest seems of no great importance beside it.'

2. K.M.'s letter of 18 November 1920: 'for this one occasion I have the use of the Corona', conveys her bitter reaction to his 'blunder'.

3. Alpers paraphrases this letter on pp. 322–323.

4. Wife of the writer and critic Bonamy Dobrée (1891–1974).

5. This is all of the letter that is extant. K.M. appears to reply on 12 December:

'A letter has come from you in which you say you are "annihilated" and tell me of Madame la Princesse because you think . . . your meeting her may have had something to do with my illness'.

January; and May – June 1921

Shortly after receiving K.M.'s wire of 15 December: 'Pay no heed to my letters illness exasperated me are you arriving Tuesday if so won't write again fondest love reply Tig', Murry set out for Menton. There he decided to give up the editorship of the *Athenaeum* and live abroad with his wife. Three weeks later, on 11 January 1921, he left for London again intending, his letter suggests, not to return finally until April. Apparently, a relapse in K.M.'s health made him hurry back, only to visit London briefly again in February.

In May Katherine and L.M. moved to Baugy, Switzerland, while Murry went to Oxford to deliver his lectures on the 'Problem of Style'. Murry's letters to K.M. were written during this separation in May and June.

[176]   [Villa Isola Bella,
                                          Menton.]
                                          [11 January, 1921.]

My own beautiful darling,

I've just got two minutes while you are getting up to say my secret word. I am going away with absolute peace in my heart, and the knowledge, certain & sure, like a warm thing curled up in side me, that I love you more, far more than ever. With all its horrors these three weeks have been a taste of our true serenity. I've no fears of anything – not one; but only a confidence that seems always on the point of breaking out into a smile deep down.

Trust me as though I were part of your own heart: I am part of your heart. I wanted you to have this [to] read after we've said good-bye. Know that all things are quite straight & plain in front of me – I am planted in 'the direct forthright'.

And now I have you in my arms my wonderful Wig-wife. You will be there always till I come in April.

Good-bye

Your

Veen.[1]

1. K.M. replies 11 January: 'I shall never forget your beautiful gesture in handing me that letter'.

---

[177]

Gd. Hotel Beau Rivage

Bandol (Var)

6 May [1921]

Darling,

Just after lunch. I'm waiting for (or rather expecting) your telegram.

There won't be much meat in my letters: I'm putting most of that in your blue cahier. I meant originally to tear out the pages and send them to you; but that seems so cruel to that lovely book. I expect I shall fill it before I get to Paris, and I'll send it you as it is.

I went to see the Allègres[1] this morning. I found an old man working wearily in the garden and I asked: Est ce que Monsieur All. habite toujours ici? To my confusion he said 'Oui, c'est moi'. He's a 100 years older. Four months ago his left side was paralysed. I could see his left wrist, dark purple, where it left his coat sleeve. An old woman, whom I didn't remember (Mme. Allègre's sister) brought us out two funny little chairs, and we sat in the sun and talked of the war and prices. He said that Bandol was much more frequented: Pauline was always let winter & summer at 250 fr. a month. Oh, but he was so *old*! Always on the tip of my tongue was some question about topinambours: Et vos topinambours, Monsieur, sont-ils toujours bien? But he was too old to ask.

Then Mme. Allègre came in from market. She hasn't changed much – but she couldn't remember whether it was 1, 2 or 3 years ago that you came to see her. I didn't stay long: it was triste: not because of Pauline, which simply basked in the heat of the sun, but because of poor M. Allègre. I know I shall never see him alive again.

Then I walked to Graviers – across the fields past our dream house with the green shutters. They are still shut; but the vines are cultivated in the field: silky, exquisite green – beautiful.

I had forgotten part of the road to Graviers – and above all I had forgotten how *red* all the ground is on the way. But I had not forgotten the smell – pines & rosemary mixed – I have never smelt anything to compare with it. I sat down on the big pebbles at Graviers and looked at the sea. Bandol is not an atom bit less beautiful than my memory made it: and one is so quiet and remote that the sweetest and absurdest thoughts come tumbling like bumble bees into one's brain.

I went to the chemist's to buy a tooth-brush. I don't think it's the same man – if it is, he too has aged terribly. I didn't dare to ask him, because I had seen that M. Allègre noticed that I didn't recognise him; and I didn't want to repeat the gaffe. The people at the tobacco shop have changed – so have the people at the general stationer's shop opposite the butcher's. I couldn't see into the butchers. Sometime this afternoon I'll go & buy some chocolate at the Epicerie Gamel – the sign is still there – & see if Thérèse is still alive.

It seems wrong that people should grow old & die in such a place as this.

Your telegram about the packet reached me just before I was leaving. I put it in an envelope & put a franc's worth of stamps on it. I couldn't register it – because it was Ascension Day.

I won't post this till your telegram has come. My plan is to leave here for Arles at 1 o'clock to-morrow – arriving at Arles at 6.30

I send you a post card to remind you, darling.

Boge.[2]

3 o'clock. I'm going off to post this, although the telegram hasn't come, in case I miss the post.

1. The owners of the Villa Pauline in Bandol.
2. K.M. replies 9 May: 'It was a great pleasure to hear from you to-day . . .'.

---

[178]   [Arles,
                                                          France.]
                                                   [7 May, 1921.]
Saturday 6 p.m.

I got the telegram safely. I left Bandol this morning at 9 p.m. and arrived here at 3.30. I've found a little hotel with rooms at 6 francs. It *looks* the pattern of cleanliness; nous verrons. This place where I'm sitting is the Place du Forum. Opposite me is a statue of Mistral,[1] on ne peut plus slouch hat & baggy trousers. There's a yellow stucco house beyond that with the inevitable lime trees, the tops just catching fire in the setting sun. Yes, Provence is a country: but one needs to have nothing to do & plenty to drink.

Good-bye darling – after the cobbles Tis [?Tisane] is the only thing Boge

1. Frédéric Mistral (1830–1914), French poet who won the Nobel Prize in 1904.

---

[179]   ·   Hotel de l'Univers
                                        rue Gay-Lussac. Paris
                                          [9 May, 1921.]

Monday

My darling,
    Early yesterday morning at Arles it began to pour with rain. It teemed all the morning. When the train got to Avignon, to Orange, to Vienne – it was always pouring: and I hadn't the courage to face getting out & looking for a hôtel. So I simply let myself be carried on in the slow train to Paris. I got a room – very dear – in an old hôtel. I fancy its the same room that we had for 6 francs – now 14. I am seeing Valéry[1] this evening & leaving to-morrow or Wednesday night: the latter if it keeps as fine as it is now. It's rather – very – pleasant sitting about now that I've got my luggage across to the Gare du Nord and have been well washed. But this place seems – as far as the people go – quite changed. The air is beautiful as ever, so is the Luxembourg. I'll have to think over *what* it is. Can it be merely that I have passed the trentaine. I lunched at Duval's: the waitress seemed as nice as ever
    I must spend from tea to dinner writing up my journal. I'll post it before I leave. It's rather beastly not having any news from you. I feel absolutely cut off
    My pieds are very tired: it's no use asking how you are. I shall be gone by the time you reply.

                              Your darling
                                 Boge[2]

1. Paul Valéry (1871–1945), French poet and man of letters whose poems, *La Jeune Parque*, Murry had reviewed in the T.L.S. in 1917. Valéry contributed *La Crise de l'Esprit* to the *Athenaeum* in 1919.

2. K.M. replies 12 May: 'The inventory came from Pope's last night'.

---

[180]   Write always to 10 Adelphi Terrace
                                        [2 Acris Street,
                                        London.]
                                        [12 May, 1921.]
                                        Thursday Afternoon 6.30.

My own darling,[1]

Your two letters at the office were – well, I felt that you were touching me. They were wonderful. I felt also very repentant of my measly postcards: but darling I was rushed off my legs. It was all I could do to keep my journal up, and I thought you'd sooner have the journal complete than half & half. I haven't finished the days in Paris. I left last night at 11.55 and arrived here this morning. In one fell swoop between 6 & 9 p.m. on Thursday evening I met – in order – Clive Bell, Anne Rice & Drey, & Duncan Grant. As I had been with Valéry & Dubos[2] (who were both – for Frenchmen – delightful) until 4 p.m., the last chance of finishing the journal in time to send to you was gone. However, it shall go off without fail to-morrow.

I am writing in the drawing-room of 2 Acris Street. My father is away, house-hunting at Hastings. Only my mother is here. It is all spring-cleaned and queer. Clocks ticking at odd angles, against one another: a late afternoon sun trickling in at the back window: remote sounds of motorbuses. I'm very dépaysé – and yet if I'm not with you I'd sooner be here than anywhere else. Right down inside me is a little fountain of happiness which your letters set going. You darling! What happiness there is for us! I've been telling my mother about what we are going to do with Broomies.

I called into the office, of course, on my way here & lunched with Tommy. He admires 'The Daughters of the Late Colonel'[3] immensely – and don't you find this letter of Mrs. Hardy very gratifying? Tommy says that you are regarded on every side with immense respect.

It amused me to find that Sullivan who only turned up a week ago has been playing the role of the tragic hero rather heavily. – ruthlessly abandoned by the darling of his heart[4] – life utterly ruined – nothing more to look forward to – must behave like a white man in spite of a broken heart. I felt that was a little too thick – so I blew the gaff rather gently to Tommy, who was staggered at the true story. However I swore him to secrecy, for Tommy says that Massingham is fed up with S. and if he hadn't been impressed with the tragedy would have given him the boot. Perhaps, by the way, that's the explanation of Sullivan's 'lay'. He may have sensed the atmosphere and played tragedy for all he was worth. At all events, it was a comic shock to be told by Tommy that Sullivan was 'feeling it terribly' – had 'almost broken down' – nearly a wreck.

I found a letter from Schiff – invited to lunch on Sunday: typewritten – evidently written by the Secretary.

Ah, Worm, I love you – Il me tarde d'être avec vous. Depend upon it, I shan't stay here a day longer than I can help. All you say of Switzerland excites me enormously. That Riviera South doesn't offer enough chance of Recueillement for me. You have to be born a Southerner – I imagine – to get the full possibilities of work out of it.

Once more darling, I do hope my measly post cards weren't too much of a disappointment. But you will have understood the difficulties.

I'm going to take my Ma to the Cinema this evening.

Boge.[5]

1. J.M. replies to K.M.'s letters of 7 May: 'I have been walking round and round this letter . . .'; and 9 May: 'It was a great pleasure to hear from you today . . .'.
2. Charles Du Bos (1882–1939), French critic and man of letters.
3. Written in December 1920 and published in the *London Mercury* in May 1921.
4. Sullivan's wife left him.
5. K.M. replies 15 May: 'I got back from Sierre about 7.30 last night'.

[181]   [2 Acris Street,
                                                      London.]
                                                  [13 May, 1921.]
                                                  Friday Afternoon.

My darling,

Your wire 'Tout va bien' was at the office. I read all I could into it: I hope not too much.

I haven't seen anybody except Tomlinson. The chief business is this affair of Arthur. It's very difficult, and Arthur doesn't make [it] very much easier.

The position is this. My father & mother will go into the country if Arthur is earning enough to keep himself in London. Of course, it's desirable & necessary that they should go into the country: not merely for themselves, but for Arthur's sake, for you can imagine that while they are kept from going into the country by Arthur's failure to earn enough to live on, the relations between A. & my father and the whole atmosphere at home are not exhilarating.

The simplest solution would be for Arthur to get that Slade Scholarship – but it's certain that my father in the present condition will never sign the necessary papers. He's absolutely opposed to the idea of the boy becoming an artist. And here Arthur isn't particularly helpful. I saw Cobden-Sanderson this afternoon: and he told me he had done all he could to put Arthur in the way of forming a connection for bookplate designing and odd jobs of the kind. In one case he got Arthur a definite commission for a book-plate (to be paid 4 guineas). Arthur simply didn't produce it – it was only after several months that Cobden-Sanderson himself simply forced A. to do it. I find that very alarming. It's true I haven't had A's version of it. But that's another difficulty. A. simply doesn't tell me what he is doing. As you know – though of course my mother & Father don't – he only works in the morning at Cobden-Sanderson's: but precisely what he does in the afternoons I haven't the least idea. He comes home at 10 or so

I wanted to have a long talk with him – I shan't have much other opportunity: but I can't get hold of him. That's what I mean when I say he makes things difficult

If his mind is set on becoming an artist (in parenthesis its quite possible that the reason why he tells me nothing is that he doesn't want to worry me) – then I propose that I should tell my Father & Mother that he has received a rise from Cobden-Sanderson. He could keep himself on £2.10.0 or £2.15.0 a week. I will pay Cobden-S. the extra £1 a week at any rate for a year. By that time my Mother & Father will have settled themselves in the country and perhaps we shall be within call. At any rate we can consider the situation again after a year. What does alarm [me] a little is the suggestion made by Cobden-Sanderson, who's devoted to Arthur, that he's slack while he's at the office. He's awfully good at the things he puts his mind to; the trouble is to get him to put his mind to them. Well, that's not my idea of an artist.

And with that disturbing element I can't make up my mind whether

this idea of subsidising Arthur is really a good thing. £50 a year is
rather a mouthful out of what I get, and though I'll pay it like a bird if
A's on the right road, the mere idea that he isn't makes me feel that my
idea *may* be absolutely wrong. I may be helping to disintegrate him;
and it *may* be the best thing that he should face facts as Gaudier did by
entering a place as a commercial designer.

But besides the truth that Cobden-Sanderson says in any ordinary
office he'd get the sack for his forgetfulness and moodiness, it's no fun
making people face facts. I have a feeling that people ought not be
made to face them. But at the same time I have a feeling that A. is
letting me down by not being careful & exact & reliable in the office.
We don't want him to grow up to believe that to be an artist is to be
careless and inexact & unreliable.

Those are the facts my darling. I haven't thought about much else
for the last 24 hours. I thought I'd put them before you. I want your
advice before I take any decision – and above all I must have a long talk
with himself.

I shall be tremendously glad to be back with you and at work again.
I'm not looking forward to Oxford one little bit. On second thoughts I
am inclined to stay there for the whole of the time – with a possible 3
days at home here in the middle. London's no place for me & I don't
like London town. I think by staying in Oxford I might get a bit of
work done. The drawback is that it may be expensive.

Good-bye darling

Boge.

[182]

The Nation

and the

Athenaeum

10, Adelphi Terrace, W.C.2

[London]

[14 May, 1921]

Saturday Morning

My darling,

Will you send me a word saying exactly what are the things that I
shall buy for you – combine [?combinations]: milanese Silk stockings
– these two I remember & the Morny June Rose – but I feel sure that
there was something else.

Boge.

[183]   chez Jenkinson à Oxford.
                                                                 [15 May, 1921.]
                                                                 Sunday 7.15

My darling,

I am here nearly a day before I wanted to come. They very wickedly, put my lecture at 12 o'clock – and nowadays owing to the strike there is only one train a day or thereabouts so that it was necessary for me to come up on Sunday afternoon. I am now sitting dressed for dinner – but *without any braces*, which I forgot, together with a tooth-brush – in Jenkinson's study.

Saturday was an awful day. First it was oppressively hot: secondly I was on my feet nearly all day, buying summer underclothes, trying to find out about trains – eventually I had to make a journey to Paddington at 11 p.m. to make sure. I finished up tuckered out. I was fit as a bird, however, this morning. Sydney Schiff had invited me to lunch, whither accordingly I went. He & Violet were as nice as usual – I have very oddly completely lost all feeling of méfiance in their regard, and I think we got on particularly well together. Your Mr. Tinayre was there – also Ada Levison[1] – three other ladies – 2 other men – one called as far as I cd. make out Dr. Rumschitzky – but it's a queer looking name. He played the piano. Sydney took your address.

Thence hither. Oh, Lord. I forgot. They are both *delighted* with your story. They think it's the best thing you've [done] so my opinion of their good taste went up with a leap & a bound.

But this is a busy life – there's no breathing space. Travelling takes hours & hours – and I've utterly lost the habit of towns. To work quietly with you is my only happiness.

However, it's so busy that it doesn't give me time to be nervous about these lectures – thank God.

I haven't made up my mind what to do. The best thing wd. be to take rooms in Oxford but this is Eights' week & things will be so cursedly expensive. Moreover tomorrow being Bank Holiday, there's no chance of looking about till Tuesday. Failing some moderately cheap & decent rooms here, I shall go back to my mothers where it costs me practically nothing. If I were sensible, I suppose I shd. suggest myself at Garsington as a P.[aying] G.[uest] – but I'm frightened. I'll tell you the moment I settle anything.

How are you, precious? I think of you *continually*.

                                                                 Boge.[2]

1. Ada Leverson (1862–1933), a sister of Violet Schiff, was a prolific writer who had been the close friend of Oscar Wilde.
2. K.M. replies (?) 19 May: 'Read this criticism'.

---

[184]   c/o A. J. Jenkinson
                                                      Stanford House,
                                                           Oxford.
Monday: after lunch.   [16 May, 1921.]

My darling,
   The first ordeal is over – an hour ago. Of course, it's Whit Monday, & I believe, impossible to send a telegram. However, I will go & see as soon as I have written this.
   There was an enormous audience – I mean not less than 250 people. But I don't suppose there will be more than half that next time: for it was obviously above the heads of half the audience. It's not the fashion to applaud in Oxford; otherwise I should interpret the dead silence into which my conclusion fell as a bad omen. Roughly, I should say that half the audience enjoyed it, while to the other half it was double Dutch: and I imagine that one half the audience will persevere to the end.
   In a sense I'm sorry that I wrote the lectures out; but I couldn't trust myself to work from notes alone. Otherwise it would probably have been better. Also, as I read, it seemed to me that the lecture[1] was packed too full of material; it was, in fact, much more an essay than a lecture. However – it can't be helped; and if I can't call it a success, it certainly wasn't a failure.
   Jenkinson has cordially invited me to stop on here till Monday next – therefore I shall. After next Monday I shall pay my visit to Hardy and then return to London. I shall come up here to lecture on Friday 27th. & then go for the week-end to Sydney Waterlow.
   I feel in an odd way very much out of my element here. There's not very much in common between myself and Oxford, I'm afraid; but still the experience is worth having. Last night at dinner I met a ridiculous old tutor of mine – called Grundy – you may have heard Goodyear & me speaking of him. I had come to believe he was a legendary figure, and that we had invented all his absurdities; but not at all. He is just as richly and unconsciously comic as I remembered him. I could hardly avoid bursting into laughter when I saw him – and heard him.

Alas, there's no chance of a letter from you to-day, & not much to-morrow: on Whit-Monday the office will be closed so that nothing will be forwarded. That's a horrible long time to wait.

It's awful – I believe a kind of fatality attends me. The first night I slept in the nice clean bed here, I had a wet dream and there this morning were the two accusing splodges. It was enough to make me blush with shame.

I must somehow say how much I love you. Our lovely months together have made me feel the pain of separation much more keenly. Of course it can't be helped, but still. I want the weeks to pass quickly. I only feel a half of a being: and though it's wonderful to know that the other half is there waiting for me to join on again – I don't like the separation, Wig, I don't like it.

But, by the Holy Poker, what a time we will have together, working & talking. I hope I shan't be overworked any more, & that we shall really have time to breathe in unison.

Goodbye darling

Boge.[2]

Don't forget to send me a card saying the things you want me to bring.

1. Murry's first lecture in a series of six on 'The Problem of Style' was on 'The Meaning of Style'.

Virginia Woolf cogitated her feelings about Murry in her *Diary* on 5 June 1921: 'I don't know – at this moment I incline to think him a damned swindler – only a swindler so plausible that he'll become Professor of English literature in the University at Oxford'. On 7 June she discussed him with T. S. Eliot: ' "He will be very successful" said Eliot. "He's been giving 6 lectures on style at Oxford – as though it were a duty. He takes the crown as soon as he's offered it. But he's not satisfied with that" '.

2. K.M. replies 19 May: 'I can't tell you how Tigs love to be told they are missed . . .'.

[185]   c/o A. J. Jenkinson
                                              Stanford House
                                              Oxford
                                              [17 May, 1921.]
Tuesday afternoon.

My darling,
    This is a goodly sheet of examination paper.
    I've spent the morning writing my article[1] for the *Nation* – the
afternoon walking along the towpath with Jinks watching the Eights.
    On the whole I'm in a pretty comatose condition. There's some-
thing about Oxford, which unless you take to it quite naturally,
simply dulls all one's perceptions. I was beginning to notice things a
bit; here I see nothing. I feel that the only event of real importance to
chronicle is that the bedroom here is roomy enough for me to do my
Muller exercises completely once more. Since I left Menton I've only
been able to perform fragments.
    Beyond that nothing. The Jenkinsons are extremely nice, and do
their best to make me feel a great man; but I'm not very convinced.
    Besides, not having had a letter from you since Friday – which was
inevitable, I know – has rather banked my fires. I want so much to
know how you are – and to have one of those astonishing letters which
I drink in at every pore.
    I am absolutely fit – clear eyes and all the rest – but ever so
fish-out-of-watery. Thank God, I never became a Don!
                              Boge.

    1. 'The personal in criticism', a review of *Literary Impressions* by Jules
Lemaître, appeared on 21 May.

----

[186]   at Stanford House
                                              Oxford.
                                              [19 May, 1921.]
Thursday

My darling,[1]
    This morning came your letter with Stephani's[2] report – and about
Montana.
    I simply long to spend a year – two years – a lifetime of years with

you at Sierre. It sounds & looks divine. I know I shall be terribly happy there. I'm all for a little chalet.

I think you know all about me now; but perhaps you don't know *quite* how much I miss you – how deeply and quietly happy I have been with you this year. I find myself continually thinking of you. That has never happened before. Honestly I don't think an hour ever passes without my imagining that we are together again. When I do my exercises in the morning, it seems to me impossible that you shouldn't be seeing my feet waggling in the wardrobe glass.

However, the weeks are going quickly.

For some reason or other, I can't give you an account of my doings in Oxford. It's all so awfully unreal. Not that the people aren't very nice to me – and Jenkinson himself a perfect angel – but it's a world I left years & years ago. I love Oxford; but in the way I love my father. We're utterly strange to each other. Sometimes, when I'm dining at the high table the clock stops ticking and I hear everything from an incredible distance – and it's so strange.

Yesterday afternoon I went to see the cricket in the Parks – it was lovely. Great tall trees, smooth grass, bright sunshine, a slow clapping when a man came out to bat, the muffled click as he hit the ball. A dream game – so remote it was from me. And how I enjoyed my own remoteness!

How intimately I have *grown in* to you lately! With everyone else, everywhere else I am a kind of bemused spectator. Life seems like the slow dropping of water into a deep well. Fascinating and very far away. A curious deep happiness is hidden somewhere inside me.

Well, darling – we've had a strangely mixed time together – but if it had been a time of unmixed suffering it would still have been worth the price to get to the condition we're in now.

I can't really write anything: I should only be rhapsodical.

If you just feel how much, how deeply, how calmly & steadily, I love you – that's all I want

Boge.[3]

My present plans are to leave Oxford on Tuesday 24 – stay at Wandsworth – return Oxford Friday 27 staying the night – 28–29 week end with Sydney Waterlow. 30 lecture, return London afternoon. Friday June 3 last lecture. Sat. 4 down to Hardy staying the night. Sunday return London. Monday–Tuesday 6–7 Broomies. 8th. depart for Clarens. Perhaps I may need 1 day more, but that's all.

1. J.M. replies to K.M.'s letters of 14 May: 'I am in the middle of one of my *Giant Coups*'; and 15 May: 'I got back from Sierre at about 7.30 last night'.
2. A doctor from Montana whom K.M. consulted.
3. K.M. replies 21 May: 'I am rather conscious that my letters have fallen off . . .'.

---

[187]   at Stanford House
                                                        Oxford.
                                                  [20 May, 1921.]
                                                        Friday

My darling,

I have just been revising my second lecture[1] which I have to deliver in three-quarters of an hour.

This morning came your letter about Arthur.[2]

Since I wrote yesterday morning I have been worrying because I made no mention in my letter of Stephani's report.

I find it so hard to say anything about your illness. It's some shyness or delicacy that prevents me. I feel I am so clumsy; and that all I can say is Darling, Darling. I hope you felt I was saying that.

I am overjoyed that you have seen Stephani – a real specialist. Do you remember the Consul at Geneva said he was the most famous of all the lung specialists in Switzerland. And to think that you feel confidence in him & that he is going to look after you is meat & drink to me.

It sometimes seems to me that when I write to you of any old thing – Arthur's troubles, cricket matches and the rest – you may think that I am forgetting that you are ill, and what you've been through. I am always thinking about it, worm; and my heart floods with love for you, and confidence that our life is going to be mysteriously happy & wonderful. We weren't put through this for nothing: we haven't fought our way to this state of grace for nothing. It is just a simple certainty with me. Having it has changed my life.

If you knew how constantly I think of your beauty. Wig, you don't know *how* beautiful you are. Honestly, I never dreamed that a woman could be so completely beautiful as you are. So exquisite without and within. I get away from you & I see you as something miraculous. As one has to stand away sometimes from a Velasquez picture. And in thinking of & looking at you my breath comes in jumps.

You have utterly spoiled me for the ordinary world. Everything I say or do up here, for instance, seems ever so slightly silly – as though I had descended from a star, & were trying to speak a very clumsy language I have long since forgotten. It makes me smile & smile. I feel you sitting in the armchair & listening with that tiny wrinkle on your forehead above your nose – and a great lump of happiness sticks in my throat. 'Let me get back to her'. Darling, darling!

And then just writing this makes me so absurdly happy. I feel fortunate, fortunate – blessed by Heaven. Ah, one day – perhaps soon I will write such a love poem to you, Worm – that the stars themselves will wonder when they wink whether they are laughing or crying.

And then *what* a writer you are! Good god, I was looking at 'The Daughters of the late Colonel' just now. It's *fairy*. There's nothing been done to touch it these dozen years. I swear it. If it's not true, I'm mad. It's the same golden ring as Shakespeare & Chaucer – they're echoing in my mind now – so I make no mistake. You *beauty* again!

Your devoted & humbly

admiring

Boge.[3]

Oh, I kiss you – on the eyelids – the tenderest kiss of all.

1. 'The Psychology of Style'.
2. In Murry's handwriting here is written 'missing'.
3. K.M. replies 24 May: 'Last evening came your perfect letter written on Friday'.

---

[188]   [Stanford House]
Oxford.
[23 May, 1921.]
Monday

My darling,

I am returning to London to-morrow morning for 3 days – coming back here on Friday, May 27, staying the night, then going (provisionally) to Sydney Waterlow's for the week-end. Here again on Monday, May 30 and leaving the same afternoon for London. There I stay May 31, June 1, June 2. Return Oxford Friday June 3, stay the night with Walter Raleigh,[1] stay the night of June 4 with Hardy, return London June 5, Broomies June 7, start for Clarens June 8 or 9. These are my final arrangements. I thought you would like to know them.

Last night I dined in College with Walter Raleigh. He is, as his reputation goes – a good talker. Beside him I made a very silent Boge. However, it was quite enjoyable and we didn't quarrel. Perhaps even we got on fairly well.

You ask me in the last card I had from you – *ever* so long ago – am I happy? I reply, quite simply, only in thinking of you. I don't say I'm miserable here. The weather has been divine of late; but I feel a kind of malaise, compounded of many elements: the biggest is separation from you, which becomes more oppressive the longer it lasts: next comes the sense of not quite fitting my milieu: and after that the nervous strain of lecturing to an audience that – I am sure – doesn't really understand what I am driving at at all.

I'm afraid the truth is that you & I have carried our thoughts in literature ever so much farther than any of our contemporaries. It's not to be wondered at that I'm not particularly intelligible, I suppose. And at any rate the lectures will be a succès d'estime anyhow.

Goodbye, darling.

Boge.[2]

1. Walter Raleigh (1861–1922), Professor of English Literature at Oxford since 1904, at whose invitation Murry was delivering his lectures on style.
2. K.M. replies 25 May: 'In a small letter from you last night you seem to suggest that my letters weren't arriving'.

---

[189]   [on the train between London & Dorchester.]
                                   [24 May, 1921.]
                            Tuesday – 2 pm

I am in the train on the way to Hardy – the day had to be changed, because it suited Mrs. H. better. The weather has been marvellous ever since I arrived in London.

I had 2 letters from you this morning.[1] About that bill of Bouchage's[2] – I can *easily* give you £20 instead of £12.10.0 on June 1, if that will be any help. I mean *easily*.

The lectures have been jogging on comfortably – I've finished 3 of them[3] now – and as the first 3 were the dullest and they have the reputation of being brainy, I imagine I shall get away without any loss of prestige.

That review[4] by W. J. Turner was the limit. What *are* you to do with people who simply don't know what good writing is. Merely this

merely that! Good God. I'd like to set the fool to write a single one of
your sentences. I'd give him a year to do it. But you remember his
blithering poem, don't you?

I just looked up and there was a lovely big white horse cut out in
chalk on the Wiltshire Downs – I'd never seen it before – now I've got
so far to one side that it begins to look like a giraffe. Then it gradually
disappeared under the brow of a green hill. Now it's up again.

Goodbye, darling. You didn't say anything about health.

Boge

1. J.M. replies to K.M.'s letters of 17 May: 'About the Journal'; and 19
May: 'Read this criticism'.
2. Dr. A. Bouchage had been treating K.M. in Menton. She wrote to
Murry on 17 May about receiving a 'letter from Bouchage and his bill (2000
francs). Awfully nasty.'
3. Murry's third lecture was on 'Poetry and Prose'.
4. W. J. Turner (1889–1946), music critic of the *New Statesman*, dramatic
critic of the *London Mercury* and later editor of the *Daily Herald* had reviewed
'Daughters of the late Colonel'.

---

[190]   at 2 Acris Street
                                             [London.]
                                             [26 May, 1921.]
                                             Thursday.

My darling,[1]

I'm sorry I couldn't send you anything yesterday. I didn't arrive
back from Hardy's till about 5, and then I had to get to Wandsworth
and change my clothes in order to dine with Sydney W. There was just
time to write a letter, and I employed it in writing one to your father. It
seemed most important that I should get it off immediately, because
it's monstrous that you should be so worried by the thought that he
may cut you off. I explained everything as nicely as I could, said that
you had not written because (1) you had been too ill & (2) had not
wanted to worry him – *he* ought to appreciate that argument, – and I
told him the truth as nearly as I could about your condition. I thought
it was foolish to delay, because unless I do these things immediately I
don't do them at all. I enclose the sole contents of the letter that
frightened you.[2] It's very nice of your Pa to return it as sent apparently
in error – I mean that's a gentleman's behaviour – but by what earthly

right does Alex. Kay send a copy of your private account to New Zealand? If I were you, Tiggy, I would bank all other moneys except the allowance with another bank.

I can't tell you all about Hardy just now, as I've got to sit down to an article which I must finish by lunch time (I'm in the little sitting room at Wandsworth – it's nearly 10 o'clock.) But there are two important things. We got on well. He was so splendidly simple. It was exactly as you thought – jam & egg-wegs³ – a condition of life into which one slides with a sigh of relief. The old man was everything I had dreamed – everything. The second thing was that he had read 'Bliss' & 'The Daughters of the Late Colonel' – and with regard to this second he told me to take you this message. He thought it wonderfully well done – you had given him those two women – and you were to go on, treating that as a prelude, and continue the story of their lives. Mrs. Hardy told me he had laughed & laughed at the interview between Cyril and the old man. That ought to be sweet to you, darling.

I don't like this old Swiss chill, my precious. Is it better yet?

The weather here too has been hot, hot, hot. In the railway carriages it has been stifling, & the job of carting one's luggage about simply terrific – but still, it is lovely weather for all that. It's the weather for us to be living quietly in our cottage at Broomies really, or in our little chalet in the Sierre.

There's not much in this letter. If I once began on Hardy I should never finish. I must just save it up and when I get a moment which won't happen till Monday next as far as I can see, try to put it down properly.

Yes, I think *Troilus & Cressida* and *Hero & Leander* two of the most beautiful things in the world. But that old man Chaucer is a sheer miracle – no less. How would you like him for a godfather?

Good-bye darling

Boge.

1. J.M. replies to K.M.'s letter of 21 May: 'I am rather conscious that my letters have fallen off . . .'; and of 23 May: 'I feel certain this letter from father contains that Blow I am always expecting'.

2. K.M.'s letter of 23 May (not published by Murry) encloses a letter from her father which she is afraid of opening. She asks him to wire her – 'Don't spare me any of Pa's letter. I can hear anything from you' – and to write to her father reporting what Dr. Stephani has said: 'There is still hope, *provided* I have no more fever [and] *provided* I can get strong enough to stand treatment'. K.M.'s fears about her father were unfounded. His letter contained a copy of

her passbook (forwarded by Kay, the London manager of the Bank of New Zealand to him) with a note indicating that it had been sent in error.

3. K.M. had written of the Hardys on 21 May: 'I feel they are simple. There'll be no need to explain things. The kind of people who understand making jam . . . I liked so what she said about their way of living. It was almost egg-weggs for tea.'

---

[191]   Oxford again
[27 May, 1921.]
Friday afternoon.

My darling,

Your telegram saying that whooping cough was a Swiss Canard came yesterday. I hadn't read anything about whooping cough in your letters – but only about a chill. So I didn't quite know what to make of it. I did know what to make of BE NAPY with which the telegram ended. The picture of myself engaged in being Napy is gorgeous & fantastic. The telegraph men are wonderful.

But I wish I knew more about the other part of the wire.

I must be feeling Napy just now. I'm quite contented – I'm trying in vain to think out an 'address' I have to deliver to the College Literary Society to-night. All that happens is that I yawn tremendously and have a feverish desire to be Napy in an armchair – in fact, to go to sleep. I don't know what that's due to. It may be the change in the weather, which has suddenly become dull & rainy and not half so hot. The last is rather a relielf [sic] (I can't spell for toffee this afternoon) for it was terribly exhausting travelling about in railway trains.

How are you, my darling? I have never been so impatient to get back to you before. It's only lately – these last three months – that I've realised how completely my home is at your side. I grow more & more silent here. I feel I can't talk to anybody at all. They don't seem to understand the simplest things.

I had tea with Sullivan yesterday. Thank God, he's decided to make his headquarters in London and become an assiduous journalist. I don't know whether he intends to come for that walking month still. Anyhow I am freed from the nightmare of having him near us – it was becoming really oppressive.

Oh Lord, darling, I'm altogether too Napy to write. *I must go to sleep, loving you absolutely – instead I've got to go out to tea.* The 4th.

lecture[1] delivered to-day was, I think, a great success. But I'm sick of Oxford.

Your Boge.

That doesn't make you <u>wince</u>?

1. 'The Central Problem of Style'.

---

[192]   Oxford – Saturday Morning
                                            [28 May, 1921.]

My darling,

It's quite cold here now. I've just got a quarter of an hour before I catch the train to Sydney Waterlow's, where I hope there will be a letter from you. I told Adelphi Terrace to forward everything there.

I made a speech at the College Literary Society last night. It was an extraordinarily bad one, because I suddenly developed a headache. However, it went down quite well. It's a very queer sensation to find all the undergraduates addressing you as 'Sir'.

I believe I told you that there is a young Don here called Taylor who is a great admirer of your work. He's rather a remarkable fellow: he's a science Don: and he's got a very unusual knowledge of modern literature. It was quite pleasant to talk to him.

So I didn't get to bed until a quarter to 1, which is ever so much too late for me. I've got so into the habit of early hours that I feel like a stranded fish in the morning. I've become very much the simple lifer, in fact.

Why on earth is it that I haven't anything to write? I sat for quite a minute or two staring at my last line. My feeling is that away from you I gradually become emptied: the water runs out of me, and there's no-one to fill me up again. Thank Heavens I'm well past half-way now.

I love you, love you, love you. There's no one but Wig for me. I've said it so many times that I'm almost ashamed of saying it again – but there; it's the only thing really in my mind. Every day I realise it more & more. My darling!

Boge.

[193]   At Sydney Waterlows.
                                         [Oare,
                                            Wiltshire.]
                                           [29 May, 1921.]
                                              Sunday

My darling,[1]

When I arrived here yesterday, I found a divine letter from you –
the one which, in tiny writing at the end, explained your whooping
cough telegram.

Yes, darling, we certainly shall be together watching the fruit
gathered. Perhaps we shall be allowed to go into the vineyards and eat
our fill for a franc. But my feeling is that it simply doesn't matter what
we plan to do – we have only to be together for everything to be
wonderful. The idea of looking out of a window in a room in which
you are – excites me. I don't really ask more of life than that – and that
seems to me an enormous thing to have given one by life.

Sullivan is down here with me. Both he & Sydney are very nice –
and though I am convinced that it wouldn't be any good if Sullivan
were to live near us, I am nevertheless glad that he – with all his
absurdities & lack of refinements – is alive and our friend. And it's the
same with old Sydney. My affection for them both is very real.

We – Sydney & I: not Sullivan – went for one of his tremendous
walks this morning. He went faster than ever. Luckily I was able to
keep up – but I wish he wouldn't go quite so fast. One simply doesn't
have time to look at anything.

I brought my camera with a roll of film – just in order to try my hand
– so that my photographs of Broomies shan't be failures. If they come
out, I'll send you the prints across.

Now Sullivan's coming up to read me a review he's just written for
the *Literary Supplement* in order that I may tell him whether it is, or is
not, too vigorous.

It wasn't – but it wasn't very good. Now Sydney has come up.

Goodbye, my darling. I have to get up at an unearthly hour
to-morrow morning in order to get to Oxford – then I shall have ticked
off Number 5[2] – thank Heaven.

                                        Your own
                                          Boge.

1. J.M. replies to K.M.'s letter of 24 May: 'Last evening came your perfect
letter written on Friday'.
2. 'The Process of Creative Style'.

2 Acris Street
                                              [London.]
                                              [30 May, 1921.]
                                              Monday. 7.30

My darling,[1]

I got back to London from Oxford this afternoon at 6 – went to the office, where I found a letter and a postcard from you: and here I am. I utterly agreed with you about the disappointment of many of the stories in the last Tchehov book.[2] Except 'Ward No. 6' itself, they all seemed to me uninteresting and unimportant. Perhaps there was one other but I can't remember. Luckily, I had taken the *Duel* volume[3] with me: otherwise the cold douche of the last volume + the icebath of the *Notebooks*[4] would have quite put me off speaking about him at Oxford.

Still, one has to remember this, darling. Poor old Tchehov never had any choice. I haven't the faintest doubt he would have kicked half his stories out; utterly disowned them. Probably he had to write them for money. At all events, it's certain that they were all gathered together by foreign & impious hands after his death. One mustn't be hard on him.

On the other hand – he is *lemonade* compared to Tolstoy. But then he said it himself; he said wonderful & beautiful things about Tolstoy; he was a true artist not least because he had reverence, that angel of the world.

But there's no getting away from the fact that Tolstoi is of the same size as Shakespeare – or that the novel is a greater form than the short story: just as the play is a greater form than the lyric poem. Not because it's actually bigger (tho' that has something to do with it) but because you can get so much more into it. Into a novel you can, if you try terribly hard, get the whole of yourself Tchehov never got the whole of himself into anything – not even into the 'Duel' or 'The Lady with the Dog' perhaps he came nearest in 'The Steppe'.

Again, I absolutely agree with you about difficulty. The most difficult thing is the best thing, because it is the only really necessary thing. The writer who plays beneath his hand, becomes a smaller writer: to play right up to your strength, that is writing. The whole job & nothing but the job. It seems to me obvious that all absolutely first class writing must be terribly hard to do – terribly hard to keep simple and yet convey all that complexity inside one. And it also seems to me that the problem has never been fought out in England since Shakespeare. I think *Antony & Cleopatra* is one of the things that is *completely worked out*. But in the 19th. century it's been terrible how great gifts have been frittered away. If people had complicated things to say, felt complicated emotions, they wrote complicatedly: which is unpardonable.

The wonderful thing is that you have the genius to get over all kinds of extremely rare and difficult emotions quite simply: there's no-one else can touch you. Whether I shall be able to do it, I don't know: but it won't be for want of trying. Yes, we'll sit down and write novels – big ones – hand in hand.

I love you
Boge.

1. J.M. replies to K.M.'s letter of 25 May: 'In a small letter from you last night you seem to suggest that my letters weren't arriving'.
2. *The Horse-Stealers and other Stories*, translated by Constance Garnett (1921).
3. *The Duel and other Stories*, translated by Constance Garnett (1916).
4. *The Note-books of Anton Tchekhov Together with Reminiscences of Tchekhov by Maxim Gorky* (translated by S. S. Koteliansky and Leonard Woolf; Hogarth Press, 1921).

---

[195]

The Athenaeum,
10, Adelphi Terrace,
London, W.C.2.
[1 June, 1921.]

Wednesday afternoon – in haste.

I found your letter[1] & the cheque here when I called at 3 this afternoon. I just had time – shooting off – to get to the Bank before it closed.

They will send you a cheque book on Friday so soon as your cheque on the B.N.Z. is cleared. It will probably take another week (i.e. Friday week) before they will have the arrangement through with the Banque Populaire Suisse at Montreux. They say they can't do it any quicker.

I'm terribly sorry that you say you have lost touch with me. It's only due to my wandering life.

I couldn't have done the Bank Business quicker darling.

Your letter to Kay was quite allright but you had better write to him telling him to cancel altogether the arrangement by which you cash B.N.Z. cheques on the Banque Populaire. You don't want two arrangements of the sort – and Kay may get suspicious.

Boge who loves you
terribly.

1. J.M. replies to K.M.'s letter of 23 May: 'I have been trying to write out a long explanation of the reasons why I have felt out of touch with you'.

---

[196]   [2 Acris Street,
                                                London.]
                                        [2 June, 1921.]
                                  Thursday – Morning.

My darling,

I'm just going off to see about my passport. Sydney Waterlow has given me a letter which should make things fairly easy. If there's any time left to-day I shall try to do some shopping. Then to-morrow comes my last lecture,[1] and I believe I am staying the night at Oxford with Raleigh. On Monday I shall finish up the shopping – on Tuesday go to Broomies: and I hope to start for Clarens on to-day week Thursday.

As soon as your cheque is cleared & the arrangement for cashing cheques in Switzerland completed, I should write to Kay and tell him what you think of him for sending your pass-book (or a copy of it) to your Father. It's an absolute breach not only of ordinary decency, but of the law. I asked the manager of Barclay's about it, and he said that if you wanted to you could bring an action for breach of contract against Kay. It makes me furious.

But I shouldn't worry about any possible effect on your father. He can't possibly cut off your allowance because you have a substantial balance:[2] what on earth would you do without a substantial balance? Really, Wig, I think you're much too frightened of what your Father may do. I am perfectly certain he would never dream of cutting off your allowance for such a cause.

One other thing. If you find my letters scrappy and unsatisfactory, just think that I hardly ever have a moment's calm in which to write. Getting things done is a terrible curse to me at all times, but now with the coal-strike on and the trains & buses & tubes working at half-pressure, it's an awful business getting from one part of London to another. What used to take half an hour takes an hour – and so, it becomes a continual rush. The whole space between lunch-time and dinner is taken up with doing two things – then come these infernal journeys to Oxford – and a whole day goes in a mouthful. I toil after parting Time in vain. It's a silly, wearing life.

However, my oasis of calm is getting very near now. I feel that I shall come like Tartarin of Tarascon[3] with my collapsible bath hung round my neck with a string. I have also bought a knickerbocker suit (quite nice & cheap) which will to some extent solve the problem of clothes. English knickerbockers – not Swiss ones – with bare knees.

But I feel you are worrying terribly about this money business. Don't darling: I'm absolutely convinced there's no cause for alarm – none at all.

Goodbye, you precious darling. Don't say you're out of touch with me. Then I feel you are that little girl who used to walk home from school to Karori in the ditch. You are completely hidden in the dock-leaves – and I can't see you anywhere. I have to call: Wig – Wig! where are you?

Boge.

1. 'The English Bible; and the Grand Style'.
2. Due to the success of *Bliss*.
3. The boastful hero of Alphonse Daudet's novel *Tartarin de Tarascon* (1872).

---

[197]   [2 Acris Street,
                                           London.]
                                         [5 June, 1921.]
                                         Sunday. 8 p.m.

My darling,

I've been to lunch with Sydney Schiff and tea with T. S. Eliot, and I've just got back to Wandsworth to find the house empty (they've probably gone for a Sunday walk). I've changed into my old blue suit, and here I am.

I didn't manage, as I thought I might have done, as I thought I had done, to control my feeling about your chill. It's haunted me ever since.

I don't know whether this note will reach you before I do; but it may buy a day,[1] if the posts really take only 48 hours. And the strange thing is that when I feel that my letters must carry love to you, I can't express it.

Really, I believe that when one is wholly given to love, as I am to love of you, it's not possible to give it a direct expression. Our love comes out in the little odd things we say to each other – the wonderful things you show to me, like the goldfinch shouldering arms with your fountain pen. And now I shall never see him.

My darling heart, you know how utterly sleeping & waking, thinking & talking, I am yours. I don't want ever to fail you, & I don't believe I ever shall. But there was something so sad in your last letter, & your confession that you felt you had lost touch with me, that I add to my anxiety about you an endless search into my own heart to find whether there is anything which may have disappointed you – anything I couldn't put my hand deep in my trousers pocket and show you. No, Wig, nothing – I don't believe I *really* think about anything except you.

Goodbye my treasure.

Boge.

1. Murry indicates here that he expects to be back with K.M. in three days; and F. A. Lea is probably correct in writing (in *The Life of John Middleton Murry*, p. 85) that 'June 9 found them once more together, at the Chalet des Sapins, Montana'. Alpers in his chronology, however, gives 9 June as the date when Murry left London.

January – February 1922

Murry was reunited with Katherine, now living at the Chalet des Sapins in Montana, Switzerland, by 9 June 1921. The months that followed, when they were both living and working together, have been reckoned the most fruitful in K.M.'s working life.

But in December 1921 she heard about a new treatment for tuberculosis being given by Dr. Manoukhine in Paris. In search of the miracle that would save her life, she insisted on leaving Montana for Paris on 30 January 1922. Murry, who was at work on a novel, remained behind in the hope that K.M. would return after an initial examination. Instead, she decided to embark immediately on a course of fifteen 'séances'. Some ten days later, Murry followed her to Paris.

[198]   Chalet des Sapins
                                        Montana-sur-Sierre
                                              Valais
                                     [31 January, 1922.]

Tuesday morning 9.40.
My darling precious,
    To-day's as grey as yesterday was blue; so it was fortunate that your going away was yesterday. After you'd gone I ski-ed down to Elizabeth's,[1] but it wasn't much fun. The snow was too thick, soft & fresh and by the time I got there I had to start home. Got back for tea at five. E. said she had been at Randogne to see if you were in the train. She looked in every window but couldn't see you. I didn't conclude that you'd fallen out, however, because she was wearing such a thick green veil that she looked no more recognizable than a Margaret Morris[2] water-nymph.
    When I got back, Wingley turned up after tea. The only way to describe his attitude is to say that he was highly offended, like an old man in a club who finds his favourite arm chair gone. He squealed about everywhere, and wouldn't stay a moment where I put him.

However, at about 9 o'clock I went down to the kitchen to get a box of matches and I found Ernestine[3] reading the *Illustration* with Wingley perfectly happy on her lap. And again when I woke up this morning he was in his usual place on your bed: so I conclude he's getting reconciled.

No letters came this morning. I rose with the lark at ten minutes past 8 and went up to get myself some cigarettes. I took possession of your room last night and I hope to get some real work done this morning. I'm longing to hear from you.

Boge.[4]

Just as I was putting this in the envelope I had a note from Woodifield[5] to say you had told him to tell me your heart was much better in Sierre. Good! Wingley I've just found on your bed again. It's his home. I'm going off to the post. It's snowing hard & fine just now.

1. Elizabeth von Arnim lived nearby in Randogne.
2. Margaret Morris, (b. 1891) learned Greek dancing from Isadora Duncan's brother, Ronald. An influential exponent of 'free' dance in England, she founded her own dance school in 1910. Her young pupils were remembered for the performances they gave dressed as wood nymphs in masses of muslin veil. An acquaintance of Ottoline Morrell's, she married Murry's artist-friend, J. D. Fergusson.
3. A Swiss woman who helped with housework and cooking.
4. K.M. replies 3 February: 'Your telegram came yesterday as a complete surprise . . .'. When Murry came to date his own and K.M.'s letters for this period, he was out by one day. The correct dates are given in these references.
5. Woodifield, whose name K.M. used for an ailing old man in her last great story, 'The Fly', was a tuberculosis patient and friend of L.M.'s at the Palace Hotel in Montana.

---

[199]
Chalet des Sapins
Montana-sur-Sierre
Valais
[1 February, 1922.]
Wednesday Morning 9.35

My darling,

Just as I was coming away from the P.O. yesterday afternoon, after posting your letter, our postman appeared out of a back door & called out 'Monsieur Mansfield!' and gave me your telegram, at which I rejoiced. After seeing yesterday & to-day I can't help believing that the aspegs for your journey were extra-special. These two days have been rotten, above all in contrast with that magnificent Monday. It snowed again heavily last night, and the snow cap with the fringe of icicles outside our bedroom window now hangs down at least six feet all on its own. The birds yesterday managed to push both cocoanuts overboard. One I rescued. The other I can't see anywhere; it must have been buried under a fall of snow. We shall find its bleached bones in the spring. This snow makes the birds extremely hungry. Yesterday when I was quite a hundred yards away from the house I heard one banging away at the nut. For a moment I really couldn't believe it was just a bird; it must be someone mending the roof. But no, there he was, two inches tall making two miles of noise.

Wingley disappears every night; but in the morning I find him on your bed in the usual place. He's there now, looking rather cleaner than he has done lately. A faint sun has just peeped through. I like your window to work at immensely: you do get a splendid sight of the birds. The tufty ones are quite the nicest, I agree, they're so *very* small & charming and they aren't rough like some of the others. I'm afraid some small birds are hooligans while others are Kezias. A pity one has other things to do; it would be pleasant to study bird temperament out of this window.

I long to hear of your interview with Manoukhin.[1] Perhaps I shall to-day. I put in a real working day yesterday – eight hours. Ernestine turned up a very good but oh, such a big fig pudding. It gave me quite a shock to think of her eating up three-quarters of it all by herself. Little Black Cap and white mole waistcoat has just turned up. He's very charming; next best to Tufty and hardly any bigger. The vigour with which he pegs away at the nut is superb: he puts his whole soul & body in chipping it. Like Prince Hal 'a would have made a good Pantler'.[2]

There were no letters yesterday – Tuesday

All my love

Boge[3]

7.30 p.m.

I'm just going off to the Post with this. I am terribly anxious to hear about M. It came over me just after lunch – that awful feeling in the pit of the stomach.

1. Koteliansky had told K.M. about Dr. Manoukhine, a Russian living in Paris, who claimed to be able to cure tuberculosis by irradiating the spleen

with X-rays. The treatment proved exhausting, very expensive – and worthless.

2. A pantryman or butler.

3. K.M. replies 3 February: 'Your telegram came yesterday as a complete surprise . . .'.

———————

[200]   Chalet des Sapins
                                         Montana-sur-Sierre
                                         Valais
Thursday Morning 9.30   [2 February, 1922.]

My darling,[1]

Your letter came yesterday afternoon. It *was* cheering. To think that 6 months of Montana had done all that in the way of strengthening your heart; it is tremendous. It sounds just like a little miracle. Don't get excited about it and do anything rash; I feel like doing something rash myself on the strength of it. Bless the day when we came up here, I say. I never really believed old Hudson[2] when he said you'd feel quite different when you got down below – now I'm beginning to have a great respect for him.

I'm bursting to hear about Manoukhin now. Yesterday turned out a brilliant day after all, and to-day the sky is cloudless again. That snow-cap on our house fell with a terrific crash at lunch-time yesterday: a very respectable avalanche, I should call it, and I fancy it wrenched a few slates or whatever they are off the roof. Wingley was very annoyed at being disturbed in his beauty sleep on the lunch table. Ernestine, who looks after me beautifully – you've no idea how much Ida's tuition has improved her now she's on her own again – bought me some Cross & B. Shrimp paste for tea yesterday. Wingley went mad about it; he thought shrimp flies were dee-lucious.

The day goes very quietly. I get through a good deal of work of one kind & another. The snow's too sticky for pleasant ski-ing so far, though it may be better to-day. I enclose all the letters that came – amounting in all to nothing. You can see, by the date on this, that I begin quite early in the morning. But then I have too. E. is as punctual as an express train. She serves lunch on the very stroke of half past twelve; supper on the stroke of seven. Tufty-nob is at your cocoanut, now. If I didn't draw the curtain I should never do any work for the delight of watching them – such queer important little personalities birds are.

I think a great deal about our house. It seems to me I'm completely domesticated. I don't believe I really want to see anybody, in spite of what Elizabeth says. I thought I should be pleased at the idea of dining at the Palace[3] to-morrow; but not at all. I'd much sooner stay here and go up to your room after supper and read.

I've nothing to say except that I love you & am very happy

Boge.

1. J.M. replies to K.M.'s letter of 31 January: 'Although I have not seen Manoukhin yet . . . I must write you a little note . . .'.
2. The English doctor at Montana who attended K.M.
3. An expensive hotel for invalids in Montana.

---

[201]   Chalet des Sapins
                                          Montana-sur-Sierre
                                          Valais
Thursday Afternoon,   [2 February, 1922.]

My darling,[1]

I wired to you as soon as I got your letter. It seems to me that there aren't two choices, really. You must do what M. says, begin the treatment now, come back here for the summer in May and go back and finish the treatment in September. Quite honestly, I think it would be criminal for you to come back now. And we shouldn't really gain anything to set off the obvious loss. I can't see how we should be really happy while we were both thinking: She might be being cured now. The thing is as plain as a pikestaff in my mind as regards you. And what terrific news it is! And surely its an omen that by the same post came this letter from Pinker saying Cassells have bought 'A Cup of Tea' for ten guineas and that's exactly the kind of story they want. Ever since you started for Manoukhin your luck seems really to have begun at last. That's how I feel.

Now there's the question of me – quite a minor affair really; but I want to keep my head about it. What I feel is – I want to stay here. If I come and try to live in a hotel in Paris, I shan't really be able to work. I can't have my books and I shan't be able to settle down to the regular grind of my novel.[2] This place suits me, dead quiet & all. I've got masses of work to do and I want to get it done. Moreover, we've paid the rent here.

But I don't feel anything very definite about it. If you have a better idea don't hesitate. But if you think mine is the best, tell me. What I should then propose is that in about a week's time I should come 3rd. class to Paris, talk things over, & stay with you while Ida comes back here and gets all the things you are sure to want. Then I should come back and stay here the three months, and return to fetch you when the treatment is over. Then, perhaps, we would take the Oiseau Bleu[3] for 4 months and then I would come back & stay with you in Paris in the autumn. I should have the bulk of my year's work done then. It would only be a matter of weekly articles.

I hope, darling, you won't think this very cold & calculating. But I feel that if I don't work now, I never shall; and that if I don't break the back of my year's work, it will drag on & on.

But as I say I'm not so much in love with my own idea that I can't believe in a better one.

Anyhow, speak to me as frankly as I have spoken to you. I mean, if you would rather I stayed in Paris now, say so straight out. Don't in any case let L.M. come back until I arrive in Paris. After all, there's not the faintest hurry to settle things here, and you have enough things for a fortnight. The main point – that you should stay & have the treatment now is quite clear. After all, this other thing is a flea-bite beside it.

Your loving
Boge[4]

I shan't move from here, anyhow, till I get an answer to this letter. So please in reply quote Ref. No. Letter X.

You are a darling:
And it's plain
You're beginning to be
A great success.

I corrected the proof of 'The Garden Party'[5] & sent it straight back to Pinker; it was cleverly divided into 3 instalments.

1. J.M. replies to K.M.'s letter of 31 January: 'I went to see M. tonight'. K.M. reported that Manoukhine had said: 'I can promise to cure you – to make you as though you never had this disease'. He urged her to start the treatment immediately, instead of returning to Montana after the preliminary examination.

2. *The Voyage* (Constable, 1924).

3. A chalet, in the next village to Montana, which they were thinking of taking over after the lease of the Chalet des Sapins expired.

4. K.M. replies 4 February: 'Your letter came as a suprise to me . . .'.

5. 'The Garden Party' was published in The *Westminster Gazette* in 1922 in three instalments: 4, 11, 18 February.

---

[202]   [Chalet des Sapins,
                                         Montana-sur-Sierre,
                                         Valais.]
                                         [3 February, 1922.]
                                         Friday 5 p.m.

My darling,

Since last night another three feet of snow have fallen and the funicular is not working, so I've had no letters and I suspect the letter to you (Ref. No X) which I posted this morning has not gone off.

(Saturday morning) It didn't stop snowing all day yesterday and it's still going on. I've had enough snow now, please. No post, no funicular, and, as it's pouring just now, it doesn't look as though there will be either to-day. The shops in the village have perfect mountains of snow in front of them, and they've given up trying to keep the road open there till the snow really stops.

I imagine this is what Russia is really like, and I can't help thinking what amazing good fortune you had in choosing Monday. Since then there's never been a really good day and the last three have been absolutely impossible. For the first time for ages I couldn't go out yesterday afternoon. I made two journeys to the village, one in the morning to post my letter, the other in the afternoon to buy one or two cakes for Woodifield, and of course one in the evening to the Palace to dinner and debate. They asked me whether I would put on *my dress clothes*. Considering the path up to the Palace was one huge snowdrift – into which I fell – the idea seemed to me dotty, and I spurned it accordingly.

However, I managed to get back without losing myself. I had told Ernestine she could have her afternoon off on the Friday, so that she wouldn't have to be in for dinner. So she had arranged some sort of corroboree with her sister down in Sierre. It took her, she says, nearly 3 hours to get down there, and just before I went to the Palace she telephoned me to say she didn't think she could get back that night. However she did, somehow, because they told her there wasn't much chance of the funicular being open to-day. Which was noble of her, and a great relief to me.

The debate went off all right I think. Our side won, and one man, a Commander Bury, I suppose a naval man, made a very amusing, dry speech – quite one of the best of the kind I've heard.

They told me at the Palace last night that a post had come in; but I've seen no sign of it. Perhaps they aren't delivering it. If nothing comes this morning, I'll go down to the P.O. after lunch & find out.

I felt at first that you were well out of this weather; but then I thought if it's snowing up here in this beastly way it must be raining & sleeting in Paris. I wonder

Your loving
Boge.[1]

1.45 p.m. I'm just going off to the post. Only 3 mouldy papers came – and still that snow pours down. J'en ai soupé de neige. It's long past a joke.

1. K.M. replies 6 February: 'I have just received your Friday–Saturday letter . . .'.

---

[203]   Chalet des Sapins
                                         Montana-sur-Sierre
                                         Valais
                                         [5 February, 1922.]

Sunday morning,
   No letter came yesterday; but then all that did come was this p.c. from Brett and a letter of acknowledgement from my bank. I couldn't tell whether it was a real post or not. However, the snow has stopped snowing, and this morning there's actually some sun. In the last 3 days at least 1½ times as much snow as there was when you left has fallen; and I don't want to see any more. Neither does Wingley. He was very miserable about it; but he came into my bed early this morning and that cheered him up. He's still there.

   I haven't said anything about Manoukhin's promise that he can cure you absolutely – simply because I'm afraid to. Life & the world would be so different, so marvellous, that I just have to put it out of my mind. That's all.

And I don't know at all about this plan of mine for staying here. It's all right when I'm immersed in work and there's a grain of sun. But when it snows and snows, and one can't go out, and there's nothing to do but glue one's nose onto the window pane and watch the incessant fall – it's not so pleasant. For the life of me I don't really know what's best. I do want to break the back of this novel; I do want to get some articles done. But at the same time just as sincerely I want to be with you if I'm any help – even if it's only as a cribbage partner. So I rely on you to tell me faithfully what your mind is. I'm going down to Elizabeth's to tea this afternoon and taking Shaw Page with me as I once promised

I hope I get a letter from you at the P.O. this morning. I haven't had one since Thursday.

Your loving
Boge.[1]

1. K.M. replies 8 February: 'I do not "understand" why you have sent this telegram . . .'.

---

[204]
Chalet des Sapins
Montana-sur-Sierre
Valais
[6 February, 1922.]

Monday Morning.

My darling,

Instead of a letter from you what arrived yesterday was one *Daily News* & one *London Mercury*. I haven't had a letter of any sort or kind since Thursday. Elizabeth whom I saw yesterday said that only one funicular had come up since the snow began. If so, that explains it. Certainly we're still practically cut off. Even the road from here to the village is impassable for a cart of any kind, and our wood-supply has given out. Worst of all it's all grey & dark to-day, and it looks very much as though a lot more snow were coming.

I managed to get down to E. yesterday. It was hard work; and I had to go down to Montana Village first and then climb up again. She said she had had a letter from you on Saturday; but it didn't seem to have been written later than the last one I had from you. It must, at any rate, have been sent before our telegrams.

I'm at your table; Wingley is on your long chair beside me. The snow makes him very querulous. I don't wonder; it does almost the same for me. Poor Elizabeth hasn't been outside the house for a week, and she says she's getting very short-tempered. Speaking of Elizabeth: she showed me a review of the Bibesco's book[1] in the *Daily News* of Thursday by Rose Macaulay[2] in which R.M. said (1) that she 'followed Katherine Mansfield' and (2) that she wasn't anything like as good. She could no more have written *Prelude* than flown. Now I couldn't understand why I hadn't seen that in the *D.N.* I rescued our copy of the Thursday number when I came back – and it wasn't in it anywhere. It's most mysterious. However, I asked E. over the telephone to send her copy up to me and I'll send it on.

However, the chief things are (1) that I want a letter. I am still all in the dark as to what you would like me to do (2) that I'm perfectly well and as happy as one can be without a letter (3) Wingley is also well, though, as I said, very querulous (4) That the birds have worked your cocoanut off the window-sill and it's fallen into a snowdrift, quite invisible. (5) Two Tchehovs have arrived – *The Schoolmaster*[3] & *The Schoolmistress*[4] – and we've read *both of them* before.

Your loving
Boge.[5]

1. Elizabeth Bibesco's first collection of short stories *I have only myself to blame* appeared in 1921; *Balloons* in 1922.
2. Rose Macaulay (1881–1958), novelist, whose books *What Not* K.M. reviewed on 4 April 1919, and *Potterism* on 4 June 1920.
3. *The Schoolmaster and other stories* (1921). Translated by Constance Garnett.
4. *The Schoolmistress and other stories* (1920). Translated by Constance Garnett.
5. K.M. replies 8 February: 'I do not "understand" why you have sent this telegram . . .'. In a P.S. she said: 'Don't send the *Daily News* about E.B.'.

[205]   Chalet des Sapins
                                              Montana-sur-Sierre
                                                    Valais
                                              [6 February, 1922.]

Monday.

My darling Wig,[1]

As I was working at half past six the telephone bell rang. Ernestine was there; the Post Office had rung up to say a courier had got through by the first funicular that's been all the way since Wednesday night. I stumped off to the Post – and I was rewarded. Two letters from you – one Wednesday; the other Friday – one where you asked to see M & Donat[2] together – the other at your first real examination.

Darling, they did me good. How one feeds on letters! I don't think other people understand – not even Elizabeth – the dull paralysing emptiness that comes – *even when one believes everything's all right* – when days pass without letters. My power to work completely disappears; I just *can't* concentrate. Something nudges at my consciousness all the while.

I can't describe my state of mind after reading your letters through. I can sincerely say – with all my heart – say that I do believe, absolutely. But what I can't do is to project myself into the future – a future totally different from the past four years. That's – at present – beyond my powers; just as though I were writing something and couldn't grasp it, couldn't get it in front of my eyes. That's as near as I can get to the truth of my feeling.

Then there's another thing. I feel my letter to you (Ref No X) about my staying here may have sounded rather cold – partly because I was making an effort to see things calmly, partly because I was struggling hard with my novel – trying to come to grips with it, not to lose the thread. The result is that I feel I did not make it clear that my course of action really does depend entirely on what you would rather have me do. What I mean is that there won't be an atom-bit of regret if you say you'd rather have me staying in Paris. Not that I want to put the burden of decision on to you. But, whatever happens, we mustn't get this wholly minor thing tangled up. I sincerely and from the bottom of my heart say that you must regard me as as easily movable as Wingley – more easily, because I can come myself.

You see, I said pretty plainly in my letter that I would prefer to stay here, after having come to see you. But that, I now realise, was because I was unconsciously influenced by [my] attitude towards my novel; I felt frightened of breaking off. Well, I now realise I don't feel frightened. I'm sure I can take it up again whenever I have the opportunity. So that the absolute, cross my heart straight dinkum truth of the situation, is this: that I *want* to do whatever will *positively* help most.

That's all, my blessed darling; I don't think I can put it more plainly, or more honestly. Goodnight, and flights of angels tend thee to thy rest – me also. It's just half past ten.

Your

Boge.[3]

You have *no* conception, as Aunt Li would say, of the *enormous* amount of snow here now. I positively declare, without exaggerating, that the heaps in the village street are *as* huge *as* icebergs.

There's another notion which occurs to me. I might come & see you now, return here, and come back to Paris for the last month or three weeks you are there. I only put it forward as a notion – no more.

'The Doll's House'[4] is in the *Nation*, which I send with this.

1. J.M. replies to K.M.'s letters of 1 February: 'I rested all day . . .'; and 3 February: 'Your telegram came yesterday . . .'.
2. Dr. Donat, Manoukhine's French partner, whose apparent scientific knowledge and complete support of the treatment impressed K.M.
3. K.M. replies 8 February: 'I do not "understand" why you have sent me this telegram . . .'.
4. 'The Doll's House' appeared in the *Nation* on 4 February 1922.

---

[206]   Chalet des Sapins
                                         Montana-sur-Sierre
                                         Valais
                                         [February, 1922]

Tuesday,

Worm darling,[1]

Your reply to my letter (Ref no. X) came this afternoon. I never heard a more obvious 'Oh!'; I saw the very smallest, invisible tear in the corner of your eyes and it went on shining all through the letter. I could no more stay here after that than I could fly. So that's *settled*, darling.

I shall roll along at the end of this week. I shall wait for a reply to this letter (Ref no. Y) because I'm rather in the air about what to bring. You say leave it all to L.M. But does that mean Come with a rucksack and a small suit-case. No, I must bring more than that; I must bring some books; I can't work without them & I must bring the greater part of my clothes. It would be useless to leave either of these things to L.M. I should never be able to explain what I wanted.

Still, even so, I don't see why I should wait for a reply. I shan't. I shall start off on Friday. I'll send you a wire as soon as I know the train. I'll bring my trunk, my small suit-case and the typewriter. Oh, Lord, I'm forgetting; I haven't enough Swiss Money to see me through. I shall have to cash a cheque first.

I've just sent Ernestine with one to the Bazar. But I don't suppose the money will be there until Saturday. You won't worry if I don't get off till then will you my precious? Friday, Saturday, Sunday or Monday – one of those days. I'll be with you at latest by to-day week.

And now I'll tell you a secret. It came over me yesterday that it was all very well my talking cheerfully about staying here – but the fact was I couldn't do it. For a day or two it seems quite possible – that's because your presence still hangs about the place. Then gradually it fades away. Your beautiful room becomes my untidy room – and I begin to feel hellishly lonely. I try not to give way: I try to get on with my work; but it's no good. C'est plus fort que moi. And, though I tried to repress it, I knew yesterday that by the end of a fortnight I should be in Paris. Now, it's to be at the end of a week – that's all. But there's nothing like confession.

I'd like to do it on the cheap if possible. A tiny little room will suit me, so long as it's warm – if it had a set of bookshelves so much the better. And I'd like to be *en pension*.

I'll make my preparations leisurely, beginning with to-morrow, when I'll clear up my room. I also must write another article for the *Nation* before I leave. I shan't do the Tchehov[2] till I get to you. And on Tuesday next at latest we'll resume our cribbage.

I am assuming that won't be too late. You took away enough things for a fortnight, didn't you? It won't matter if we don't settle all the bills, will it before I leave? L.M. can do that.

Boge.

You are an awful darling, you know – if you only knew the great wave of love that came over me when I read your letter and saw that very faint little tear, you'd think I wasn't such a bad sort after all.

I've written to Mrs. Maxwell[3] by this post asking if we may sublet, & telling her to reply to Paris.

1. J.M. replies to K.M.'s letter of 4 February: 'Your letter came as a complete suprise to me . . .'.
2. 'The Method of Tchekhov', Murry's review of Tchekhov's *The School-master, and other stories* and *The Cook's Wedding, and other stories*, appeared in *The Republic* (New York) on 22 March 1922; in the *Nation and Athenaeum* on 8 April 1922.
3. Mrs Maxwell, mother of Dr. Hudson, owned the Chalet des Sapins. The Murrys' lease did not expire for another five months.

[207]   Chalet des Sapins
                                         Montana-sur-Sierre
                                         Valais
                                         [8 February, 1922.]
Wednesday Morning,

I'm just going off to the post with this, & to telegraph to you. It occurs to me you may think I'm coming because I think you want me to come chiefly – this is only to say that it's because I want to come chiefly. I couldn't possibly stop here.

They say the money will be here on Saturday morning. If so, I shall try & leave by the same 2.0 funicular – but anyhow I shall take it quietly & not kill myself if that's difficult.

                                         Boge.

[208]   Chalet des Sapins
                                         Montana-sur-Sierre
                                         Valais
                                         [8 February, 1922.]
Wednesday.

My darling,
You are an upsetting soul.[1] After I spent all the morning writing & posting letters with my new address, & tidying up, & the afternoon in going to Chalet Soleil[2] to get E. to cash a cheque, the same old telegram awaits me on my return. I almost expected it; it's come so often before.

Well, I am coming, simply *because I don't want to stay here*, darling. But just as I'd arranged things comfortably so that I could get off on Friday to have your wire telling me Ida is arriving on Saturday is confusing, above all as I particularly asked you not to send L.M. before I came. I don't quite know what to do – whether to wait till she comes or start off on Friday as I had arranged. The only thing to do is to telegraph again, which I'll do first thing to-morrow morning.

But what I do want to make quite clear is that I have, of my own free will and in my right mind, calm as ever I hope to be, decided to come to Paris till your fifteen séances[3] are over. I suppose you 'beg me not to come' because you imagine that I am doing something I don't want to do myself, for your sake. Well, I'm not. I have realised that I shall be intensely miserable here by myself so far from you, that I shan't be able to work, and as I explained that my first burst of feeling that I could be a hermit doing 8 hours a day was simply due to the fact that I hadn't yet realised that you were gone. That sounds mysterious, but I've noticed it many times before it takes me 3 or 4 days to get the full flavour of your absence.

All the same, I wish you hadn't sent that wire. I was trundling along so nicely: and now I'm suspended again. However, I recognise that the original fault was my own. I miscalculated my own feelings – not for the first time. However, that's enough of that.

To-day was the first fine day we've had since the Monday when you left. E. (i.e. Elizabeth, not Ernestine) has never been out of the house since.

Boge.

There's not much love in this letter, but there's plenty in my heart.

1. Murry added the marginal note here: 'This sounds angry – you know it's not meant to be'.
2. The Randogne home of Elizabeth von Arnim.
3. Manoukhine had told K.M. that she would need fifteen 'séances', after which she would feel 'perfectly well', then a 'period of repose'.

---

[209]   [Chalet des Sapins,
                               Montana-sur-Sierre,
                               Valais.]
                               Thursday evening February 9 1922.

My darling Worm,[1]

I must write to you though the letter will never be posted.[2] Your express letter has just arrived in answer to my telegram. I must somehow kill the time by thinking that I am near you.

I deserve the letter. It's the most awful one you've ever sent me.

I deserve the letter. I mean my action deserves the letter. But my soul doesn't. Darling, I'm a difficult person. I don't understand myself. I don't know myself. You know me better than I do, probably. But I'll try to explain.

I hadn't prepared myself at all for the possibility of your staying there. Subconsciously, I shirked it. When I knew you were going to stay there, I instinctively shirked it again – the change, the uprooting.

And I was able to, simply because your presence was in the house with me. We weren't apart. (There's an enormous difference, darling, in feeling between the one who stays and the one who goes. The one who stays is in a familiar place – everything here told me of your presence.) The day after I sent that letter,[3] I knew it was all wrong. It was meant to be true: it wasn't put up. But that was just because I wasn't yet free to feel your absence. The next day I knew it was impossible for us to be apart. I began to be anxious every hour of the day: I had lost my mate.

Don't say I was 'claiming my freedom as an artist' – such an idea never entered into my head. If you think that, you've got it all wrong. I wasn't claiming any freedom; I don't want, never have for a year now even dreamed of wanting 'freedom'. I was just shirking, shrinking from being uprooted. That was bad enough, I know; but it's better at any rate than claiming 'freedom as an artist'. If I pleaded my novel, I pleaded it (unconsciously) only as an excuse for my shrinking. As a matter of fact, it took me exactly four days to realise that I *couldn't work at all* without your presence. I worked just so long as your presence remained, not a moment longer.

I hate defending myself to you, my darling. I feel I'm not worth it; you're a so much finer being than I am. But yet I want you to know the truth about me. I'm not bad. I do believe in the last year most of the badness has gone out of me, and that I am in most ways your worthy Boge. But one thing, instead of growing better, grows worse & worse. I am more and more frightened of the world: more terrified of moving: of venturing a finger into the cogs. The last four years have taken away what little courage I had – and I never had any. That is a ghastly confession to make for a man who is well, to his wife who is ill. I am utterly ashamed. But what can I do? I fight against it. But when the moment comes I'm just petrified with fear. I *can't* move.

And I forsake you. It's terrible; it's even more terrible that I somehow deceive myself. If you had said to me, as you very nearly did, 'Bogey, why don't you come *with me* to Paris?' the only answer I could have made, if I'd been honest, was: 'I'm *afraid, afraid*'. Well, I've confessed – there's nothing else to confess. It's my very soul. It's fear makes me a miser even. I'm terrified of what may happen.

There's only one thing greater than my fear – that is my love. My love will always conquer my fear – but it can't do it immediately. It needs the full force of my love to do it and it takes days for that to emerge out of its dark hiding places. And in these days you have despaired of me again.

Wig precious, I shall never write anything truer of myself than this. Don't lose faith in me; I couldn't live unless you believed in me. But remember my fear – help me to fight it.

Your

Boge.

1. J.M. replies to K.M.'s letter of 8 February: 'I do not "understand" why you have sent this telegram . . .'.

2. K.M. must have received the letter for Murry wrote afterwards at the top: 'K. had pasted this in her Shakespeare which she bequeathed to Elizabeth'.

3. His letter of 2 February.

Murry spent the next four months with K.M. in a Paris hotel, L.M. being sent to close up the Chalet des Sapins. In June, after Katherine had completed her initial fifteen 'séances' with Dr. Manoukhine, she and Murry set out for Randogne. The journey was a terrible one; K.M.'s health deteriorated – as did her relationship with Murry – and L.M. was summoned back from England. While he remained in Randogne, the two women moved to Sierre. No extant letters from Murry record the separation.

In August 1922, instead of returning to continue her treatment in Paris, K.M. suddenly decided to visit London. Murry, who accompanied her, says that her real purpose was not so much to consult Dr. Sorapure as to make contact with Ouspensky and his English followers whom she had heard about from Orage. Murry was quite unable to share, or condone, his wife's new preoccupation with the mystical teachings of Gurdjieff's disciple, Ouspensky. While she attended Ouspensky's lectures with Orage and other friends, therefore, they lived apart. In September he went to live in Selsfield with his friend, Vivian Locke Ellis.

Ostensibly to resume the Manoukhine treatment, Katherine returned to Paris on 2 October. But it was the spiritual salvation offered by Gurdjieff rather than the hope of a physical remedy that now drove her on. The same day that she embarked on her final journey to the Gurdjieff Institute at Fontainebleau – 16 October – she telegraphed her farewell to Murry and to England: 'Dear house dear friends accept my love Katherine'.

Very few of the letters Murry wrote to Katherine in the closing months of her troubled life remain. Undoubtedly his painful sense of helplessness during this period was worsened by an inability to understand the choice she had made. Even so, his very last letters indicate that far from cutting himself off from Katherine, Murry was becoming reconciled to her decision, attempting one final time to follow where she led.

[210]   Selsfield House
                                          [East Grinstead,
                                              Sussex.]
                                          [14 October, 1922.]
                                              Saturday

My darling Wig,[1]

Your letter has disturbed me very much. Your going to Gurdjeff's[2] institute may be everything that you think: I'm sure you know & I don't. But to give up Manoukhin, as you evidently are doing, though you don't say so, seems to me criminal. I really mean wrong, utterly wrong.

However, I feel it's quite hopeless for me to say anything: and perhaps useless of me to try to say anything. I simply don't understand what you are doing – but then I haven't understood very much ever since Uspensky began. I've trusted in it & you as something beyond me. Now I don't trust in it. The horrid thing is that I had a feeling that this was going to happen which I dismissed.

Oh, please don't imagine me as scolding. I'm terribly disappointed about Manoukhine.

But then I feel I don't *know* anything. You've passed clean out of my range & understanding: and so suddenly, Wig.

That's the only fact worth thinking about. I can't make head or tail of it. I haven't changed, you have: so probably you're right. But I feel our ships are sailing away from each other, & that we're just waving.

Be happy. You know whether you are right. I can let you have £20 a month if that wd. help.[3]

1. J.M. replies to K.M.'s letter of 13 October: 'That was a massive 1st instalment from Newcassel'.
2. George Gurdjieff (1872–1949), born near Armenian Russia, was a widely travelled mystic who had founded his quasi-psychological Institute for the Harmonious Development of Man in Moscow in 1914. With Ouspensky he left Russia about 1921, establishing himself at La Prieuré, a former Carmelite monastery at Fontainebleau. Gurdjieff's disciples at Fontainebleau were mostly well-to-do Russian and English 'intellectuals'.
3. Murry's footnote to this letter reads: 'Not sent'.

[211]   Wayside Cottage
                                               Ditchling Sussex
                                               [17 December, 1922.]

Sunday

My precious darling,[1]

Of course, the moment I'd posted my last, yours came. As a matter
of fact I have begun to read something Eastern, or rather something
odder than Eastern, which Bill Dunning (i.e. Mrs. Dunning) gave
me for a present. And in a queer way I was *very much* impressed by it.
Moreover I've promised Dunning that I will read an Indian book on, I
think, Rama Yoga, which he's going to give me soon. But mostly I
listen to Dunning.[2] I sit in their kitchen-sitting room in the evenings,
and we talk. I don't know how to describe it – it's so very simple.
Sometimes it reminds me of the times when you & I used to sit with
the Lawrences in their kitchen. But the differences are so tremendous
that that is rather misleading than otherwise. There's no *agitation* at,
[sic] it's all very calm & pure. And I too shall never be able to lead the
old life again or anything like it. Mine will have to be some kind of
going on from this life I lead now.

So you see, darling, if you have your Salzmann's,[3] whom I should
dearly love to know, I have my Dunnings, whom I would dearly love
you to know. And every letter of yours that I get now makes me feel
more than ever that we are marching along parallel paths – parallel
paths which converge, and that the day is not so terribly far distant
when we shall be ready for one another. And then, I know, life will be
quite simple. There simply will not be any difficulties.

We're having some most amazing weather. The climate in this part
of Sussex is really remarkable, though. I can never really believe that it
is winter.

My only real regret is that I have no garden of my own. But then,
just at present, I couldn't manage both my housework and my
gardening – so it's probably as well. And I've never been happy like
this before – that is certain.

I have to go to London on Thursday until Sunday, to finish up this
Sickert essay,[4] also to buy some Xmas presents for the Dunning
children, – also to see Kot, with whom I have – also quite simply –
become reconciled, & for whom I'm doing some work of late.

                         With all my love, my darling,
                              Your own Boge.[5]

1. J.M. replies to K.M.'s letter of 9 December: 'I have never had a letter from you that I so "understood" . . .'.
2. Murry was now living next door to the Dunnings at Ditchling.
3. Alexander Salzmann, a painter and friend of Chekhov's widow, decorated the white-washed walls and ceiling of the gallery in the cow-house assigned to Katherine at Fontainebleau.
4. 'The Etchings of Walter Sickert' appeared in *Print Collectors' Quarterly*, February 1923.
5. K.M. replies 23 December: 'Just a note to wish you a Happy Xmas'.

---

[212]   Wayside Cottage
                                               Ditchling [Sussex.]
                                               New Year's Eve. [1922.]
9 p.m.

My precious darling,[1]

New Year's Eve. Sullivan is away. I've just come back from the Dunnings', where I've been having supper, to write this letter. Afterwards, I'm going back to see the New Year in. I can't help thinking of the New Year you & I saw in – so long ago – at Rose Tree Cottage, do you remember?

I'm so glad you liked the drawing. I liked it. And then someone said, just before I sent it off, – oh, yes, it was Mrs. Jones – that it wasn't like me: so I was afraid you wouldn't care for it.

The Old Adam didn't last very long, thank Goodness. I'd forgotten all about him by the time I got your letter – and I couldn't really remember what I'd been talking about. But now I do. I wrote at the end of a day when I had been tense and irritable: and such a thing hasn't happened to me for so long that I felt rather depressed about it. I discovered eventually that the cause was that I couldn't get away by myself at all, and that the continual interruption made it impossible for me to relax. It's very hard for me to relax at the best of times: but I do make some progress. On this day I just felt that everything was in league against me. But it passed away completely.

I agree absolutely with you that the question to answer is Who am I? And that it can't be settled by the head. And like you I'm learning *how* unreal I am. (By the way, Dunning has lent me a deeply interesting Eastern book on this, called *Raja Yoga*: it's absorbing and very exciting. It makes me feel that I want to lose no time, to go terribly fast to the goal. But that, I know, is all wrong. There's no way of going fast.) But for heaven's sake, Wig, don't think you bore me by writing about these things: they're the only things which really interest me.

I don't a bit like the glimpse of Sullivan's activities I got through your letter *viâ* Brett. In some way he's very restive. While he's down here, and towards me, he is *very nice indeed*. I'm not exaggerating. He makes a real effort to be considerate, and to try to get rid of the horrid, uncouth, masculine intellectual pride that is the worst thing in him: it's so utterly unworthy of himself at his best moments. But then it seems he rebels against his efforts, and when he goes up to London sometimes (not always) breaks out into a real unregenerate Adam. But you mustn't imagine those moments are typical of him. I know of them only by what comes round to me. In all our direct relations he's very different, believe me.

So you also have a man who's keen on Astrology. Dunning sometimes talks a good deal about that also. For a long while he has been asking me to find out the exact date of my birth so as to have my horoscope cast. And some destiny or other makes me always forget when I see my mother.

When Beresford came here the other day he inquired a great deal about you. He also said he had given up Uspensky:[2] he said that Uspensky's wasn't true mysticism, it was occultism. I didn't understand that at all – it seemed by the way to me that Beresford was trying to understand it all with his *head* – and I asked him what he meant. He gave me a definition of the difference between mysticism & occultism: mysticism is an effort to get beyond the self and to come to union with a higher, outer reality: occultism is an attempt to penetrate into the self, inwardly, and involves a withdrawal & isolation from human life. Well, that didn't convince me at all. Of course, I don't know how far Le Prieuré[3] is connected with Uspensky: but what I do know of your life there suggests the very opposite of a withdrawal & isolation. And, moreover, according to my ideas – or rather instincts – a true penetration of the self, a true realisation is quite essential to mysticism. Only by doing that can you come into union with a higher reality – that part of it which is manifested in you.

However, I took it along to Dunning & asked him what he thought of Beresford's definition. I was glad that he said it was all nonsense.

I suppose you couldn't tell me whether you do any exercises, & what they are.

I've had a letter from L.M. She's doing cows, & is enthusiastic about them.

The motor-car (a 10 H.P. Citroën – the make, I seem to remember, that L.M. wanted me to have) is coming to-morrow. I'm going to spend the morning (I hope) trying to drive it. I want to be an expert driver by the time you come back.

I *adore* Michael Dunning – the youngest – I'll tell you about him next time. Ever your own

Boge.

1. J. M. replies to K.M.'s letter of 26 December: 'I think the drawing of you [by Rothenstein] is extraordinarily good . . .'.
2. P. D. Ouspensky, a Russian mathematician and disciple of Gurdjieff, who gave lectures in London based on his own book, *Tertium Organum* (1920).
3. Gurdjieff's headquarters at Fontainebleau.

---

[213]   Wayside Cottage
                            Ditchling [Sussex.]
                          [5 January, 1923.]
Friday

My precious darling,[1]

I'm overjoyed at the idea of coming over next week to see you & Le Prieuré. I would have arrived on Monday had it not been that I've promised a leader for *The Times Supplement*, and I'm not sure that I should be able to finish it.

I shall come by Newhaven. It saves my having to go back to London. I shall take the night boat on Monday arrive in Paris early on Tuesday, collect your things from Mrs. Nelson who is taking them over for me,* & come on I suppose about midday.

*Apparently it occurred to Brett – very sensibly – that if I were to carry some new shoes & clothes among my things which obviously belonged to a woman, I should or might be badly held up. At all events the arrangement is that Mrs. Nelson is to take them, & I'm to call for them at 16 rue de Seine on Tuesday morning.

Au revoir my darling
Your own
Boge.

1. J. M. replies to K.M.'s letter of 31 December: 'My fountain pen is mislaid, so as I am in a hurry to write please forgive this pencil'.

January 9, 1923

Four days later, on the afternoon of Tuesday January 9, 1923, Murry arrived at Fontainebleau as planned. He and Katherine spent a happy afternoon together, meeting the friends she had made at Le Prieuré and talking about the ways in which her thinking had changed. Murry recorded:

> She told me she had felt that her love for me had had to die. 'It was killing us both', she said. And it had died. 'I felt that I could not bear it, – tearing my heart away from yours. But I managed to do it'. I gathered somehow that it was part of the spiritual discipline of the place, as she conceived it, thus to sacrifice one's earthly affections. But I made no comment. I was happy to see her happy. 'But now I have come through, at last', she said. 'My love for you has all come back to me, renewed and purified – and greater than ever. That was why I wanted you to come.'

About ten o'clock that night, suddenly forgetting herself, Katherine tried to run up the stairs to bed. Horrified, Murry looked on as a fit of coughing turned into a violent haemorrhage. Within half an hour she was dead. Murry was only thirty-three; he was to live on for another thirty-three years. In a sense, however, it could be said that a part of him had died when Katherine Mansfield died – in 1923.

Chronology

1889
August: John Middleton Murry was born.

1901
January: Murry entered Christ's Hospital on a scholarship.

1907
Murry saved up enough money to go with a school friend on a walking-tour of Brittany.

1908
The winning of an exhibition and scholarship enabled Murry to enter Brasenose College, Oxford.

1910–1911
During the Christmas vacation in Paris on the Left Bank, Murry met the painter, J. D. Fergusson and discussed the idea of a new literary magazine to be called *Rhythm*. He became romantically involved with a French girl, Margueritte.

1911
Easter: Murry returned to Paris with Michael Sadleir where they planned the opening number of *Rhythm*. The affair with Margueritte continued.
June: the first issue of *Rhythm* appeared.
December: Murry met Katherine Mansfield at the home of W. L. George.

1912
April: Murry came down from Oxford and became K.M.'s lodger at 69 Clovelly Mansions, London. J. A. Spender, editor of the *Westminster Gazette*, took Murry on as a reviewer.
September: Murry and K.M. rented Runcton Cottage, near Chichester.

October: 'Stephen Swift', the publisher of *Rhythm*, absconded leaving a debt of £400.

November: They moved from Runcton Cottage to 57 Chancery Lane, London. Edward Marsh helped *Rhythm* financially.

December: K.M. & J.M. visited Paris.

1913

March: They rented 'The Gables' at Cholesbury, Bucks. Murry commuted to London.

May: Rhythm was reconstituted as *The Blue Review*.

July: The Blue Review closed down after three issues. J.M. and K.M. moved to Chaucer Mansions, Baron's Court, London.

December: They moved to 31 Rue de Tournon, Paris, K.M. met Francis Carco.

1914

February: Murry declared bankruptcy and with K.M. returned to London.

July: Murry and Katherine were witnesses at the marriage of D. H. Lawrence and Frieda.

October: After several changes of address in London, K.M. and J.M. moved to Rose Tree Cottage, The Lee, near Great Missenden, Bucks. The Lawrences lived nearby. Murry began writing a novel, *Still Life*.

December: They attended a Christmas party at the Cannans' mill house.

1915

February: K.M. left Murry to visit Francis Carco in France. Murry came down with influenza and went to the Lawrences' to be nursed.

March: K.M. visited Paris – to write.

May: Murry took rooms at 95 Elgin Crescent, London. K.M. returned to Paris to write.

June: They took a house at 5 Acacia Road, St. John's Wood, London.

Autumn: With Lawrence, Murry started the short-lived magazine, *Signature*. K.M.'s only brother, Leslie Beauchamp, visited them on leave.

October: Leslie was accidentally killed.

November: Murry escorted Katherine, grief-stricken, to Bandol in France.

December: Having returned to England, Murry spent Christmas at Garsington.

1916
January: Murry joined K.M. at the Villa Pauline in Bandol. While she worked on *The Aloe*, he embarked on his study of Dostoevsky.
April: Urged by the Lawrences, K.M. and J.M. came back to England to a cottage at Zennor in Cornwall.
June: They moved away from the Lawrences to Sunnyside Cottage, Mylor, Cornwall.
July: K.M. visited Lady Ottoline Morrell at Garsington for the first time.
August: Murry was taken on as a translator at the War Office. His *Fyodor Dostoevsky: A Critical Study* was published.
September: He and K.M. took rooms at 3 Gower Street, Bloomsbury.
December: Still Life was published. Murry and Katherine joined a Christmas house-party at Garsington.

1917
February: K.M. rented a studio in Church Street, Chelsea, while Murry moved to 47 Redcliffe Road, Fulham.
May: Their friend Frederick Goodyear was killed.
November: Murry was suspected of tuberculosis and given two months' sick leave, which he spent at Garsington.
December: After a visit to Garsington, a spot on K.M.'s lung was diagnosed.

1918
January: K.M. set off alone for Bandol, where she became seriously ill.
April: Accompanied by Ida Baker, K.M. finally arrived back in London.
May: K.M. and J.M. were married. Two weeks later, she went to Looe, Cornwall.
June: Murry negotiated the lease and redecoration of a house at 2 Portland Villas, Hampstead.
July: After a short holiday with her in Cornwall, Murry brought K.M. back to London. They lived together at 2 Portland Villas until September 1919.

December: Murry's *Poems 1917–18* was published by himself and his brother on the Heron Press, Hampstead.

1919
Spring: Murry was appointed editor of the *Athenaeum*, and resigned from his position as Chief Censor at the War Office.
April: The first number of the *Athenaeum* edited by Murry appeared.
September: Murry escorted K.M. and Ida Baker to Ospedaletti on the Italian Riviera.
October: He returned to England. His long poem, *The Critic in Judgement; or Belshazzar of Baron's Court* was published by the Hogarth Press.
December: K.M.'s unhappiness made Murry decide unexpectedly to join her for Christmas.

1920
January: Murry returned to London.
April: K.M. and Ida Baker came back to 2 Portland Villas for the summer.
May: Murry's verse play, *Cinnamon and Angelica*, was published.
June: Aspects of Literature was published.
September: K.M. and Ida Baker left London for the Villa Isola Bella in Menton. Murry's *Poems 1916–20* was published.
December: Relations between J.M. and K.M. became strained because of his friendship with Elizabeth Bibesco. Murry went out to see K.M. in Menton.

1921
January: Murry returned briefly to London, having decided to give up his editorship of the *Athenaeum*.
February: The *Athenaeum* was merged with the *Nation*. Murry visited London briefly, returning to Menton.
May: K.M. moved with Ida Baker to Baugy, Switzerland while Murry went to Oxford where he gave six lectures on *The Problem of Style*.
June: Murry returned to K.M. in Switzerland. They moved to the Chalet des Sapins in Montana-sur-Sierre.

1922
January: K.M. left Montana for Paris to undergo Dr Manoukhine's treatment for tuberculosis.

February: Murry joined K.M. in a Paris hotel.

March: The Problem of Style and Murry's novel, *The Things We Are*, were published.

June: K.M. and Murry left Paris. He stayed in Randogne while she and Ida Baker went to Sierre. Murry's *Countries of the Mind: Essays in Literary Criticism* was published.

August: Murry accompanied K.M. back to London. They lived apart.

September: Murry moved to Selsfield with Vivian Locke Ellis.

October: K.M. returned to Paris, and after two weeks entered the Gurdjieff Institute at Fontainebleau.

1923

January: At Katherine's invitation Murry went to visit her at Fontainebleau. On the evening of their reunion she died.

Appendix of Unpublished Letters and Telegrams

This appendix lists all the known letters of John Middleton Murry to Katherine Mansfield that have not been included in the present book. For the sake of clarity, the dates and addresses (some of which were not given in full in the letters but which have been ascertained from internal evidence) have been standardized. However, when Murry wrote more than once to Katherine Mansfield on the same day, his own indication of the time of writing has been given. The address of letters written on official *Athenaeum* notepaper, or headed "the office", is given as: 10, Adelphi Terrace, London. A question-mark prefixes dates which could not be accurately established. Murry's telegrams to Katherine Mansfield are included in this appendix and are marked by "T".

1913

T	Wednesday 14 May	London

1914

T	Thursday 12 February	London
T	Thursday 12 February	Brighton
T	Saturday 14 February	London

1915

	Monday 10 May	95 Elgin Crescent, London
T	Monday 10 May	London

1915

	Wednesday 12 May	95 Elgin Crescent, London
T	Wednesday 12 May	London
	Friday 14 May	95 Elgin Crescent, London
	Wednesday 8 December	Paris
	Thursday 9 December	c/o Koteliansky, London
	Monday 13 December	c/o Koteliansky, London
	Tuesday 14 December	c/o Koteliansky, London
	Wednesday 15 December	23 Worsley Road, London
	Friday 17 December	23 Worsley Road, London
	Wednesday 22 December	23 Worsley Road, London
	Friday 24 December	Garsington Manor, Oxford
	Saturday 25 December	Garsington Manor, Oxford
	Monday 27 December	Garsington Manor, Oxford

1918

	Thursday 17 January	47 Redcliffe Road, London
	Friday 18 January	47 Redcliffe Road, London
	Monday 21 January	47 Redcliffe Road, London
	Tuesday 22 January	47 Redcliffe Road, London
	Wednesday 23 January	47 Redcliffe Road, London
	Thursday 24 January	47 Redcliffe Road, London
	Friday 25 January	47 Redcliffe Road, London
	Sunday (morning) 27 January	47 Redcliffe Road, London
	Sunday (8 p.m.) 27 January	47 Redcliffe Road, London
	Monday 28 January	47 Redcliffe Road, London
	Tuesday 29 January	47 Redcliffe Road, London
	Thursday 31 January	47 Redcliffe Road, London
	Sunday 3 February	47 Redcliffe Road, London
	Monday 4 February	47 Redcliffe Road, London
T	Wednesday 6 February	London
	Wednesday (morning) 6 February	47 Redcliffe Road, London
	Wednesday (9 p.m.) 6 February	47 Redcliffe Road, London
T	Friday 8 February	London
	Monday 11 February	47 Redcliffe Road, London

	Tuesday 12 February	47 Redcliffe Road, London
	Wednesday (8.30 p.m.) 13 February	47 Redcliffe Road, London
	Wednesday (10.45 p.m.) 13 February	47 Redcliffe Road, London
	Sunday (11.15 a.m.) 17 February	47 Redcliffe Road, London
	Sunday (10.55 p.m.) 17 February	47 Redcliffe Road, London
	Tuesday 19 February	47 Redcliffe Road, London
	Wednesday 20 February	47 Redcliffe Road, London
	Friday 22 February	47 Redcliffe Road, London
	Sunday 24 February	47 Redcliffe Road, London
	Tuesday 26 February	47 Redcliffe Road, London
	Wednesday 27 February	47 Redcliffe Road, London
	Thursday 28 February	47 Redcliffe Road, London
	Saturday 2 March	47 Redcliffe Road, London
	Sunday 3 March	47 Redcliffe Road, London
T	Sunday 3 March	London
	Monday 4 March	47 Redcliffe Road, London
	Wednesday 6 March	47 Redcliffe Road, London
T	Wednesday 6 March	London
	Thursday 7 March	47 Redcliffe Road, London
	Friday 8 March	47 Redcliffe Road, London
	Monday 11 March	47 Redcliffe Road, London
	Tuesday 12 March	47 Redcliffe Road, London
	Thursday 14 March	47 Redcliffe Road, London
T	Saturday 16 March	London
	Monday (morning) 18 March	47 Redcliffe Road, London
	Monday (11.45 p.m.) 18 March	47 Redcliffe Road, London
	Wednesday 20 March	47 Redcliffe Road, London
	Friday 22 March	47 Redcliffe Road, London
	Sunday 24 March	47 Redcliffe Road, London
	Monday 25 March	47 Redcliffe Road, London
	Tuesday 26 March	47 Redcliffe Road, London
	Wednesday 27 March	47 Redcliffe Road, London
	Thursday 28 March	47 Redcliffe Road, London
	Friday 29 March	47 Redcliffe Road, London
	Saturday (morning) 30 March	47 Redcliffe Road, London
	Saturday (8.20 p.m.) 30 March	47 Redcliffe Road, London

	Sunday 31 March	47 Redcliffe Road, London
	Tuesday 2 April	47 Redcliffe Road, London
	Wednesday (Early Spring)	10 Adelphi Terrace, London
	Wednesday 3 April	47 Redcliffe Road, London
	Thursday 4 April	47 Redcliffe Road, London
	Saturday 6 April	47 Redcliffe Road, London
	Sunday 7 April	47 Redcliffe Road, London
	Tuesday 9 April	47 Redcliffe Road, London
	Wednesday 10 April	47 Redcliffe Road, London
T	Friday 12 April	London
	Sunday 19 May	47 Redcliffe Road, London
	Tuesday 21 May	47 Redcliffe Road, London
	Thursday 23 May	47 Redcliffe Road, London
	Monday 27 May	47 Redcliffe Road, London
T	Tuesday 28 May	London
	Wednesday 29 May	47 Redcliffe Road, London
	Friday 31 May	47 Redcliffe Road, London
	Saturday (morning) 1 June	47 Redcliffe Road, London
T	Saturday 1 June	London
	Monday 3 June	The War Office, London
	Monday (night) 3 June	47 Redcliffe Road, London
	Tuesday (afternoon) 4 June	The War Office, London
	Tuesday (9.15 p.m.) 4 June	47 Redcliffe Road, London
	Thursday 6 June	The War Office, London
	Friday 7 June	47 Redcliffe Road, London
	Sunday 9 June	47 Redcliffe Road, London
	Monday (afternoon) 10 June	The War Office, London
T	Monday 10 June	London
T	Tuesday 11 June	London
	Wednesday (morning) 12 June	47 Redcliffe Road, London
	Wednesday (evening) 12 June	47 Redcliffe Road, London
	Thursday (morning) 13 June	47 Redcliffe Road, London
	Thursday (evening) 13 June	47 Redcliffe Road, London
	Friday 14 June	47 Redcliffe Road, London
	Monday 17 June	47 Redcliffe Road, London
	Tuesday (morning) 18 June	47 Redcliffe Road, London
	Tuesday (night) 18 June	47 Redcliffe Road, London
	Wednesday 19 June	47 Redcliffe Road, London

1919

Sunday 9 March	Garsington Manor, Oxford
Monday 10 March	Garsington Manor, Oxford
Wednesday 1 October	Vintimiglia, Italy
Friday 3 October	2 Portland Villas, London
Saturday 4 October	2 Portland Villas, London
Sunday 5 October	2 Portland Villas, London
Monday 6 October	10 Adelphi Terrace, London
Monday (night) 6 October	2 Portland Villas, London
Wednesday 8 October	2 Portland Villas, London
Sunday 12 October	2 Portland Villas, London
Monday 13 October	2 Portland Villas, London
Tuesday 14 October	2 Portland Villas, London
Wednesday 15 October	2 Portland Villas, London
Thursday 16 October	2 Portland Villas, London
Saturday 18 October	2 Portland Villas, London
Wednesday 22 October	2 Portland Villas, London
Thursday 23 October	2 Portland Villas, London
Saturday 25 October	2 Portland Villas, London
Sunday 26 October	2 Portland Villas, London
Monday 27 October	2 Portland Villas, London
Wednesday 29 October	2 Portland Villas, London
Thursday 30 October	2 Portland Villas, London
Friday 31 October	2 Portland Villas, London
Sunday 2 November	2 Portland Villas, London
Monday 3 November	2 Portland Villas, London
Tuesday 4 November	2 Portland Villas, London
Wednesday 5 November	10 Adelphi Terrace, London
Thursday 6 November	2 Portland Villas, London
Friday 7 November	2 Portland Villas, London
Saturday 8 November	2 Portland Villas, London
Monday 10 November	2 Portland Villas, London
Wednesday 12 November	10 Adelphi Terrace, London
Saturday 15 November	2 Portland Villas, London
Tuesday 18 November	2 Portland Villas, London
Wednesday 19 November	2 Portland Villas, London
Monday 24 November	2 Portland Villas, London
Wednesday 26 November	10 Adelphi Terrace, London
Friday 28 November	2 Portland Villas, London

Saturday 29 November	2 Portland Villas, London
Sunday 30 November	2 Portland Villas, London
Tuesday 2 December	2 Portland Villas, London
Wednesday 3 December	2 Portland Villas, London
Thursday 4 December	2 Portland Villas, London
Sunday 7 December	2 Portland Villas, London
Wednesday 10 December	2 Portland Villas, London
Sunday 14 December	2 Portland Villas, London

1920

Sunday 4 January	2 Portland Villas, London
Tuesday 6 January	2 Portland Villas, London
Wednesday 7 January	2 Portland Villas, London
Thursday 8 January	2 Portland Villas, London
Saturday 10 January	Oare, Somerset
Sunday 11 January	Oare, Somerset
Monday 12 January	2 Portland Villas, London
Wednesday 14 January	2 Portland Villas, London
Thursday 15 January	2 Portland Villas, London
Friday 16 January	2 Portland Villas, London
Sunday 18 January	Easton Glebe, Dunmow, Essex
Tuesday 20 January	2 Portland Villas, London
Friday 23 January	10 Adelphi Terrace, London
Saturday 24 January	The Crown Inn, Lewes, Sussex
Saturday (night) 24 January	The Crown Inn, Lewes, Sussex
Tuesday 27 January	In the train to London
Wednesday 28 January	10 Adelphi Terrace, London
Friday 30 January	2 Portland Villas, London
Saturday 31 January	The George Inn, Battle, Sussex
Wednesday 4 February	2 Portland Villas, London
T Tuesday 10 February	London
Sunday 15 February	East Grinstead, Sussex
Friday 20 February	Fleur de Lis Hotel, Canterbury, Kent
Friday (6 p.m.) 20 February	Fleur de Lis Hotel, Canterbury, Kent
Saturday 21 February	2 Portland Villas, London
Thursday 26 February	2 Portland Villas, London

Friday 27 February	2 Portland Villas, London
Saturday 28 February	2 Portland Villas, London
Sunday 29 February	2 Portland Villas, London
Tuesday 2 March	10 Adelphi Terrace, London
Wednesday 10 March	10 Adelphi Terrace, London
Thursday 11 March	10 Adelphi Terrace, London
Friday 12 March	2 Portland Villas, London
Tuesday 16 March	2 Portland Villas, London
Friday 19 March	2 Portland Villas, London
Saturday 27 March	2 Portland Villas, London
Monday 29 March	2 Portland Villas, London
Tuesday 30 March	2 Portland Villas, London
Saturday 3 April	2 Portland Villas, London
Sunday 4 April	2 Portland Villas, London
Wednesday 7 April	10 Adelphi Terrace, London
T Friday 9 April	London
Saturday 10 April	2 Portland Villas, London
Sunday 11 April	2 Portland Villas, London
Tuesday [? 13] April	2 Portland Villas, London
Saturday 17 April	2 Portland Villas, London
Wednesday 21 April	Shakespeare Hotel, Stratford-on-Avon, Warwick
Thursday 22 April	Shakespeare Hotel, Stratford-on-Avon, Warwick

Index